A Collaborative Approach to Eating Disorders

While many aspects of eating disorders remain a mystery, there is growing evidence that collaboration is an essential element for treatment success. This book emphasises and explains the importance of family involvement as part of a unified team approach towards treatment and recovery.

A Collaborative Approach to Eating Disorders draws on up-to-date evidence-based research as well as case studies and clinical vignettes to illustrate the seriousness of eating disorders and the impact on both the sufferer and their loved ones. Areas of discussion include:

- current research including genetic factors, socio-cultural influences and early intervention
- clinical applications such as family-based dialectical and cognitive behavioural treatments
- treatment developments for both adolescents and adults with a range of eating disorders
- building collaborative alliances at all levels for treatment and ongoing recovery.

With contributions from key international figures in the field, this book will be a valuable resource for students and mental health professionals including family doctors, clinicians, nurses, family therapists, dieticians and social workers.

June Alexander is an Australian writer and former newspaper editor who has a forty-year career in journalism and has battled eating disorders since the age of 11.

Janet Treasure is Director, South London and Maudsley NHS Trust, Eating Disorder Unit, and Professor of Psychiatry, King's College London.

D1465127

A Collaborative Approach to Eating Disorders

Edited by
June Alexander and Janet Treasure

Routledge
Taylor & Francis Group

LONDON AND NEW YORK

First published 2012
by Routledge
27 Church Road, Hove, East Sussex BN3 2FA

Simultaneously published in the USA and Canada
by Routledge
711 Third Avenue, New York, NY 10017

*Routledge is an imprint of the Taylor & Francis Group, an Informa
business*

This publication has been produced with paper manufactured to strict
environmental standards and with pulp derived from sustainable forests.

British Library Cataloguing in Publication Data
A catalogue record for this book is available from the British Library

Library of Congress Cataloging-in-Publication Data

A collaborative approach to eating disorders / edited by June Alexander
and Janet Treasure.
    p. ; cm.
  Includes bibliographical references.
  ISBN 978-0-415-58145-5 (hardback)—ISBN 978-0-415-58146-2 (pbk.)
    1. Eating disorders—Psychological aspects. 2. Eating disorders—
Treatment. 3. Physician and patient. 4. Family psychotherapy.
I. Alexander, June, 1950- editor. II. Treasure, Janet, editor.
[DNLM: 1. Eating Disorders—psychology. 2. Eating Disorders—
therapy. 3. Family Relations. 4. Family Therapy—methods.
5. Professional-Patient Relations. WM 175]
  RC552.E18C638 2010
  616.85'26—dc22   2010046833

ISBN: 978-0-415-58145-5 (hbk)
ISBN: 978-0-415-58146-2 (pbk)
ISBN: 978-0-203-81669-1 (ebk)

Typeset in Times New Roman by RefineCatch Limited, Bungay, Suffolk
Printed and bound in Great Britain by TJ International, Padstow, Cornwall
Paperback cover design by Andrew Ward

Contents

Contributors

Carrie Arnold is a freelance science writer whose work has appeared in the *Washington Post* and *Scientific American*. She is in recovery from anorexia and the author of *Running on Empty* and *Next to Nothing*. She blogs daily at www.edbites.com

Ursula F. Bailer is Associate Professor of Psychiatry and Director of the Eating Disorders Outpatient Clinic and Research Program at the Medical University of Vienna, and currently Visiting Associate Professor at the University of California, San Diego.

Donald H. Baucom is Richard Simpson Distinguished Professor of Psychology at the University of North Carolina at Chapel Hill. His primary interests are in relationship functioning, developing treatments for couples, and interaction between individual psychological difficulties and interpersonal interactions.

C. Laird Birmingham is Professor of Psychiatry and an associate member of the Departments of Medicine, Health Care and Epidemiology, and Pharmacology and Therapeutics at the University of British Columbia. He was British Columbia Provincial Director for Eating Disorders until 2008 and is now Medical Director of the Woodstone Residence. He has published 124 refereed articles, twenty invited chapters, and eight books.

Solfrid Bratland-Sanda is a researcher at the Modum Bad Psychiatric Center, Norway. Her research interests include physical activity and exercise among males and females with eating disorders. Solfrid has worked as an exercise physiologist in the Norwegian Olympic Sports Training Center's eating disorders treatment team.

Allegra Broft is Assistant Professor of Clinical Psychiatry at the Columbia University Medical Center, and a psychiatrist in the Eating Disorders Research Unit, conducting studies on neurobiology of eating disorders.

Cynthia M. Bulik is Jordan Distinguished Professor of Eating Disorders in the Department of Psychiatry, Professor of Nutrition, and Director of the University of North Carolina Eating Disorders Program.

Susan Byrne is a clinical psychologist and Associate Professor at the University of Western Australia, School of Psychology (M.Psych/PhD from UWA and DPh from Oxford University). She leads research projects which aim to identify causal pathways to eating disorders and obesity, and to test new treatments. Dr Byrne's team provides evidence-based psychological treatment for eating and weight disorders in children, adolescents and adults.

Mari Campbell is a clinical psychologist at the Child and Adolescent Eating Disorders Service, South London and Maudsley NHS Foundation Trust, London, and Section of Family Therapy, Institute of Psychiatry, King's College London. Her research interests include dropout in eating disorders and factors affecting maintenance of adolescent eating disorders.

Jacqueline C. Carter is Staff Psychologist in the Eating Disorder Program at Toronto General Hospital and Associate Professor in Psychiatry at the University of Toronto. Her research focus is recovery and relapse in anorexia nervosa and development of novel psychological treatments.

Angela Celio Doyle is a Clinical Associate at the University of Chicago. Her research interests include early intervention and treatment of eating disorders and obesity in youth.

Angélica M. Claudino is head of the Eating Disorders Programme (PROATA), Department of Psychiatry, Federal University of São Paulo (UNIFESP), São Paulo, Brazil. She was previously a Postdoctoral Fellow at the Eating Disorders Section, Institute of Psychiatry, King's College London (2008). Her research focus is eating disorders treatment, especially bulimic-type disorders such as binge eating disorder (BED).

Leora David is a research coordinator at the Eating Disorders Research Unit of Columbia University Medical Center (CUMC), with a special interest in medication treatment of eating disorders.

Emma Dove is a research psychologist at the University of Western Australia. Her research interests include psychological approaches to treatment of obesity, disordered eating and management of type 2 diabetes. Emma helped to establish the UWA Weight Management Programme (UWA WMP), a cognitive behavioural treatment for adult obesity. She is currently working on an Australia-wide trial of treatment for eating disorders, on research in obese, diabetic and bariatric surgery populations, and on the UWA WMP.

Peter M. Doyle is a Postdoctoral Fellow in the Eating Disorders Program at the University of Chicago. His research interests include early response to treatment in eating disorders.

Ivan Eisler is Professor of Family Psychology and Family Therapy at the Institute of Psychiatry, King's College London and Joint Head of the Child and Adolescent Eating Disorders Service at the South London and Maudsley NHS Foundation Trust, London.

Jane Evans is Highly Specialist Clinical Psychologist at the Vincent Square Eating Disorders Service, Central and North West London NHS Foundation Trust. Her clinical work is primarily with adult outpatients with eating disorders, using a cognitive-behavioural approach.

Anita Federici, PhD York University, is Director of the Dialectical Behavior Therapy program at the Cleveland Center for Eating Disorders. With Dr Lucene Wisniewski, Anita's research and clinical work focus is developing innovative and empirically sound eating disorder treatments for complex and multi-diagnostic patients.

Stefanie Gilbert is a Harvard-educated clinical psychologist with a private practice in Bethesda, Maryland. A former tenured professor at Howard University, Dr Gilbert has been a Board Member of the Washington Society for the Study of Eating Disorders since 1998 and served six years as the organization's president.

Elizabeth Goddard is a New Zealander completing her PhD at the Eating Disorders Unit, Institute of Psychiatry, King's College London. She is investigating the neuropsychological profile of parents of people with eating disorders and working on a trial evaluating the effectiveness of intervention for carers of inpatients with anorexia nervosa.

Lynn S. Grefe is President and Chief Executive Officer of the National Eating Disorders Association, USA. She is a leading advocate in raising global awareness and providing education, resources and support, and instrumental in setting policy nationally. She aims to promote healthy body image, prevent eating disorders and ensure access to quality care and support.

Susan Hart is a dietitian, with twelve years' experience in eating disorders, now Program Manager of a new Day Program in Sydney, Australia. Her research interests include nutritional management of eating disorders, and establishing an evidence base for practice in this area. Susan won the Dietitians Association of Australia Emerging Researcher Award, 2009.

Natalie Kanakam is a PhD student by MRC scholarship under Professor Janet Treasure. Her research focus is on twins, investigating how genetic predisposition interacts with environment. The research examines the neurocognitive profile associated with eating disorders and whether this is heritable.

Debra K. Katzman is Professor of Pediatrics, Head of the Division of Adolescent Medicine, Department of Pediatrics and University of Toronto, Medical Director of the Eating Disorders Program at the Hospital for Sick Children and Senior Associate Scientist at the Research Institute at the Hospital for Sick Children. Her research focus is to understand the unique physiologic, psychological, and developmental issues in children and adolescents with eating disorders. Dr Katzman was the 2010–2011 President of the Academy for Eating Disorders.

Walter H. Kaye is Professor of Psychiatry and Director of the Eating Disorder Treatment and Research Program at the University of California, San Diego (UCSD). Dr Kaye, Dr Bailer and Ms Klabunde study the neurobiology of eating disorders using brain imaging and genetics with the intention of applying this knowledge towards new treatments.

Jennifer S. Kirby is Research Assistant Professor of Psychology at the University of North Carolina at Chapel Hill. Her research focus is the treatment of intimate relationships and the interplay between individual distress and relationship functioning.

Megan Klabunde is completing her PhD in clinical psychology. Her research focus includes the neuropathophysiology of eating disorders and its application towards creating new therapies. Megan has managed several of Dr Walter Kaye's research studies at the University of California, San Diego.

Anna Konstantellou is a PhD student at the Institute of Psychiatry, King's College London. Her research focus is anxiety factors in eating disorders, especially intolerance of uncertainty in adolescents with anorexia nervosa.

Ann M. Laverty is Associate Director (Counselling) at the Wellness Centre, University of Calgary, and specializes in individual and group psychotherapy. Her research focus is eating disorders treatment, clinical supervision of graduate students and health promotion within a post-secondary context.

Daniel Le Grange is Professor of Psychiatry and Director of the Eating Disorders Program at The University of Chicago. His research interests include treatment outcome of adolescent eating disorders.

Laura (Collins) Lyster-Mensh is Executive Director of FEAST, an international non-profit organization supporting parents of eating disorder patients. The author of *Eating With Your Anorexic*, Laura blogs at the *Huffington Post* and *HealthyPlace.com* on mental health and parenting issues.

Sloane Madden is co-director of the Eating Disorder Service at the Children's Hospital at Westmead, Australia's largest public eating disorder service. He specializes in the treatment and management of eating disorders in children. His research has three major foci: early onset eating disorders, treatment of anorexia nervosa and neurobiology of eating disorders.

Stephanie Milstein is a clinical psychologist at Dennis & Moye & Associates in Bloomfield Hills, Michigan. She specializes in treating eating disorders, and provides Maudsley parent/family/group coaching and treatment. She is a group facilitator for the Parent Coaching Program at Beaumont Hospital, and a member of the FEAST professional advisory panel and National Eating Disorders Association (NEDA).

Christina M. Morgan is a clinical psychologist and supervisor of psychologist trainees on the Eating Disorders Programme (PROATA) of the Federal University of São Paulo. Her research training (PhD) at the National Institute of Mental Health in the USA focused on children with binge eating.

John F. Morgan is head of the Yorkshire Centre for Eating Disorders in Leeds and Senior Lecturer, St George's University of London. He is a member of the Eating Disorder Research Society and a fellow of the Academy for Eating Disorders. His research has examined treatment, risk management and early intervention. Professor Morgan authored the first self-help book for males with eating disorders.

Ashley Moskovich is a graduate student at Duke University Medical Center, Duke University, North Carolina.

Marion P. Olmsted is Director of the Eating Disorder Program at Toronto General Hospital and Professor in Psychiatry at the University of Toronto. Her research interests include rates and predictors of relapse and evaluation of treatment interventions.

Julie O'Toole is founder and director of the Kartini Clinic for Disordered Eating in Portland, Oregon. She is a paediatrician and adolescent medicine doctor, specializing in very young patients with anorexia nervosa and food phobia; and she maintains parents do not cause neurobiological brain disorders known as eating disorders and children do not choose to have them.

Susan J. Paxton is Professor and Head of the School of Psychological Science, La Trobe University, Australia. Her major research focus is prevention, risk factors and early intervention for body image and eating disorders. She was President of the Academy for Eating Disorders, 2009–2010.

Kathleen M. Pike is Assistant Dean for Research and Professor of Psychology at Temple University, Japan. Her research focus is treatment outcome and culture and risk factors in eating disorders development.

Simone Raenker is from Germany, and is completing her PhD at the Eating Disorders Unit, Institute of Psychiatry, King's College London. Her research focus is the role of fathers in the care and management of eating disorders, and a trial evaluating the effectiveness of an intervention for carers of inpatients with anorexia nervosa.

Renee Rienecke Hoste is Assistant Professor of Psychiatry at the University of Chicago. Her research interests include the role of expressed emotion in treatment outcome of eating disorders.

Susan Ringwood is Chief Executive of Beat, the UK charity supporting people affected by eating disorders. She is an Advisory Board member of the Academy for Eating Disorders; she initiated the World Wide Charter for Action on Eating Disorders; and she is a member of the Royal College of Psychiatrists Eating Disorders Section Executive Committee.

Janice Russell is Clinical Professor of Psychiatry, University of Sydney and Medical Director of Eating Disorders Programs at Royal Prince Alfred Hospital and the Northside Clinic, Greenwich, both teaching hospitals of Sydney Medical School. She is an Executive Committee member of the Boden Institute for Obesity, Nutrition, Exercise and Eating Disorders, University of Sydney, and Secretary of the Section for Eating Disorders of the World Psychiatric Association. Her clinical research focus is psychoneuroendocrinology of eating disorders.

Angela Smyth is Clinical Associate and Medical Director of the Eating Disorders Program at the University of Chicago. Her research interests include treatment of adolescent and adult eating disorders.

Jorunn Sundgot-Borgen is Professor in the Department of Sports Medicine, Norwegian School of Sports Sciences, Norway. Her research interests include prevention and treatment of eating disorders in sports. She established and ran an eating disorders treatment team at the Norwegian Olympic Sports Training Center.

Mary Tantillo is a fellow of the Academy for Eating Disorders, Associate Professor of Clinical Nursing at the University of Rochester School of Nursing, Clinical Associate Professor of Psychiatry at the University of Rochester School of Medicine, and Director of the Western New York Comprehensive Care Center for Eating Disorders.

Janet Treasure is Director, South London and Maudsley NHS, Trust Eating Disorder Unit, and Professor of Psychiatry, King's College London. She is a fellow of both the Academy for Eating Disorders and Beat, the UK's leading eating disorders charity. Her research interests include carers of people with eating disorders, treatment and aetiology of eating disorders, and neurobiology, particularly anorexia nervosa.

Chevese Turner is founder and Chief Executive Officer of the non-profit Binge Eating Disorder Association (BEDA), providing resources and education to treatment providers and people with BED.

Eric van Furth, PhD is a clinical psychologist and psychotherapist and Clinical Director of the Center for Eating Disorders Ursula in Leidschendam, the Netherlands. He has been working clinically with patients with eating disorders for twenty-five years. After holding a seat as the Chair of the Dutch Multidisciplinary Treatment Guideline Workgroup on Eating Disorders, he is currently a Fellow and Past-President of the Academy for Eating Disorders and co-initiator of www.Proud2Bme.nl.

Claire Vickery is founder and executive chairperson of the Butterfly Foundation, Australia's largest charity supporting people with eating disorders and negative body image. Butterfly funds individuals for treatment, delivers prevention programmes, enhances treatment facilities, funds research and promotes cultural change through advocacy and philanthropy.

Mallory Vinson, MSW, is a project coordinator for Duke University Medical Center's Department of Psychiatry. Her research interests include early onset and intervention in eating disorders in children and adolescents.

Kristin M. von Ranson is Associate Professor in the Clinical Psychology Program, Department of Psychology, University of Calgary. Her research focus is the gap between researchers' recommendations and practitioners' choices of psychotherapies for eating disorders, associations of eating problems with comorbid psychopathology and personality, and conceptualization of eating disorders as addictions.

Tracey D. Wade completed her Masters in Clinical Psychology at the Australian National University in 1992, her PhD at Flinders University in 1998, and a post-doctoral fellowship in the USA during 1999 at the Virginia Institute for Psychiatric and Behavioural Genetics. A clinician in eating disorders for over twenty years, she is currently Professor in the School of Psychology, Flinders University. Her research interests include the aetiology, prevention and treatment of eating disorders; and she has more than 100 publications in peer-reviewed journals.

Alison Wakefield is an Advanced Accredited Practising Dietitian. She developed the *Practice Recommendations for the Nutritional Management of Anorexia Nervosa in Adults*, DAA; and she is an author/presenter on the dietitian's role in eating disorder management. She has been an Academy for Eating Disorders (Australia/New Zealand) executive; and a consultant on the first postgraduate general practitioner diploma on anorexia nervosa and the Australian and New Zealand Clinical Practice Guidelines for Anorexia Nervosa.

Glenn Waller is a consultant clinical psychologist with the Vincent Square Eating Disorders Service, Central and North West London NHS Foundation Trust, and Visiting Professor of Psychology at the Institute of Psychiatry, King's College London. His clinical specialty and core research area is cognitive behavioural therapy for eating disorders.

B. Timothy Walsh is Ruane Professor of Psychiatry at Columbia University Medical Center, and Founding Director of the Columbia Eating Disorders Research Unit. He has conducted studies on the treatment of eating disorders for more than thirty years.

Hunna J. Watson is a senior research psychologist at the Eating Disorders Program, Princess Margaret Hospital for Children, Western Australia; a research psychologist at the Centre for Clinical Interventions, Department of Health, in WA; and an adjunct research fellow at the School of Paediatrics and Child Health, University of WA. Her research interests include thinking styles and traits that could act as causal and maintaining factors of eating disorders, and dissemination of evidence-based therapies in naturalistic clinical practice.

Karli Watson received her PhD from the California Institute of Technology and is a post-doctoral fellow in neurobiology at Duke University. Her research interests include primate neuroethology, social decision-making, and eating disorders.

Hazel Williams is a dietitian specializing in nutritional management of eating disorders. She is senior dietitian at the Beumont Centre for Eating Disorders in the teaching hospital of Sydney University. She developed the *Practice Recommendations for the Nutritional Management of Anorexia Nervosa in Adults*, DAA; she is an author/presenter on the dietitian's role in eating disorder management; and she is a former Academy for Eating Disorders (Australia/ New Zealand) executive.

Lucene Wisniewski is Clinical Director and co-founder of the Cleveland Center for Eating Disorders (CCED), adjunct assistant professor at Case Western Reserve University, and an Academy for Eating Disorders fellow.

Nancy Zucker is Assistant Professor of Psychiatry and Behavioral Science at Duke University Medical Center, Adjunct Assistant Professor of Psychology and Neuroscience at Duke University, and Director, Duke Center for Eating Disorders. Her research interests include developmental neuroscience of body awareness and visceral sensitivity to understand self and others.

Preface

A Collaborative Approach to Eating Disorders is about increasing awareness in the general practitioner field and building a bridge between research and practice. It is about encouraging established clinicians to consider new approaches based on research, and to provide instances of collaborative care treatments to clinicians-in-training. It describes how clinicians, researchers, carers and patients are forming collaborative recovery models of care that emphasise shared responsibility, autonomous choices and collaboration. This recovery model involves optimism, empowerment and interpersonal support and a focus on collaborative treatment approaches. *A Collaborative Approach to Eating Disorders* is one of the first steps on this journey and the authors hope it will lead to more productive roles for all involved in the future. The contributors are world leaders in their fields of research, treatment, advocacy and family support. Case studies illustrate the outcomes of their approach.

A Collaborative Approach to Eating Disorders is essential reading for general practitioners and non-specialised clinicians who wish to update and broaden their knowledge of new approaches in eating disorder treatment and care, and for specialised clinicians updating their knowledge of this standard of care.

This book establishes parameters on what is needed to achieve the best outcomes in research and treatment of eating disorders. An example is family-based treatment, where the family/carers are integral to the recovery approach, and teamwork by clinicians applying their respective model of care. The eating disorder field is necessarily multi-disciplinary – more so than perhaps any other field. Add to this the necessity of a higher degree of family involvement than almost any other field (autism perhaps being the closest) and the need for the collaborative approach becomes clear. The text has a strong emphasis on family and Maudsley/family-based treatment because evidence-based research has shown this to be one of the most effective ways to treat eating disorders, particularly with early intervention in children and adolescents. This book will assist those making or completing a paradigm shift in recognising that family-based treatment is not separate from the rest of the eating disorder field, but part of it. Contributors explain empirical research leading to family-based, dialectical and cognitive behavioural treatments. They explore and illustrate the influence of genetics, personality traits and environment in the development of an eating disorder. They discuss comorbidities, the risk of relapse and why family – in whatever form – is integral in recovery efforts.

A Collaborative Approach to Eating Disorders is written primarily for health professionals who want to better understand, diagnose and guide the management of eating disorders. It underscores the need for more research, education and training of health practitioners in providing early diagnosis and care guidance. Case studies provide insights into eating disorder diagnosis and care and emphasise the need for research outcomes to more quickly reach family doctor and health practitioner consulting rooms, clinics and hospitals, where they are needed most. While introducing some collaborative therapies in use today, this book does not pretend to provide all the answers to eating disorder illnesses – illnesses for which there is not yet knowledge of a cause or cure.

The co-editors exemplify the book's collaborative theme. June Alexander is a writer who battled eating disorders for four decades from the age of 11; Janet Treasure is a Professor of Psychiatry conducting world-leading research into the causes and treatment of eating disorders. The concept for *A Collaborative Approach to Eating Disorders* evolved when June was considering a sequel to her book *My Kid Is Back – Empowering Parents to Beat Anorexia Nervosa*. Research revealed an enthusiastic call for a book to help close the gap of knowledge between research and practice. Concern was expressed that in the field of eating disorders researchers and clinicians often do not speak the same language. *A Collaborative Approach to Eating Disorders* paves the way.

June Alexander developed anorexia nervosa at the age of 11 in 1962 and transitioned to bulimia nervosa. Her illness was not correctly diagnosed for twenty-one years. Her memoir *A Girl Called Tim – Escape from an Eating Disorder Hell* (2011) chronicles her eating disorder journey. In *My Kid Is Back – Empowering Parents to beat Anorexia Nervosa,* June writes about the Maudsley Approach in collaboration with Professor Daniel Le Grange of the University of Chicago. www.junealexander.com.

Janet Treasure, PhD, FRCP, FRCPsych, is Director, South London and Maudsley NHS Trust, Eating Disorder Unit, and Professor of Psychiatry, King's College London. Professor Treasure has authored numerous books on eating disorders (www.eatingresearch.com).

Foreword

Those of us who work in the field of eating disorders live in exciting times. Knowledge of the nature and causes of eating disorders across the spectrum of age and illness is increasing; new, more effective developmentally appropriate treatments are being developed; and clinical and educational services for people with these disorders are growing in scope and complexity.

For these reasons, the time is right for *A Collaborative Approach to Eating Disorders* edited by June Alexander and Janet Treasure. A comprehensive, compassionate account of the current state of knowledge about eating disorders derived from interdisciplinary collaboration, this unique new book integrates findings from evidence-based research with the knowledge that comes from clinical experience and practice. Contributors include international experts in clinical care, research, advocacy, and family support, as well as carers and people who have had an eating disorder.

This book provides an excellent discussion of collaborative treatment approaches to improving the health of patients with eating disorders. The authors illustrate how providing collaborative care uses the unique skills of healthcare professionals working together with patients and families, and how this care results in better outcomes and, ultimately, a better quality of life for patients.

The scholarly, yet practical, accessible discussions of the research for the material presented are one of the strengths of this text. Editors June Alexander and Janet Treasure, and the authors, support our assumptions about the aetiology, prevention, and treatment of eating disorders with current research, and translate this information into clinical practice. The content skilfully bridges the appreciable gap between research findings and clinical practice.

The book is divided into four sections: understanding risk and resilience for eating disorders, treatment, clinical presentations, and changing the culture. The first section describes the current research into our understanding of eating disorders, including biological and psychosocial risks, behavioural effects, and cultural factors in the genesis of an eating disorder. The second section provides an overview of various successful treatment modalities, including family approaches, and a variety of psychotherapeutic and psychopharmacologic approaches. The third section focuses on the presentation of eating disorders in clinical populations that are often neglected: children and adolescents, African-American women, athletes, and males. The final section deals with the need for a cultural shift in the way our communities and healthcare systems understand eating disorders. The authors use clinical cases to bring the chapters to life, then follow the cases with the insights of interdisciplinary experts who present the evidence and its application to clinical practice. This format is a compelling, effective way of engaging healthcare professionals' understanding of the content which should facilitate its application to meet the needs of patients and their families.

Our knowledge of eating disorders is changing rapidly. The editors and authors of this book should be congratulated for putting together an important, indispensable resource for interdisciplinary trainees and healthcare professionals who wish to update their understanding, treatment and care of people with eating disorders. *A Collaborative Approach to Eating Disorders* successfully promotes collaboration between the clinician, researcher, advocate, carer and patient, and translates research into practice. In the process, this book raises a number of important questions that should stimulate further research and scholarly work.

A Collaborative Approach to Eating Disorders provides the necessary tools healthcare professionals need to meet the challenges facing people who suffer with eating disorders.

Debra K. Katzman

Acknowledgements

The following people are acknowledged for courageously and generously sharing their experience with an eating disorder for consideration and inclusion as case studies: Raye-Ann deRegnier; Marilyn Colón Asencio and Jeannette Marie Rodriquez; Therese Waterhous; Julia; Carolin Gray; Kelly; Veronica Kamerling, Peter Kamerling, Vanessa and Henrietta Kamerling; Stephanie and Kate; Bek Simmons and family; Chevese Turner; Suzanne, Mark, Amy, Jessica and Ellie van de Ven; Jennifer Marsh (*in honour of Aimee McArthur – we continue the fight against eating disorders, in your memory*); Cathy; Leslie Long; Pam and Sarah Macdonald; Sarah C; Beth, Brian and Holly; J.V. Maddison, Barbara Dawkin; Anna Marie Hopewell, Kate and John, Stephanie and Josh; Denise Clancy; Amanda F. Kleinman; Lynne, Andy, Rachel and Lucy; Angela E. Lackey; Marina, Grant and Sarah; Karin Sabina Drucker; Lydia (*with gratitude for my brave and remarkable daughter and everything she taught me on our journey*); Duncan Strachan; Fiona and Zoe; Patrick Bergstrom; Monica and Jenna; Kate Le Page; Russell Cooper; Amanda and Sarah Cattrall; Bridget Bonnin; Colleen Sidlovsky; Diane Israel; Lisa; Wendy.

Compilation of the case studies has been a great international, collaborative effort by patients, patients in recovery, families, support groups and clinicians. Almost all interviews were accomplished via telephone, Skype and the internet – in the United Kingdom, elsewhere in Europe, North America and Australia.

I wish to thank Belinda Dalton, Jane Cawley (www.maudsleyparents.org/), Laura Collins (www.feast-ed.org/), Carrie Arnold (ed-bites.blogspot.com/) and members of the eating disorder unit at Guy's Hospital, London (Gillian Todd, Liz Goddard and Wendy Whitaker) for 'spreading the word' in seeking appropriate case studies. The international support has been amazing. Within hours of a call being posted, patients and carers generously and bravely responded, offering to share their stories to help others.

Authors have contributed from around the globe – the UK, elsewhere in Europe, Canada, the United States, Brazil, Japan and Australia –with the internet providing the major form of communication. The textbook is an amazing feat in international collaboration.

I thank Laura Collins and Jane Cawley for their friendship and encouragement at all times, and for assistance in research and reading the manuscript.

Above all, I thank co-author Professor Janet Treasure, Department of Academic Psychiatry, Bermondsey Wing, Guy's Hospital, London, and my editors, Joanne Forshaw and Jane Harris, for believing in me.

June Alexander

Furthermore:

Jane Evans and Glenn Waller would like to thank 'Sarah' for kindly agreeing to her story being told, and for her much appreciated input towards development of their chapter.

Walter Kaye, Ursula Bailer and Megan Klabunde wish to acknowledge that funding for their work was provided by the National Institute of Mental Health (NIMH) MH046001, MH042984, MH076286, MH086017, the Hilda & Preston Davis Foundation and the Price Foundation.

Elizabeth Goddard, Simone Raenker and Janet Treasure wish to acknowledge that their work was funded by a Department of Health NIHR Programme Grant for Applied Research (reference number RP-PG-0606-1043). This work was also supported by the NIHR Biomedical Research Centre for Mental Health, South London and Maudsley NHS Foundation Trust, Institute of Social Psychiatry and Institute of Psychiatry, King's College London. The views and opinions expressed within their chapter do not necessarily reflect those of DH/NIHR.

Part I

Understanding risk and resilience for eating disorders

Introduction

Carrie Arnold

A revolution in genetics and neuroscience is dramatically altering the way eating disorders are understood and treated. We know now that eating disorders are illnesses, not a lifestyle choice. This knowledge, while a giant step forward, opens the door to many new challenges. In the United States, about 11 million people suffer from an eating disorder, and about one in every twenty people will suffer an eating disorder during their lifetime. The causes remain unclear, but numerous risk factors have been identified, including exposure to the thin body ideal, body dissatisfaction (Stice *et al.*, in press), negative affect (Rivinus *et al.* 1984), female gender (Jacobi *et al.* 2004), and variations in serotonin genes (Calati *et al.,* in press). Yet some of the strongest risk factors are the presence of an anxiety disorder, such as social anxiety disorder and obsessive-compulsive disorder, and a family history of eating disorders. Research reveals that genetics comprise up to 86 per cent of the reason a person develops an eating disorder (Klump *et al.* 2001; Lilenfeld *et al.* 1998). Together, these studies indicate a strong biological basis for eating disorders.

Ramifications are far-reaching. When researchers presented eating disorders as biologically based mental illnesses, caused primarily by genetics, college students viewed sufferers with more compassion than if they were told eating disorders were essentially a cultural phenomenon (Crisafulli *et al.* 2008: 333). And the biological basis of anorexia can determine who gets treatment. In the state of New Jersey in the United States, health insurers could legally deny paying for anorexia treatment because it wasn't classified as a biologically based mental illness. A recent class action lawsuit caused this provision to be overturned and anorexia and bulimia treated on a par with depression, bipolar disorder, and schizophrenia (Rothman 2008).

When I began treatment for anorexia nervosa a decade ago, treatment providers didn't inform me of these biological studies. They didn't explain that something in my brain was compelling me to starve, purge, and over-exercise. They said my eating disorder was a choice, and so was my recovery. From the inside, however, my eating disorder was a Byzantine array of rules and rituals that paralyzed me with fear of food. Following numerous hospital admissions, several lengthy stays in residential treatment, and multiple trips to the emergency room, therapists said I would recover 'when I was ready'.

Their theories colored how my eating disorder was treated and how I viewed my illness. Ultimately, I blamed myself: I should be able to pull myself out of this; I shouldn't need help to eat. But all the insight in the world couldn't overcome my fear of food. After essentially kissing my twenties goodbye, food is simply food again. It's food because I found a therapist who didn't waste time on 'why'. Well-versed in the latest evidence-based treatment for eating disorders, she said: 'You need to eat, and eat regularly.' I needed to normalize my eating and exercise habits now, not later. And my parents were the best people to help me. I began to realize my eating disorder was driven not by society or some error in my psyche, but by something deeper and more primal. As explained in the following chapters, my eating disorder was a biologically based mental illness that I didn't choose and my parents (and society) didn't cause.

References

Calati, R., De Ronchi, D., Bellini, M., and Serretti, A. (2011) 'The 5-HTTLPR Polymorphism and Eating Disorders: A Meta-Analysis', *Int J Eat Disord* 44, 3: 191–9.

Crisafulli, M., Von Holle, A., and Bulik, C. (2008) 'Attitudes Towards Anorexia Nervosa: The Impact of Framing on Blame and Stigma', *Int J Eat Disord* 41, 4: 333–9.

Jacobi, C., Hayward, C., de Zwaan, M., Kraemer, H.C., and Agras, W.S. (2004) 'Coming to Terms with Risk Factors for Eating Disorders: Application of Risk Terminology and Suggestions for a General Taxonomy', *Psychol Bull* 130, 1: 19–65.

Klump, K.L., Miller, K.B., Keel, P.K., McGue, M., and Iacono, W.G. (2001) 'Genetic and Environmental Influences on Anorexia Nervosa Syndromes in a Population-Based Twin Sample', *Psychol Med* 31, 4: 737–40.

Lilenfeld L.R., Kaye, W.H., Greeno, C.G., Merikangas, K.R., Plotnicov, K., Pollice, C., Rao, R., Strober, M., Bulik, C.M., and Nagy, L. (1998) 'A Controlled Family Study of Anorexia Nervosa and Bulimia Nervosa: Psychiatric Disorders in First-Degree Relatives and Effects of Proband Comorbidity', *Arch Gen Psychiatry* 55, 7: 603–10.

Rivinus, T.M., Biederman, J., Herzog, D.B., Kemper, K., Harper, G.P., Harmatz, J.S., and Houseworth, S. (1984) 'Anorexia Nervosa and Affective Disorders: A Controlled Family History Study', *Am J Psychiatry* 141, 11: 1414–18.

Rothman, C.J. (2008) 'Insurer Agrees to $1.2M Settlement in Anorexia Lawsuit', *New Jersey Star-Ledger*, 25 November.

Stice, E., Ng, J., and Shaw, H. (2010) 'Risk Factors and Prodromal Eating Pathology', *J Child Psychol Psychiatry* 51, 4: 518–25.

Chapter 1

The family context: cause, effect or resource

Anna Konstantellou, Mari Campbell and Ivan Eisler

Introduction

Historically, interest in families of people with eating disorders developed from clinical accounts of 'anorexic families' (Minuchin *et al.* 1978), suggesting such families were rigid, had poor communication and parents who were over-involved with their children's lives (Yager 1982). These accounts were often persuasive and seemed to offer a way of understanding an important part of the causal pathway in development of the illness, and some research studies appeared to support the conclusions (Latzer and Gaber 1998; McGrane and Carr 2002). However, as many authors indicate, generalizing from clinical accounts or small cross-sectional studies about the nature of aetiological processes is highly problematic, does little to improve our understanding of treatments and can undermine the positive role the family can have in helping the ill patient (Eisler 1995; Le Grange *et al.* 2010). From a research perspective, the findings also tend to oversimplify complex mechanisms and take little account of reciprocal processes between development of the illness and family functioning (Eisler 1995).

In 1995, Eisler conducted a review which examined family factors and their relationship with eating disorders. He found few consistent differences between families who had a son or daughter with an eating disorder (ED) and those who did not (Eisler 1995). The review also highlighted methodological issues with the research, including a lack of prospective data and comparison groups, samples consisting largely of chronically ill patients treated in specialist services, and lack of control for influences from other relevant factors such as depression. This chapter will update readers on research examining the family and eating disorders.

Personality and psychopathology in family members

Increasingly, research has studied parental and family psychopathology and personality traits in relation to eating disorders (see Chapter 2, on genes and personality). For instance, higher levels of overall psychopathology have been found in parents and relatives of patients with eating disorders when compared to parents of healthy individuals (Fassino *et al.* 2003, 2009; Lilenfeld *et al.* 1998; Steiger *et al.*

1995, 1996). In particular, higher levels of perfectionism have been reported in parents of patients with anorexia nervosa (AN) and bulimia nervosa (BN) when compared to parents with healthy offspring (de Amusquibar and De Simone 2003; Lilenfeld *et al.* 2000; Woodside *et al.* 2002). Raised levels of perfectionism in parents could indicate a genetic predisposition to a trait considered a risk factor for eating disorders but could also have an effect through its influence on parenting (Woodside *et al.* 2002). Other traits reported in mothers of daughters with AN behaviour include alexithymia (the inability to identify and process emotions; Espina 2003), depression (de Amusquibar and De Simone 2003) and lack of empathy (Guttman and Laporte 2000). Parental behaviour-related psychopathology will be covered in the next section. The above studies are predominately cross-sectional in nature and therefore no causal inferences can be made. Our understanding of the potential impact of parental psychopathology on offspring and in particular its contribution to development of behaviour psychopathology remains limited.

Family eating behaviours and comments about weight and shape

Many studies have examined family members, particularly mothers, and the effect of their eating behaviours or comments about weight and shape on behaviour symptoms or dieting and weight concerns in children and adolescents. As we will explain, evidence is conflicting. We look first at the relationship between parental eating-related factors in eating disorders and behaviour-related symptoms, and then at the effect of such parental factors on dieting and weight concerns in offspring.

Parental scores on the Eating Disorders Inventory (EDI) were found to be related to the development of behaviour symptoms in young adolescents in a two-stage community study (Canals *et al.* 2009), although associations were relatively weak and the parental EDI scores were generally considerably lower than those found in clinical populations. Adult patients with AN behaviour have also been found to more often have mothers who dieted or restricted their food intake than healthy individuals (Andrews and Brown 1999). Some studies have found that family preoccupation with weight and appearance and pressure to diet either by friends or family are associated with body dissatisfaction, restrained eating and bulimic behaviours (Fairburn *et al.* 1997; Keel *et al.* 1997; Leung *et al.* 1996; Pauls and Daniels 2000; Vincent and McCabe 2000; Young *et al.* 2004).

While these studies contain a fair degree of consistency, there are several caveats. First, the methodological quality of the studies was variable. While some larger, community-based studies were well designed, others, in particular those comparing a patient's recollections of parental behaviours with controls, were not always well matched or did not control for possible confounding variables. Second, the association between parental (particularly mothers') behaviours and attitudes appears clearer for patients with BN than for patients with AN (Benninghoven *et al.* 2007). Third, several studies found that the role of family factors was either mediated by other factors such as anxiety (Davis *et al.* 2004) or was reduced to non-significance when other factors such as depression, body dissatisfaction and peer influences were controlled for (Young *et al.* 2004).

Many studies have examined the effect of parents' own eating behaviours and attitudes towards weight and food on the dieting and weight and shape concerns of their offspring. For instance, female body image was predicted by levels of negative feedback from mothers, maternal disapproval of their daughter's figure, and the mothers' own eating behaviours and attitudes as perceived by daughters (Cooley *et al.* 2008). Body dissatisfaction and restrained eating have been associated with children's perception of mothers' encouragement to be thin (Anschutz *et al.* 2009). Furthermore, negative comments from mothers regarding their child's weight have been associated with weight-controlling behaviours in adolescents (Tremblay and Larivière 2009). It has also been identified that emotional eating (eating more in response to stress) is more present in daughters whose mothers emotionally eat (Blissett and Meyer 2006; Elfhag and Linne 2005; Snoek *et al.* 2007). Mothers and daughters have been found to share similar eating concerns and to place the same amount of importance on thinness (Steiger *et al.* 1996; Stice 1998). An internalized thin ideal appears to mediate the relationship between family concern about weight and looks, and body dissatisfaction, in a non-clinical sample of girls with low self-esteem (Senra *et al.* 2007). In a large prospective study, children's perception of the importance that fathers and mothers placed on being thin was found to be a factor that influenced dieting in both girls and, albeit less so, boys, and had a stronger influence than the attitudes of their peers, although surprisingly the perception of mothers' attitudes seemed to have a smaller role than that of fathers' (Field *et al.* 2001). Another study found a moderate association between comments about weight from parent to child, and losing weight and body esteem, in both boys and girls (Smolak *et al.* 1999). However, body mass index (BMI) was not controlled for and it has been shown that BMI mediates the relationship between parental comments on weight and dieting behaviours in children (Thelen and Cormier 1995). Possibly some children may have needed to lose weight and comments from parents may have been appropriate. There has been suggestion that socio-cultural influences could mediate the effects of parents' critical comments about weight and shape on children (Cordero and Israel 2009).

In contrast to the above literature, other studies fail to find an association between parents' and children's weight-restricting behaviours and body dissatisfaction (Davison *et al.* 2000; Ogden and Elder 1998; Ogden and Steward 2000). Parental views on weight and the importance placed on appearance were not strong predictors of disordered eating in 11- to 13- year-old girls (Kanakis and Thelen 1995). Similarly, adolescents' dieting and body image were not associated with mothers' own body image and dieting behaviours, nor did mothers' body image and dieting behaviours predict girls' dieting behaviours after a one-year follow-up (Byely *et al.* 2000). Longitudinal research has also not found an association between parents' dieting and their children's dieting (Snoek *et al.*

2009). In other words, family members may present certain similar dieting behaviours but there is no direct evidence of a transmission of such behaviours between parents and children (Snoek *et al.* 2009). Several studies have failed to find links between eating problems in children or adolescents and eating attitudes or eating pathology in mothers (Barbin *et al.* 2002; Chatoor *et al.* 2000; Cooper *et al.* 2001; Sanftner *et al.* 1996).

There are inconsistencies in the literature regarding the effect of parents' own behaviour symptoms, and attitudes and behaviours towards weight and shape, on their children. Moreover, we know little regarding possible pathways. Initial research seems to show that comments made by parents about food and weight have a stronger effect on their offspring than parents' modelling of inappropriate eating patterns (Baker *et al.* 2000; Byely *et al.* 2000; Ogden and Steward 2000; Thelen and Cormier 1995).

Family functioning and the family environment

Focus on family environment and family functioning has continued in relation to the development and maintenance of eating disorders. Cross-sectional research suggests that young females with AN behaviour perceive their family environment as lacking in warmth, support and cohesiveness when compared to healthy females (Bonne *et al.* 2003; Cunha *et al.* 2009). In a community-based sample, females with high scores on BN-related behaviours perceived their family environment as low in cohesion compared to those who showed less bulimic symptoms (Pauls and Daniels 2000).

Some studies reveal that criticism, hostility and/or emotional over-involvement (as assessed using the Expressed Emotion (EE) scales; Leff and Vaughn 1985) in families with an adolescent suffering from AN behaviour predict poorer outcome at end of therapy and at one-year follow-up, with maternal criticism being the best predictor of treatment outcome (van Furth *et al.* 1996). Eisler *et al.* (2007) have found similar results for adolescents with AN, with maternal critical comments at assessment predicting poorer engagement in treatment and outcome at end of treatment and at five-years follow-up, particularly if they received conjoint family therapy when compared to separated family therapy. Levels of EE, however, at end of treatment did not predict outcome at follow-up (Eisler *et al.* 2007). Similarly, inpatients with BN from high EE family backgrounds had higher levels of BN symptoms at discharge, at two-years-follow-up and, to some extent, at six-years follow-up compared to patients with low EE (Hedlund *et al.* 2003).

Of note is that although EE seems to affect treatment response, it is not particularly high at the beginning of treatment in adolescent AN samples (van Furth *et al.* 1996). This is different from adults with eating disorders where families with a patient with AN behaviour show high levels of expressed emotion (using a self-report measure of EE, the Family Questionnaire; Wiedemann *et al.* 2002) when compared to healthy control families (Kyriacou *et al.* 2008).

Some studies fail to find support for an association between family functioning and eating-related psychopathology. One study found family functioning, as reported by both patients with AN and BN and their mothers, to be in the normal range (Benninghoven *et al.* 2007). Family functioning has also not been found a significant predictor of bulimic behaviour in a non-clinical sample of female students (Young *et al.* 2001), nor did patients suffering from AN show more dysfunctional family patterns than healthy families (Cook-Darzens *et al.* 2005). However, families with a youngster suffering from AN reported feeling more disengaged and more dissatisfied with family connectedness than 'healthy' families (Cook-Darzens *et al.* 2005). Dissatisfaction with levels of connectedness may partly reflect the actual level of connectedness but also could reflect expectations or what the family member would wish for and both of these could be influenced by AN behaviour. The complexity of interplay between the illness and family environment and its effect on family functioning is important to keep in mind.

Parent–offspring relationships

Relationships between parents and their offspring have also been examined and reports are similar to those described in the previous section. Several, relatively small, cross-sectional studies comparing individuals suffering from an eating disorder with controls have identified differences in perceived relationships with parents. For example, patients with BN perceive their family relationships more negatively than healthy controls but not more negatively than a comparison clinical group (Benninghoven *et al.* 2003); while more positive, close relationships with both parents, as reported by a non-clinical sample of adolescent girls, were negatively associated with problematic eating attitudes (Swarr and Richards 1996). Furthermore, Latzer *et al.* (2009) report that daughters with AN behaviour tended to perceive their relationship with their parents to be poor, and Tata *et al.* (2001) report modest but statistically significant correlations between eating attitudes and ratings of parental overprotective behaviours in female students. The usual caveats about the limitations of interpreting findings from small, cross-sectional studies (to be addressed in the discussion section) are reinforced in this case by findings from two further studies.

An interesting prospective study of seventy-seven adolescent girls and their mothers (Byely *et al.* 2000) examined the relationship between body image concerns and dieting in adolescents and perceptions of family relationships, maternal dieting and maternal body image concerns. They found an evolving relationship between these factors over the course of a year. At initial assessment an association was found between negative perceptions and dieting, but this was largely mediated by body image which reduced the association between family relationships, and dieting to non-significance. At follow-up, however, the initial perceptions of family relationships rather than body image, predicted increased dieting (accounting for approximately 7 per cent of the variance), suggesting a negative perception of family relationships may have a cumulative effect over time. However, note that this accounts for a tiny proportion of the dieting behaviour changes.

The second set of data comes from Lehoux and Howe's 2007 study of differences in perception of family environments of forty women with BN and their well sisters. The study's methodology draws on the notion of non-shared family environments (Rowe and Plomin 1981) which explores factors that differentiate between siblings. Note however, that the study found more similarities than differences in perceptions between women with BN and their sisters. No differences were found in perceptions of maternal or paternal affection, women with BN rated both parents as displaying equally controlling behaviours (discipline, attention) towards themselves and their sisters, whereas the sisters were more likely to rate both parents as having been slightly more controlling towards their sibling with BN than towards themselves. The sibling relationships were rated equally on closeness, antagonism and caring but women with BN perceived themselves as being more jealous than their sisters, although this was not reflected in the siblings' ratings of jealousy. Another difference identified was higher ratings of insecure attachment assigned to fathers from women with BN, though no difference was found in attachment patterns of mothers.

Several studies have examined the role of attachment in eating disorders. Studies using various self-report measures of attachment (Broberg *et al.* 2001; Tereno *et al.* 2008; Ward *et al.* 2000) have found that patients with AN and BN generally rate their attachment relationships with parents as higher in anxiety and avoidance when compared with control groups. Ringer and Crittenden (2007) and Ward *et al.* (2001) used the more robust methodology of assessing attachment with the Adult Attachment Interview (George *et al.* 1985/1996) and found that patients with eating disorders in their sample were almost all rated as insecurely attached (most commonly dismissing or preoccupied attachment). Finally, some studies have found that attachment patterns are predictive of engagement in and response to treatment (Tasca *et al.* 2004, 2006; Tereno *et al.* 2008). These have a potentially important bearing on interpretation of attachment literature. Given that most research has been conducted in chronically ill patients, insecure attachment could be over-represented as it may moderate the course of the illness.

Impact on the family of having a child with an eating disorder

In the past, it has been assumed that differences identified between families with AN behaviour and control families indicate that certain family characteristics may be implicated in the causation of eating disorders. An equally plausible explanation, not examined to the same extent, is that a child with AN behaviour can contribute to the differences found between families. Support for this alternative pathway comes from a longitudinal study that found a direct effect of the ill person on the relationship between mother and daughter, while support for the reverse pathway was not found (Archibald *et al.* 2002). There is also evidence that caring for someone with AN behaviour can produce great amounts of emotional strain and as much stress and burden on the family as caring for someone with a physical illness (Gilbert *et al.* 2000; Sim *et al.* 2009). This is due to the life-threatening nature of the illness, its physical complications and associated psychological problems (Harris and Barraclough 1998; Hoek 2006; Papadopoulos *et al.* 2009). Therefore AN is likely to affect family relationships (Gilbert *et al.* 2000) and research suggests it affects parents in five areas (Hillege *et al.* 2006). These include behaviours either uniting the family or dividing it; parents struggling to cope due to experiencing high levels of emotional burden; inconsiderate comments from significant others increasing pressure on parents; social isolation from friends and health professionals; and financial strains (Hillege *et al.* 2006).

Family protective factors

Research has increasingly started to examine family factors that can have a positive impact on the illness and act as protective factors against young people developing eating disorders. A positive family environment and positive relationships within the family have been linked to less behaviour-related psychopathology and better outcome (Botta and Dumlao 2002; Byely *et al.* 2000; McVey *et al.* 2002; North *et al.* 1997; Swarr and Richards 1996). Healthy family eating patterns have been found to act as a shield against the development of eating disorders (Krug *et al.* 2009). A father–daughter relationship that has good conflict resolution and open communication has been shown to act as a protective factor against AN (Botta and Dumlao 2002) whereas lack of a father's support has been associated with disordered eating (McVey *et al.* 2002).

Discussion

The overall picture is of many disparate studies providing relatively few consistent findings. The difficulties are to some extent methodological but to a much larger degree conceptual.

Most studies tend to continue to employ small sample sizes, use a cross-sectional design, and compare families with an individual who has an eating disorder and families without a member of the family having an eating disorder. Invariably, authors of studies acknowledge the limitations of such a design but too often draw 'cautious' or 'tentative' conclusions that ignore these limitations. The problem is not the methodology but the lack of clear conceptualization informing such studies. There is nothing wrong with cross-sectional design *per se*, if it fits the question addressed by the research. Too often, such designs are chosen because they are the easiest to implement, resulting in research driven by the method rather than the research question.

Historically, a desire to elucidate putative family aetiological processes has driven family research. Many authors have pointed out (e.g. Schmidt and Treasure 2006;

Shafran and de Silva 2003) that understanding aetiological mechanisms tells relatively little about what to do in treatment; indeed one could argue they tell nothing at all unless they happen to coincide or overlap with maintenance mechanisms. The distinction between causal and maintaining mechanisms is important (and too often ignored) and should lead to different research designs. For instance a cross-sectional design comparing cases of brief duration with cases of long duration of illness would tell little about causal factors but might suggest possible factors connected with maintenance. Understanding causal pathways for development of eating disorders is of course a valid issue in its own right. There is rich literature on how such research is best conducted and the pitfalls it needs to avoid in relation to eating disorders (see Jacobi *et al.* 2004; Kazdin *et al.* 1997; Kraemer *et al.* 1997; Rutter 2000, 2005). Unfortunately, little family research in eating disorders has heeded this literature.

The other important distinction that can helpfully focus questions of research design is to differentiate between factors that may have a role in maintaining the illness and factors that moderate the effects of treatment. For instance, as we discussed earlier, parents of adult patients with AN, with a long illness duration, have been rated higher on criticism when compared to controls, whereas the same results have not been found in adolescent AN samples. However, both groups reveal consistent evidence that raised levels of criticism predict engagement in and response to treatment. The low levels of criticism in adolescent AN suggest it is not a risk factor for the illness, but the difference between the two samples indicates it may be a maintaining factor, and the relationship between criticism and poor engagement in treatment is more consistent with this factor being a moderator of treatment. Similarly, as we noted earlier, much research on attachment and eating disorders, showing high levels of insecure attachment, is usually interpreted as providing evidence of a possible aetiological pathway. However, it is equally plausible (and in some ways more consistent with existing data) that insecure attachment is more related to chronicity either as an illness-maintaining factor or a treatment-moderating factor.

Conclusions

In reviewing the literature on families and eating disorders we have been disappointed with the extent to which the question of the family's role in eating disorder development continues to dominate family research and the lack of conceptual and methodological sophistication that seems to accompany this. Research evidence continues to not support the notion that the family causes eating disorders. While some research might indicate possible family risk factors, these tend to be non-specific or play a relatively minor role in the disorder's development compared to other factors (and often have been shown to be associated only with increased dieting or body dissatisfaction rather than the actual behaviour).

Our main argument is that family research needs to be more theoretically driven, leading to more specific and more clearly defined questions which in turn should lead to more appropriate choice of research methodology. Where researchers continue to question the development of eating problems or eating disorders they should focus on protective as well as risk factors, and make better use of the range of research approaches and fit them to their specific questions.

From a clinical point of view we would like to see more research effort focused on the mechanisms of illness maintenance and family factors that might operate as moderators or mediators of treatment. Understanding better how the families' attempts to help can become counterproductive and reinforce rather than overcome problems, knowing more about what family factors predict which kind of treatment might be most useful, and above all understanding what family processes may need to be mobilized or changed as part of effective treatments are of central importance. At present we may have good evidence for the efficacy of family interventions but our knowledge of how such interventions work and how they can be enhanced remains in its infancy.

References

Andrews, B. and Brown, C. (1999) 'The role of infant characteristics and maternal behaviour in the development of later eating disorders', *Eur Eat Disord Rev* 7: 279–85.

Anschutz, D. J., Kanters, L. J., Van Strien, T., Vermulst, A. A., and Engels, R. C. (2009) 'Maternal behaviors and restrained eating and body dissatisfaction in young children', *Int J Eat Disord* 42: 54–61.

Archibald, A. B., Linver, M. R., Graber, J. A., and Brooks-Gunn, J. (2002) 'Parent-adolescent relationships and girls' unhealthy eating: Testing reciprocal effects', *J Res Adolesc* 12: 451–61.

Baker, C. W., Whisman, M. A., and Brownell, K. D. (2000) 'Studying intergenerational transmission of eating attitudes and behaviors: Methodological and conceptual questions', *Health Psychol* 19: 376–81.

Barbin, J. M., Williamson, D., Stewart, T., Thaw, J., Guarda, A., and Reas, D. (2002) 'Psychological adjustment in the children of mothers with a history of eating disorders', *Eat Weight Disord* 7: 32–8.

Benninghoven, D., Schneider, H., Strack, M., Reich, G., and Cierpka, M. (2003) 'Family representations in relationship episodes of patients with a diagnosis of bulimia nervosa', *Psychol Psychother Theor Res Pract* 76: 323–36.

Benninghoven, D., Tetsch, N., Kunzendorf, S., and Jantschek, G. (2007) 'Body image in patients with eating disorders and their mothers, and the role of family functioning', *Compr Psychiatry* 48: 118–23.

Blissett, J. and Meyer, C. (2006) 'The mediating role of eating psychopathology in the relationship between unhealthy core beliefs and feeding difficulties in a nonclinical group', *Int J Eat Disord* 39: 763–71.

Bonne, O., Lahat, S., Kfir, R., Berry, E., Katz, M., and Bachar, E. (2003) 'Parent–daughter discrepancies in perception of family function in bulimia nervosa', *Psychiatr Interpers Biol Process* 66: 244–54.

Botta, R. A. and Dumlao, R. (2002) 'How do conflict and communication patterns between fathers and daughters contribute to or offset eating disorders?', *Health Comm* 14: 199–219.

Broberg, A. G., Hjalmers, I., and Nevonen, L. (2001) 'Eating disorders, attachment and interpersonal difficulties: A comparison between 18- to 24- year-old patients and normal controls', *Eur Eat Disord Rev* 9: 381–96.

Byely, L., Archibald, A. B., Graber, J., and Brooks–Gunn, J. (2000) 'A prospective study of familial and social influences on girls' body image and dieting', *Int J Eat Disord* 28: 155–64.

Canals, J., Sancho, C., and Arija, M. (2009) 'Influence of parent's eating attitudes on eating disorders in school adolescents', *Eur Child Adolesc Psychiatry* 18: 353–9.

Chatoor, I., Ganiban, J., Hirsch, R., Borman-Spurrell, E., and Mrazek, D. A. (2000) 'Maternal characteristics and toddler temperament in infantile anorexia', *J Am Acad Child Adolesc Psychiatry* 39: 743–51.

Cook-Darzens, S., Doyen, C., Falissard, B., and Mouren, M.-C. (2005) 'Self-perceived family functioning in 40 French families of anorexic adolescents: Implications for therapy', *Eur Eat Disord Rev* 13: 223–36.

Cooley, E., Toray, T., Wang, M. C., and Valdez, N. N. (2008) 'Maternal effects on daughters' eating pathology and body image', *Eat Behav* 9: 52–61.

Cooper, M., Galbraith, M., and Drinkwater, J. (2001) 'Assumptions and beliefs in adolescents with anorexia nervosa and their mothers', *Eat Disord* 9: 217–23.

Cordero, E. D. and Israel, T. (2009) 'Parents as protective factors in eating problems of college women', *Eat Disord* 17: 146–61.

Cunha, A. I., Relvas, A. P., and Soares, I. (2009) 'Anorexia nervosa and family relationships: Perceived family functioning, coping strategies, beliefs, and attachment to parents and peers', *Int J Clin Health Psychol* 9: 229–40.

Davis, C., Shuster, B., Blackmore, E., and Fox, J. (2004) 'Looking good – family focus on appearance and the risk for eating disorders', *Int J Eat Disord* 35: 136–44.

Davison, K., Markey, C., and Birch, L. (2000) 'Etiology of body dissatisfaction and weight concerns among 5-year-old girls', *Appetite* 35: 143–51.

de Amusquibar, A. and De Simone, C. (2003) 'Some features of mothers of patients with eating disorders', *Eat Weight Disord* 8: 225–30.

Eisler, I. (1995) 'Family models of eating disorders', in G. I. Szmukler and C. Dare (eds) *Handbook of Eating Disorders: Theory, Treatment and Research* (pp. 155–76), Chichester: John Wiley & Sons.

Eisler, I., Simic, M., Russell, G. F. M., and Dare, C. (2007) 'A randomised controlled treatment trial of two forms of family therapy in adolescent anorexia nervosa: A five-year follow-up', *J Child Psychol Psychiatry* 48: 552–60.

Elfhag, K. and Linne, Y. (2005) 'Gender differences in associations of eating pathology between mothers and their adolescent offspring', *Obes Res* 13: 1070–6.

Espina, A. (2003) 'Alexithymia in parents of daughters with eating disorders: Its relationships with psychopathological and personality variables', *J Psychosom Res* 55: 553–60.

Fairburn, C. G., Welch, S. L., Doll, H. A., Davies, B. A., and O'Connor, M. E. (1997) 'Risk factors for bulimia nervosa: A community-based case-control study', *Arch Gen Psychiatry* 54: 509–17.

Fassino, S., Amianto, F., Daga, G., Leombruni, P., Garzaro, L., Levi, M., and Rovera, G. (2003) 'Bulimic family dynamics: Role of parent's personality – a controlled study with the temperament and character inventory', *Compr Psychiatry* 44: 70–7.

Fassino, S., Amianto, F., and Abbate-Daga, G. (2009) 'The dynamic relationship of parental personality traits with the personality and psychopathology traits of anorectic and bulimic daughters', *Compr Psychiatry* 50: 232–9.

Field, A. E., Camargo Jr, C. A., Taylor, C. B., Berkey, C. S., Roberts, S. B., and Colditz, G. A. (2001) 'Peer, parent, and media influences on the development of weight concerns and frequent dieting among preadolescent and adolescent girls and boys', *Pediatrics* 107: 54–60.

George, C., Kaplan, N., and Main, M. (1985/1996) *Adult Attachment Interview: Interview Protocol*, Berkeley, CA: University of California.

Gilbert, A. A., Shaw, S. M., and Notar, M. K. (2000) 'The impact of eating disorders on family relationships', *Eat Disord* 8: 331–45.

Guttman, H. A. and Laporte, L. (2000) 'Empathy in families of women with borderline personality disorder, anorexia nervosa, and a control group', *Fam Process* 39: 345–58.

Harris, E. C. and Barraclough, B. (1998) 'Excess mortality of mental disorder', *Br J Psychiatry* 173: 11–53.

Hedlund, S., Fichter, M., Quadflieg, N., and Brandl, C. (2003) 'Expressed emotion, family environment, and parental bonding in bulimia nervosa: A 6-year investigation', *Eat Weight Disord* 8: 26–35.

Hillege, S., Beale, B., and McMaster, R. (2006) 'Impact of eating disorders on family life: Individual parents' stories', *J Clin Nurs* 15: 1016–22.

Hoek, H. W. (2006) 'Incidence, prevalence and mortality of anorexia nervosa and other eating disorders', *Curr Opin Psychiatry* 19: 389–94.

Jacobi, C., Hayward, C., de Zwaan, M., Kraemer, H., and Agras, W. (2004) 'Coming to terms with risk factors for eating disorders: Application of risk terminology and suggestions for a general taxonomy', *Psychol Bull* 130: 19–65.

Kanakis, D. M. and Thelen, M. H. (1995) 'Parental variables associated with bulimia nervosa', *Addict Behav* 20: 491–500.

Kazdin, A. E., Kraemer, H. C., Kessler, R. C., Kupfer, D. J., and Offord, D. R (1997) 'Contributions of risk-factor research to developmental psychopathology', *Clin Psychol Rev* 17: 375–406.

Keel, P. K., Heatherton, T. F., Harnden, J. L., and Hornig, C. D. (1997) 'Mothers, fathers, and daughters: Dieting and disordered eating', *Eat Disord* 5: 216–28.

Kraemer, H., Kazdin, A., Offord, D., Kessler, R., Jensen, P., and Kupfer, D. (1997) 'Coming to terms with the terms of risk', *Arch Gen Psychiatry* 54: 337–43.

Krug, I., Treasure, J., Anderluh, M., Bellodi, L., Cellini, E., Collier, D., Bernardo, M. D., Granero, R., Karwautz, A., Nacmias, B., Penelo, E., Ricca, V., Sorbi, S., Tchanturia, K., Wagner, G., and Fernandez-Aranda, F. (2009) 'Associations of individual and family eating patterns during childhood and early adolescence: A multicentre European study of associated eating disorder factors', *Br J Nutr* 101: 909–18.

Kyriacou, O., Treasure, J., and Schmidt, U. (2008) 'Expressed emotion in eating disorders assessed via self-report: An examination of factors associated with expressed emotion in carers of people with anorexia nervosa in comparison to control families', *Int J Eat Disord* 41: 37–46.

Latzer, Y. and Gaber, L. B. (1998) 'Pathological conflict avoidance in anorexia nervosa: Family perspectives', *Contemp Fam Ther* 20: 539–51.

Latzer, Y., Lavee, Y., and Gal, S. (2009) 'Marital and parent–child relationships in families with daughters who have eating disorders', *J Fam Issues* 30: 1201–20.

Leff, J. and Vaughn, C. (1985) *Expressed Emotion in Families*, New York: Guilford Press.

Le Grange, D., Lock, J., Loeb, K., and Nicholls, D. (2010) 'Academy for eating disorders position paper: The role of the family in eating disorders', *Int J Eat Disord* 43: 1–5.

Lehoux, P. M. and Howe, N. (2007) 'Perceived non-shared environment, personality traits, family factors and developmental experiences in bulimia nervosa', *Br J Clin Psychol* 46: 47–66.

Leung, F., Schwartzman, A., and Steiger, H. (1996) 'Testing a dual-process family model in understanding the development of eating pathology: A structural equation modelling analysis', *Int J Eat Disord* 20: 367–75.

Lilenfeld, L. R., Kaye, W. H., Greeno, C. G., Merikangas, K. R., Plotnicov, K., Pollice, C., Rao, R., Strober, M., Bulik, C. M., and Nagy, L. (1998) 'A controlled family study of anorexia nervosa and bulimia nervosa: Psychiatric disorders in first-degree relatives and effects of proband comorbidity', *Arch Gen Psychiatry* 55: 603–10.

Lilenfeld, L., Stein, D., Bulik, C., Strober, M., Plotnicov, K., Pollice, C., Rao, R., Merikangas, K., Nagy, L., and Kaye, W. H. (2000) 'Personality traits among current eating disordered, recovered and never ill first-degree female relatives of bulimic and control women', *Psychol Med* 30: 1399–1410.

McGrane, D. and Carr, A. (2002) 'Young women at risk for eating disorders: Perceived family dysfunction and parental psychological problems', *Contemp Fam Ther* 24: 385–95.

McVey, G. L., Pepler, D., Davis, R., Flett, G. L., and Abdolell, M. (2002) 'Risk and protective factors associated with disordered eating during early adolescence', *J Early Adoles* 22: 75–95.

Minuchin, S., Rosman, B. L., and Baker, B. L. (1978) *Psychosomatic Families: Anorexia Nervosa in Context*, Cambridge, MA: Harvard University Press.

North, C., Gowers, S., and Byram, V. (1997) 'Family functioning and life events in the outcome of adolescent anorexia nervosa', *Br J Psychiatry* 171: 545–9.

Ogden, J. and Elder, C. (1998) 'The role of family status and ethnic group on body image and eating behavior', *Int J Eat Disord* 23: 309–15.

Ogden, J. and Steward, J. (2000) 'The role of the mother–daughter relationship in explaining weight concern', *Int J Eat Disord* 28: 78–83.

Papadopoulos, F. C., Ekbom, A., Brandt, L., and Ekselius, L. (2009) 'Excess mortality, causes of death and prognostic factors in anorexia nervosa', *Br J Psychiatry* 194: 10–17.

Pauls, B. S. and Daniels, T. (2000) 'Relationship among family, peer networks, and bulimic symptomatology in college women', *Can J Counsel* 34: 260–72.

Ringer, F. and Crittenden, P. M. (2007) 'Eating disorders and attachment: The effects of hidden family processes on eating disorders', *Eur Eat Disord Rev* 15: 119–30.

Rowe, D. C. and Plomin, R. (1981) 'The importance of nonshared (E_1) environmental influences in behavioural development', *Dev Psychol* 17: 517–31.

Rutter, M. (2000) 'Psychosocial influences: Critiques, findings, and research needs', *Dev Psychopathol* 12: 375–405.

Rutter, M. (2005) 'Environmentally mediated risks for psychopathology: Research strategies and findings', *J Am Acad Child Adolesc Psychiatry* 44: 3–18.

Sanftner, J. L., Crowther, J. H., Crawford, P. A., and Watts, D. D. (1996) 'Maternal influences (or lack thereof) on daughters' eating attitudes and behaviors', *Eat Disord* 4: 147–59.

Schmidt, U. and Treasure, J. (2006) 'Anorexia nervosa: Valued and visible. A cognitive-interpersonal maintenance model and its implications for research and practice', *Br J Clin Psychol* 45: 343–66.

Senra, C., Sanchez-Cao, E., Seoane, G., and Leung, F. Y. (2007) 'Evolution of self-concept deficits in patients with eating disorders: The role of family concern about weight and appearance', *Eur Eat Disord Rev* 15: 131–8.

Shafran, R. and de Silva, P. (2003) 'Cognitive-behavioural models', in J. Treasure, U. Schmidt, and E. van Furth (eds) *Handbook of Eating Disorders*, Chichester: Wiley.

Sim, L. A., Homme, J. H., Lteif, A. N., Vande Voort, J. L., Schak, K. M., and Ellingson, J. (2009) 'Family functioning and maternal distress in adolescent girls with anorexia nervosa', *Int J Eat Disord* 42: 531–9.

Smolak, L., Levine, M. P., and Schermer, F. (1999) 'Parental input and weight concerns among elementary school children', *Int J Eat Disord* 25: 263–71.

Snoek, H. M., Engels, R. C., Janssens, J. M., and van Strien, T. (2007) 'Parental behaviour and adolescents' emotional eating', *Appetite* 49: 223–30.

Snoek, H. M., van Strien, T., Janssens, J. M., and Engels, R. C. (2009) 'Longitudinal relationships between fathers', mothers', and adolescents' restrained eating', *Appetite* 52: 461–8.

Steiger, H., Stotland, S., Ghadirian, A., and Whitehead, V. (1995) 'Controlled study of eating concerns and psychopathological traits in relatives of eating-disordered probands: Do familial traits exist?', *Int J Eat Disord* 18: 107–18.

Steiger, H., Stotland, S., Trottier, J., and Ghadirian, A. (1996) 'Familial eating concerns and psychopathological traits: Causal implications of transgenerational effects', *Int J Eat Disord* 19: 147–57.

Stice, E. (1998) 'Modeling of eating pathology and social reinforcement of the thin-ideal predict onset of bulimic symptoms', *Behav Res Ther* 36: 931–44.

Swarr, A. E. and Richards, M. H. (1996) 'Longitudinal effects of adolescent girls' pubertal development, perceptions of pubertal timing, and parental relations on eating problems', *Dev Psychol* 32: 636–46.

Tasca, G. A., Taylor, D., Bissada, H., Ritchie, K., and Balfour, L. (2004) 'Attachment predicts treatment completion in an eating disorders partial hospital program among women with anorexia nervosa', *J Pers Assess* 83: 201–12.

Tasca, G. A., Ritchie, K., Conrad, G., Balfour, L., Gayton, J., Daigle, V., and Bissada, H. (2006) 'Attachment scales predict outcome in a randomized controlled trial of two group therapies for binge eating disorder: An aptitude by treatment interaction', *Psychother Res* 16: 106–21.

Tata, P., Fox, J., and Cooper, J. (2001) 'An investigation into the influence of gender and parenting styles on excessive exercise and disordered eating', *Eur Eat Disord Rev* 9: 194–206.

Tereno, S., Soares, I., Martins, C., Celani, M., and Sampaio, D. (2008) 'Attachment styles, memories of parental rearing and therapeutic bond: A study with eating disordered patients, their parents and therapists', *Eur Eat Disord Rev* 16: 49–58.

Thelen, M. H. and Cormier, J. F. (1995) 'Desire to be thinner and weight control among children and their parents', *Behav Ther* 26: 85–99.

Tremblay, L. and Larivière, M. (2009) 'The influence of puberty onset, body mass index, and pressure to be thin on disordered eating behaviors in children and adolescents', *Eat Behav* 10: 75–83.

van Furth, E. F., van Strien, D. C., Martina, L. M., van Son, M. J., Hendrickx, J. J., and van Engeland, H. (1996) 'Expressed emotion and the prediction of outcome in adolescent eating disorders', *Int J Eat Disord* 20: 19–31.

Vincent, M. A. and McCabe, M. P. (2000) 'Gender differences among adolescents in family, and peer influences on body dissatisfaction, weight loss, and binge eating behaviors', *J Youth Adolesc* 29: 205–21.

Ward, A., Ramsay, R., Turnbull, S., Benedettini, M., and Treasure, J. (2000) 'Attachment patterns in eating disorders: Past in the present', *Int J Eat Disord* 28: 370–6.

Ward, A., Ramsay, R., Turnbull, S., Steele, M., Steele, H. and Treasure, J. (2001) 'Attachment in anorexia nervosa: A transgenerational perspective', *Br J Med Psychol* 74: 497–505.

Wiedemann, G., Rayki, O., Feinstein, E., and Hahlweg, K. (2002) 'The family question-naire: Development and validation of a new self-report scale for assessing expressed emotion', *Psychiatry Res* 109: 265–79.

Woodside, D., Bulik, C. M., Halmi, K. A., Fichter, M. M., Kaplan, A., Berrettini, W. H., Strober, M., Treasure, J., Lilenfeld, L., Klump, K., and Kaye, W. H. (2002) 'Personality, perfectionism, and attitudes towards eating in parents of individuals with eating disorders', *Int J Eat Disord* 31: 290–9.

Yager, J. (1982) 'Family issues in the pathogenesis of anorexia nervosa', *Psychosom Med* 44: 43–60.

Young, E. A., McFatter, R., and Clopton, J. R. (2001) 'Family functioning, peer influence, and media influence as predictors of bulimic behavior', *Eat Behav* 2: 323–37.

Young, E. A., Clopton, J. R., and Bleckley, M. (2004) 'Perfectionism, low self-esteem, and family factors as predictors of bulimic behavior', *Eat Behav* 5: 273–83.

Chapter 2

The links between genes and the environment in the shaping of personality

Janet Treasure and Natalie Kanakam

Eating disorders in the family

This chapter will discuss how genetic factors might contribute to the development of an eating disorder. Usually in psychological disorders, the genetic effects which impact on brain structure and function are modified by the social, family, developmental and ecological environments. Genetic effects may directly increase the risk, for example in eating disorders, by impacting on appetite control networks, or have indirect effects by influencing information processing traits and temperamental features which form personality.

The two case reports in this chapter illustrate complexities in this area. In the first family, two sisters have an eating disorder, one anorexia nervosa (AN) and the other bulimia nervosa (BN). The mother also has eating issues. The second case involves an eating disorder within the context of pronounced obsessive compulsive and autistic spectrum disorder traits that were present in childhood and have remained after recovery from the eating disorder.

Background

Genetic factors that produce their effects within the brain can affect information processing in cognitive, affective, perceptual and behavioural domains. These innate tendencies shape the reaction to environmental events and contribute to the formation of identity and personality. For most psychological/psychiatric traits/disorders several genes, each with a small effect, contribute to vulnerability. Single genes with major effect seem less likely to be relevant. Humans have a long phase of dependency with later maturation and therefore the interpersonal environment is particularly relevant in shaping brain development. During adolescence the individual starts to make choices about their own environment, which in turn affects development. Also in adolescence higher aspects of cognitive function (social cognition, decision making) and other complex affective, perceptual and behavioural processes mature as the frontal lobes develop. Eating disorders have their onset during this critical phase of biological and social maturation. This probably has relevance as the context in which eating disorders are triggered. Also eating disorder symptoms, in particular their nutritional consequences, can disrupt this process.

The underpinning evidence relating to genetic factors is in a phase of continuing active progress and there is much uncertainty. We include a short summary of this and interactions between genetic and environmental factors. Finally, we discuss temperament and personality, a final product of gene–environment interactions throughout development.

Our case studies illustrate the mix of factors that contribute to the causes and maintenance of eating disorders. They illustrate the process of clinical formulation. First we consider predisposing factors, which include the genetic and temperamental template, and environmental factors that impinge on the developing individual from conception until illness onset. Next we consider triggering factors – the developmental and environmental effects associated with onset. Finally the formulation considers maintaining factors that allow symptoms to stick.

Summary of evidence relating to genetic risk for anorexia nervosa

Many studies have confirmed that genetic factors have an important role in the aetiology of eating disorders and indeed many genes linked to obesity regulate processes in the brain. Eating is one major way in which many body systems can interact and interface with the environment. For example, the amount of serotonin available for release by nerve cells depends on the amount of tryptophan taken in the diet. The brain itself requires 500 Kcal of energy daily in the form of glucose and is central in controlling this supply through complex and multifactorial processes.

The genetics of eating disorders

Twin and family studies suggest that AN, BN and Binge Eating Disorder (BED) are complex genetic disorders and for each disorder the estimated levels of heritability are 50–83 per cent (Bulik et al. 2007: 265–6; Bulik and Tozzi 2004; Javaras et al. 2008: 177). This genetic vulnerability is not specific for eating disorders; rather a third of the risk is shared with depression (Wade et al. 2000: 2), anxiety disorders (Keel et al. 2005: 102) and addictive disorders (Baker et al. 2007: 676).

Technologies used to interrogate the genetic underpinning of eating disorders have been increasing in sophistication. Linkage studies aim to identify the genomic regions that are inherited more frequently in affected relatives than is expected by chance alone. The search can be narrowed within this space for potential candidate genes (Bulik et al. 2007: 267). Another approach is to examine for an association between a particular gene and the disorder in question. Initially, particular genes theoretically implicated in dysregulated pathways were chosen. More recently, it has been possible to use more sophisticated mathematical modelling and multiple testing across the genome, in so-called genome wide associations studies (GWAS).

Linkage studies have identified loci for AN, BN and associated behavioural traits such as compulsivity (Bacanu *et al.* 2005: 5; Bergen *et al.* 2003b: 46–7; Bulik *et al.* 2003: 204). Grice and colleagues (2002: 789) found some evidence for linkage to a marker at chromosome 1. Association studies suggest genes that code for components within serotonin, dopamine, opioid systems and the brain-derived neurotrophic factor may be relevant to eating disorders. However great uncertainty remains because findings between studies are inconsistent, often because studies are small and associations may occur by chance alone. Results from genome wide associations studies in large populations with an eating disorder are awaited, as are approaches such as seeking copy number variations or epigenomic factors.

The interaction between genes and the environment

Interactions between genetic and environmental factors have been found to enhance the risk for various psychiatric disorders. The first interaction described was between the 5HTTLPR polymorphism and stressful life events which increased the risk of developing depression (Caspi *et al.* 2003: 388). This interaction with a stressful environment also occurs with the neurobiological variables underlying personality, shaping vulnerability and the path of development. The stressor may be external (dangerous neighbourhoods), within the family (conflict, neglect) or within a carer (paternal style), or physiological (poor nutrition and stress in utero). In animals, for example, the mother's behaviour to her offspring can programme behavioural and endocrine responses to stress that endure throughout the life span with effects mediated by an alteration in gene expression (epigenetic effects or DNA methylation).

Twins and sisters

Research on first-degree relatives (who share 50 per cent of genes) or monozygotic twins (who share 100 per cent of genes) offers an opportunity to parse out genetic and environmental risk factors. In these families it is possible to examine traits that increase eating disorder risk, i.e. certain ways of processing information that may be investigated by neuropsychology testing and/or brain scanning. Affected relatives would be expected to share the same risk traits but unaffected relatives have a 50 per cent chance of carrying the same vulnerabilities. It is interesting to examine how those with the same risk traits have shown resilience and not developed an eating disorder. How have they been protected? This kind of research is in its infancy.

The twin studies have enabled examination of risk factors or components of the illness that appear part of the genetic risk. For example genetic factors account for half of the tendency to show 'body dissatisfaction' and 'drive for thinness' (Keski-Rahkonen *et al.* 2005: 195; Rutherford *et al.* 1993: 431). Interestingly there is an interaction with age. For example, body dissatisfaction and weight preoccupation were more influenced by additive genetic factors in post-pubertal twins, whereas in pre-pubertal twins they were more influenced by environmental factors (Klump *et al.* 2002: 289).

Development of temperament, personality and identity

Genetic and biological influences, together with learning from our environment, shape the organisation of cognitive, affective, perceptual and behavioural factors leading to identity and personality formation. Approximately 60 per cent of patients with an eating disorder have a personality disorder, twice the level of the comparison population. Temperamental features that contribute to the formation of personality can appear in childhood and these traits remain after recovery from the illness. Five major traits are thought to contribute to the emergent personality: neuroticism, extraversion, social closeness, rejection sensitivity and conscientiousness. These relate to neurobehavioural systems and are modified by experience (Depue 2009: 1037). The traits of neuroticism, rejection sensitivity and conscientiousness contribute to the personality categories commonly associated with eating disorders. Aspects of serotonin functioning (increased 5HT) probably relate to the biological underpinning associated with conscientiousness. This trait may be linked to an ability to remain focused on a task and to follow rules systematically and not to be derailed by the 'noise' of other environmental events.

Serotonin function as moderated by the transporter 5HTT is linked to the neuroticism trait. This high sensitivity to threat may produce a negative bias in relationship with environmental events and a tendency to avoid new experiences. The biochemistry underpinning rejection sensitivity is uncertain, whereas social closeness, which may be reduced in people with eating disorders, with less reward to affiliative stimuli, is associated with the mu opiate system (Depue and Morrone-Strupinsky 2005: 345, 318). Interestingly, genetic anomalies in this system have been found in people with eating disorders (Bergen *et al.* 2003a: 400; Brown *et al.* 2007: 369).

Obsessive compulsive disorder (OCPD)

Traits that characterise OCPD include a preoccupation with details, rules, organisation and schedules, rigidity and inflexibility in thinking, perfectionism and conscientiousness. Approximately one-third of people with eating disorders manifest some of these traits in childhood (Anderluh *et al.* 2003: 245). The neurobiological traits underpinning this are poor set-shifting (Roberts *et al.* 2007: 1075, 2010: 3; Tchanturia *et al.* 2004a: 516–17, 2004c: 549) and a detail-focused information processing style (Lopez *et al.* 2008a: 144, 2008b: 1401, 2009: 122). Shifting difficulties are accentuated in the acute phase of the illness and are less marked following weight gain and after recovery (Holliday *et al.* 2005: 2271; Roberts *et al.* 2007, 2010: 4; Tchanturia *et al.* 2004c: 549). These traits are also present in non-affected sisters of those with eating disorders, suggesting they may be part of the genetic vulnerability (Roberts *et al.* 2010: 4).

Autism spectrum disorder

People with autistic spectrum disorder (ASD) have high levels of obsessive compulsive traits. This may explain the comorbidity between eating disorders and ASD noted by Gillberg and his group. In addition, people with ASD have problems in social cognition. These traits are also shared with people with eating disorders who are often shy with few friends (Fairburn *et al.* 1999: 470) and have clinical levels of distress with social phobia (Kaye *et al.* 2004: 2220). The underpinning neurobiological traits include impairments in social and emotional tasks, such as difficulties inferring high-level mental or emotional states in others when currently ill (Oldershaw *et al.* 2010: 476; Tchanturia *et al.* 2004b: 364) and increased sensitivity to anger and neutral faces (Harrison *et al.* 2010b: 6). These problems are accentuated in the acute illness state and it is uncertain whether this feature represents a genetic vulnerability or a starvation consequence.

Anxious, fearful-avoidant, dependent personalities

Premorbidly, people who develop AN are overanxious (Raney *et al.* 2008: 328–9) with high levels of negative affect (Pike *et al.* 2008: 1448) and neuroticism with sensitivity to punishment (Harrison *et al.* 2010a: 6). This may be part of an inherited disposition, since it was found to be elevated in non-affected twins of those with an eating disorder (Wilksch and Wade 2008: 817).

Case study 1: Family

Two sisters develop an eating disorder. The older sister, Henrietta, develops BN but this is not obvious to family members for several years, whereas when the younger sister Vanessa develops AN, this is quickly detected and medical help sought.

Predisposing factors

The risk of developing an eating disorder increases tenfold if another family member is affected. Shared genes contribute to this risk but separating out environmental effects is difficult. The reports from all family members identify the shared vulnerability between eating disorder and self-esteem. Some family members consider this part of a genetic vulnerability but others consider it a learned response to interpersonal relationships.

As a family we have been caught up in this illness that is eating disorders. We have all suffered low self-esteem due to our parents, and I was a nightmare to my children while trying to cope myself and manifested this in a variety of eating behaviours.

Veronica (mother)

I would perhaps describe Veronica as a 'border line anorexic'.

Peter (father)

My relationship with food has been distinctly suspect, always about control.

Veronica (mother)

My low self-esteem is partly a result of my mother's attitudes and behaviours around food, weight and shape.

Daughter Henrietta – BN

I was convinced I was useless at everything, ugly and no one liked me.

Daughter Vanessa – AN

The common thread woven throughout these accounts is of low self-esteem and the tendency to strive and persist to obtain goals. The striving tendency may be linked to perfectionism and the trait of conscientiousness. Self-esteem, however, is a complex construct and is unlikely to be linked to any one gene or personality trait.

A common background feature for people with an eating disorder is for food and weight to have a particular meaning and value. If thinness is highly valued by individuals in their social network then critical comments or comparisons about body size may lead to experiencing disgust and shame about their body, particularly in those sensitive to threat or social rejection.

I felt a huge amount of jealousy toward my sister, especially as she had trouble keeping weight on. I wanted to be like her.

I was also heavier than most girls in my peer group. I felt the odd one out and as though I wasn't good enough. I have always felt shame about my weight.

Taking on these beliefs when small, they became my internal tape; my behaviour and coping mechanisms developed around them. Letting them go – the idea that I am not lovable or acceptable – is incredibly difficult.

Daughter Henrietta – BN

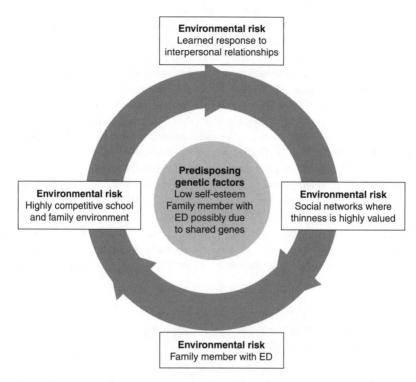

Figure 2.1 A depiction of how a genetic predisposition to low self-esteem and eating disorder can interact with environmental factors, such as competitive environments, social networks where thinness is highly valued and observing other family members' responses to food, to bring about the development of an eating disorder.

Henrietta was 'sandwiched' between her two-year-older brother, our 'Golden Boy', and Vanessa, two years her junior, who from birth suffered serious medical problems. She felt that she got a disproportionately small share of parental attention. In hindsight we gave too much attention to Henrietta's brother and her sickly little sister, making Henrietta feel left out and unloved. Later she told me she had started to equate being heavily built ('fat') with being unloved. From that early moment, food which she loved (and still does!) became an issue for her.

Peter (father)

We are not given information about pregnancy or perinatal events in this family. However Vanessa's physical problems led to prolonged engagement with medical services with overt physical scarring and possible emotional scarring. These events had repercussions for the family and both parents wondered with hindsight whether Henrietta had suffered neglect as a consequence. These adversities in childhood may have interacted with neural networks and altered later functioning.

Environments that foster interpersonal competition over collaboration, and striving over compassion, may also contribute to an eating disorder's onset, particularly in those with extremes on traits related to interpersonal rejection or social closeness. Schools (ballet schools, particularly) can be high-risk environments for those with extremes on social dispositions.

Both sisters attended boarding school and were exposed to a high intensity of peer interactions with less opportunity for modification by parenting. Some schools have a highly competitive ethos that fosters social ranking and lower affiliation and where the distinction between winners and losers is salient. This subsequently impacts on self-esteem. Interestingly, these sisters had areas of demarcation with Vanessa more interested in sport and Henrietta in academic abilities.

> But my boarding school was also rife with eating disorders, which constantly went untreated.
>
> Daughter Vanessa – AN

> My sister and I will always have an element of competition – because we are both very insecure people – we want to feel we are getting it right – we compete for a sense of approval and affection from family and friends. I am more sporty, Henrietta more academic. Her friends knew her at school as a workaholic. She would be found in the library, and I would be in the gym. She is very bright. I am more sporty and a workaholic.
>
> Daughter Vanessa – AN

Precipitating factors

Stressful life events and difficulties trigger some eating disorders but in other cases the normal transitions that occur during this period or chance remarks may trigger onset.

> A boy who I had briefly dated mentioned I was looking a little 'podgy'. When I went on holiday a few weeks later ... I decided to get fit so started

> doing lengths in the pool every day. I would always try and beat my previous record. By the end of the five-day holiday I had reached 100 laps a day.
>
> Daughter Vanessa – AN

Perpetuating factors

Schmidt and Treasure (2006: 345) have developed a model describing four domains that can cause an eating disorder to be perpetuated. Two of these domains relate to factors that the individual brings to the illness, i.e. traits that are relevant throughout development and may be genetically determined. Obsessive compulsive personality traits such as rigidity and a focus on detail are one predisposing domain and are possibly linked to the trait of constraint and conscientiousness. The other includes social and emotional factors such as an over-sensitivity to punishment leading to anxiety, low self-esteem and difficulties relating to others (high sensitivity to rejection and low levels of affiliation). The illness accentuates these traits and the individual becomes further rule-bound and unable to see the big picture. The two other domains relate to the secondary effects that emerge as a response by the individual (a sense of mastery) or her social network (over-protection) to the illness.

> I began to realise I was quite good at this losing weight thing and initially enjoyed the buzz it gave me.
>
> Daughter Vanessa – AN
>
> My sister and I have always been highly competitive towards each other and this was heightened when she also developed an eating disorder.
>
> Daughter Vanessa – AN
>
> I have since met many parents who are over-smothering, wanting to do everything. But helping a child recover from an eating disorder is about setting and recognising the boundaries and being open to being told how to do things. Many carers have difficulty accepting this – perhaps due to how they are told. It is very difficult for them. When you learn what you have to do – the next step is putting it into practice and this is definitely a leap of faith.
>
> Veronica (mother)

This family's early and energetic response to signs of Vanessa's illness may have contributed to its early resolution. More hidden, Henrietta's illness persisted for several years. It is noteworthy that mother Veronica recognised how her behaviour might have inadvertently contributed to the problem. Once she got help and stepped back, Henrietta was able to make steps forward.

> **Case study 2: Eating disorder traits, also associated with autistic spectrum disorder**
>
> Louise is a woman with extreme obsessive compulsive traits that predated her illness. Despite this she attained academic excellence, obtaining a PhD and employment in a university. However she found the demands of her job made it difficult to maintain her health and she retired due to ill health.

Predisposing factors

> My mother describes how, as a four year old, I would only eat three types of food: boiled eggs, bread and a particular type of chocolate biscuit.
>
> When I started school packed lunches were not allowed and I refused to eat school lunch prepared on site. I felt nauseated when I looked at the food and would go the whole school day without eating.
>
> Louise

Also Louise had difficulties fitting in socially with other children.

> I was a target for bullying because of my awkwardness, and because I was advanced academically compared to other children of my age.
>
> Louise

Precipitating factors

The transition through puberty led to more difficulties understanding other people and stressful events triggered the onset of eating disorder behaviours.

> I never felt I fitted in with other children, except with very close friends with whom I shared common interests.
>
> Comments like 'you're growing into a pretty young woman' reinforced my fears that I was growing up – i.e. people could see the physical evidence and would expect me to behave normally. Perhaps the crunch came when a male teacher said in a one-to-one session: 'You have a lovely figure; if I were twenty years younger I'd fall for you'. I didn't know how to

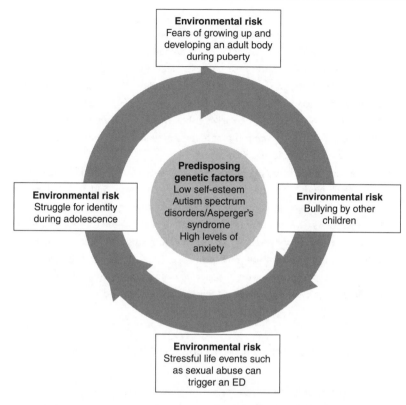

Figure 2.2 A depiction of how a genetic predisposition to obsessive compulsive traits, high levels of anxiety or Asperger's syndrome can interact with environmental factors, such as being bullied, the reinforcement of exercise or a demanding career, to bring about the development of an eating disorder.

respond and feared he wanted to rape me; just as another man had done several years earlier. I began to fear that ALL men wanted to rape me.

Having always been an anxious child, my anxiety levels 'skyrocketed'. I started to hate myself, feeling desperate, worthless and extremely unhappy. Life felt chaotic and I was terrified of the future.

Louise

Perpetuating factors

In this case as in many others, high levels of exercise reduced anxiety. Exercise became reinforcing and served to maintain the disorder.

When running, my worries lifted. The motion was tranquilising. I ran daily at 7 am and 4.30 pm for exactly thirty minutes and then added a thirty-minute cycle ride. Besides exercising to feel better and dissociate from intrusive thoughts, the routine and predictability of my exercise regime added order to my life. This felt safe. However, over-exercising led to weight loss. This didn't particularly bother me and I viewed it as a sign of my fitness. I decided I wanted a career as a runner and thought by eating a 'healthy' diet I would become fitter.

I started to read books on 'healthy eating' and cut 'bad' foods out of my diet. ('Bad' foods contained high proportions of sugar and fat.) I derived immense enjoyment planning my diet, making lists of 'good' foods, collecting healthy recipes – writing down everything I ate. I calculated calories, grams of fat, protein and carbohydrate in my diet and in recipes. My diet and exercise behaviours felt to constitute a life plan – i.e. rules of 'how to live'. I ate and exercised at specific times and in a specific manner, to help me feel in control. I was 12 years old. Meanwhile, my weight steadily dropped.

Louise

Louise did not have the more typical concerns about body shape and weight.

My problems didn't revolve around my body image; rather I was stuck in patterns of compulsive behaviours and was scared of life outside my anorexia and generally scared of interacting with people.

I was terrified of changing my diet and exercise rituals and suffering the accompanying panic of losing my routines. Dependence upon my anorexia behaviours, more than fear of weight gain, trapped me in my illness. I feared weight gain only because weight was a numerical gauge of my success at performing my diet and exercise rituals. I feared I would lose part of my identity if I didn't perform these rituals on a daily basis.

Louise

Understanding her underlying traits and a possible additional diagnosis has helped Louise adjust to her illness and find an environment more compatible with her strengths and weaknesses.

I was relieved when my psychiatrist discussed autism spectrum disorders/ Asperger's syndrome because this explained why I have struggled to fit in, as well as my other eccentricities. Reading literature on Asperger's syndrome has been accompanied by 'Eureka' moments. Everything seems to fit into place.

My personality is similar to that of my father and brother and I have accepted my inherent traits and eccentricities as being 'me'. Although changing behaviours has been extremely difficult, I am glad I persisted. I avoid gyms because I am liable to develop ritualistic and dangerous behaviour patterns around exercise. Exercise only feels right when done to exhaustion. I'm all or nothing about exercise. I always need an eating plan otherwise I am liable to under-eat.

I see my anorexia as having been a brain illness/neurological phenomenon and not a product of popular culture. It was in many ways an extension of my obsessive and compulsive behaviours in earlier childhood. My anorexia had nothing to do with beauty or vanity, or feeling pressured by society to have a perfect body.

Louise

Conclusion

This chapter presents some evidence which supports the role of genetic factors in eating disorders. One pathway may involve cognitive, emotional and perceptual traits forming particular styles of personality, which may trigger the onset or allow the perpetuation of the problem. Thus weak set-shifting and coherence and obsessive compulsive traits are risk factors that become more marked as a consequence of the eating disorder symptoms themselves. Sensitivity to punishment and high anxiety are another risk factor. Eating disorder symptoms themselves impact on social cognition and interpersonal function, which may accentuate the sense of anxiety. Therefore, in the acute state, people with eating disorders may resemble individuals with autism spectrum disorders more closely. However, this similarity usually disappears after full weight recovery.

Understanding how genetic and environmental factors interact to form personality and identity and the risk of developing an eating disorder is important for clinical formulations (see case studies). This can guide the choice of behaviours to target in treatment, for both professional and non-professional carers.

Understanding aetiological risk factors may help people process and cope with environmental adversities (Case 2) and enable them to adjust their environment to minimise unhelpful interactions between their genetic propensities and their ecological context. For example, someone with high trait anxiety may choose to ensure they have high levels of safety, a close support network and low-risk goals. Others who are somewhat rigid will flourish best in an environment where rules are predictable and unchanging. An ability to concentrate on the detail of a task and not be deviated by the bigger picture can also be helpful.

References

Anderluh, M. B., Tchanturia, K., Rabe-Hesketh, S., and Treasure, J. (2003) 'Childhood obsessive-compulsive personality traits in adult women with eating disorders: Defining a broader eating disorder phenotype', *Am J Psychiatry* 160: 242–7.

Bacanu, S. A., Bulik, C. M., Klump, K. L., Fichter, M. M., Halmi, K. A., Keel, P., Kaplan, A. S., Mitchell, J. E., Rotondo, A., Strober, M., Treasure, J., Woodside, D. B., Sonpar, V. A., Xie, W., Bergen, A. W., Berrettini, W. H., Kaye, W. H., and Devlin, B. (2005) 'Linkage analysis of anorexia and bulimia nervosa cohorts using selected behavioral phenotypes as quantitative traits or covariates', *Am J Med Genet B Neuropsychiatr Genet* 139: 1–8.

Baker, J. H., Mazzeo, S. E., and Kendler, K. S. (2007) 'Association between broadly defined bulimia nervosa and drug use disorders: Common genetic and environmental influences', *Int J Eat Disord* 40: 673–8.

Bergen, A. W., van den Bree, M. B., Yeager, M., Welch, R., Ganjei, J. K., Haque, K., Bacanu, S., Berrettini, W. H., Grice, D. E., Goldman, D., Bulik, C. M., Klump, K., Fichter, M., Halmi, K., Kaplan, A., Strober, M., Treasure, J., Woodside, B., and Kaye, W. H. (2003a) 'Candidate genes for anorexia nervosa in the 1p33–36 linkage region: Serotonin 1D and delta opioid receptor loci exhibit significant association to anorexia nervosa', *Mol Psychiatry* 8: 397–406.

Bergen, A. W., Yeager, M., Welch, R., Ganjei, J. K., ep-Soboslay, A., Haque, K., van den Bree, M. B., Goldman, D., Berrettini, W. H., and Kaye, W. H. (2003b) 'Candidate gene analysis of the Price Foundation anorexia nervosa affected relative pair dataset', *Curr Drug Targets CNS Neurol Disord* 2: 41–51.

Brown, K. M., Bujac, S. R., Mann, E. T., Campbell, D. A., Stubbins, M. J., and Blundell, J. E. (2007) 'Further evidence of association of OPRD1 and HTR1D polymorphisms with susceptibility to anorexia nervosa', *Biol Psychiatry* 61: 367–73.

Bulik, C. M., and Tozzi, F. (2004) 'The genetics of bulimia nervosa', *Drugs Today (Barc)* 40: 741–9.

Bulik, C. M., Devlin, B., Bacanu, S. A., Thornton, L., Klump, K. L., Fichter, M. M., Halmi, K. A., Kaplan, A. S., Strober, M., Woodside, D. B., Bergen, A. W., Ganjei, J. K., Crow, S., Mitchell, J., Rotondo, A., Mauri, M., Cassano, G., Keel, P., Berrettini, W. H., and Kaye, W. H. (2003) 'Significant linkage on chromosome 10p in families with bulimia nervosa', *Am J Hum Genet* 72: 200–7.

Bulik, C. M., Slof-Op't Landt, M. C., van Furth, E. F., and Sullivan, P. F. (2007) 'The genetics of anorexia nervosa', *Annu Rev Nutr* 27: 263–75.

Caspi, A., Sugden, K., Moffitt, T. E., Taylor, A., Craig, I. W., Harrington, H., McClay, J., Mill, J., Martin, J., Braithwaite, A., and Poulton, R. (2003) 'Influence of life stress on depression: Moderation by a polymorphism in the 5-HTT gene', *Science* 301: 386–9.

Depue, R. A. (2009) 'Genetic, environmental, and epigenetic factors in the development of personality disturbance', *Dev Psychopathol* 21: 1031–63.

Depue, R. A., and Morrone-Strupinsky, J. V. (2005) 'A neurobehavioral model of affiliative bonding: Implications for conceptualizing a human trait of affiliation', *Behav Brain Sci* 28: 313–50.

Fairburn, C. G., Cooper, Z., Doll, H. A., and Welch, S. L. (1999) 'Risk factors for anorexia nervosa: Three integrated case-control comparisons', *Arch Gen Psychiatry* 56: 468–76.

Grice, D. E., Halmi, K. A., Fichter, M. M., Strober, M., Woodside, D. B., Treasure, J. T., Kaplan, A. S., Magistretti, P. J., Goldman, D., Bulik, C. M., Kaye, W. H., and Berretini, W. H. (2002) 'Evidence for a susceptibility gene for anorexia nervosa on chromosome 1', *Am J Hum Genet* 70: 787–92.

Harrison, A., O'Brien, N., Lopez, C., and Treasure, J. (2010a) 'Sensitivity to reward and punishment in eating disorders', *Psychiatry Res* 177: 1–11.

Harrison, A., Sullivan, S., Tchanturia, K., and Treasure, J. (2010b) 'Emotional functioning in eating disorders: Attentional bias, emotion recognition and emotion regulation', *Psychol Med* 27: 1–11.

Holliday, J., Tchanturia, K., Landau, S., Collier, D., and Treasure, J. (2005) 'Is impaired set-shifting an endophenotype of anorexia nervosa?', *Am J Psychiatry* 162: 2269–75.

Javaras, K. N., Laird, N. M., Reichborn-Kjennerud, T., Bulik, C. M., Pope, H. G. Jr., and Hudson, J. I. (2008) 'Familiality and heritability of binge eating disorder: Results of a case-control family study and a twin study', *Int J Eat Disord* 41: 174–9.

Kaye, W. H., Bulik, C. M., Thornton, L., Barbarich, N., and Masters, K. (2004) 'Comorbidity of anxiety disorders with anorexia and bulimia nervosa', *Am J Psychiatry* 161: 2215–21.

Keel, P. K., Klump, K. L., Miller, K. B., McGue, M., and Iacono, W. G. (2005) 'Shared transmission of eating disorders and anxiety disorders', *Int J Eat Disord* 38: 99–105.

Keski-Rahkonen, A., Bulik, C. M., Neale, B. M., Rose, R. J., Rissanen, A., and Kaprio, J. (2005) 'Body dissatisfaction and drive for thinness in young adult twins', *Int J Eat Disord* 37: 188–99.

Klump, K. L., McGue, M., and Lacano, W. G. (2002) 'Differential heritability of eating attitudes and behaviours in prepubertal versus pubertal twins', *Int J Eat Disord* 33: 287–92.

Lopez, C., Tchanturia, K., Stahl, D., Booth, R., Holliday, J., and Treasure, J. (2008a) 'An examination of the concept of central coherence in women with anorexia nervosa', *Int J Eat Disord* 41: 143–52.

Lopez, C., Tchanturia, K., Stahl, D., and Treasure, J. (2008b) 'Central coherence in eating disorders: A systematic review', *Psychol Med* 38: 1393–404.

Lopez, C., Tchanturia, K., Stahl, D., and Treasure, J. (2009) 'Weak central coherence in eating disorders: A step towards looking for an endophenotype of eating disorders', *J Clin Exp Neuropsychol* 31: 117–25.

Oldershaw, A., Hambrook, D., Tchanturia, K., Treasure, J., and Schmidt, U. (2010) 'Emotional theory of mind and emotional awareness in recovered anorexia nervosa patients', *Psychosom Med* 72: 73–9.

Pike, K. M., Hilbert, A., Wilfley, D. E., Fairburn, C. G., Dohm, F. A., Walsh, B. T., and Striegel-Moore, R. (2008) 'Toward an understanding of risk factors for anorexia nervosa: A case-control study', *Psychol Med* 38: 1443–53.

Raney, T. J., Thornton, L. M., Berrettini, W., Brandt, H., Crawford, S., Fichter, M. M., Halmi, K. A., Johnson, C., Kaplan, A. S., Lavia, M., Mitchell, J., Rotondo, A., Strober, M., Woodside, D. B., Kaye, W. H., and Bulik, C. M. (2008) 'Influence of overanxious disorder of childhood on the expression of anorexia nervosa', *Int J Eat Disord* 41: 326–32.

Roberts, M. E., Tchanturia, K., Stahl, D., Southgate, L., and Treasure, J. (2007) 'A systematic review and meta-analysis of set-shifting ability in eating disorders', *Psychol Med* 37: 1075–84.

Roberts, M. E., Tchanturia, K., and Treasure, J. L. (2010) 'Exploring the neurocognitive signature of poor set-shifting in anorexia and bulimia nervosa', *J Psychiatr Res* 14: 1–7.

Rutherford, J., McGuffin, P., Katz, R. J., and Murray, R. M. (1993) 'Genetic influences on eating attitudes in a normal female twin population', *Psychol Med* 23: 425–36.

Schmidt, U. and Treasure, J. (2006) 'Anorexia nervosa: Valued and visible. A cognitive-interpersonal maintenance model and its implications for research and practice', *Br J Clin Psychol* 45: 343–66.

Tchanturia, K., Anderluh, M. B., Morris, R. G., Rabe-Hesketh, S., Collier, D. A., Sanchez, P., and Treasure, J. L. (2004a) 'Cognitive flexibility in anorexia nervosa and bulimia nervosa', *J Int Neuropsychol Soc* 10: 513–20.

Tchanturia, K., Happe, F., Godley, J., Treasure, J., Bara-Carril, N., and Schmidt, U. (2004b) '"Theory of mind" in anorexia nervosa', *Eur Eat Disord Rev* 12: 361–6.

Tchanturia, K., Morris, R. G., Anderluh, M. B., Collier, D. A., Nikolaou, V., and Treasure, J. (2004c). 'Set shifting in anorexia nervosa: An examination before and after weight gain, in full recovery and relationship to childhood and adult OCPD traits', *J Psychiatr Res* 38: 545–52.

Wade, T. D., Bulik, C. M., Neale, M., and Kendler, K. S. (2000) 'Anorexia nervosa and major depression: Shared genetic and environmental risk factors', *Am J Psychiatry* 157: 469–71.

Wilksch, S. M. and Wade, T. D. (2008) 'An investigation of temperament endophenotype candidates for early emergence of the core cognitive component of eating disorders', *Psychol Med* 39: 811–21.

Chapter 3

Neurobiology explanations for puzzling behaviours

Walter H. Kaye, Ursula F. Bailer and Megan Klabunde

Case study

Alisa was 15 years old when admitted to the emergency room after collapsing during a school volleyball game. Although about the same weight and height (a body mass index (BMI) of around 19.5 kg/m^2) as her best friend Jodie, both girls had decided to diet when they were 14. They wanted to lose weight especially around their bellies and their thighs. They started to skip lunch at school, stopped eating sweet things and became vegetarians. After about a month Jodie could not restrict her food intake anymore; she felt exhausted, weak and sad about not being able to eat her favourite chocolate, and returned to her original meal patterns.

Alisa, however, felt that her dieting and constant weight loss made her stronger. She lost 5 kg in five months. Compared to Jodie, who appeared an easygoing person, Alisa was very hard on herself. This was especially true in school. She achieved excellent grades, but never felt happy, always worrying about not making things perfect. Even as a child, Alisa always felt very anxious. She had severe difficulties being separated from her parents and had frequent fears about what could happen to them.

Dieting, however, eased her anxiety. Additionally, Alisa started to exercise excessively. She tried to expend as many calories as she consumed each day, plus an additional 1,000 calories. After she lost her menstrual cycle at a BMI of 17 kg/m^2, her worried parents took her to their primary care physician. When confronted about her weight loss and excessive exercise, Alisa denied she had a problem. However, she promised to eat lunch at school again, to ease her parents' concern. After another five months of dieting and losing another 7 kg, Alisa's pathological eating worsened. She ate nothing during the day and only one apple and one tub of non-fat yoghurt at night.

Additionally she ran and cycled for about four hours after school. She spent 90 per cent of her time counting calories and thinking about her food and weight. She started storing large bags of cookies in her closet, nightstand and desk drawers and kept them after the use-by dates expired. She collected recipes, food magazines and flyers advertising food products. When teachers and peers confronted Alisa about her low weight, she denied the seriousness of her medical problems. This may be because, although weighing 38 kg, she still felt fat. Even during the emergency room assessment, Alisa denied being ill. When a doctor said her weight was at a very low and medically risky BMI of 15 kg/m^2, she continued to perseverate on being fat and repeatedly denied her collapse was related to her low weight. Though initially hesitant about starting treatment, Alisa finally engaged in an outpatient behavioural family therapy programme. The treatment comprised nine months of behavioural family therapy. Alisa's menstrual cycle restored when she was at a BMI of 18 kg/m^2 and she regained most of her weight in the first six months.

Therapist

Introduction

People with anorexia nervosa (AN) exhibit a highly rigid, ritualized, and inadequate intake of food and consequently become severely underweight. How can they consume a few hundred calories per day and maintain an extremely low weight for many years, when most people struggle to lose a few pounds?

People with AN tend to resemble each other in many ways. For example, there is a narrow range of age of onset (early adolescence), similar presentation of symptoms and course, and this disorder tends to occur mostly in females (American Psychiatric Association 1994). People with AN exhibit a resistance to eating and a powerful pursuit of weight loss, yet are paradoxically preoccupied with food and eating rituals to the point of obsession. They have a distorted body image, and even when underweight tend to see themselves as 'fat', express denial of being underweight, and compulsively over-exercise. They are often resistant to treatment and lack insight regarding the seriousness of the disorder's medical consequences. The similarity of symptoms supports the possibility that underlying neurobiological contributions drive such behaviours.

Two types of eating-related behaviour are seen in AN. Restricting-type anorexics (AN) lose weight purely by dieting without binge eating or purging. Binge-eating/purging-type anorexics (AN-BN) also restrict their food intake to lose weight, but have a periodic disinhibition of restraint and engage in binge eating and/or purging as also occurs in bulimia nervosa (BN). Considering that transitions often occur between syndromes, it has been argued that AN and BN share some risk and liability factors (Lilenfeld *et al.* 1998; Walters and Kendler 1995). Because of space considerations, this chapter will focus on restricting-type AN.

Cause and consequence

Although AN is characterized as an eating disorder, it remains unknown whether there is a primary disturbance of brain systems that regulate appetite, or whether disturbed appetite is secondary to other factors, such as anxiety or obsessional preoccupation with weight gain. Starvation and weight loss have powerful effects on the functioning of the brain and other organ systems. They cause neurochemical disturbances that could exaggerate pre-existing traits (Pollice *et al.* 1997), adding symptoms that maintain or accelerate the disease process. For example, AN patients have a reduced brain volume (Katzman *et al.* 1996), altered metabolism of brain regions known to modulate emotion and thought (frontal, cingulate, temporal, and parietal regions) (Kaye *et al.* 2006), and a return to childhood levels of female hormones (Boyar *et al.* 1974). The fact that such disturbances tend to normalize after weight restoration suggests these alterations are a consequence, and not a cause, of AN.

There has been considerable interest in the role of regions of the brain such as the hypothalamus in food and weight regulation in AN. This is where well-known chemicals, such as insulin and leptin, act, in sending messages about hunger and energy balance. Insulin and leptin and other such chemicals reach abnormal levels when people lose weight. However, evidence reveals such changes are driven by starvation, and serve to conserve energy or stimulate hunger and feeding (Schwartz *et al.* 2000). Although the hypothalamus is an important regulator of food intake and body weight, most evidence suggests that changes in this region are secondary to starvation, and not the cause of AN. Now, studies in animals and healthy humans are leading to a new understanding of uniquely human, higher brain regions that may be able to override lower regions such as the hypothalamus. This is important because when people with AN starve, they appear to be able to override, or ignore, signals from lower brain regions, such as the hypothalamus, that say their body has insufficient stores of 'fuel' and they need to eat. Importantly, these higher brain regions play an important role in emotions, personality, and rewards – factors also thought to be important in AN.

What are these vulnerabilities that might cause AN?

Several studies show that genes play a major role in causing eating disorders (Berrettini 2000; Bulik *et al.* 2006; Walters and Kendler 1995). However, there is not a centre in the brain that causes AN. Instead, genes may contribute to a range of emotional, personality, and reward 'traits' that put people at risk for developing AN. Note that the genes responsible for such traits remain unknown. However, a considerable number of studies in the past decade suggest that people who develop AN tend to have a certain personality and temperament in childhood, years before they develop AN in adolescence. For example, these studies (Anderluh *et al.* 2003; Lilenfeld *et al.* 2006; Stice 2002) describe anxiety and depression, behavioural inhibition, perfectionism, drive for thinness, altered interoceptive awareness, and obsessive-compulsive personality as common traits in childhood that precede an eating disorder onset and persist after recovery (see below). Regarding the latter, obsessive personality traits tend to involve an over-concern for symmetry and exactness (Kaye 1997). For example, these children may have colour-coded clothes in their closet, have specific spots for items in their room and may get upset if things are moved. From another perspective, these children tend to be achievement-oriented, compliant, and are exceptional students. Children who later develop AN are typically described as 'the best little girl in the world'. Like Alisa, they tend to be rule-abiding, rigid and anxious children, high in 'harm avoidance'. Harm avoidance is a personality trait characterized by a tendency to criticize and doubt past thoughts and behaviours, worry about the future and struggle with uncertainty (Cloninger *et al.* 1994). Finally, studies suggest these traits are heritable, can be present in unaffected family members, and are independent of body weight (Bulik *et al.* 2007), providing further evidence that they confer risk for AN development. Note that not everyone who develops AN has all these traits. Some may not have any. Still, our experience is that most people who develop AN have such personality and temperament in childhood.

Do biological changes in AN patients reflect state or trait?

Designing studies to find traits that may cause AN in the first place has been difficult. Prospective, longitudinal studies are difficult given the young age of potential subjects, the rarity of the disorder, and the need to follow them for many years. An alternative strategy is to study individuals who have recovered from AN, thus avoiding the confounding influence of malnutrition and weight loss on biological systems. No agreed-upon definition of recovery from AN exists, but in our research we employ a definition that includes stable and healthy body weight for at least a year, with stable nutrition, the relative absence of dietary abnormalities, and normal menstruation. Although the process of recovery in AN is poorly understood and, in most cases, protracted, approximately 50 to 70 per cent of patients will eventually have complete or moderate resolution of the illness, although this may not occur until their early to mid-twenties (Steinhausen 2002; Strober *et al.* 1997; Wagner *et al.* 2006). Studies have described temperament and character traits that persist after long-term recovery from AN, such as negative emotionality, harm avoidance and perfectionism, desire for thinness, and mild dietary preoccupation. Such persistent symptoms are posssibly 'scars' caused by chronic malnutrition. However, the fact that such behaviours (Casper 1990; Srinivasagam *et al.* 1995; Wagner *et al.* 2006) are similar to those described in children who will go on to develop AN (Anderluh *et al.* 2003; Lilenfeld *et al.* 2006; Stice 2002) argues that they reflect underlying traits that contribute to risk of developing AN.

Neurobiology and behaviour

Common comorbid behaviours found in both recovered and ill AN patients, such as inhibition, anxiety, depression and obsessionality, and puzzling symptoms such as body image distortion, perfectionism and anhedonia, are often expressed in concert. Our group has been interested in discovering how these behaviours are coded in the brain. Note that it is over-simplified to think these traits are encoded in brain chemicals, or brain regions. The human brain is far too complex. Rather, these behaviours could be encoded in pathways that modulate emotion, reward, and the ability of humans to think about consequences and the future. In fact, we know that two neural pathways, called 'limbic' and 'cognitive circuits', modulate and integrate neuronal processes that are related to appetite, emotionality and cognitive control.

While this is highly technical, we will briefly describe each circuit. A ventral (limbic) neurocircuit that includes the amygdala, insula, ventral striatum and ventral regions of the anterior cingulate cortex (ACC) and orbita frontal cortex (OFC) seems important for identifying the emotional significance of stimuli and for generating an affective response to these stimuli (Phillips *et al.* 2003a, 2003b). A dorsal (cognitive) neurocircuit is thought to modulate selective attention, planning, inhibition, and effortful regulation of affective states, and includes the hippocampus, dorsal regions of the ACC, dorsolateral prefrontal cortex (DLPFC), parietal cortex and other regions (Phillips *et al.* 2003a, 2003b). Indeed, earlier brain imaging studies have shown that recovered AN patients have altered activity in frontal, ACC, and parietal regions (I. Gordon *et al.* 1997; Rastam *et al.* 2001; Uher *et al.* 2003).

Neurocircuitry of appetite

If people with AN have dysregulated feeding behaviour, where should we look? This is complicated because appetite comprises many signals coming from nerves and hormones from the gastrointestinal tract, fat and sugar stores in the body, and many parts of the brain (Figure 3.1). There are many reasons to think that higher brain structures may be particularly involved in altered appetite control in AN. In terms of the brain, recent studies suggest the motivation to eat (or not eat) is related to food's rewarding properties, to whether a person's energy stores are reduced in the body, and to the cognitive ability to favour alternative (to eating) behaviours (Elman *et al.* 2006; Kelley 2004; Saper *et al.* 2002).

Appetite is clearly disturbed in AN. People with AN dislike high-fat foods (Drewnowski *et al.* 1988; Fernstrom *et al.* 1994), report sucrose as aversive when satiated, and fail to rate food positively when hungry (Garfinkel *et al.* 1979; Santel *et al.* 2006). These responses tend not to change following weight regain. Moreover, there is evidence that dietary restraint reduces anxiety and that eating results in an anxious and/or depressed mood (Kaye *et al.* 2003; Strober 1995; Vitousek and Manke 1994). Moreover, food-related behaviours in AN are

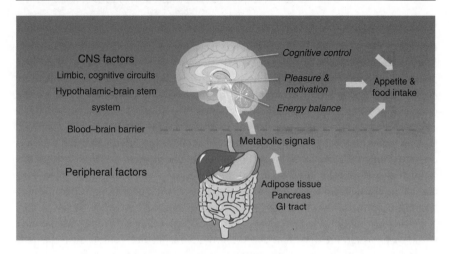

Figure 3.1 Systems determining food and weight regulation.

relatively unique, tend to be similar in most people with AN, and have a relentless expression, supporting the possibility of reflecting some aberrant function of neural circuits involved in regulating eating behaviour.

Although a sweet-taste perception task does not test the complexity of food choices (Small 2006), it can be used in brain imaging studies to activate brain areas involved in appetite regulation. Sweet-taste perception (Figure 3.2) is peripherally mediated by tongue receptors that respond to a sweet taste (Chandraskekar *et al.* 2006) and then send a signal through the brain stem and lower brain regions to an area described as the primary taste centre, in the anterior insula (Faurion *et al.* 1999; Ogawa 1994, Schoenfeld *et al.* 2004; Scott *et al.* 1986; Yaxley *et al.* 1990), a part of the brain adjacent to the frontal and temporal lobes. By primary taste centre, we mean this is the first cortical region to recognize that we have tasted something sweet (or salty or sour). The insula and a related network, comprising the ventral neurocircuits that are interconnected with the insula (Figure 3.2), including the amygdala, the ventral ACC and the OFC, help to determine whether we find that taste pleasant or unpleasant. The insula and these regions appear to become more active when one is hungry, and less active when one is full (Kringelbach *et al.* 2003; Morris and Dolan 2001; Small *et al.* 2001; Tataranni *et al.* 1999; Uher *et al.* 2006). Food tastes 'better' and we have a greater drive to eat when very hungry. And while food may taste pleasant, it tends to be less rewarding when we are full. A phenomenon called sensory specific satiety explains why we grow 'tired' of eating one food during a meal and switch to another food. And food can become unpleasant. For example eating a small piece of chocolate cake may be pleasant but being forced to eat the whole cake could be unpleasant. These regions connect to a subcortical region, the ventral striatum, which is important for carrying out motivated behaviour. Together, these regions are responsible for sensing the pleasurable and motivating

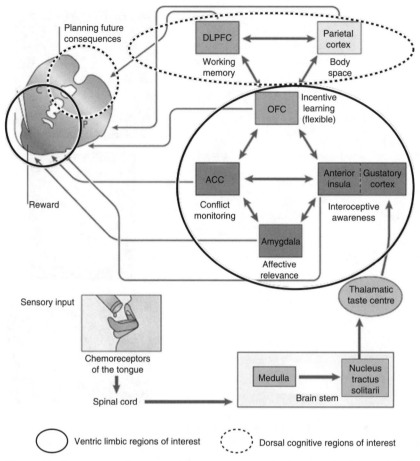

Figure 3.2 Receptors on the tongue detect a sweet taste that is transmitted through brain-stem and thalamic taste centers to the primary taste cortex in the anterior insula, which is part of a 'ventral (limbic) neurocircuit.' The sensory aspects of taste are primarily an insula phenomenon, whereas higher cortical areas modulate pleasure, motivation and cognitive aspects of taste. (From Kaye, Fudge, & Paulus, 2009.) Used with permission.

value of food, and how this value may change, depending on whether we are hungry or full.

Findings in anorexia nervosa

Studies using brain imaging show that people who have recovered from AN have a reduced activation of the insula (Figure 3.3), ACC and striatum when tasting a sugar compared to control subjects (Wagner *et al.* 2008). Other brain imaging studies, which look at pictures of food, also show altered activity in the insula, the OFC, the mesial temporal and parietal cortex and the ACC in underweight AN

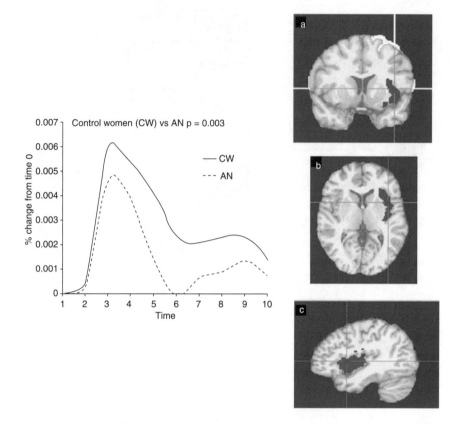

Figure 3.3 Left insula/OFC response to sucrose.

(Ellison *et al.*1998; C. M. Gordon *et al.* 2001; Naruo *et al.* 2000; Nozoe *et al.* 1993; Uher *et al.* 2004) and in AN after recovery (Uher *et al.* 2003). Moreover, the more that healthy controls thought the sugar tasted pleasant, the more activity they showed in their insula, ACC and striatum (Wagner *et al.* 2008), supporting the idea that these regions are important for sensing 'reward'. Consistent with the idea that the ability to perceive a palatable taste is fundamentally altered in AN, people recovered from AN showed no relationship between the taste of sugar and the activity of these regions.

Although simplified, we think the decreased signal in the anterior insula, and other parts of this network, suggests people with AN have reduced ability to 'sense' the taste of sugar, and/or reduced reward and/or motivation to approach food. In other words, people with AN may have a reduced drive of systems that modulate a complex of sensory-hedonic-motivation signals that respond to hunger. This may explain why they can pursue emaciation to the point of death. When people normally become hungry, this network should become more active, making

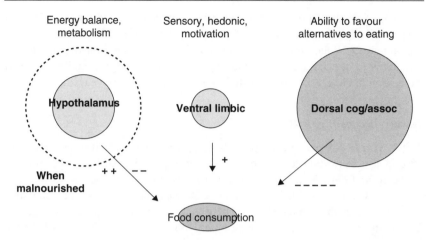

Figure 3.4 Understanding appetite in anorexia nervosa: incentive motivational drive to seek and consume food.

food taste more rewarding and driving the motivation to eat. In Figure 3.4, this simplified diagram suggests that people with AN may have a reduced sensor-reward signal. If this is true when they are hungry, the drive to eat may be reduced, and override lower brain regions, such as the hypothalamus, signalling depletion of the body's fuel stores.

A central role for the anterior insula?

Besides affecting taste, the insula is critically involved in a concept called interoception (Craig 2009; Critchley *et al.* 2004; Paulus and Stein 2006) which involves one's ability to detect and be aware of bodily states. Interoceptive signals include a range of sensations beyond taste, including the perception of pain, temperature, itch, tickle, sensual touch, muscle tension, air hunger and intestinal tension. Integration of these internal feelings provides an integrated sense of the physiological condition of the entire body and one's overall homeostasis (Craig 2009). That is, the insula plays a critical role in making us aware of our body processes. Moreover, the insula signals where there is a change in some body process, and says there is a change, 'do something about it'. As noted, the insula becomes more active when hungry, but also responds to air hunger, thirst or other changes in the body.

There are theories that altered interoceptive awareness might be a precipitating and reinforcing factor in AN (Bruch 1962; Fassino *et al.* 2004; Garner *et al.* 1983; Lilenfeld *et al.* 2006). Our group's studies support the idea that altered function of the anterior insula goes beyond taste. That is, there may be a generalized alteration of insula activity involving many other interoceptive signals. This raises the question of whether altered insula function contributes to a fundamentally and physiologically altered sense of self in AN (Pollatos *et al.* 2008). Indeed, many symptoms of AN, such as distorted body image, lack of recognition of malnutrition symptoms (e.g. a failure to respond appropriately to hunger), and diminished motivation to change, could be related to disturbed interoceptive awareness.

Reward processing in AN

People with AN often exercise compulsively, are anhedonic and ascetic, and find little in life rewarding aside from weight loss pursuit (American Psychiatric Association 1994). Such temperament persists, in a more modest form, after recovery (Klump *et al.* 2004; Wagner *et al.* 2006), indicating these characteristics are traits rather than state-related. There is considerable evidence that altered function of the neurotransmitter dopamine (DA) occurs in AN (Kaye *et al.* 2009). Thus DA, which plays a key role in striatal circuits, might contribute to altered reward and affect, decision-making, and executive control, as well as over-exercise and decreased food ingestion, in AN patients (Frank *et al.* 2005).

To determine whether people who have recovered from AN have fundamentally different responses to reward compared to healthy controls, our group did a brain imaging study while participants performed a simple choice and feedback task (Wagner *et al.* 2007). The task was adapted from a well-characterized 'guessing-game' protocol (Delgado *et al.* 2000) which is known to activate the ventral striatum and ACC, with control participants showing differential activity in these areas in response to winning and losing money. For example, if you gambled in Las Vegas and won $100,000, you would feel a lot differently than if you lost $100,000. The ventral striatum contains a 'reward centre' that may be particularly important in explaining how people discriminate between positive and negative feedback. In controls, the signal for a win differed greatly from the loss signal. In comparison, in recovered AN subjects, brain activity in the ACC and its ventral striatal target was similar during positive and negative feedback (Wagner *et al.* 2007). This suggests that patients with AN might have difficulty discriminating between positive and negative feedback. In turn, these data support the possibility that ability to identify the emotional significance of stimuli might be impaired (Phillips *et al.* 2003a), and this could be important in understanding why motivating patients with AN to engage in treatment or appreciate consequences of their behaviours is difficult (Halmi *et al.* 2005).

Moreover, the recovered AN women had exaggerated activation in the caudate-dorsal striatum and in the 'cognitive' cortical regions that project to this area, specifically the DLPFC and the parietal cortex (Wagner *et al.* 2007). These regions are activated by tasks in which there is both a perceived connection between action and outcome and some uncertainty about whether the action will lead to the desired outcome (Tricomi *et al.* 2004). In the absence of appropriate reward processing via ventral striatal/DA paths, people who have recovered from AN might focus on a detailed strategy rather than the overall picture.

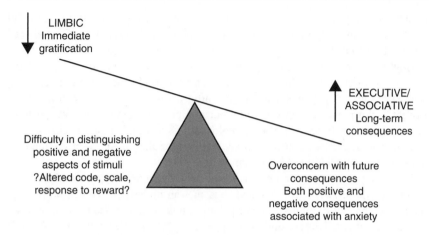

LIMBIC
Immediate
gratification

EXECUTIVE/
ASSOCIATIVE
Long-term
consequences

Difficulty in distinguishing
positive and negative
aspects of stimuli
?Altered code, scale,
response to reward?

Overconcern with future
consequences
Both positive and
negative consequences
associated with anxiety

Figure 3.5 Altered balance in anorexia nervosa?

From another perspective, control women appropriately 'lived in the moment'. That is, they realized they had to make a guess and move on to the next task. By contrast, AN patients tend to worry about consequences of their behaviours, looking for 'rules' when there are none, and are overly concerned about making mistakes. A recent functional magnetic resonance imaging study, using a set shifting task, showed relatively similar findings in ill AN patients (Zastrow *et al.* 2009), namely hypoactivation in the ventral ACC-striato-thalamic loop, with predominant activation of fronto-parietal networks. Together these data suggest that people with AN might be less able to precisely modulate affective response to immediate stimuli, but have increased activity in neurocircuits concerned with planning and consequences (Figure 3.5).

Importantly, also note that cortical regions included in the dorsal neurocircuit – such as the DLPFC, the parietal cortex, and the posterior insular region, mediate executive (e.g. cognitive) functions such as planning and sequencing. These regions send inputs to other subcortical striatal regions, which might interface and overlap with ventral striatal areas (Chikama *et al.* 1997; Fudge *et al.* 2005). Together, these inputs are thought to modulate the striatal activity that underlies the approach or avoidance of food. We speculate that there is an overactivity of the inhibitory aspects of this cognitive circuit. Consequently AN individuals are able to suppress and override signals about bodily needs, such as hunger.

Conclusions

AN is thought to be a disorder of complex aetiology, in which genetic, biological, psychological and socio-cultural factors, and interactions between them, seem to contribute significantly to susceptibility (Connan *et al.* 2003; Jacobi *et al.* 2004; Lilenfeld *et al.* 2006; Stice 2002). Because no single factor has been shown to be either necessary or sufficient for causing AN, a multifactorial threshold model might be the most appropriate model (see the excellent review by Connan and colleagues (2003)). Typically, AN begins with a restrictive diet and weight loss during teenage years, which progresses to an out-of-control spiral. Thus, individuals might cross a threshold in which a premorbid temperament, interacting with stress and/or psychosocial factors, progresses to an illness with impaired insight and a powerful, obsessive preoccupation with dieting and weight loss. Adolescence is a time of profound biological, psychological and socio-cultural change, and demands a considerable degree of flexibility to successfully manage the transition into adulthood (Connan *et al.* 2003).

Psychologically, change might challenge the perfectionism, harm avoidance, and rigidity of those at risk for AN and thus fuel an underlying vulnerability. The biological changes of adolescence or puberty might also increase the risk of onset of eating disorders. This possibility is supported by twin studies (Klump *et al.* 2007) which implied that puberty might play a role in activating the genetic predisposition for eating disorder symptoms. Moreover, biological changes associated with adolescence differ in males and females and could explain the sexual dimorphism of AN. For example, menarche is associated (Connan *et al.* 2003) with a rapid change in body composition and neuropeptides modulating metabolism. Little is known about whether the rise in oestrogen levels associated with puberty in females is contributory to AN, but it could affect neuromodulatory systems such as serotonin (Rubinow *et al.* 1998) or neuropeptides (Torpy *et al.* 1997) that affect feeding, emotionality, and other behaviours. Brain changes associated with puberty might further challenge these processes. For example, orbital and dorsolateral prefrontal cortex regions develop greatly during and after puberty (Huttenlocher and Dabholkar 1997), and increased activity of these cortical areas might be a cause of the excessive worry, perfectionism, and strategizing in AN patients. Stress and/or cultural and societal pressures might contribute by increasing anxious and obsessional temperament. People with AN find restricting food intake powerfully reinforcing because it provides a temporary respite from dysphoric mood. They enter a vicious cycle – which could account for the chronicity of this disorder – because eating exaggerates, and food refusal reduces, an anxious mood.

Importantly, the temperament and personality traits that might create a vulnerability to develop AN might also have a positive aspect. These traits include attention to detail, concern about consequences, and a drive to accomplish and succeed. Our clinical experience shows that many people who recover from AN do well in life. It is tempting to speculate that the ability to plan ahead, control impulses, and avoid harm might have had highly adaptive value for ancestors who lived in environments where food supplies were constrained by long periods of cold weather (e.g. worry in July about food supplies in January). Adolescence is a time of transition: individuals leave the security of their home environment and must learn to balance immediate and long-term needs and goals to achieve independence (Connan *et al.* 2003). For such individuals, learning to flexibly interact with and master complex and mixed cultural and societal messages and pressures and cope with stress might be difficult and overwhelming, which could exacerbate possible underlying traits of harm avoidance, and a desire to achieve perfection.

References

American Psychiatric Association (APA) (1994) *Diagnostic and Statistical Manual of Mental Disorders*, Washington DC: American Psychiatric Association.

Anderluh, M. B., Tchanturia, K., Rabe-Hesketh, S., and Treasure, J. (2003) 'Childhood Obsessive-Compulsive Personality Traits in Adult Women with Eating Disorders: Defining a Broader Eating Disorder Phenotype', *Am J Psychiatry* 160: 242–7.

Berrettini, W. (2000) 'Genetics of Psychiatric Disease', *Annu Rev Med* 51: 465–79.

Boyar, R. K., Finkelstein, J., Kapen, S., Weiner, H., Weitzman, E., and Hellman, L. (1974) 'Anorexia Nervosa. Immaturity of the 24-Hour Luteinizing Hormone Secretory Pattern', *NEJM* 291: 861–5.

Bruch, H. (1962) 'Perceptual and Conceptual Disturbances in Anorexia Nervosa', *Psychosom Med* 24: 187–94.

Bulik, C., Sullivan, P. F., Tozzi, F., Furberg, H., Lichtenstein, P., and Pedersen, N. L. (2006) 'Prevalence, Heritability and Prospective Risk Factors for Anorexia Nervosa', *Arch Gen Psychiatry* 63: 305–12.

Bulik, C., Hebebrand, J., Keski-Rahkonen, A., Klump, K., Reichborn-Kjennerud, K. S., Mazzeo, S., and Wade, T. (2007) 'Genetic Epidemiology, Endophenotypes, and Eating Disorder Classification', *Int J Eat Disord* 40 (Suppl): S52–60.

Casper, R. C. (1990) 'Personality Features of Women with Good Outcome from Restricting Anorexia Nervosa', *Psychosom Med* 52: 156–70.

Chandraskekar, J., Hoon, M., Ryba, N., and Zuker, C. (2006) 'The Receptors and Cells for Mammalian Taste', *Nature* 444: 288–94.

Chikama, M., McFarland, N., Armaral, D., and Haber, S. (1997) 'Insular Cortical Projections to Functional Regions of the Striatum Correlate with Cortical Cytoarchitectonic Organization in the Primate', *J Neurosci* 17: 9686–705.

Cloninger, C., Przybeck, T., Svrakic, D., and Wetzel, R. (1994) *The Temperament and Character Inventory (TCI): A Guide to its Development and Use*, St. Louis, MO: Washington University Center for Psychobiology of Personality.

Connan, F., Campbell, I., Katzman, M., Lightman, S., and Treasure, J. (2003) 'A Neurodevelopmental Model for Anorexia Nervosa', *Physiol Behav* 79: 13–24.

Craig, A. (2009) 'How Do You Feel – Now? The Anterior Insula and Human Awareness', *Nat Rev Neurosci* 10: 59–70.

Critchley, H., Wiens, S., Rotshtein, P., Ohman, A., and Dolan, R. (2004) 'Neural Systems Supporting Interoceptive Awareness', *Nat Rev Neurosci* 7: 189–95.

Delgado, M., Nystrom, L., Fissel, C., Noll, D., and Fiez, J. (2000) 'Tracking the Hemodynamic Responses to Reward and Punishment in the Striatum', *J Neurophysio* 84: 3072–7.

Drewnowski, A., Pierce, B., and Halmi, K. (1988) 'Fat Aversion in Eating Disorders', *Appetite* 10: 119–31.

Ellison, Z., Foong, J., Howard, R., Bullmore, E., Williams, S., and Treasure, J. (1998) 'Functional Anatomy of Calorie Fear in Anorexia Nervosa', *The Lancet* 352: 1192.

Elman, I., Borsook, D., and Lukas, S. (2006) 'Food Intake and Reward Mechanisms in Patients with Schizophrenia: Implications for Metabolic Disturbances and Treatment

With Second-Generation Antipsychotic Agents', *Neuropsychopharmacology* 31: 2091–120.

Fassino, S., Piero, A., Gramaglia, C., and Abbate-Daga, G. (2004) 'Clinical, Psychopathological and Personality Correlates of Interoceptive Awareness in Anorexia Nervosa, Bulimia Nervosa and Obesity', *Psychopathology* 37: 168–74.

Faurion, A., Cerf, B., Van De Moortele, P. F., Lobel, E., MacLeod, P., and Le Bihan, D. (1999) 'Human Taste Cortical Areas Studied with Functional Magnetic Resonance Imaging: Evidence of Functional Lateralization Related to Handedness', *Neurosci Lett* 277: 89–192.

Fernstrom, M. H., Weltzin, T. E., Neuberger, S., Srinivasagam, N., and Kaye, W. H. (1994) 'Twenty-Four-Hour Food Intake in Patients with Anorexia Nervosa and in Healthy Control Subjects', *Biol Psychiatry* 36: 696–702.

Frank, G., Bailer, U. F., Henry, S., Drevets, W., Meltzer, C. C., Price, J. C., Mathis, C., Wagner, A., Hoge, J., Ziolko, S. K., Barbarich, N., Weissfeld, L., and Kaye, W. (2005) 'Increased Dopamine D2/D3 Receptor Binding After Recovery from Anorexia Nervosa Measured by Positron Emission Tomography and [11C]Raclopride', *Biol Psychiatry* 58: 908–12.

Fudge, J., Breitbart, M., Danish, M., and Pannoni, V. (2005) 'Insular and Gustatory Inputs to the Caudal Ventral Striatum in Primates', *J Comp Neurol* 490: 101–18.

Garfinkel, P., Moldofsky, H., and Garner, D. M. (1979) 'The Stability of Perceptual Disturbances in Anorexia Nervosa', *Psychol Med* 9: 703–8.

Garner, D. M., Olmstead, M. P., and Polivy, J. (1983) 'Development and Validation of a Multidimensional Eating Disorder Inventory for Anorexia and Bulimia Nervosa', *Int J Eat Disord* 2: 15–34.

Gordon, C. M., Dougherty, D. D., Fischman, A. J., Emans, S. J., Grace, E., Lamm, R., Alpert, N. M., Majzoub, J. A., and Rausch, S. L. (2001) 'Neural Substrates of Anorexia Nervosa: A Behavioural Challenge Study With Positron Emission Tomography', *J Pediatr* 139: 51–7.

Gordon, I., Lask, B., Bryant-Waugh, R., Christie, D., and Timimi, S. (1997) 'Childhood-Onset Anorexia Nervosa: Towards Identifying a Biological Substrate', *Int J Eat Disord* 22: 159–65.

Halmi, K., Agras, W. S., Crow, S., Mitchell, J., Wilson, G., Bryson, S., and Kraemer, H. C. (2005) 'Predictors of Treatment Acceptance and Completion in Anorexia Nervosa', *Arch Gen Psychiatry* 62: 776–81.

Huttenlocher, P., and Dabholkar, A. (1997) 'Regional Differences in Synaptogenesis in Human Cerebral Cortex', *J Comp Neurol* 387: 167–78.

Jacobi, C., Hayward, C., De Zwaan, M., Kraemer, H., and Agras, W. (2004) 'Coming to Terms with Risk Factors for Eating Disorders: Application of Risk Terminology and Suggestions for a General Taxonomy', *Psychol Bull* 130: 19–65.

Katzman, D. K., Lambe, E. K., Mikulis, D. J., Ridgley, J. N., Goldbloom, D. S., and Zipursky, R. B. (1996) 'Cerebral Gray Matter and White Matter Volume Deficits in Adolescent Girls With Anorexia Nervosa', *J Pediatr* 29: 794–803.

Kaye, W. H. (1997) 'Anorexia Nervosa, Obsessional Behaviour, and Serotonin', *Psychopharmacol Bull* 33: 335–44.

Kaye, W. H., Barbarich, N. C., Putnam, K., Gendall, K. A., Fernstrom, J., Fernstrom, M., Mcconaha, C. W., and Kishore, A. (2003) 'Anxiolytic Effects of Acute Tryptophan Depletion in Anorexia Nervosa', *Int J Eat Disord* 33: 257–67.

Kaye, W., Wagner, A., Frank, G., and Uf, B. (2006) 'Review of Brain Imaging in Anorexia and Bulimia Nervosa', in S. Wonderlich, J. Mitchell, M. De Zwaan, H. Steiger (eds)

AED Annual Review of Eating Disorders, Part 2 (pp. 113–30), Abingdon: Radcliffe Publishing Ltd.

Kaye, W., Fudge, J., and Paulus, M. (2009) 'New Insight into Symptoms and Neurocircuit Function of Anorexia Nervosa', *Nat Rev Neurosci* 10: 573–84.

Kelley, A. E. (2004) 'Ventral Striatal Control of Appetite Motivation: Role in Ingestive Behaviour and Reward-Related Learning', *Neurosci Biobehav Rev* 27: 765–76.

Klump, K., Strober, M., Johnson, C., Thornton, L., Bulik, C., Devlin, B., Fichter, M., Halmi, K., Kaplan, A., Woodside, D. B., Crow, S., Mitchell, J., Rotondo, A., Keel, P., Berrettini, W. H., Plotnicov, K., Pollice, C., Lilenfeld, L. R., and Kaye, W. (2004) 'Personality Characteristics of Women Before and After Recovery from an Eating Disorder', *Psychol Med* 34: 1407–18.

Klump, K., Burt, S., McGue, M., and Iacono, W. (2007) 'Changes in Genetic and Environmental Influences on Disordered Eating Across Adolescence. A Longitudinal Twin Study', *Arch Gen Psychiatry* 64: 1409–15.

Kringelbach, M. L., O'Doherty, J., Rolls, E., and Andrews, C. (2003) 'Activation of the Human Orbitofrontal Cortex to a Liquid Food Stimulus is Correlated with its Subjective Pleasantness', *Cereb Cortex* 13: 1064–71.

Lilenfeld, L. R., Kaye, W. H., Greeno, C. G., Merikangas, K. R., Plotnicov, K., Pollice, C., Rao, R., Strober, M., Bulik, C. M., and Nagy, L. (1998) 'A Controlled Family Study of Anorexia Nervosa and Bulimia Nervosa: Psychiatric Disorders in First-Degree Relatives and Effects of Proband Comorbidity', *Arch Gen Psychiatry* 55: 603–10.

Lilenfeld, L., Wonderlich, S., Riso, L. P., Crosby, R., and Mitchell, J. (2006) 'Eating Disorders and Personality: A Methodological and Empirical Review', *Clin Psychol Rev* 26: 299–320.

Morris, J. S. and Dolan, R. J. (2001) 'Involvement of Human Amygdala and Orbitofrontal Cortex in Hunger-Enhanced Memory for Food Stimuli', *J Neurosci* 21: 5304–10.

Naruo, T., Nakabeppu, Y., Sagiyama, K., Munemoto, T., Homan, N., Deguchi, D., Nakajo, M., and Nozoe, S. (2000) 'Characteristic Regional Cerebral Blood Flow Patterns in Anorexia Nervosa Patients With Binge/Purge Behaviour', *Am J Psychiatry* 157: 1520–2.

Nozoe, S., Naruo, T., Nakabeppu, Y., Soejima, Y., Nakajo, M., and Tanaka, H. (1993) 'Changes in Regional Cerebral Blood Flow in Patients with Anorexia Nervosa Detected Through Single Photon Emission Tomography Imaging', *Biol Psychiatry* 34: 578–80.

Ogawa, H. (1994) 'Gustatory Cortex of Primates: Anatomy and Physiology', *Neurosci Res* 20: 1–13.

Paulus, M. and Stein, M. B. (2006) 'An Insular View of Anxiety', *Biol Psychiatry* 60: 383–7.

Phillips, M., Drevets, W. R., Rauch, S. L., and Lane, R. (2003a) 'Neurobiology of Emotion Perception I: The Neural Basis of Normal Emotion Perception', *Biol Psychiatry* 54: 504–14.

Phillips, M., Drevets, W. R., Rauch, S. L., and Lane, R. (2003b) 'Neurobiology of Emotion Perception II: Implications for Major Psychiatric Disorders', *Biol Psychiatry* 54: 515–28.

Pollatos, O., Kurz, A.-L., Albrecht, J., Schreder, T., Kleemann, A., Schopf, V., Kopietz, R., Weismann, M., and Schandry, R. (2008) 'Reduced Perception of Bodily Signals in Anorexia Nervosa', *Eat Behav* 9: 381–8.

Pollice, C., Kaye, W. H., Greeno, C. G., and Weltzin, T. E. (1997) 'Relationship of Depression, Anxiety, and Obsessionality to State of Illness in Anorexia Nervosa', *Int J Eat Disord* 21: 367–76.

Rastam, M., Bjure, J., Vestergren, E., Uvebrant, P., Gillberg, I. C., Wentz, E., and Gillberg, C. (2001) 'Regional Cerebral Blood Flow in Weight-Restored Anorexia Nervosa: A Preliminary Study', *Dev Med Child Neurol* 43: 239–42.

Rubinow, D. R., Schmidt, P. J., and Roca, C. A. (1998) 'Estrogen-Serotonin Interactions: Implications for Affective Regulation', *Biol Psychiatry* 44: 839–50.

Santel, S., Baving, L., Krauel, K., Munte, T., and Rotte, M. (2006) 'Hunger and Satiety in Anorexia Nervosa: FMRI During Cognitive Processing of Food Pictures', *Brain Res* 1114: 138–48.

Saper, C. B., Chou, T. C., and Elmquist, J. K. (2002) 'The Need to Feed: Homeostatic and Hedonic Control of Eating', *Neuron* 36: 199–211.

Schoenfeld, M., Neuer, G., Tempelmann, C., Schussler, K., Noesselt, T., Hopf, J., and Heinze, H. (2004) 'Functional Magnetic Resonance Tomography Correlates of Taste Perception in the Human Primary Taste Cortex', *Neuroscience* 127: 347–53.

Schwartz, M. W., Woods, S. C., Porte, D. Jr., Seeley, R. J., and Baskin, D. G. (2000) 'Central Nervous System Control of Food Intake', *Nature* 404: 661–71.

Scott, T. R., Yaxley, S., Sienkiewicz, Z., and Rolls, E. (1986) 'Gustatory Responses in the Frontal Opercular Cortex of the Alert Cynomolgus Monkey', *J Neurophysiol* 56: 876–90.

Small, D. (2006) 'Central Gustatory Processing in Humans', *Adv Otorhinolaryngol* 63: 191–220.

Small, D., Zatorre, R., Dagher, A., Evans, A., and Jones–Gotman, M. (2001) 'Changes in Brain Activity Related to Eating Chocolate: From Pleasure to Aversion', *Brain* 124: 1720–33.

Srinivasagam, N. M., Kaye, W. H., Plotnicov, K. H., Greeno, C., Weltzin, T. E., and Rao, R. (1995) 'Persistent Perfectionism, Symmetry, and Exactness After Long–Term Recovery from Anorexia Nervosa', *Am J Psychiatry* 152: 1630–4.

Steinhausen, H. C. (2002) 'The Outcome of Anorexia Nervosa in the 20th Century', *Am J Psychiatry* 159: 1284–93.

Stice, E. (2002) 'Risk and Maintenance Factors for Eating Pathology: A Meta-Analytic Review', *Pychopharm Bull* 128: 825–48.

Strober, M. (1995) 'Family-Genetic Perspectives on Anorexia Nervosa and Bulimia Nervosa', in K. Brownell and C. Fairburn (eds) *Eating Disorders and Obesity: A Comprehensive Handbook* (pp. 212–18), New York: Guilford Press.

Strober, M., Freeman, R., and Morrell, W. (1997) 'The Long-Term Course of Severe Anorexia Nervosa in Adolescents: Survival Analysis of Recovery, Relapse, and Outcome Predictors Over 10–15 Years in a Prospective Study', *Int J Eat Disord* 22: 339–60.

Tataranni, P. A., Gautier, J. F., Chen, K., Uecker, A., Bandy, D., Salbe, A. D., Pratley, R. E., Lawson, M., Reiman, E. M., and Ravussin, E. (1999) 'Neuroanatomical Correlates of Hunger and Satiation in Humans Using Positron Emission Tomography', *Proc Natl Acad Sci USA* 96: 4569–74.

Torpy, D., Papanicolaou, D., and Chrousos, G. (1997) 'Sexual Dismorphism of the Human Stress Response May Be Due to Estradiol-Mediated Stimulation of Hypothalamic Corticotropin-Releasing Hormone Synthesis', *J Clin Endocrinol Metab* 82: 982.

Tricomi, E. M., Delgado, M. R., and Fiez, J. A. (2004) 'Modulation of Caudate Activity by Action Contingency', *Neuron* 41: 281–92.

Uher, R., Brammer, M., Murphy, T., Campbell, I., Ng, V., Williams, S., and Treasure, J. (2003) 'Recovery and Chronicity in Anorexia Nervosa: Brain Activity Associated with Differential Outcomes', *Biol Psychiatry* 54: 934–42.

Uher, R., Murphy, T., Brammer, M., Dalgleish, T., Phillips, M., Ng, V., Andrew, C., Williams, S., Campbell, I., and Treasure, J. (2004) 'Medial Prefrontal Cortex Activity Associated with Symptom Provocation in Eating Disorders', *Am J Psychiatry* 161: 1238–46.

Uher, R., Treasure, J., Heining, M., and Brammer, M. J. (2006) 'Cerebral Processing of Food-Related Stimuli: Effects of Fasting and Gender', *Behav Brain Res* 169: 111–19.

Vitousek, K. and Manke, F. (1994) 'Personality Variables and Disorders in Anorexia Nervosa and Bulimia Nervosa', *J Abnorm Psychol* 103: 137–47.

Wagner, A., Barbarich, N., Frank, G., Bailer, U., Weissfeld, L., Henry, S., Achenbach, S., Vogel, V., Plotnicov, K., McConaha, C., Kaye, W., and Wonderlich, S. (2006) 'Personality Traits After Recovery From Eating Disorders: Do Subtypes Differ?', *Int J Eat Disord* 39: 276–84.

Wagner, A., Aizenstein, H., Venkatraman, M., Fudge, J., May, J., Mazurkewicz, L., Frank, G., Bailer, U. F., Fischer, L., Nguyen, V., Carter, C., Putnam, K., and Kaye, W. H. (2007) 'Altered Reward Processing in Women Recovered from Anorexia Nervosa', *Am J Psychiatry* 164: 1842–9.

Wagner, A., Aizenstein, H., Frank, G. K., Figurski, J., May, J. C., Putnam, K., Bailer, U. F., Fischer, L., Henry, S. E., McConaha, C., and Kaye, W. H. (2008) 'Altered Insula Response to a Taste Stimulus in Individuals Recovered from Restricting-Type Anorexia Nervosa', *Neuropsychopharmacology* 33: 513–23.

Walters, E. E. and Kendler, K. S. (1995) 'Anorexia Nervosa and Anorexic-Like Syndromes in a Population-Based Female Twin Sample', *Am J Psychiatry* 152: 64–71.

Yaxley, S., Rolls, E., and Sienkiewicz, Z. (1990) 'Gustatory Responses of Single Neurons in the Insula of the Macaque Monkey', *J Neurophysiol* 63: 689–700.

Zastrow, A., Kaiser, S. S., Walthe, S., Herzog, W., Tchanturia, K., Belger, A., Weisbrod, M., Treasure, J., and Friederich, H. (2009) 'Neural Correlates of Impaired Cognitive-Behavioural Flexibility in Anorexia Nervosa', *Am J Psychiatry* 166: 608–16.

Chapter 4

Emotions and empathic understanding: capitalizing on relationships in those with eating disorders

Nancy Zucker, Ashley Moskovich, Mallory Vinson and Karli Watson

Case study

Angelina, aged 20, has a history of anorexia nervosa (AN) since the age of 14. Prior to the onset of AN, Angelina struggled with profound fears of social disapproval and remained isolated even in her experience of interpersonal discomfort. Her desire for achievement, particularly in running and academics, made her stifle relationship fears and suffer silently while continuing to participate in these organized social activities. The thought of describing discomfort to others 'never occurred' to her. Years later, when Angelina and her family were in therapy for treatment of her AN, purging subtype, both parents were surprised to learn of Angelina's subjective reports of social anxiety in childhood as, to all appearances, she was coping 'well'.

Angelina in fact was a very lonely child. She lacked intimate friendships and did not have a best friend. In terms of Angelina's learning history, her father struggled with a chronic history of debilitating social anxiety that, despite significant improvement, continues to interfere with all domains of functioning (e.g. prevents employment). His early learning history was notable for severe violations in interpersonal boundaries leading to maladaptive beliefs and behaviours regarding the degree of control and responsibility one has over another's emotional experience. His frustrations with his own ability to help his daughter and difficulty apprehending Angelina's experiences led to explosive anger outbursts followed by days of silence and threats of abandonment. Arguments were rarely resolved and over time, Angelina developed a conditioned fear of anger in others, a pattern of learning that made her vulnerable to patterns of abuse (emotional, sexual) in interpersonal relationships.

Her eating disorder history has been particularly malignant. Intense experiences of shame prompted dangerous behaviours: binge eating, purging, cutting and burning. She has maintained a dangerously low body mass index (BMI) throughout her illness.

> The slightest thought of making a mistake or disappointing someone – falling short of my expectations of perfection – conjures intense feelings of fear and anxiety. My eating disorder developed as an escape, a collection of methods designed to numb and protect myself from overwhelming emotions. Converting emotional pain into physical pain [by purging or cutting] makes it tangible, and therefore easier to deal with. Additionally, I've used my 'illness' as an excuse to avoid, the theory being that if I didn't try, I couldn't fail. The most essential thing has been learning to recognize what is truly important to me – the comforting emptiness as an emotionless zombie, or pursuing my goals of relationships, academics.
>
> Angelina

Relationships and eating disorder treatment

Enhancing relationships is essential for effective treatment of eating disorders (Rieger *et al.* 2010). Perhaps this is best illustrated by examining the legacy of family involvement in the treatment of adolescent AN: outcomes for this dangerous disorder have improved dramatically since families, particularly parents, have been integrated as part of the treatment process. This development was due to promising long-term outcome data from clinical trials examining family-based treatment developed by researchers at the Maudsley Hospital in London (Eisler *et al.* 2007; G. F. M. Russell *et al.* 1992) and intensified efforts to disseminate this original model to the US (Lock *et al.* 2001). Prior to such shift in emphasis, families were largely excluded from the treatment process, an exclusion that stifled progress and alienated families from potential benefits of psychotherapy. One critical emphasis of this treatment model is that the family team battles together against a personified enemy, 'the eating disorder' that has taken their child 'hostage' (Loeb *et al.* 2009). This emphasis, a technique borrowed from narrative therapy (White and Epston 1990), is critical as it helps shift blame and negative affect from the child to the illness. Addressing barriers that limit caregiver effectiveness is essential for the next iteration of treatments for eating disorders.

Yet, some families may be a poor fit for family-based psychotherapy. Families with elevations in expressed emotion do not fare as well as other families (Szmukler *et al.* 1985; van Furth *et al.* 1996). Expressed emotion is a pattern of heightened critical communication directed towards the individual with a diagnosis (Vaughn and Leff 1976). Zucker *et al.* (2007) have previously argued that expressed emotion may reflect a complex array of deficits including impaired theory of mind and poor emotion regulation skills. Theory of mind is the capacity to understand that others have a mind separate from one's own and hence a different frame of reference – with different motivations to act, different reactions to experiences, etc. (Focquaert *et al.* 2008; Vogeley *et al.* 2001). Parents with impairments in this capacity may not comprehend the difficulties their child is experiencing, despite extreme devotion to their child and strong motivation to assist recovery. Further, challenges regulating their own emotional arousal, i.e. not allowing emotional experience to interfere with goal-directed actions, may affect their ability to effectively implement a treatment plan (Ochsner and Gross 2005). Thus, we propose that the combination of impaired theory of mind and poor emotion regulation may facilitate the display of expressed emotion. In this chapter, we describe how these capacities are linked and how interventions directed towards adaptive emotion regulation may indirectly improve empathic understanding of others.

However, improvement in interpersonal communication is not only relevant to enhance family functioning; such improvements may also facilitate willingness to improve eating disorder symptoms. Consider data that indicate that social anxiety often precedes the onset of AN (Godart *et al.* 2000; Raney *et al.* 2008) and evidence that social stressors often instigate the intentional or accidental weight loss that begins the cascade of events that ultimately culminate in AN (Schmidt *et al.* 1997). Angelina's experience further illustrates the interaction of these processes. Combined, such data suggest that symptoms of AN, irrespective of the complex biological cocktail that precipitates illness onset, may help to manage social fears via facilitated avoidance and emotional distancing from others. For individuals like Angelina to desire to re-engage fully in life events without the numbing isolation afforded by starvation, we need to increase self-efficacy in their capacity to form and maintain interpersonal relationships (Rieger *et al.* 2010; Zucker *et al.* 2007). Further, we need to help patients with AN maintain their independence of thought, belief, and emotional experience in the presence of such intimacy. We will illustrate the inextricable link between emotional experience and emotional perception and illustrate how enhancing emotion regulatory capacities may also enhance empathic attunement. We further illustrate how the starvation of AN may compromise certain facets of social perception.

Empathy and the experience of emotion

You see a woman sobbing over her sick child and feel a deep pit of dread in your gut and anxious fluttering of your heartbeat. Such sensual embodiment of another's experience is a pivotal foundation of empathy, the capacity to accurately attune to the cognitive, visceral, and emotional experiences of another person (Decety and Meyer 2008). Research investigating the nature of empathic experience is increasingly revealing that attuning to the experience of others requires a virtual re-enactment of their felt sense: we understand the pit of dread in our friend's gut, in part, because we too have experienced such somatic sensations and partially embody those experiences as we seek to connect with others (you hurt, I hurt) (Decety and Meyer 2008). The embodiment of empathic experience is receiving increased attention as technological advances permit researchers to probe the limits of shared experiences by comparing the distributed neural circuitry of perceiving relative to experiencing a given event (Iacoboni *et al.* 2005). This pattern of results has prompted an increase in studies differentiating the nuances of empathic experience and elucidating the limitations of the framework of mirror neurons (i.e. neurons that fire when both performing and observing an action) (Hickok 2009). We raise this connection to illustrate an intriguing point about enhancing empathic responding in those with eating disorders and their families: we can improve our empathic capacities by improving capacities to sense our own emotional experience.

Emotions and parent competence

Increasing parent confidence and expertise in understanding and responding to their own emotional experience may have a twofold purpose: it may also help them apprehend the experiences of their children. Caregivers assist their children in learning to understand and respond to emotional needs by the way in which they respond to their own and their child's emotional experience (Propper and Moore 2006). For example, in a group skill-based intervention for parents of children with eating disorders, parents are taught to recognize the intensity of their own emotional arousal and to match their choice of emotion regulatory strategy based on their level of arousal. The intention is to help caregivers prevent the intensity of emotional experience from compromising effectiveness. Caregivers learn to decrease arousal and proceed on their intended action (Zucker 2005, 2006). The metaphor of an emotional wave is used to represent the degree of intensity of affective experience: climbing the wave is the experience of intensifying emotions while surfing the wave is not allowing the intensity of emotional experience to interfere with goal-directed actions (Merwin, personal communication). The Logic Line (Figure 4.1) symbolizes the relative balance between cognition and emotional experience: as intensity of emotions increases, rational cognition becomes increasingly compromised. Parents are taught to recognize this trade-off and the implications for using various emotion regulation strategies. Crossing the Logic Line renders certain emotion regulation strategies relatively ineffective, especially strategies that rely heavily on cognitive processes (i.e. it is hard to reason with someone experiencing an intense emotional episode).

In Phase One, parents learn to recognize the intensity of their affective arousal and to not allow the intensity of emotional experiences to decrease their effectiveness in managing their child's disorder. Further, as their self-efficacy in recognizing their own emotional experience increases, they improve their ability to recognize variations of emotional intensity in their child. Such recognition facilitates the ability to match their approach to their child's level of arousal. In this manner, caregivers are both modelling effective emotion regulation and gently shaping such regulation in their children (Zucker, in press).

In Phase Two, parents learn the value of emotions: motivated states that communicate information. Emotions are communication devices: the expression of fear signals danger to others; displays of sadness signal the need for support, nurturance, and recuperation (Elfenbein and Ambady 2002). Just as emotions are

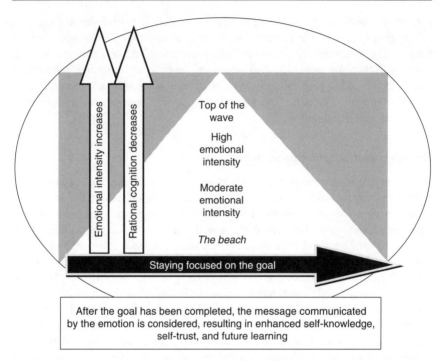

Figure 4.1 A model of the emotional wave, a metaphor used to enhance parental compe-
tence in identifying, attuning, and regulating their own emotional experience
and that of their children. The model emphasizes the interplay of cognition
and emotion as a simplified heuristic to increase parent awareness of their
relative efficacy and capacities for judgement as affective intensity increases.

interpersonal signalling devices, they are also intrapersonal signalling devices:
learning to attune to our own emotional experience gives us information about our
preferences and needs. The back and forth of attuning to one's own emotional
experience may thus facilitate development of a self-concept: 'when this happens, I
feel this way. I like this. I get nervous when this happens.' Similar to the role-
modelling/shaping strategy of Phase One, Phase Two is role modelling and shaping
as parents learn the communicative value of affective signals. Angelina's mother Jane
became adept at recognizing her own emotional experience and being authentic with
her feelings about her daughter's illness. This allowed her to learn more about her
own interests: her dissatisfaction with her current employment, her love of crafts.
Irrespective of her daughter's progress, Jane became an increasingly better role model
of adaptive self-regulation, improving her own quality of life and that of her other
children. The communicative value of emotions both provides information to guide
the behaviour of others and is instructive regarding our own motivational drives. Over
time, the back and forth communicative dance of affective signals and adaptive
responses results in solidification of a cohesive frame of reference: the common
denominator of this dance is the 'me' for whom all these signals have relevance.

Starvation, emotions, and social information processing

Of course, if emotions communicate, one must be able to perceive these affective signals for optimal interpersonal interactions to ensue. Social perception is thus the essential counterpart to apprehending one's own emotional experience. Deficits on either side of the equation may compromise empathic attunement. While investigators increasingly agree there are significant deficits in social functioning among patients with AN (Jansch *et al.* 2009; Kucharska-Pietura *et al.* 2004; Oldershaw *et al.* 2010; T. M. Russell *et al.* 2009; Zucker *et al.* 2007), contributions to these deficits are less clear. Jansch *et al.* (2009) found that individuals with AN reported less ability to decipher their own emotional experience compared to healthy controls. This study also found that those with AN had more trouble classifying and correctly identifying emotions on a facial recognition task (Jansch *et al.* 2009). These findings were replicated by Kucharska-Pietura *et al.* (2004) who also reported deficits in identifying affect in voice prosody. There are reports that people with AN endorse higher levels of alexithymia, an inability to discriminate and label states of subjective emotional arousal; however, this study noted that facial emotion recognition was not related to alexithymia (Kessler *et al.* 2006), a pattern of results that differed in healthy controls. These findings indicate that those with AN may develop different strategies to decipher the emotional experiences of others, strategies with implications for their capacity to empathize.

To date, investigation exploring the capacities of those with AN to empathically attune to the emotional experiences of others has been limited. Empathy is conceptually related to theory of mind, and Oldershaw *et al.* (2010) found that affective or emotional theory of mind was impaired in currently ill patients with AN, but not significantly impaired in recovered patients. Two other studies also found that patients currently diagnosed with AN performed more poorly on theory of mind tasks compared to healthy controls (T. M. Russell *et al.* 2009; Tchanturia *et al.* 2004). Of course, performance on tasks that require abilities to decipher the experience of others may differ from one's subjective evaluation of one's capacities. Hambrook *et al.* (2008) predicted that women suffering from AN would endorse lower scores on a measure tapping their perceived capacities to empathize with others; however, they failed to find significant differences in those with AN relative to healthy controls. The group with AN did endorse elevated symptoms on a continuous measure of symptoms of the autism spectrum, a disorder characterized, in part, by deficits in reciprocal social interactions. However, autism spectrum disorders are complex illnesses characterized by multiple symptom clusters including deficits in communication, and rigid, repetitive behaviours often characterized by an insistence on sameness (Happe *et al.* 2006). As rigid and repetitive behaviours are often part of the phenotypic presentation of AN, and often exacerbated by starvation, it is notable that the AN group differed specifically on subscales related to social skills and imagination – but not communication. Also notably, this pattern of results was replicated in our laboratory: a lack of significance on self-report measures of empathy, but significant differences on the autism quotient in a sample of sixty-six individuals (forty-four with current or prior histories of AN).

Several hypotheses could explain this pattern of results and highlight areas for research. First, as noted by Hambrook *et al.* (2008), sample sizes have been small and replication is needed with larger samples. An alternative hypothesis is that people with AN may indeed have equivalent capacities to empathize with others but may have to use different strategies. If true, they may have to work harder to achieve an equivalent result, processes that may compromise their capacities during rapid and dynamic interpersonal interactions. In contrast, laboratory tasks and questionnaires are often poor imitations of such real-world complexity, though they provide essential first steps in segregating the components of social perception and emotional experience. Thus, more precise methodologies may be needed. Finally, measures asking those with AN to appraise their own abilities may have limited utility as people may have limited insight into their own capacities, particularly if they have no intimate friendship from which to compare current relationships. Discerning true capacities from perceived abilities and characterizing differential processes despite similar outcomes is essential to develop tailored strategies to facilitate affectively intimate relationships in those with AN.

Targets and features of visually-guided attention may differentiate those with AN despite having similar performance outcomes. Too many visual stimuli impinge on an organism for all potential stimuli to be accessible to conscious thought at any given moment. Rather, people make choices, both consciously and unconsciously, regarding where to direct visual attention. Examining where people choose to look provides an index of what is motivationally salient to that individual (a child obsessed with trains may first focus on a toy train while his mother directs her attention to all breakable things in the store). Given the communicative function of emotions, facial affective expressions not only provide vital information about current conditions of both the person and their context, but certain facial features are particularly vital to achieve this function. Eyes are particularly salient social signals and prior work has indicated that individuals can discern complex emotional states of another individual when only the eyes are available to view. Given this, the relative time individuals spend gazing at the eyes of another has been used as an index of aberrant patterns of visually-guided attention. For example, Watson *et al.* (manuscript under review) reported that people with a prior history of AN spent less time gazing at the eyes of female photos and more time looking at the mouth than those without such history. As the mouth is less informative in discerning the actor's feelings, differential attention allocation to this facial affective signal may have implications for a person's ability to decipher the emotional experience of others.

There are also important neurodevelopmental consequences to such patterns of viewing (Klin *et al.* 2002). In young infants, eye-contact is proposed to facilitate robust connectivity between the fusiform gyrus and amygdala, neural regions specialized for detection and recognition of salient stimuli, with potential specialization for the perception of faces (Volkmar *et al.* 2005). Over time, such enhanced connectivity would lead to even greater detection and recognition, while the absence of such eye-contact would putatively impact such adaptive neural development (Dziobek *et al.* 2010). The neurodevelopment of visually-guided attention in AN has been a limited focus of study and may provide vital information to guide development of novel intervention strategies.

The starvation and related malnourishment that hallmarks AN and is a potential sequela of bulimia nervosa (BN) may in and of itself compromise social perception. When people feel threatened, they direct their attention to potential sources of threat. This is adaptive as it enables them to be prepared to escape in an emergency. Starvation is a state of vulnerability: a starved animal is less protected than a nourished one. Thus, the very nature of eating disorders increases stress and vulnerability and has implications for the capacity to detect threat. For example, Zucker *et al.* (manuscript under review) reported that patients with AN were better at perceiving anger from biological motion cues (body gestures and stimuli portraying moving bodies), but worse at perceiving sadness. The authors discuss these implications in relation to family dynamics: while parents may have difficulty expressing their emotions effectively, their children may be oversensitive to signals of anger, a combination that may perpetuate conflict and tension. There is much to learn about how the ill state of eating disorders perpetuates, exacerbates, and/or creates problems in empathically attuning to others.

Conclusion

Let us return to Angelina and her chronic difficulties in forming intimate relationships. Relative even to others with AN, Angelina scored a standard deviation higher on a task tapping abilities to notice details embedded in complex stimuli, a local bias of visually-guided attention. Such results indicate Angelina is excellent at noticing features, and may notice such features at the expense of the surrounding context. Angelina also scored above average on a task in which she had to identify the affect in facial expressions. Notably, unlike some people with AN who evidence difficulties shifting between cognitive sets, Angelina did not evidence decrements in this area. She could arrange and execute plans, when not compromised by states of heightened affect. Finally, Angelina scored extremely high on a measure of rejection sensitivity – even relative to others with AN. Given her father's frequent anger outbursts, Angelina may be in a context in which she is better at detecting anger and frequently sees angry expressions (and thus gets more practice). These capacities and experiences may combine to communicate to Angelina that the world is indeed a threatening place. Incorporating a person's capacity to sense both one's own emotional experience and that of others, patterns of visually-guided attention, and the integrity of complex cognitive functions, will be critical to advance our treatments. The increasing precision with which we can match individual capacities with their narratives will be critical for the next phase of tailored interventions for those with eating disorders and their families and to help those with eating disorders form rewarding, intimate relationships.

References

Decety, J. and Meyer, M. (2008) From emotion resonance to empathic understanding: A social developmental neuroscience account. *Development and Psychopathology*, 20(4), 1053–80.

Dziobek, I., Bahnemann, M., Convit, A., and Heekeren, H. R. (2010) The role of the fusiform-amygdala system in the pathophysiology of autism. *Archives of General Psychiatry*, 67(4), 397–405.

Eisler, I., Simic, M., Russell, G. F., and Dare, C. (2007) A randomised controlled treatment trial of two forms of family therapy in adolescent AN: a five-year follow-up. *Journal of Child Psychology and Psychiatry*, 48(6), 552–60.

Elfenbein, H. A. and Ambady, N. (2002) On the universality and cultural specificity of emotion recognition: A meta-analysis. *Psychological Bulletin*, 128(2), 203–35.

Focquaert, F., Braeckman, J., and Platek, S. M. (2008) An evolutionary cognitive neuroscience perspective on human self-awareness and theory of mind. *Philosophical Psychology*, 21(1), 47–68.

Godart, N. T., Flament, M. F., Lecrubier, Y., and Jeammet, P. (2000) Anxiety disorders in AN and bulimia nervosa: co-morbidity and chronology of appearance. *European Psychiatry*, 15(1), 38–45.

Hambrook, D., Tchanturia, K., Schmidt, U., Russell, T., and Treasure, J. (2008) Empathy, systemizing, and autistic traits in AN: A pilot study. *British Journal of Clinical Psychology*, 47, 335–9.

Happe, F., Ronald, A., and Plomin, R. (2006) Time to give up on a single explanation for autism. *Nature Neuroscience*, 9(10), 1218–20.

Hickok, G. (2009) Eight problems for the mirror neuron theory of action understanding in monkeys and humans. *Journal of Cognitive Neuroscience*, 21(7), 1229–43.

Iacoboni, M., Molnar-Szakacs, I., Gallese, V., Buccino, G., Mazziotta, J. C., and Rizzolatti, G. (2005) Grasping the intentions of others with one's own mirror neuron system. *Plos Biology*, 3(3), 529–35.

Jansch, C., Harmer, C., and Cooper, M. J. (2009) Emotional processing in women with AN and in healthy volunteers. *Eating Behaviours*, 10, 184–91.

Kessler, H., Schwarze, M., Filipic, S., Traue, H. C., and von Wietersheim, J. (2006) Alexithymia and facial emotion recognition in patients with eating disorders. *International Journal of Eating Disorders*, 39(3), 245–51.

Klin, A., Jones, W., Schultz, R., Volkmar, F., and Cohen, D. (2002) Defining and quantifying the social phenotype in autism. *American Journal of Psychiatry*, 159(6), 895–908.

Kucharska-Pietura, K., Nikolaou, V., Masiak, M., and Treasure, J. (2004) The recognition of emotion in the faces and voice of AN. *International Journal of Eating Disorders*, 35(1), 42–7.

Lock, J., Le Grange, D., Agras, W. S., and Dare, C. (2001) *Treatment Manual for AN: A Family-Based Approach*. New York: Guilford Press.

Loeb, K. L., Hirsch, A. M., Greif, R., and Hildebrandt, T. B. (2009) Family-based treatment of a 17-year-old twin presenting with emerging AN: A case study using the 'Maudsley Method'. *Journal of Clinical Child and Adolescent Psychology*, 38(1), 176–83.

Ochsner, K. N. and Gross, J. (2005) The cognitive control of emotion. *Trends in Cognitive Sciences*, 9, 242–9.

Oldershaw, A., Hambrook, D., Tchanturia, K., Treasure, J., and Ulrike, S. (2010) Emotional theory of mind and emotional awareness in recovered AN patients. *Psychosomatic Medicine*, 72, 73–9.

Propper, C. and Moore, G. A. (2006) The influence of parenting on infant emotionality: A multi-level psychobiological perspective. *Developmental Review*, 26(4), 427–60.

Raney, T. J., Thornton, L. M., Berrettini, W., Brandt, H., Crawford, S., Fichter, M. M., *et al.* (2008) Influence of overanxious disorder of childhood on the expression of AN. *International Journal of Eating Disorders*, 41(4), 326–32.

Rieger, E., Van Buren, D. J., Bishop, M., Tanofsky-Kraff, M., Welch, R., and Wilfley, D. E. (2010) An eating disorder-specific model of interpersonal psychotherapy (IPT-ED): Causal pathways and treatment implications. *Clinical Psychology Review*, 30(4), 400–10.

Russell, G. F. M., Dare, C., Eisler, I., and Le Grange, P. D. F. (1992) Controlled trials of family treatments in anorexia nervosa. In K. A. Halmi (ed.) *Psychobiology and Treatment of Anorexia Nervosa and Bulimia Nervosa* (pp. 237–62). Arlington, VA: American Psychiatric Press.

Russell, T. M., Schmidt, U., Doherty, L., Young, V., and Tchanturia, K. (2009) Aspects of social cognition in AN: Affective and cognitive theory of mind. *Psychiatry Research*, 168, 181–5.

Schmidt, U., Tiller, J., Blanchard, M., Andrews, B., and Treasure, J. (1997) Is there a specific trauma precipitating AN? *Psychological Medicine*, 27(3), 523–30.

Szmukler, G. I., Eisler, I., Russell, G., and Dare, C. (1985) AN, parental 'expressed emotion' and dropping out of treatment. *British Journal of Psychiatry*, 147, 265–71.

Tchanturia, K., Happe, F., Godley, J., Treasure, J., Bara-Carril, N., and Schmidt, U. (2004) 'Theory of Mind' in AN. *European Eating Disorders Review*, 12(6), 361–6.

van Furth, E. F., van Strien, D. C., Martina, L. M., van Son, M. J., Hendrickx, J. J., and van Engeland, H. (1996) Expressed emotion and the prediction of outcome in adolescent eating disorders. *International Journal of Eating Disorders*, 20(1), 19–31.

Vaughn, C. and Leff, J. (1976) Measurement of expressed emotion in families of psychiatric-patients. *British Journal of Social and Clinical Psychology*, 15, 157–65.

Vogeley, K., Bussfeld, P., Newen, A., Herrmann, S., Happe, F., Falkai, P., *et al.* (2001) Mind reading: Neural mechanisms of theory of mind and self-perspective. *Neuroimage*, 14(1), 170–81.

Volkmar, F., Chawarska, K., and Klin, A. (2005) Autism in infancy and early childhood. *Annual Review of Psychology*, 56, 315–36.

Watson, K., Werling, D., Zucker, N., and Platt, M. L. (manuscript under review) Altered social reward and attention in AN.

White, M. and Epston, D. (1990) *Narrative Means to Therapeutic Ends*. New York: Norton.

Zucker, N. L. (in press) *A Parent Skills Program for the Treatment of Eating Disorders*. Oakland, CA: New Harbinger.

Zucker, N. L., Ferriter, C., Best, S., and Brantley, A. (2005) Group parent training: a novel approach for the treatment of eating disorders. *Eating Disorders: The Journal of Treatment and Prevention*, 13(4), 391–405.

Zucker, N. L., Marcus, M. D., and Bulik, C. (2006) A group parent training program: A novel approach for eating disorder management. *Eating and Weight Disorders: Studies on Anorexia, Bulimia and Obesity*, 11, 78–82.

Zucker, N., Losh, M., Bulik, C., LaBar, K. S., Piven, J., and Pelphrey, K. A. (2007) AN and autism spectrum disorders: guided investigation of social cognitive endophenotypes. *Psychological Bulletin*, 133(6), 976–1006.

Zucker, N., Moskovich, A., Wagner, H. R., Bulik, C. M., Merwin, R., Piven, J., *et al.* (manuscript under review) Perception of affect in biological motion cues in AN.

Chapter 5

Modifiable risk factors that can be translated into prevention or resilience

Susan J. Paxton

Case study

I was about 13 when I became aware of being 'different' from other girls. My body began to change and develop overnight. I felt a deep-seated fear as everything in the mirror before me twisted and shifted and I lost complete control over my body. Being a young black girl, growing up in a mostly white-middle-class neighbourhood, surrounded by white classmates, there weren't many examples, outside my family, of what a girl my age of African descent should look like.

My body looked 'wrong'. Puberty was hard on me and I hated that my new body no longer was straight all the way down, but now curved and bulged and was difficult to dress. I was fat and ugly.

Reflecting, I see that what I thought was 'fat' was only the 'puppy fat' of adolescence, but negative body image thoughts had already begun to take hold.

I was a good student and drove myself to perfection academically. I was rarely satisfied even when I did well. I was creative and loved to write music and short stories and sing, but my need to control every creative element, began to suck the joy out of my art.

Food became my refuge and comfort: a diversion from pain I was feeling about difficult situations in my home life. Food became my voice: what I couldn't bring myself to say, I ate. Food helped me control my fears: whenever I felt lost, scared or insecure, I ate. Eating became a quick escape, a way of avoiding the messiness of learning how to say 'no' and a blanket for managing emotions. I started binging late at night and began to lie to cover my tracks.

In my teens, I became obsessed with dieting and exercise and an expert on every weight loss approach. During my 'diets' I would deny myself for days on end – then splurge towards the end of the week. I would starve myself until I could no longer feel the hunger pangs and think that meant success. Then I'd undo all the work by eating all seven days' worth of meals in one sitting. My metabolism probably didn't know what hit it.

In university, away from family and friends, I discovered laxatives. Now I could secretly binge and purge and no one would know the difference. To the outside world I was functioning, full of ambition and drive, 'going places!' But on the inside I was a mess. In a line-up of ED sufferers, you'd miss me every time, and yet I was suffering.

Later, working full-time in the media as a freelance journalist, the images surrounding me were of [mostly white] slim, happy-looking women – none black or fat like me. Women like me didn't seem to exist and if we did, no one wanted to see us in coloured print. My one example was Oprah Winfrey – and while in some ways an excellent role model, she also represented everything I despised in myself – a woman constantly struggling with her weight. Several times people tried to compliment me by saying I reminded them of her – but this confirmed my biggest fear. The thought I would *always* struggle and never would be truly beautiful ....

Anna

Introduction

Prevention is essential to reduce the enormous burden of eating disorders like the disorder suffered by Anna. In this chapter, underlying concepts of prevention will first be described. Next, different types of promising prevention approaches will be described. Finally, important issues in relation to prevention will be discussed.

Concepts of prevention

As Anna's story illustrates, eating disorders are the end point of a pathway from relatively healthy body image and eating behaviours, to emerging body image and eating problems, and finally to a clinical eating disorder. Prevention interventions aim to stop movement up this pathway. Ideally, prevention takes place before any symptoms develop, e.g. before Anna became distressed about her adolescent body shape. However, in some instances, early eating disorder symptoms may already be present. In this situation, the goal of prevention is to prevent the development of a clinical eating disorder and to reduce existing symptoms, e.g. after Anna had developed body image concerns but before her eating disorder symptoms occurred.

Three major types of prevention intervention have been identified (National Research Council and Institute of Medicine 2009: 66). Universal prevention refers to an intervention that is targeted at whole populations without any consideration of whether early symptoms are present (e.g. a media advertising programme or curriculum for the whole school). Selective prevention is specifically for high-risk groups but again is delivered without any consideration of whether early symptoms are present (e.g. a body image programme for all girls in a grade seven class). Indicated or targeted prevention is an intervention specifically designed for high-risk individuals already displaying early symptoms for the disorder (e.g. grade seven girls with high levels of body image concerns).

For prevention, first it is essential to identify variables that increase the likelihood of movement up the eating disorder pathway, i.e. risk factors for an eating disorder, and those that reduce the likelihood of movement, i.e. protective factors. Unmodifiable risk factors for eating disorders include genetic predisposition, perfectionistic temperament, depressive tendencies, traumatic life experiences, living in an industrialised country, and being female (Jacobi et al. 2004). As these risk factors cannot be changed, they are not appropriate foci for prevention. However, potentially modifiable individual risk factors have also been identified. These include body dissatisfaction, extreme weight loss behaviours, higher weight, adoption of the socially endorsed thin body ideal as a personal standard (i.e. internalisation of the thin body ideal), and placement of an undue emphasis on weight and shape in evaluation of the self (Jacobi et al. 2004; Neumark-Sztainer et al. 2006a; Stice 2002). These variables are potential foci for prevention.

Risk and protective environments have also been identified. Family, peer, and sport or professional environments, in which there is a focus on thin appearance, dieting and encouragement of unhealthy weight loss strategies, increase risk for body dissatisfaction and eating disorders (Jones 2004; Paxton et al. 1999; Rodgers and Chabrol 2009; Thompson and Sherman 2010). Appearance teasing and bullying is a particularly important environmental risk factor (e.g. Wertheim et al. 2001). On the other hand, more frequent family meals protect against the development of extreme weight loss behaviours (Neumark-Sztainer et al. 2008). Finally, our media environment, which promotes a narrow and typically unachievable image of beauty, sells the message that achieving this appearance is the only way to happiness and success, and encourages stigmatisation of larger body sizes, provides a backdrop for the development of body dissatisfaction and eating disorders. In vulnerable girls, like Anna, exposure to these messages increases body dissatisfaction and contributes to the belief that achieving thinness will be a means to self-esteem, control, and freedom from problems (Wertheim et al. 2009). Prevention interventions can either endeavour to change the way in which a person responds to a risk environment or, alternatively, endeavour to change the environment itself.

Anna's story illustrates several of these risk factors. Anna most likely had a genetic predisposition for perfectionism and a fuller body shape. But she was living in a world that held a narrow view of the ideal body – thin and Caucasian –and she did not fit. Despite her desire for perfection and the centrality of the thin ideal to Anna's life, this ideal could not naturally be achieved. Food became a comfort, extreme weight loss behaviours alternated with binging, and a bulimic cycle became established.

Prevention approaches

Most body image and eating disorder prevention approaches evaluated to date have tried to change individual body image attitudes and eating behaviours and to provide coping strategies to manage the many pressures to conform to the current body image ideal. These have typically been conducted in school or college settings and take the form of classroom curricula, and the most promising types of intervention are described below. More recently, some governments have adopted public policy approaches to prevention of body dissatisfaction and eating disorders, and examples are described.

Prevention curricula

Media literacy

Media literacy is an approach to prevention that aims to reduce the risk factor of internalisation of the thin body ideal. Although body ideals are propagated through a range of social environments, media images are an important means of transmission. Media literacy is based on inoculation theory which suggests that strategies to resist social persuasion can be acquired – in this case, skills to resist pressure from media to adopt media body ideals can be learnt (Wilksch *et al.* 2008: 940).

An important element of media literacy is the deconstruction of advertising images. Usually through their own investigation of media images, participants learn how unrealistic and lacking in diversity the body shapes, sizes and colours in the media are and to identify ways in which media images have been manipulated to distort reality. Compelling video clips are frequently used, such as those produced by Dove to illustrate the transformation of images from reality to fantasy using different techniques (Dove Campaign for Real Beauty). To reinforce knowledge about the manipulation of images, participants may be asked to engage in media activism, i.e. trying to change the situation by action such as writing to a magazine editor to complain about an image. Anna, for example, could have explored the lack of diversity in ethnicity in media images and written to a magazine editor to complain. Media Smart is a particularly promising media literacy programme for grade seven and eight students which has been shown to result in lower shape and weight concerns, dieting and body dissatisfaction in participants than in a control group at a thirty-month follow-up assessment (Wilksch and Wade 2009).

Cognitive dissonance approaches

Cognitive dissonance approaches to prevention build on dissonance theory. This theory proposes that possessing inconsistent views on a topic is an uncomfortable state. Under these circumstances an individual is motivated to change his or her views to make them more consistent with each other (Festinger 1957). Cognitive dissonance approaches aim to capitalise on this phenomenon. They 'encourage adolescent girls and young women who subscribe to the thin ideal to critique it in a series of verbal, written and behavioural group-based exercises' (Stice *et al.* 2008b: 116). Thus, this approach has been used with participants who have already been identified as having high levels of body dissatisfaction and internalisation of the thin ideal (i.e. targeted prevention), and the main risk factor addressed is internalisation of the thin ideal.

Cognitive dissonance programmes use discussion to raise the issue of the thin ideal and discuss how pressures from family, peers, partners and media perpetuate it. Participants engage in exercises such as writing a letter to a hypothetical younger person that discusses the costs of endorsing the thin ideal. In this way, they are arguing against an attitude which they themselves hold (Stice *et al.* 2008b). This approach has been found to be effective in decreasing internalisation of the thin ideal, body dissatisfaction, negative affect and eating disorder symptoms over a two- to three-year follow-up period (Stice *et al.* 2008a) and in college sororities (Becker *et al.* 2008).

Peer interactions and environments

Peer environments can be critical in the development of body image and eating disorders. The first prevention study to emphasise change of the peer environment was conducted by Piran (1999) in the context of a ballet school. Piran worked to assist peers to form support groups to combat the expression of prejudices and inequalities. Norms were established around appropriate comments about the body. The change in the peer environment reduced body image and eating problems within the community. Another promising brief intervention for grade seven girls helps participants learn about the negative impact of appearance conversations, appearance teasing and 'fat-talk' on internalisation of the thin ideal and self-esteem, and learn ways to change these environmental risk factors (Richardson and Paxton 2010). An intervention of this kind in Anna's school could have helped create an environment that did not emphasise appearance and reduced comparisons made on the basis of appearance.

Psycho-education approaches and cognitive behavioural therapy

Psycho-education refers to providing education about the nature of eating disorders while cognitive behavioural therapy (CBT) approaches teach strategies to change attitudes and behaviours. These approaches tend to be used together. Programmes of this kind have been most effective with adolescents and young women with high weight and shape concerns and eating disorder symptoms, of the kind Anna displayed in her mid-teens (i.e. as a targeted intervention). One example is Food, Mood and Attitude (Franko *et al.* 2005), an interactive programme in which participants hypothetically serve as a peer counsellor and 'meet' a series of young people with eating disorder symptoms. In so doing, participants learn about eating disorders and develop skills for managing different situations themselves. Student

Bodies (Taylor *et al.* 2006) is another combined programme which is most effectively used in college students with high weight and shape concerns. This programme has been found to reduce weight and shape concerns and also the development of eating disorders in a high-risk sub-group, for up to two years (Taylor *et al.* 2006).

Targeted preventions have not been widely used in high-school girls. However, they can be beneficial. One internet-delivered psycho-education and CBT programme that addresses body dissatisfaction and healthy eating and coping strategies has resulted in clinically significant improvements in body dissatisfaction, eating disorder and depressive symptoms (Heinicke *et al.* 2007). As Anna's symptoms developed during early adolescence, an early intervention programme such as this could have been helpful in preventing her ongoing clinical eating disorder.

Public policy prevention interventions

A public policy intervention is a decision or action of any level of government, city, state or national, to address a particular problem. Although many governments are yet to perceive prevention of body image and eating disorders as a worthwhile goal, some have taken first steps in implementing prevention strategies (Paxton, in press).

Legislative action has been taken in several instances. In 2010, the Spanish government passed a law to prevent advertising on television before 10 pm for cosmetic surgery or chemical ways to achieve the perfect body. The government argued that exposure of children to messages suggesting a perfect body can be achieved by these drastic means increased the likelihood of body dissatisfaction and eating disorders. In another example, the lower house of the French government passed legislation banning the provocation of a person to achieve excessive thinness by encouraging prolonged restriction of nourishment. This legislation is specifically designed to ban 'pro-ana' website exposure which could contribute to the development of eating disorders.

Some governments have called on media and fashion companies to endorse voluntary codes of conduct, to make a commitment to present a diverse range of body types in the media, and not to engage in media manipulation of images that create unrealistic body image expectations. Countries taking this step include Italy, France, Canada (Quebec; Quebec Government 2009), and Australia (Victoria; Victorian Government, Australia 2008). Being voluntary, no enforcement of the commitments is made, but these actions raise awareness within the industries of their role in the development of eating disorders.

The Victorian government in Australia has implemented two social marketing campaigns. The first, Fad Diets Won't Work, aimed to discourage unhealthy weight loss behaviours, specifically fad diets (Victorian Government, Australia 2006). Anna might have benefitted from such information. The second campaign, Real Life Doesn't Need Retouching (Victorian Government, Australia 2009), aimed to challenge unrealistic images of beauty presented in the media. Although these campaigns were of short duration, they represent a first step in using social marketing to convey prevention messages. Unfortunately, it will be some time until we create an environment more supportive of fuller-shaped people like Anna.

Issues in prevention

Do no harm

Patients sometimes report they have learnt about eating disorder symptoms from school classes or informational material intended to be preventive and have tried the particular behaviour in order to lose weight. Research evidence for this effect is only indicative (e.g. Mann *et al.* 1997). However, professionals in the field warn of providing detailed information about eating disorder symptoms and, rather, suggest talking about eating disorders more generally.

Relationship between eating disorder and obesity prevention

It has been proposed that eating disorder and obesity prevention have contradictory messages – that eating disorder prevention encourages body acceptance and satisfaction rather than dieting while obesity prevention encourages dissatisfaction with weight and engaging in weight loss attempts. They may be contradictory if presented inappropriately. However, if presented appropriately, eating disorder and obesity prevention should both aim to teach healthy eating behaviours, weight management and body satisfaction. Higher weight is a risk factor for eating disorders, as in Anna's situation, and use of unhealthy dieting approaches is a risk factor for both eating disorders and weight gain (e.g. Neumark-Sztainer *et al.* 2006b). Moreover, a positive attitude towards one's body is more likely to encourage nurturing through healthy eating and physical activity (Neumark-Sztainer 2009). Planet Health, a nineteen-month school-based nutrition and physical exercise programme designed to prevent obesity, illustrates close links between obesity and eating disorder prevention (Austin *et al.* 2007). At the programme's completion, researchers observed that 1 per cent of girls in intervention schools compared to 4 per cent of girls in control schools reported onset of the eating disorder symptoms of purging or laxative/diet pill use.

Interventions to change family and school environments

The early family environment in relationship to weight and shape concerns is frequently crucial in contributing to poor body image and low self-esteem that eventually lead to eating disorders. To date, we have done little to provide parents of young children with information that will help them create body-image-friendly family environments. Excellent resources are available for parents who seek it (e.g. Neumark-Sztainer 2005), but this information will reach a relatively small number. Interventions need to be considered that reach parents when their children are very young. For example, maternal health and playgroup organisations could be valuable preventive settings.

Most young people spend a substantial amount of time in school and in the associated peer environment. Thus, it is particularly important that schools provide a body-image-friendly environment. Support needs to be provided to schools to ensure that they implement policies that facilitate acceptance of diversity, appropriate teacher training, developmentally appropriate prevention curricula, and parent information (National Advisory Group on Body Image 2009).

Conclusion

Although encouraging steps have been taken in relatively small-scale prevention studies, there is great need for further research and development. In particular, we need to identify developmentally appropriate interventions that can be instituted at every year level so that interventions can have a cumulative positive effect. More importantly, we need to identify ways in which whole school, family and community environments can be changed to encourage acceptance and celebration of diversity in appearance. To make a real difference to eating disorder incidence, substantial funding and government support are required to enable wide implementation of effective strategies.

References

Austin, S.B., Kim, J., Wiecha, J., Troped, P.J., Feldman, H.A., and Peterson, K.E. (2007) 'School-based overweight preventive intervention lowers incidence of disordered weight-control behaviours in early adolescent girls', *Arch Pediatr Adolesc Med* 9: 865–9.

Becker, C.B., Bull, S., Schaumberg, K., Cauble, A., and Franco, A. (2008) 'Effectiveness of peer-led eating disorders prevention: A replication trial', *J Consult Clin Psychol* 76: 347–54.

Dove Campaign for Real Beauty. 'Evolution'. Online. Available: http://www.dove.us/#/features/videos/default.aspx[cp-documentid=7049579] (accessed 29 August 2010).

Festinger, L. (1957) *A Theory of Cognitive Dissonance*, Palo Alto, CA: Stanford University Press.

Franko, D.L., Mintz, L.B., Villapiano, M., Green, T.C., Mainelli, D., Folensbee, L., Butler, S.F., Davidson, M.M., Hamilton, E., Little, D., Kearns, M., and Budman, S.H. (2005) 'Food, Mood, and Attitude: Reducing risk for eating disorders in college women', *Health Psychol* 24: 567–78.

Heinicke, B.E., Paxton, S.J., McLean, S.A., and Wertheim, E.H. (2007) 'Internet-delivered targeted group intervention for body dissatisfaction and disordered eating in adolescent girls: A randomized controlled trial', *J Abnorm Psychol* 35: 379–91.

Jacobi, C., Hayward, C., de Zwaan, M., Kraemer, H.C., and Agras, S. (2004) 'Coming to terms with risk factors for eating disorders: Application of risk terminology and suggestions for a general taxonomy', *Psychol Bull* 130: 19–65.

Jones, D. (2004) 'Body image among adolescent girls and boys: A longitudinal study', *Dev Psychol* 40: 823–35.

Mann, T., Nolen-Hoeksema, S., Burgard, D., Huang, K., Wright, A., and Hanson, K. (1997) 'Are two interventions worse than none? Joint primary and secondary prevention of eating disorders in college females', *Health Psychol* 16: 215–25.

National Advisory Group on Body Image (2009) 'A Proposed National Strategy on Body Image', Canberra, ACT: Commonwealth of Australia. Online. Available: http://www.youth.gov.au/Documents/Proposed-National-Strategy-on-Body-Image.pdf (accessed 27 August 2010).

National Research Council and Institute of Medicine (NRCIM) (2009) *Preventing Mental, Emotional, and Behavioural Disorders Among Young People: Progress and Possibilities,* Washington, DC: National Academics Press.

Neumark-Sztainer, D. (2005) *"I'm, Like, So Fat!": Helping Your Teen Make Healthy Choices about Eating and Exercising in a Weight-Obsessed World*, New York: Guilford Press.

Neumark-Sztainer, D. (2009) 'Preventing obesity and eating disorders in adolescents: What can health care providers do?', *J Adolesc Health* 44: 206–13.

Neumark-Sztainer, D., Paxton, S.J., Hannan, P.J., Haines, J., and Story, M. (2006a) 'Does body satisfaction matter? Five-year longitudinal associations between body satisfaction and health behaviours in adolescent females and males', *J Adolesc Health* 39: 244–51.

Neumark-Sztainer, D., Wall, M., Guo, J., Story, M., Haines, J., and Eisenberg, M. (2006b) 'Obesity, disordered eating and eating disorders in a longitudinal study of adolescents: How do dieters fare five years later?', *J Am Diet Assoc* 106: 559–68.

Neumark-Sztainer, D., Eisenberg, M. E., Fulkerson, J.A., Story, M., and Larson, N.I. (2008) 'Family meals and disordered eating in adolescents: Longitudinal findings from Project EAT', *Arch Pediatr Adolesc Med* 162: 17–22.

Paxton, S.J. (in press) 'Public policy approaches to prevention', in T.F. Cash and L. Smolak (eds) *Body Image: A Handbook of Science, Practice, and Prevention*, 2nd edn, New York: Guilford Press.

Paxton, S.J., Schutz, H.K., Wertheim, E.H., and Muir, S.L. (1999) 'Friendship clique and peer influences on body image concerns, dietary restraint, extreme weight-loss behaviours, and binge eating in adolescent girls', *J Abnorm Psychol* 108: 255–66.

Piran, N. (1999) 'Prevention in a high risk environment: An intervention in a ballet school', in N. Piran, M.P. Levine and C. Steiner-Adair (eds) *Preventing Eating Disorders: A Handbook of Interventions and Special Challenges* (pp. 148–9), New York: Brunner/Mazel.

Quebec Government (2009) 'Quebec Charter for a Healthy and Diverse Body Image'. Online. Available: http://www.mcccf.gouv.qc.ca/fileadmin/documents/actualites/annexe1_charte.pdf, http://www.telio.com/pdf/chartreEN.pdf (accessed 27 August 2010).

Richardson, S.M. and Paxton, S.J. (2010) 'An evaluation of a body image intervention based on risk factors for body dissatisfaction: A controlled study with adolescent girls', *Int J Eat Disord* 43: 112–22.

Rodgers, R. and Chabrol, H. (2009) 'Parental attitudes, body image disturbance and disordered eating amongst adolescents and young adults: A review', *Eur Eat Disord Rev* 17: 137–51.

Stice, E. (2002) 'Risk and maintenance factors for eating pathology: A meta-analytic review', *Psychol Bull* 128: 825–48.

Stice, E., Marti, N., Spoor, S., Presnell, K., and Shaw, H. (2008a) 'Dissonance and healthy weight eating disorder prevention programs: Long-term effects from a randomized efficacy trial', *J Consult Clin Psychol* 76: 329–40.

Stice, E., Shaw, H., Becker, C.B., and Rohde, P. (2008b) 'Dissonance-based interventions for the prevention of eating disorders: Using persuasion principles to promote health', *Prev Sci* 9: 114–28.

Taylor, C.B., Bryson, S., Luce, K.H, Cunning, D., Doyle, A.C., Abascal, L.B., Rockwell, R., Dev, P., Winzelberg, A.J., and Wilfley, D.E. (2006) 'Prevention of eating disorders in at-risk college-age women', *Arch Gen Psychiatry* 63: 881–8.

Thompson, R.A. and Sherman, R.T. (2010) *Eating Disorders in Sport*, London: Routledge.

Victorian Government, Australia: Department of Health (2006) 'Fad Diets Won't Work'. Online. Available: http://www.goforyourlife.vic.gov.au/hav/articles.nsf/pages/Fad_diets?OpenDocument (accessed 27 August 2010).

Victorian Government, Australia: Department of Planning and Community Development (2008) 'Voluntary Media Code of Conduct on Body Image'. Online. Available: http://www.youth.vic.gov.au/Web21/ofy/rwpgslib.nsf/GraphicFiles/Body+Image+Media+Code+of+Conduct/$file/Body+Image+A4.pdf (accessed 27 August 2010).

Victorian Government, Australia: Department of Planning and Community Development (2009) 'Real Life Doesn't Need Retouching'. Online. Available: http://www.youthcentral.vic.gov.au/News+and+Features/Body+Image/Body+Image+Ad/ (accessed 27 August 2010).

Wertheim, E.H., Koerner, J., and Paxton, S.J. (2001) 'Longitudinal predictors of restrictive eating and bulimic behaviour in adolescent girls', *J Youth Adolesc* 30: 69–81.

Wertheim, E.H., Paxton, S.J., and Blaney, S. (2009) 'Body image in girls', in L. Smolak and J.K. Thompson (eds) *Body Image, Eating Disorders and Obesity in Youth*, 2nd edn (pp. 47–76), Washington, DC: American Psychological Association.

Wilksch, S.M., and Wade, T.D. (2009) 'Reduction of shape and weight concern in young adolescents: A 30-month controlled evaluation of a media literacy program', *J Am Acad Child Adolesc Psychiatry* 48: 652–61.

Wilksch, S.M., Durbridge, M.R., and Wade, T.D. (2008) 'A preliminary controlled comparison of programs designed to reduce risk of eating disorder targeting perfectionism and media literacy', *J Am Acad Child Adolesc Psychiatry* 47: 939–47.

Chapter 6

Obesity and eating disorders

Emma Dove and Susan Byrne

Case study

I am 48 years old and have felt overweight for most of my life. Looking at photos taken in my youth, however, I am not sure why I was so worried – I was probably about average weight. I suspect some of my worry about weight may have stemmed from my early family environment where there was an intense focus on weight and eating. My father was a jockey, an occupation requiring a very low body weight. In the lead up to important races Dad would be 'wasting' – eating extremely restrictively and exercising constantly. To be supportive, my mother, siblings and I would go through this process with him – we would all diet strictly for weeks at a time. After the race Dad would feast, eating large amounts of foods that he had been avoiding during his race preparation. Again, the family would join him in this celebration. I think this pattern of wasting and feasting has influenced the way I eat and think about my weight ever since. After the birth of my third child, my weight increased significantly. I began dieting strictly to lose weight, much as I had during childhood. This strategy worked in the short term, however I began to experience times when I would binge on the very foods that I was trying to avoid. To compensate for this I tried to diet even more strictly. However, I soon began periodically eating enormous amounts of food and this process felt completely unstoppable. I have now given up trying to control my weight; however I continue to binge any time that I feel sad or angry. I have stopped seeing friends and going to my book club because I am so embarrassed about my weight. I have recently started seeing a psychologist who says she would like to begin treatment with me for depression and Binge Eating Disorder.

Lisa

Introduction

Obesity and eating disorders are usually considered to be distinct conditions, with different origins, courses and approaches to prevention and treatment. Eating disorders are diagnosable psychiatric conditions with associated physical features and consequences (e.g., weight loss, symptoms of starvation, binge eating). Obesity, in contrast, is viewed as a medical condition defined by anthropometric measurement; it is not necessarily accompanied by psychopathology; and it is not associated with a consistent psychological or psychiatric profile. However, eating disorders and obesity can also be viewed as part of a spectrum of food and weight-related problems that are symptoms of our 'toxic' cultural context. On the one hand, we live in an 'obesogenic' society, where it is easy to overconsume and to be physically inactive. On the other hand, society glorifies thinness and stigmatises obesity. Therefore, it may be helpful for clinicians and researchers to consider an integrated approach to the understanding, prevention and treatment of eating disorders and obesity.

While obesity is not an eating disorder, it is common for obese people to experience an eating disorder or eating disorder symptoms. The most prevalent eating disorder in obesity is binge eating disorder (BED), and common eating disorder symptoms include excessive concern about body weight and shape and extreme dietary restraint. Adequate assessment of eating disorder symptoms in obese patients is important so that appropriate interventions, which address both the obesity and eating disorder symptoms, may be developed and prescribed (Goldschmidt *et al.* 2008: 261). In this chapter we will describe the symptoms and associated psychopathology of eating disorders in obesity. We will conclude with guidelines for the treatment of obese patients with disordered eating.

Obesity

Obesity is a condition in which a person's total body fat is excessive such that it may adversely affect health (WHO 2000: 6). A body mass index (BMI; weight in kg/height in metres^2) of 30 kg/m^2 or more typically defines obesity. Although an indirect measure, BMI is strongly correlated with body fat in the general population (Storti *et al.* 2006). Obese people are at increased risk of a range of physical health problems, including cardiovascular disease and type 2 diabetes.

Obesity is extremely common, and prevalence is increasing worldwide. In the United States 32 per cent of adults are obese and 17 per cent of children and adolescents are overweight or obese (Ogden *et al.* 2006). While eating disorders are also increasing in prevalence, they currently occur in less than 5 per cent of the population (Agras 2001), a figure that is comparatively dwarfed by obesity rates. Unlike eating disorders, obesity is equally likely in males and females (Cameron *et al.* 2003). Obesity rates are increased among older people (Lahti-Koski *et al.* 2001) and those with lower socioeconomic status (Ball and Mishra 2006).

Eating disorders in obesity

Despite the heterogeneity in factors affecting the aetiology and maintenance of obesity, a proportion of obese people experience a comorbid eating disorder or eating disorder symptoms. In Australia, 3.5 per cent of the total population (aged over 15 years) report obesity comorbid with eating disorder symptoms (binge eating, purging or strict dieting), and 20 per cent of the obese population report eating disorder symptoms (Darby *et al.* 2009). Between 1995 and 2005 in Australia the prevalence of obesity comorbid with eating disorder symptoms increased more rapidly than either obesity or eating disorder symptoms alone (Darby *et al.* 2009). The reason for this increase in comorbidity is unknown, but may be related to widespread promulgation of the dangers of obesity by the media and health professionals (Darby *et al.* 2009: 107). Recognition of the frequent comorbidity of obesity and eating disorder symptoms has led to suggestions that overweight and obese people should be routinely assessed for binge eating, unhealthy weight control behaviours and overconcern with weight and shape (Goldschmidt *et al.* 2008: 261; Neumark-Sztainer 2005: S133).

Eating disorder symptoms in obese people

Binge eating

Binge eating is the most common disordered eating behaviour found among obese individuals (Darby *et al.* 2009). Binge eating may be an important factor determining whether a person seeks treatment for obesity; data from multi-site population-based studies and obesity treatment centres indicate that 20 to 50 per cent of obese people seeking obesity treatment report binge eating (e.g. Delinsky *et al.* 2006), whereas this is the case for only 5 to 9 per cent of non-treatment-seeking obese people (Yanovski 1999).

Two theoretical frameworks have been proposed to account for the aetiology and maintenance of recurrent binge eating in adults. *Restraint theory* suggests that people who diet strictly might binge eat in response to minor transgressions of rigid and inflexible dietary rules (Polivy and Herman 1985). However, a significant proportion of obese people appear to binge eat in the context of a general tendency to overeat, rather than against a background of strict dietary restraint (Cooper *et al.* 2003). In addition, about half of obese binge eaters report that they began binge eating prior to any attempts at dietary restraint (Abbott *et al.* 1998). *Affect regulation theory* suggests that people binge eat as a means of regulating negative mood states such as anger, sadness, anxiety, loneliness or boredom or to 'block out' unpleasant thoughts (Masheb and Grilo 2006), a tendency often termed 'emotional eating'. These two theories of binge eating, one focused on dietary restraint and the other on affect regulation, may be complementary rather than competing, with both pathways operating in some people. With Lisa, binge eating initially developed in response to rigid dietary restraint, and although Lisa eventually abandoned attempts at dieting, the binge eating remained and became a maladaptive strategy for regulating her emotions.

If binge eating is sufficiently frequent, binge eating disorder (BED) may be diagnosed. BED is characterised by regular (an average of two or more episodes per week) and sustained (episodes for at least six months) binge eating, *without* regular inappropriate compensatory behaviours (such as self-induced vomiting, laxative misuse or excessive exercise). Other diagnostic criteria for BED include the experience of marked distress about binges and at least three of: (i) eating very rapidly, (ii) eating until uncomfortably full, (iii) eating large amounts of food when not physically hungry, (iv) eating alone due to embarrassment by how much one is eating, and (v) feeling disgusted or guilty after overeating (APA 2000). (See also Chapter 21, 'Unravelling binge eating disorder'.)

Studies using interview methods based strictly upon the DSM-IV diagnostic criteria have generally reported prevalence rates of BED of 1 to 19 per cent among samples of treatment-seeking obese people (e.g. Allison *et al.* 2006). In contrast to other eating disorders, BED often occurs in males and middle-aged people. Compared to obese people without BED, those with BED have an earlier onset of obesity, a higher maximum lifetime weight, a history of more frequent weight fluctuations (Yanovski *et al.* 1993), and higher rates of eating disorder psychopathology (Crow *et al.* 2002; Telch and Stice 1998) and general psychopathology, especially depression (Wilfley *et al.* 2000).

Strict dietary restraint

Extreme levels of dietary restraint are often present in obese people with very negative attitudes towards their weight and shape. This might predispose to binge eating and further weight gain (Stice *et al.* 2005: 199). Strict and inflexible dieting practices are reported by around 21 per cent of obese people with comorbid eating disorder symptoms (Darby *et al.* 2009).

Unhealthy weight control behaviours

The use of unhealthy weight control practices such as self-induced vomiting and the misuse of laxatives and diuretics is significantly more likely among obese people than among non-obese people (Boutelle *et al.* 2002). Obese people often report a history of using these unhealthy weight control methods; and current use increases the risk of developing a clinical eating disorder.

Weight and shape concern

A pervasive negative attitude towards body weight and shape is a feature of all eating disorders, and is also common in obesity. Weight and shape concern refers to a range of related constructs, including body dissatisfaction (perception of, and negative feelings about, the discrepancy between one's actual and desired body weight and shape) and overvaluation of weight and shape (undue influence of weight or shape on self-evaluation). Clearly, in Lisa's case, significant weight and shape concerns have been present since childhood.

Body dissatisfaction occurs on a continuum ranging from mild feelings of unattractiveness to an extreme preoccupation with physical appearance that impairs functioning. While some degree of body dissatisfaction is arguably normal given societal attitudes to weight and shape, a significant proportion of obese people experience distressing and problematic levels of body dissatisfaction. Studies have consistently demonstrated that compared to healthy-weight people, obese people are significantly more dissatisfied, embarrassed by and preoccupied with their physical appearance, and avoid more social situations due to their appearance (e.g. Sarwer *et al.* 1998). Among obese people, body dissatisfaction appears to be most problematic in females, and in those who were obese during childhood and experienced weight-related teasing (Grilo *et al.* 1994). However, among the obese population, there is no significant relationship between actual BMI and body dissatisfaction, indicating that excessive weight *per se* does not determine this construct. Instead, body dissatisfaction seems to fluctuate in response to mood, changes in weight and shape and perceived control over eating (Cooper and Fairburn 1993: 386).

The overvaluation of, and resulting preoccupation with, weight and/or shape is a diagnostic criterion for both anorexia nervosa and bulimia nervosa, and it has been argued that this characteristic psychopathology should also be included as a diagnostic criterion for BED, given its frequency and prominence in the disorder (Hrabosky *et al.* 2007). Overvaluation of weight and shape is a fairly stable construct that varies with self-esteem (Cooper and Fairburn 1993: 386).

Night eating syndrome

The central feature of night eating syndrome (NES) is an abnormal circadian pattern of eating, which includes evening hyperphagia, and/or eating during the night more than half of the time upon awakening. Evening hyperphagia involves consuming more than 25 per cent of daily caloric intake after the evening meal. This syndrome may also be accompanied by morning anorexia and belated intake of the first daily meal, although these symptoms are not diagnostic criteria for NES. Among population-based community samples, NES occurs in approximately 1.5 per cent of people. However, the prevalence of NES is positively associated with BMI and has been estimated to occur in 9 to 15 per cent of people presenting for weight loss treatment and in 8 to 42 per cent of those being assessed for bariatric surgery (Rand *et al.* 1997). There is some evidence to suggest that the onset of NES can be precipitated by stress and/or depression (Allison *et al.* 2005).·

Causes of eating disorders in obesity

To date, there is limited evidence identifying factors that predict the onset of eating disorders in obese people (Goldschmidt *et al.* 2008: 260). However, several risk factors are common to both obesity and eating disorders. These factors, identified by reviews and studies, include repeated dieting, media use, weight-related teasing and weight and shape concern (Haines and Neumark-Sztainer 2006; Neumark-Sztainer *et al.* 2007).

While strict dieting is the strongest risk factor for the development of an eating disorder, it is also consistently associated with weight gain and the development of obesity (Field *et al.* 2003; Neumark-Sztainer *et al.* 2006, 2007; Stice *et al.* 1999). The strong relationship between strict dieting and the development of binge eating may partly account for these findings. Weight and shape concern is an established risk factor for eating disorders, but it may also be a risk factor for, as well as a consequence of, obesity. Both weight and shape concern and body dissatisfaction are associated with binge eating and becoming overweight (Allen *et al.* 2008; Johnson and Wardle 2005; Neumark-Sztainer *et al.* 2007). This association might be explained by body dissatisfaction-induced increases in dieting behaviour or negative mood (Haines and Neumark-Sztainer 2006: 775). Body dissatisfaction is also related to lower physical activity, which may promote weight gain (Neumark-Sztainer *et al.* 2006).

The use of media and internalisation of media messages is also considered a risk factor for obesity and eating disorders (Haines and Neumark-Sztainer 2006). The physical inactivity and consumption of energy-dense food promoted by television viewing likely increases obesity risk (Robinson 1998), while internalisation of the thin ideal promoted during television viewing may lead to body dissatisfaction and eating disorders (Haines and Neumark-Sztainer 2006: 774). Weight-related teasing places people at risk for binge eating, eating disorder symptoms and becoming overweight (Brown *et al.* 1989; Neumark-Sztainer *et al.* 2007). Binge eating in response to weight-related teasing may arise through increases in depression, body dissatisfaction or dieting (Haines and Neumark-Sztainer 2006: 777), and promotes the development of eating disorders and weight gain.

Psychopathology associated with eating disorders in obesity

Obesity is strongly related to psychopathology and poor mental health. Cross-sectional studies indicate that obesity is significantly associated with depression (Heo *et al.* 2006; Onyike *et al.* 2003), and longitudinal studies show that obesity (current and past) is a risk factor for future depression (Friedman and Brownell 1995; Herva *et al.* 2006; Roberts *et al.* 2003). Eating disorders and eating disorder symptoms are also associated with depression and low self-esteem, as well as with anxiety and substance use (Crow *et al.* 2006; Decaluwe *et al.* 2003; Glasofer *et al.* 2006).

The stigmatisation of obesity likely contributes to an obese person's increased risk for psychological difficulties. There is a pervasive perception that obesity reflects negative characteristics such as laziness, self-indulgence, stupidity and emotional impairment (Cossrow *et al.* 2001; Friedman *et al.* 2005; Harris *et al.* 1982; Latner *et al.* 2005). Obese people experience discrimination in many areas of life, such as in the workplace and school, during social interactions and from health professionals (Neumark-Sztainer *et al.* 1998; Puhl and Brownell 2001). Weight bias from health professionals may decrease obese patients' willingness to seek health care or the quality of care they receive. Weight-related discrimination increases linearly with BMI and impacts negatively on self-worth, body dissatisfaction, depression and general psychiatric symptoms (Friedman *et al.* 2005).

Eating disorder symptoms are likely to exacerbate poor psychological functioning in obesity. Obese binge eaters are significantly more likely than obese non-binge eaters to report current depressive symptoms or a lifetime history of major depression, anxiety or personality disorders (Bulik *et al.* 2002; Yanovski *et al.* 1993). They also evidence lower self-esteem, more extreme concerns about shape and weight, greater body dissatisfaction and greater impairment in work and social functioning than do obese non-binge eaters (Yanovski *et al.* 1993). Among obese binge eaters, there appears to be a continuum of vulnerability for the severity of psychopathology, with the frequency of binge eating being positively associated with overconcern about eating, shape and weight, depression, and total time spent dieting over the lifetime; and negatively associated with self-esteem (Delinsky *et al.* 2006). Obese persons with NES, have also been found to exhibit higher levels of depression and poorer self-esteem than obese individuals without NES and are more likely to report a history of major depressive disorder, anxiety disorder or substance abuse/dependence (Allison *et al.* 2005).

Treatment of eating disorders in obesity

As a heterogeneous condition, a significant proportion of obese people clearly will present with BED or subclinical eating disorder symptoms. This presents a challenge for their treatment. Is it better to treat obese individuals with eating disorder symptoms using standard weight reduction techniques, or to directly address the eating disorder symptoms? This question has been debated by researchers (e.g. Stunkard and Allison 2003).

Standard obesity treatments focused on weight reduction

There are currently three major evidence-based treatments for reducing obesity, comprising surgical, pharmacological and psychological (behavioural therapy and cognitive behavioural therapy) approaches. With the exception of surgery, obesity treatments generally result in weight loss of 5 to 10 per cent in the short term (e.g. Cooper *et al.* 2010), which confers clinically significant improvements in health and disease risk (Lean *et al.* 1998) for as long as the weight loss is maintained (Simkin-Silverman *et al.* 1998). However, weight regain is almost inevitable, with about half of the weight lost regained in the first year following treatment (Wadden *et al.* 1989), and by three to five years post-treatment, about 85 per cent of patients have returned to, or exceeded, their pre-treatment weight (Crawford *et al.* 2000).

Standard obesity treatments appear to be effective for short-term weight loss irrespective of whether a patient has comorbid eating disorder symptoms. Weight loss and maintenance does not differ between binge and non-binge eaters who receive behavioural therapy (Sherwood *et al.* 1999). However, one large-scale study reported that people who ceased binge eating during a 12-month weight loss intervention lost significantly more weight than those who continued to binge eat (Gorin *et al.* 2008). The association of treatment attrition with binge eating is unclear, with some reporting a positive association (Sherwood *et al.* 1999), others no association (Wadden *et al.* 1994), and others a negative association (Delinsky *et al.* 2006).

The comparable weight reduction observed for eating disordered and non-eating disordered patients receiving standard obesity treatments might be related to an indirect effect of these treatments, or of weight loss itself, on eating disorder symptoms (Delinsky *et al.* 2006: 1247). That is, standard obesity treatments typically confer moderate *improvements* in eating disorder symptoms, such as reductions in binge eating and other eating disorder symptoms, psychological distress and depression and increases in self-esteem body image (Dalle Grave *et al.* 2007, 2010; National Task Force on the Prevention and Treatment of Obesity 2000; Van Vlierberghe *et al.* 2009). Behavioural therapy (BT) tends to result in decreased binge eating among those with BED and no onset of binge eating among those who did not binge eat prior to treatment (Porzelius *et al.* 1995; Wing *et al.* 1989).

However, with the weight regain that is common in non-surgical methods of obesity treatment, eating disorder symptoms tend to re-emerge (e.g. Werrij *et al.* 2009). In the absence of effective long-term non-surgical treatments for weight loss and maintenance, some researchers and clinicians have argued that we should focus on delivering treatments that promote reductions in eating disorder symptoms and other psychopathology, as well as encouraging perseverance with long-term weight management strategies (Werrij *et al.* 2009: 315). Given that frequent weight loss and regain increases the risk of eating disorder symptoms (Delinsky *et al.* 2006: 1246), an integrated treatment approach might even mitigate the risk of eating disorder symptoms developing through repeated obesity treatment attempts.

Integrated treatment for obesity and eating disorder symptoms

Intuitively, the development of integrated treatments that address both eating disorder symptoms and obesity is appealing, given the complementary treatment goals for these disorders. Both aim to help patients attain a healthy and moderate weight, develop healthy eating patterns and enjoy physical activity. The best established treatment approach is that of cognitive behavioural therapy (CBT). For long-term weight loss and maintenance, CBT is equally as effective as BT, with superior benefits for shape concern (Cooper *et al.* 2010: 711). Cognitive therapy may enhance the effect of dietetic treatment on weight loss, and facilitate decreases in weight and shape concern and binge eating and increases in maintenance of weight loss (Werrij *et al.* 2009: 321).

A cognitive behavioural approach addressing both obesity and eating disorder symptoms was developed by Professor Christopher Fairburn and colleagues (Cooper and Fairburn 2001; Fairburn *et al.* 2003). This treatment utilises treatment strategies that are complementary in addressing obesity and eating disorder symptoms, including self-monitoring, collaborative weighing, regular eating, decreasing binge eating and emotional eating, improving body dissatisfaction and overvaluation of weight and shape, and long-term weight maintenance. This treatment for obesity stems from Fairburn and Cooper's theory that patients' failure to engage in effective weight-control behaviour following treatment is a result of a progressive decrease in their belief that they *can* control their weight, combined with the realisation that they will achieve neither their goal weight (which is usually unrealistically low), nor many of the other benefits that they hoped would arise from losing weight (e.g. improved relationships and self-confidence).

There are several treatment approaches for reducing binge eating. These are likely to improve psychological well-being for participants, and may indirectly lead to moderate weight loss. There is substantial evidence that CBT is an effective treatment for eliminating binge eating in BED (Munsch *et al.* 2007; Wilfley *et al.* 2002). An alternative promising treatment approach is dialectical behaviour therapy, which is highly effective for ameliorating binge eating (Telch *et al.* 2001). Interpersonal therapy has also shown effectiveness in reducing binge eating (Wilfley *et al.* 2002) and it has been argued that this therapy may lead to moderate weight reduction and prevention of eating disorders (Tanofsky-Kraff *et al.* 2007). It is important that further research investigates the efficacy of these treatment approaches and modifications of them in addressing obesity and eating disorder symptoms.

Summary

Approximately 20 per cent of obese people experience a comorbid eating disorder or eating disorder symptoms. Eating disorder symptoms place obese people at increased risk of psychopathology such as depression and anxiety, as well as further weight gain. Thus, it is important that clinicians enquire about the presence of these eating disorder cognitions and behaviours during assessment and treatment of obese patients. Conceptualisation of obesity and eating disorders as part of a spectrum of weight and eating problems has led to greater focus on developing integrated approaches to the prevention and treatment of obesity and eating disorders (Neumark-Sztainer *et al.* 2007: 359). Encouragement of integrated approaches, and of collaboration between researchers from the eating disorder and obesity fields, may provide far-reaching benefits from both a public health and individual standpoint.

References

Abbott, D.W., de Zwaan, M., Mussell, M.P., Raymond N.C., Seim, H.C., Crow, S.J., Crosby, R.D., and Mitchell, J.E. (1998) 'Onset of binge eating and dieting in overweight women: Implications for etiology, associated features and treatment', *J Psychosom Res* 44: 367–74.

Agras, W.S. (2001) 'The consequences and costs of the eating disorders', *Psychiatr Clin North Am* 24: 371–9.

Allen, K.L., Byrne, S.M., McLean, N.J., and Davis, E.A. (2008) 'Overconcern with weight and shape is not the same as body dissatisfaction: Evidence from a prospective study of pre-adolescent boys and girls', *Body Image* 5: 261–70.

Allison, K.C., Grilo, C.M., Masheb, R.M., and Stunkard, A.J. (2005) 'Binge eating disorder and night eating syndrome: A comparative study of disordered eating', *J Consult Clin Psychol* 73: 1107–15.

Allison, K.C., Wadden, T.A., Sarwer, D.B., Fabricatore, A.N., Crerand, C.E., Gibbons, L.M., Stack, R.M., Stunkard, A.J., and Williams, N.N. (2006) 'Night eating syndrome and binge eating disorder among persons seeking bariatric surgery: Prevalence and related features', *Surg Obes Relat Dis* 2: 153–8.

American Psychiatric Association (APA) (2000) *DSM-IV-TR: Diagnostic and Statistical Manual of Mental Disorders* 4th edn (text revision), Washington, DC: American Psychiatric Press.

Ball, K. and Mishra, G.D. (2006) 'Whose socioeconomic status influences a woman's obesity risk: Her mother's, her father's, or her own?', *Int J Epidemiol* 35: 131–8.

Boutelle, K., Neumark-Sztainer, D., Story, M., and Resnick, M. (2002) 'Weight control behaviors among obese, overweight, and nonoverweight adolescents', *J Pediatr Psychol* 27: 531–40.

Brown, T.A., Cash, T.F., and Lewis, R.J. (1989) 'Body-image disturbances in adolescent female binge-purgers: A brief report of the results of a national survey in the U.S.A.', *J Child Psychol Psychiatry* 30: 605–13.

Bulik, C.M., Sullivan, P.F., and Kendler, K.S. (2002) 'Medical and psychiatric morbidity in obese women with and without binge eating', *Int J Eat Disord* 32: 72–8.

Cameron, A.J., Welborn, T.A., Zimmet, P.Z., Dunstan, D.W., Owen, N., Salmon, J., Dalton, M., Jolley, D., and Shaw, J.E. (2003) 'Overweight and obesity in Australia: The 1999–2000 Australian Diabetes, Obesity and Lifestyle Study (AusDiab)', *Med J Aust* 178: 427–32.

Cooper, P.J. and Fairburn, C.G. (1993) 'Confusion over the core psychopathology of bulimia nervosa', *Int J Eat Disord* 13: 385–9.

Cooper, P.J. and Fairburn, C.G. (2001) 'A new cognitive behavioural approach to the treatment of obesity', *Behav Res Ther* 39: 499–511.

Cooper, Z., Fairburn, C.G. and Hawker, D.M. (2003) *Cognitive-Behavioural Treatment of Obesity: A Clinican's Guide,* New York: Guilford Press.

Cooper, Z., Doll, H.A., Hawker, D.M., Byrne, S.M., Bonner, G., Eeley, E., O'Connor, M.E., and Fairburn, C.G. (2010) 'Testing a new cognitive behavioural treatment for obesity: A randomized controlled trial with three-year follow-up', *Behav Res Ther* 48: 706–13.

Cossrow, N.H.F., Jeffery, R.W., and McGuire, M.T. (2001) 'Understanding weight stigmatization: A focus group study', *J Nutr Educ* 33: 208–14.

Crawford, D., Jeffery, R.W., and French, S.A. (2000) 'Can anyone successfully control their weight? Findings of a three year community-based study of men and women', *Int J Obes* 24: 1107–10.

Crow, S.J., Agras, W.S., Halmi, K., Mitchell, J.E., and Kraemer, H.C. (2002) 'Full syndromal versus subthreshold anorexia nervosa, bulimia nervosa, and binge eating disorder: A multicenter study', *Int J Eat Disord* 32: 309–18.

Crow, S., Eisenberg, M.E., Story, M., and Neumark-Sztainer, D. (2006) 'Psychosocial and behavioral correlates of dieting among overweight and non-overweight adolescents', *J Adolesc Health* 38: 569–74.

Dalle Grave, R., Cuzzolaro, M., Calugi, S., Tomasi, F., and Temperilli, F., and Marchesini, G. (2007) 'The effect of obesity management on body image in patients seeking treatment at medical centers', *Obesity* 15: 2320–7.

Dalle Grave, R., Calugi, S., Petroni, M.L., Di Domizio, S., and Marchesini, G. (2010) 'Weight management, psychological distress and binge eating in obesity. A reappraisal of the problem', *Appetite* 54: 269–73.

Darby, A., Hay, P., Mond, J., Quirk, F., Buttner, P., and Kennedy, L. (2009) 'The rising prevalence of comorbid obesity and eating disorder behaviors from 1995 to 2005', *Int J Eat Disord* 42: 104–8.

Decaluwe, V., Braet, C., and Fairburn, C.G. (2003) 'Binge eating in obese children and adolescents', *Int J Eat Disord* 33: 78–84.

Delinsky, S.S., Latner, J.D., and Wilson, G.T. (2006) 'Binge eating and weight loss in a self-help behavior modification program', *Obesity* 14: 1244–9.

Fairburn, C.G., Cooper, Z., and Shafran, R. (2003) 'Cognitive behavior therapy for eating disorders: A "transdiagnostic" theory and treatment', *Behav Res Ther* 41: 509–28.

Field, A.E., Austin, S.B., Taylor, C.B., Malspeis, S., Rosner, B., Rockett, H.R., Gillman, M.W., and Colditz, G.A. (2003) 'Relation between dieting and weight change among preadolescents and adolescents', *Pediatrics* 112: 900–6.

Friedman, M.A., and Brownell, K.D. (1995) 'Psychological correlates of obesity: Moving to the next research generation', *Psychol Bull* 117: 3–20.

Friedman, K.E., Reichmann, S.K., Costanzo, P.R., Zelli, A., Ashmore, J.A., and Musante, G.J. (2005) 'Weight stigmatization and ideological beliefs: Relation to psychological functioning in obese adults', *Obes Res* 13: 907–16.

Glasofer, D.R., Tanofsky-Kraff, M., Eddy, K.T., Yanovski, S.Z., Theim, K.R., Mirch, M.C., Ghorbani, S., Ranzenhofer, L.M., Haaga, D., and Yanovski, J.A. (2006) 'Binge eating in overweight treatment-seeking adolescents', *J Pediatr Psychol* 32: 95–105.

Goldschmidt, A.B., Passi Aspen, V., Sinton, M.M., Tanofky-Kraff, M., and Wilfley, D.E. (2008) 'Disordered eating attitudes and behaviors in overweight youth', *Obesity* 16: 257–64.

Gorin, A.A., Niemeier, H.M., Hogan, P., Coday, M., Davis, C., DiLillo, V.G., Gluck, M.E., Wadden, T.A., West, D.S., Williamson, D., and Yanovski, S.Z. (2008) 'Binge eating and weight loss outcomes in overweight and obese individuals with type 2 diabetes: Results from the Look AHEAD trial', *Arch Gen Psychiatry* 65: 1447–55.

Grilo, C.M., Wilfley, D.E., Brownell, K.D., and Rodin, J. (1994) 'Teasing, body image, and self-esteem in a clinical sample of obese women', *Addict Behav* 19: 443–50.

Haines, J. and Neumark-Sztainer, D. (2006) 'Prevention of obesity and eating disorders: A consideration of shared risk factors', *Health Educ Res* 21: 770–82.

Harris, M.B., Harris, R.J., and Bochner, S. (1982) 'Fat, four-eyed and female: Stereotypes of obesity, glasses, and gender', *J Appl Soc Psychol* 12: 503–16.

Heo, M., Pietrobelli, A., Fontaine, K.R., Sirey, J.A., and Faith, M.S. (2006) 'Depressive mood and obesity in US adults: Comparison and moderation by sex, age, and race', *Int J Obes* 30: 513–19.

Herva, A., Laiteinen, J., Miettunen, J., Veijola, J., Karvonen, J.T., Laksy, K., and Joukamaa, M. (2006) 'Obesity and depression: Results from the longitudinal Northern Finland 1966 Birth Cohort Study', *Int J Obes* 30: 520–7.

Hrabosky, J.I., Masheb, R.M., White, M.A., and Grilo, C.M. (2007) 'Overvaluation of shape and weight in binge eating disorder', *J Consult Clin Psychol* 75: 175–80.

Johnson, F. and Wardle, J. (2005) 'Dietary restraint, body dissatisfaction, and psychological distress: A prospective analysis', *J Abnorm Psychol* 114: 119–25.

Lahti-Koski, M., Jousilahti, P., and Pietinen, P. (2001) 'Secular trends in body mass index by birth cohort in eastern Finland from 1972–1997', *Int J Obes* 25: 727–34.

Latner, J.D., Stunkard, A.J., and Wilson, G. (2005) 'Stigmatized students: Age, sex and ethnicity effects in the stigmatization of obesity', *Obes Res* 13: 1226–31.

Lean, M.E., Han, T.S., and Seidell, J.C. (1998) 'Impairment of heath and quality of life in people with large waist circumference', *Lancet* 351: 853–6.

Masheb, R.M. and Grilo, C.M. (2006) 'Emotional overeating and its associations with eating disorder, psychopathology among overweight patients with binge eating disorder', *Int J Eat Disord* 39: 141–6.

Munsch, S., Biedert, E., Meyer, A., Michael, T., Schlup, B., Tuch, A., and Margraf, J. (2007) 'A randomized comparison of cognitive behavioral therapy and behavioral weight loss treatment for overweight individuals with binge eating disorder', *Int J Eat Disord* 40: 102–13.

National Task Force on the Prevention and Treatment of Obesity (2000) 'Dieting and the development of disorders in overweight and obese adults', *Arch Intern Med* 160: 2581–9.

Neumark-Sztainer, D. (2005) 'Preventing the broad spectrum of weight-related problems: Working with parents to help teens achieve a healthy weight and a positive body image', *J Nutr Educ Behav* 37: S133–9.

Neumark-Sztainer, D., Story, M., and Faibisch, L. (1998) 'Perceived stigmatization among overweight African-American and Caucasian adolescent girls', *J Adolesc Health* 23: 264–70.

Neumark-Sztainer D., Paxton, S.J., Hannan, P.J., Haine, J., and Story, M. (2006) 'Does body satisfaction matter? Five-year longitudinal associations between body satisfaction and health behaviors in adolescent females and males', *J Adolesc Health* 39: 244–51.

Neumark-Sztainer, D.R., Wall, M.M., Haines, J.I., Story, M.T., Sherwood, N.E., and van den Berg, P.A. (2007) 'Shared risk and protective factors for overweight and disordered eating in adolescents', *Am J Prev Med* 33: 359–69.

Ogden, C.L., Carroll, M.D., Curtin, L.R., McDowell, M.A., Tabak, C.J., and Flegal, K.M. (2006) 'Prevalence of overweight and obesity in the United States, 1999-2004', *JAMA* 295: 1549–55.

Onyike, C.U., Crum, R.M., Lee, H.B., Lyketsos, C.G., and Eaton, W.W. (2003) 'Is obesity associated with major depression? Results from the Third National Health and Nutrition Examination Survey', *Am J Epidemiol* 158: 1139–47.

Polivy, J. and Herman, C.P. (1985) 'Dieting and binging: A causal analysis', *Am Psychol* 40: 193–201.

Porzelius, L.K., Houston, C., Smith, M., Arkin, C., and Fisher, E. (1995) 'Comparison of standard weight loss treatment and a binge eating weight loss treatment', *Behav Ther* 26: 199–234.

Puhl, R., and Brownell, K.D. (2001) 'Bias, discrimination, and obesity', *Obes Res* 9: 788–805.

Rand, C.S., Macgregor, M.D., and Stunkard, A.J. (1997) 'The night eating syndrome in the general population and amongst post-operative obesity surgery patients', *Int J Eat Disord* 22: 65–9.

Roberts, R., Deleger, S., Strawbridge, W., and Kaplan, G. (2003) 'Prospective association between obesity and depression: Evidence from the Alameda County Study', *Int J Obes* 27: 514–21.

Robinson, T.N. (1998) 'Does television cause childhood obesity?', *JAMA* 279: 959–60.

Sarwer, D.B., Wadden, T.A., and Foster, G.D. (1998) 'Assessment of body image dissatisfaction in obese women: Specificity, severity, and clinical significance', *J Consult Clin Psychol* 66: 651–4.

Sherwood, N.E., Jeffery, R.W., and Wing, R.R. (1999) 'Binge status as a predictor of weight loss treatment outcome', *Int J Obes* 23: 485–93.

Simkin-Silverman, L.R., Wing, R.R., Boraz, M.A., Meilahn, E.N., and Kuller, L.H. (1998) 'Maintenance of cardiovascular risk factor changes among middle-aged women in a lifestyle intervention trial', *Women's Health* 4: 255–71.

Stice, E., Cameron, R.P., Killen, J.D., Hayward, C., and Taylor, C.B. (1999) 'Naturalistic weight-reduction efforts prospectively predict growth in relative weight and onset of obesity among female adolescents', *J Consult Clin Psychol* 67: 967–74.

Stice, E., Presnell, K., Shaw, H., and Rohde, P. (2005) 'Psychological and behavioral risk factors for obesity onset in adolescent girls: A prospective study,' *J Consult Clin Psychol* 73: 195–202.

Storti, K.L., Brach, J.S., Fitzgerald, S.J., Bunker, C.H., and Kriska, A.M. (2006) 'Relationships among body composition measures in community-dwelling older women', *Obesity* 14: 244–51.

Stunkard, A.J., and Allison, K.C. (2003) 'Binge eating disorder: Disorder or marker?', *Int J Eat Disord* 34: S107–16.

Tanofsky-Kraff, M., Wilfley, D.E., Young, J.F., Mufson, L., Yanovski, S.Z., Glasofer, D.R., and Salaita, C.G. (2007) 'Preventing excessive weight gain in adolescents: Interpersonal psychotherapy for binge eating', *Obesity* 15: 1345–55.

Telch, C.F., and Stice, E. (1998) 'Psychiatric comorbidity in women with binge eating disorder: Prevalence rates from a non-treatment seeking sample', *J Consult Clin Psychol* 66: 768–76.

Telch, C.F. Agras, W.S., and Linehan, M.M. (2001) 'Dialectical behavior therapy for binge eating disorder', *J Consult Clin Psychol* 69: 1061–5.

Van Vlierberghe, L., Braet, C., Goossens, L., Rosseel, Y., and Mels, S. (2009) 'Psychological disorder, symptom severity and weight loss in inpatient adolescent obesity treatment', *Int J Pediatr Obes* 4: 36–44.

Wadden, T.A., Sternberg, J.A., Letizia, K.A., Stunkard, A.J., and Foster, G.D. (1989) 'Treatment of obesity by very low calorie diet, behavior therapy, and their combination: A five-year perspective', *Int J Obes* 13: 39–46.

Wadden, T.A., Foster, G.D., and Letizia, K.A. (1994) 'One-year behavioral treatment of obesity: Comparison of moderate and severe caloric restriction and the effects of weight maintenance therapy', *J Consult Clin Psychol* 62: 165–71.

Werrij, M.Q., Jansen, A., Mulkens, S., Elgersma, H.J., Ament, A.J., and Hospers, H.J. (2009) 'Adding cognitive therapy to dietetic treatment associated with less relapse in obesity', *J Psychosom Res* 67: 315–24.

WHO (2000) 'Obesity: Preventing and managing the global epidemic. Report of a WHO consultation', *WHO technical report series* 894, Geneva: World Health Organization.

Wilfley, D.E., Friedman, M.A., Dounchis, J.Z., Stein, R.I., Welch, R.R., and Ball, S.A. (2000) 'Comorbid psychopathology in binge eating disorder: Relation to eating disorder severity at baseline and following treatment', *J Consult Clin Psychol* 68: 641–9.

Wilfley, D.E., Welch, R.R., Stein, R.I., Borman Spurrell, E., Cohen, L.R., Saelens, B.E., Zoler Dounchis, J., Frank, M.A., Wiseman, C.V., and Matt, G.E. (2002) 'A randomized comparison of group cognitive-behavioural therapy and group interpersonal psychotherapy for the treatment of overweight individuals with binge-eating disorder', *Arch Gen Psychiatry* 59: 713–21.

Wing, R., Marcus, B.H., Epstein, L.H., Blair, S.N., and Burton, L.R. (1989) 'Binge eating in obese patients with type 2 diabetes', *Int J Eat Disord* 8: 671–9.

Yanovski, S.Z. (1999) 'Diagnosis and prevalence of eating disorders in obesity', in G. Ailhaud, and B. Guy-Grand *et al.* (eds) *Progress in Obesity Research*, 8 (pp. 229–36), London: John Libby & Co.

Yanovski, S.Z., Nelson, J.E., Dubbert, B.K., and Spitzer, R.L. (1993) 'Association of binge eating disorder and psychiatric comorbidity in obese subjects', *Am J Psychiatry* 150: 1472–9.

Part 2

Treatment

Creating a common language of care

Introduction

Laura (Collins) Lyster-Mensh

I often speak with parents when they first encounter what I call the 'Rabbit Hole' fall. Suddenly, this formerly unknown obstacle opens up and swallows the family whole: an eating disorder diagnosis for a loved one. Down the hole, parents are little and the children are big. Strange authorities spout odd and alarming phrases and mum and dad are left to wonder what became of normal life. In this frightening and disorienting time, parents seek authorities and authoritative sources. We want to be handed a guidebook; a dictionary; an atlas. We're willing to learn the plan, follow the leader, but the first issue is who to trust; we no longer feel we can trust ourselves.

As a parent advocate, I struggle daily with a dilemma. My moral obligation is to encourage parents to find and trust expert clinical teams. At the same time, I know the family is likely to encounter a diversity of diagnoses, treatment advice, and prognoses for the same patient. Why? There are several reasons, but an important solution is an exciting new era of collaborative and evidence-based treatment. Part 2 explores this new approach in care.

The phrase 'multidisciplinary approach' has special meaning, and risk, in the treatment of eating disorders. Used wisely, it can mean collaborative and coordinated care. To be effective, no aspect of eating disorder care can be sectioned off: treatment that addresses only one or two or even three aspects of care is insufficient and counterproductive. Eating disorders cannot be successfully treated by even the finest of care that only addresses nutrition, or offers only psychotherapy, or addresses medical care only in crisis. Weight restoration alone is as ineffective as psychotherapy in isolation. Like a boat with several holes, treatment has to fill and reinforce all weaknesses in the system to create a safe vessel and harbor.

The good news: collaborative evidence-based care is working. It is being adopted and refined in many clinics around the world, and an increasingly professional field is sharing information and refining techniques. This section's authors exemplify collaboration and interdisciplinary care by redefining eating disorders as an illness where symptoms not only affect the body but also arise as the result of physical processes. C. Laird Birmingham sets the stage by describing the physical effects on the body and how clinicians can interpret and intervene to correct them. He makes the essential point that the effects are 'ongoing' and even when 'not evident … they are gradually developing'.

Of course, many eating disorder symptoms result in, and are perpetuated by, nutritional deficits. In Chapter 8 by Hart *et al.* we are reminded: 'Food and its intake has everything to do with eating disorders from their genesis to maintenance, management and resolution.' This reality, historically undervalued and even scorned, can no longer be regarded as ancillary or additive. Clinicians treating eating disorders must become familiar with and clearly understand the relationship between eating disorder cognitions and nutritional status as a dynamic and interactive process.

Food is medicine in eating disorder care, but pharmacological medicine is a tool that clinicians and the patients' families must also consider. Research is in its infancy and is complicated by multiple factors unique to eating disorders, including nutritional status and the trajectory of recovery. The difficulty of diagnosing comorbid conditions at different stages of illness and treatment, as well as problems with compliance, continue to challenge the field regarding drug therapies. The evidence review offered by David *et al.* (Chapter 9) provides an update on pharmaceutical interventions and the important message that drug therapies are most effective when paired with evidence-based psychotherapeutic therapies.

Wade and Watson (Chapter 10) bring us up to date on evidence-based psychotherapeutic approaches for anorexia nervosa, bulimia nervosa, and binge eating disorder. The importance of evidence-based treatment – also called empirically-based treatment – is twofold. The primary reason is to increase the likelihood of effectiveness and allow personalization of treatment recommendations. A second important reason is to allow patients and their families to distinguish these treatments from those which may be in common use but represent opinion-based practices: ones that follow either tradition or philosophical beliefs about the illness.

'Truly, the tide is turning,' declare Hoste *et al.* in their chapter on family-based treatment, also known as the Maudsley approach: 'Families are an integral part of the treatment (FBT) team'. Truly collaborative care means personalizing care by using all useful resources and techniques available, and parents are integral to this. For adult patients, Goddard and co-authors continue the theme of family involvement in their description of a collaborative mode (Chapter 13) and Evans and Waller discuss compassion and alliance with the use of cognitive behavioral therapy for adults (Chapter 14). Milstein and Arnold demonstrate the wisdom of 'Recovery comes first and must be top priority' with concrete tools for families to ally with clinical teams for ongoing maintenance of treatment gains (Chapter 12). For situations with comorbid illness, high family criticism, or more complex cases, the use of dialectical behavioral therapy remains well-supported and congruent with other evidence-based techniques – including FBT, as described by Federici and Wisniewski (Chapter 15). In 'Couples therapy for anorexia nervosa', Bulik *et al.* describe an innovative couples-based therapeutic approach called UCAN.

As the growing body of data makes clear, eating disorders are a chronic predisposition that requires vigilance even in remission. We end this section with an examination of what factors predict successful long-term remission, common pathways to relapse, and strategies to prevent the tragic re-emergence of illness.

Eating disorders are a challenge to treat, but they are more than an illness. The necessity of multidisciplinary cooperation and coordination with the family complicates treatment in confounding ways. The illness, being anosognosic in nature, stymies communication by the patient to clinicians and family. The necessity for multiple competencies on the treatment team adds complexity. Family, rarely having a deep knowledge of the illness or the necessary care, struggles to support the patient and treatment recommendations.

The solution lies in adopting a common language: the language of science. Most parents enter the treatment environment assuming that care is based on established science. They are shocked to discover that where treatment guidelines exist, they are not always followed. We cannot blame individual clinicians for this, or think this is peculiar to eating disorders. The field has much to learn from the history of autism treatment and schizophrenia treatment, and the cautionary tales from both diseases where families have been disregarded or blamed in the process (Brumberg 1988; Lidz et al. 1965). Families need to know, and clinicians need to acknowledge, that medical decisions are not always based on empirical data, and psychology in particular has long relied on clinical judgment and intuition more than research. Eating disorder treatment, though, has a particular roadblock: it is inherently multidisciplinary.

Eating disorders require attention to medical, nutritional, psychological, psychiatric, and other fields of knowledge. It is a challenge for any clinician to remain up-to-date and authoritative and no one on an eating disorder team can be expert in all aspects of treatment.

Eating disorders present unique challenges and opportunities for treatment providers. The illness affects all family members, confounds the efforts of dedicated treatment providers, and thrives on isolation and compartmentalization. The team approach of truly collaborative treatment is a big step in the right direction for those we all care about: the patients.

References

Brumberg, J. J. (1988) *Fasting Girls: The Emergence of Anorexia Nervosa as a Modern Disease*, Cambridge, MA: Harvard University Press.

Lidz, Theodore, Fleck, Stephen, and Cornelison, Alice R. (1965) *Schizophrenia and the Family*, New York: International Universities Press.

Chapter 7

Physical effects of eating disorders

C. Laird Birmingham

Eating disorder patients are often turned away when they seek medical help. Are there blood tests or physical findings that would help doctors make the diagnosis of a serious eating disorder?

> **Case study: Julie**
>
> We took Julie to emergency when she was 16 years old. She had lost a lot of weight, which she denied, she was seeing her friends less often, she exercised much more than before, and we had heard her retching when she went to the bathroom after eating. The emergency doctor said her blood tests, her heart tracing (EKG), and her physical examination were normal. The doctor also told us that exercise was good, that Julie looked thin and trim. She denied vomiting and we were told to take her home.
>
> Julie's parents

Julie's diet and activity have likely been increasingly abnormal for at least a year or two – not just a month or two. Most of the physical effects of the eating disorder are not evident on history, physical, examination or laboratory testing. They develop gradually and, because Julie is young and resilient, they will not decrease her ability to exercise for some time. Imagine a car that has been left unused for years. It may look fine. Any problems with its function will only become evident with use.

Why were the laboratory tests normal?

The laboratory tests are usually normal before weight gain. Weight loss reduces metabolic rate and the need for vitamins and minerals, and the gradual weight loss allows the body to shift vitamins and minerals around between the blood and the tissues.

Which laboratory tests are most likely to be abnormal early in the eating disorder?

The serum bicarbonate may be elevated due to loss of fluid and acid from the stomach caused by vomiting. The white blood cell count is usually reduced once weight loss is about 7 kg due to the effect of malnutrition on bone marrow. Many doctors will overlook this – but it is a clue.

The heart tracing (EKG) usually shows a slow heart rate and may show an increased QTc interval (longer than 440 msec), which indicates the heart takes longer to recharge electrically. Various types of EKG abnormalities can be seen in anorexia nervosa (heart blocks, rhythm abnormalities, and non-specific changes that may appear benign) (Birmingham *et al.* 1996: 211, 1999: 219–222; Birmingham and Gritzner 2007: e7–10; Bravender *et al.* 2006: 613; Casu *et al.* 2002: 239; Lesinskiene *et al.* 2008: 86). These are not normal in young women and correct with feeding. If the EKG of a middle-aged male with chest pain had these abnormalities, the doctor would be worried. However, doctors are much less likely to consider them important in young women – because they are young women.

What physical signs might have been overlooked?

Medical doctors do not reliably diagnose the physical signs associated with eating disorders. Doctors are not taught in medical school how to examine for these signs and they would not see them often enough in their practice to continue to recognize them, even if they were (Tyler and Birmingham 2001: 343; Uyeda *et al.* 2002: 116).

One of the key diagnostic factors is weight loss of more than 5 kg in someone who does not look very ill (as they would with pneumonia or cancer), who denies dieting, and is able to exercise more than ever. If these factors occur in a young female like Julie, anorexia nervosa should be considered.

Julie's blood pressure is likely to be low and her heart rate slow (this can also be seen in elite athletes). Her heart rate will likely increase markedly when she stands up from a lying position. However, her blood pressure will remain the same because the blood vessels of young people can constrict quickly.

Julie's parotid glands are likely to be enlarged, due to her vomiting. The parotid glands are the glands that are also enlarged in mumps. They are just under the skin in front of the ears. There may be fine hair growing on her body, especially on her back and abdomen, called lanugo hair. This hair is similar to the hair on newborn babies. Yellow skin, without a yellow tinge to the whites of the eyes (hypercarotenaemia), is often present, caused by the low metabolic rate caused by malnutrition (Birmingham 2002: 222).

Compare the colour of your palms to those of Julie; her palms will be light yellow. She will have a low body temperature if she has just come in from the cold (less than 36.5 degrees centigrade) or a slightly high temperature if she has been in extreme heat. Patients with anorexia nervosa are poikilothermic (like snakes);

they cannot maintain a constant temperature (euthermic) like most humans. If Julie is using her fingers to induce vomiting there may be a red area or scar on the back of her hand. (Russell's sign) (This is usually over the knuckles of the two fingers next to the thumb on the dominant hand.)

Admission to hospital

Julie is admitted to hospital six months later. She is admitted to a medical ward where the resident doctors say she is their first case of anorexia nervosa. They seem interested but not worried.

The most dangerous time in the treatment of anorexia nervosa is the first few weeks of weight gain. This is because the body is like an unused factory that is suddenly put into overtime production.

Which physical effects of her eating disorder are unlikely to cause problems?

Her parotid glands will likely be enlarged (Clare *et al.* 2005: 61). If her mouth is kept very dry these could become infected, but this is rare. She has had generalized hair loss from her scalp; this will grow back. Her lanugo hair will disappear with recovery. There may be discoloured skin on Julie's abdomen or back (erythema ab igne) caused by her use of heat from hot water bottles or warming blankets she has used to warm herself.

Which physical effects could cause problems?

A new or worsened heart murmur (due to mitral valve prolapse) is associated with an increased chance of chest pain, palpitations, or rarely stroke and infection. This will improve with recovery. Julie may notice that her heart rate goes faster and slower, unrelated to exertion, that she sweats on and off at night, and that her bowels and bladder function abnormally. These changes indicate abnormal function of the involuntary (autonomic) nervous system. If she gains weight quickly with autonomic dysfunction she has a greater chance of developing arrhythmias of the heart. Julie complains of cold hands and feet. Her body decreases blood flow through her cold extremities to avoid cooling her organs. She needs to be warmed and to be given fluids to correct dehydration.

What are the physical effects of feeding?

The most common physical effects are weight gain, swelling, 'growing pains' and muscle aches.

Weight loss causes the body to dehydrate; as a result, the hormones that cause fluid retention increase. When fluids are given to the body it retains them (oedema). Julie's oedema will worsen during the first few days of feeding and then disappear in a week or two. The oedema will cause swelling that appears in Julie's face and fingers in the morning and moves to her feet and legs during the day.

Julie's sense of swelling is mostly due to this oedema as well as her bowels. Her bowels do not function normally and retain more gas, faeces, and fluid. Her bowels will be weak and they will bloat up 'like a balloon' when she starts to eat. All of these things will get better gradually.

Julie's growing pains and muscle aches are similar to the 'growing pains' that occur in adolescence during a 'growth spurt'. In anorexia nervosa they occur when minerals move into muscles and bones during feeding. Often extra potassium, magnesium, or phosphorus is needed.

Very important physical effects

Irregular heart beat or extra beats (arrhythmia)

The heart usually beats slower than normal in anorexia nervosa due to a low metabolic rate, as well as extreme exercise or low body temperature. Arrhythmias can occur that Julie senses as an extra beat of her heart, a fluttering in her chest, or lightheadedness. Some patients are unaware of arrhythmias even when they are severe or frequent. Arrhythmias are only rarely a danger to Julie. However, if the arrhythmia reduces blood flow resulting in dizziness, loss of consciousness, or seizure, she must be taken to emergency immediately. Arrhythmias are most likely to occur during rapid refeeding, so rapid refeeding should take place in hospital. Other factors that make arrhythmia more likely are very low potassium, very low magnesium, heart failure, severe mitral valve prolapse, a QTc interval longer than 440 msec, or a recent increase in the QTc, which may be caused by certain medications.

Hypoglycaemia

If Julie's blood sugar drops too low her body normally responds by releasing sugar from a storage depot in her liver. With severe weight loss her storage depot may be empty. Importantly, if Julie eats more, especially carbohydrate (sugar), her blood sugar will rise as the food is digested, insulin will be released from her pancreas to move sugar into the cells, and her blood sugar will then drop – but it won't stop dropping. It won't stop dropping if she has lost weight to the point that she doesn't have a store of sugar in her liver. Julie could suffer confusion, tiredness, decreased consciousness, and even coma, seizures, arrhythmia, and death. If hypoglycaemia occurs, Julie will need a constant intravenous source of sugar until her liver stores are back to normal.

Nutrient deficiencies and their physical effects

Short term (in the first few days to three weeks) the following deficiencies can occur:

- The most common deficiencies are potassium (muscle weakness, arrhythmia), magnesium (muscle weakness, muscle cramps, decreased memory, difficulty maintaining focus of the eyes, seizures, arrhythmia), and phosphorus (heart failure, muscle breakdown, weakness, failure of all organs).
- Less common deficiencies are thiamine (confusion, loss of short-term memory, difficulty walking), zinc (abnormal taste sensation, dry skin, skin cuts that won't heal and infections), iron (anaemia, tiredness, and eating non-foods), and riboflavin (sores at the sides of the mouth).

Long term (months to years) the following deficiencies can occur:

- The most common deficiency is B12 (tiredness, anaemia, confusion, weakness, dementia).
- Rarely selenium (muscle, liver and heart weakness), vitamin A (decreased vision including night vision and day vision), and niacin (diarrhoea, dementia, skin rash on legs, death) deficiencies can occur.

Male with anorexia

Case study: James

I'm a 32-year-old lawyer, and have been obsessed with my body since my teens. My doctor told me that I don't have anorexia nervosa because I don't meet the DSM criteria, anorexia is rare in men, and, 'besides, there is no treatment for men with eating disorders.'

James

Anorexia nervosa in men presents differently than in women. Men want to gain weight in the form of muscle and reduce their body fat to almost none. As a consequence they will often appear to be eating more normally than women and appear to be less fat phobic.

Physical signs

James has a marked reduction in fat beneath his skin, muscle hypertrophy, and marked definition of his visible muscles. Parotid hypertrophy, lanugo hair, and hypercarotenaemia can occur in men, but James does not have these signs. Parotid hypertrophy is most common in males who vomit. Osteoporosis is common in males. James has back pain and has had stress fractures of bones in his feet believed to be due to over-exercise.

Relapse

Case study: Helen

I'm a 40-year-old dentist, who experienced mild and stable bulimia nervosa from my twenties. Suddenly I started to binge and purge many times a day. I knew of no apparent reason for this. After T3 toxicosis (hyperthyroidism) was diagnosed and treated, my bingeing and purging improved.

Helen

A relapse of bulimia nervosa usually results from increased life stressors, co-occurring psychiatric disease, substance use, discontinuing medication, or medication interaction. When I examined Helen she had physical signs of an overactive thyroid (hand tremor, eye signs, fast heart rate). Worsening of the eating disorder can also be due to physical diseases such as inflammatory bowel disease, thyroid dysfunction, coeliac disease, cancer, occult infection, or cirrhosis of the liver.

Physical signs

The only physical signs that Helen should have with stable bulimia nervosa are parotid hypertrophy, recession of her gums, erosion of teeth, Russell's sign (if she used her fingers to induce vomiting), and mild dehydration.

Physical effects of chronic eating disorders

Case study: Carla

I'm 47 now, and have suffered anorexia nervosa binge-purge subtype since 12 years of age. I live in an apartment by myself on a disability pension. I have been plagued with recurrent bone fractures, constipation, bowel pain, and repeated infections. The infections include pneumonia, kidney infection, and bone infection (osteomyelitis). Recently, my vision worsened over a two-month period.

Carla

It may take decades to develop certain deficiencies in chronic eating disorder patients. Even though Carla has been relatively stable, her diet will continue to be abnormal. As well, every illness she has will further drain her stores of nutrients. The body normally has a seventeen-year store of vitamin A, whereas the store of thiamine only lasts weeks, B12 a few years, and there is no store of zinc in the brain. So it may take a long time to develop certain deficiencies.

Carla has abnormal immunity. She can fight viral infections better than average, but she cannot fight bacterial infections normally because the proteins in her blood that control the white cells (those that kill bacteria) are abnormal (Birmingham *et al.* 2003: 269; Brown *et al.* 2005: 261).

Carla has severe osteoporosis.

Physical effects

Carla has the typical signs of chronic anorexia nervosa with generalized wasting of her body, visible bones of her upper chest, ribs, and the sides of her head, long fine hair growth on her body (lanugo hair), yellow skin (hypercarotenaemia), slow heart rate, low blood pressure, and intermittent oedema. Other common signs and symptoms are spasm of the facial muscles induced by tapping in front of the ear (Chvostek's sign), contraction of the hand muscles when the blood pressure is kept above the systolic (high) blood pressure for one or two minutes (Trousseau's sign), weakness of the muscles (especially of the shoulders and hips), blue extremities (acrocyanosis), delayed return of blood to the skin of the hands and feet after pressure is applied and released, and other nervous system signs (Hoffman's sign, clonus, brisk tendon jerk reflexes).

Carla's vision was decreased. Decreased vision can be due to magnesium deficiency, but low magnesium only causes loss of accommodation of focus after twenty minutes or so. Carla said her vision is always decreased. Vitamin A deficiency injures the cells of the retina. Her serum vitamin A level and the level of the protein that carries vitamin A (retinal binding globulin) were both very low.

Will my baby be healthy?

Case study: Andrea

I'm 30 and I want to get pregnant. I have had an eating disorder since I was young; I have restricted and binged and purged. I want to know whether my eating disorder could reduce my fertility or complicate my pregnancy.

Andrea

Anorexia does not hurt the ovaries or make women who recover unable to get pregnant and have babies. It causes no long-term effect on the pituitary or hypothalamus that regulate most hormones in the body.

Nutrient levels should be measured if food intake is not absolutely normal. This is especially important because dietary habits like a semi-vegetarian diet can lead to B12, magnesium, iron, zinc, and protein deficiency over time, especially with the increased nutritional requirements of pregnancy.

Andrea is likely to be concerned about her continued preoccupations and whether this will have an impact on her child. This must be discussed whether she raises the issue or not.

Physical effects

If Andrea has 'not had an eating disorder for years' she should have no physical complaints and a normal physical examination. She may still eat abnormally and have certain fears and preoccupations about eating, weight, and shape.

The physical complications that can persist after an eating disorder are: chronic bowel symptoms, scars on the back of the hand (Russell's sign), the signs left by self-injurious behaviour such as cutting, erosion of teeth, and erythema ab igne (which usually decreases with time but may not clear completely) (Tyler et al. 2002).

The fine body hair (lanugo hair), hair loss on scalp (alopecia due to telogen effluveum), yellow skin (hypercarotenaemia), and parotid hypertrophy should be gone.

Andrea's body fat should be assessed either by body mass index (BMI) and inspection or special measures such as anthropometrics (calipers that pinch the thickness of the skin and body fat underneath). If she is menstruating regularly while off the birth control pill she should be fertile. Anorexics can be fertile and ovulate without menstruating, so contraception should be used before pregnancy is planned, even if she is not menstruating.

References

Birmingham, C. L. (2002) 'Hypercarotenemia', *New Engl J Med* 347, 3: 222–3.

Birmingham, C. L. and Gritzner, S. (2007) 'Heart failure in anorexia nervosa: Case report and review of the literature', *Eat Weight Disord* 12, 1: e7–10.

Birmingham, C. L., and Treasure, J. (2010) *Medical Management of Eating Disorders*, 2nd edn, Cambridge: Cambridge University Press.

Birmingham, C. L., Alothman, A. F., and Goldner, E. M. (1996) 'Anorexia nervosa: Refeeding and hypophosphatemia', *Int J Eat Disord* 20, 2: 211–13.

Birmingham, C. L., Stigant, C., and Goldner, E. M. (1999) 'Chest pain in anorexia nervosa', *Int J Eat Disord* 25, 2: 219–22.

Birmingham, C. L., Hodgson, D. M., Fung, J., Brown, R., Wakefield, A., Bartrop, R., and Beumont, P. (2003) 'Reduced febrile response to bacterial infection in anorexia nervosa patients', *Int J Eat Disord* 34, 2: 269–72.

Bravender, T., Kanter, R., and Zucker, N. (2006) 'Anorexia nervosa and second-degree atrioventricular block (Type I)', *Int J Eat Disord* 39, 7: 612–15.

Brown, R. F., Bartrop, R., Beumont, P., and Birmingham, C. L. (2005) 'Bacterial infections in anorexia nervosa: Delayed recognition increases complications', *Int J Eat Disord* 37, 3: 261–5.

Casu, M., Patrone, V., Gianelli, M. V., Marchegiani, A., Ragni, G., Murialdo G., and Polleri, A. (2002) 'Spectral analysis of R-R interval variability by short-term recording in anorexia nervosa', *Eat Weight Disord* 7, 3: 239–43.

Clare, M., Gritzner, S., Hlynsky, J., and Birmingham, C. L. (2005) 'Measuring change in parotid gland size: Test-retest reliability of a novel method', *Eat Weight Disord* 10, 3: e61–5.

Lesinskiene, S., Barkus, A., Ranceva, N., and Dembinskas, A. (2008) 'A meta-analysis of heart rate and QT interval alteration in anorexia nervosa', *World J Biol Psychiatry* 9, 2: 86–91.

Tyler, I., and Birmingham, C. L. (2001) 'The interrater reliability of physical signs in patients with eating disorders', *Int J Eat Disord* 30, 3: 343–5.

Tyler, I., Wiseman, M. C., Crawford, R. I., and Birmingham, C. L. (2002) 'Cutaneous manifestations of eating disorders', *J Cutan Med Surg* 6, 4: 345–53.

Uyeda, L., Tyler, I., Pinzon, J., and Birmingham, C. L. (2002) 'Identification of patients with eating disorders. The signs and symptoms of anorexia nervosa and bulimia nervosa', *Eat Weight Disord* 7, 2: 116–23.

Chapter 8

The role of nutrition

What has food got to do with it?

Susan Hart, Hazel Williams, Alison Wakefield and Janice Russell

---

Case study: Emma

Emma is 17½ years old with anorexia nervosa, binge-purge subtype.

> I first noticed changes in Emma three years ago, when she was 14. We had the vegetarian thing. She was a chubby adolescent and didn't want to be that way. She cried every night. I tried to help by suggesting going for walks and cutting back certain foods. She went to dance classes with two skinny friends and that's when she decided to lose weight. Six months later she weighed 45 kg.
>
> She began avoiding us, became isolated, eating in the lounge room. She would make excuses that she had eaten before dinner or up at the shops with friends in the afternoon and was full. Her mood became incredibly black, many anorexic wishes, and schedules for herself: how many calories; how many kilograms. She was sleeping on her bedroom floor, not in her bed. She went on anorexic websites and had an anorexic pen pal.
>
> Emma's mother

Introduction

Food has everything to do with eating disorders, from their genesis to their maintenance, management and resolution. Hippocrates said; 'Let your food be your medicine and your medicine be your food', and nowhere is this as true as for the eating disorders where nutritional intervention (NI) is fundamental to treatment. Core goals are getting the patient to eat again and stop weight losing behaviours to reach and maintain normal body weight. Otherwise the sufferer is locked into a vicious cycle of energy wasting by factors related to the emaciation of anorexia nervosa. These include slow gastric emptying, constipation, taste and appetite changes causing "true" anorexia and metabolic impediments to weight gain such as the energy cost of tissue repair and physical restlessness due to low levels of leptin (a hormone from fat cells). Brain changes as a result of starvation lead to anxiety and depression with rigid, repetitive, weight-obsessed thinking which precludes change (Hebebrand *et al.* 2007; Russell *et al.* 2001; Tchanturia *et al.* 2004). Alternatively when the body fights back in bulimia nervosa, binge eating is triggered by low blood glucose and maintained by high insulin levels in response to weight-losing behaviours. These include purging and overexercise which, together with bingeing, become ways of dealing with negative self-image, mood swings, despair and worsening impulse control (Johnson *et al.* 1994; Russell *et al.* 1996).

When a patient won't eat or drink

A worrying occurrence for a busy general practitioner, physician or paediatrician is the presentation of a young person who, their family says will not eat or has not eaten (and sometimes not drunk) for some days. The child's symptoms may occur in the context of a suspected eating disorder and/or emotional crisis. The first requirement is a careful (and corroborative) history and physical examination for vital signs, nutritional state, hydration, cardiovascular status and general medical condition including any illness causing acute anorexia – infectious mononucleosis (glandular fever) and hepatitis being at the top of the list. Obvious psychiatric diagnoses such as major depression, acute psychosis, substance abuse, other acute organic brain syndromes and borderline personality disorder will need to be considered. These can coexist with, be mimicked by or precipitate an eating disorder, as can a medical illness. If the patient is significantly dehydrated, heading for a state of cardiovascular collapse or in an acute psychiatric state or family crisis, urgent hospitalisation might be the only option and coercive measures might be necessary.

If this is not the case, the initial aim is to work out with the patient and carers, a structured plan for gradually increasing intake until consultation with a suitably experienced dietitian and psychiatrist, or hospitalisation to a specialised service, can be arranged. Everyone must work together to gradually help improve the patient's intake and prevent weight-losing behaviours (and possibly self-harm). Monitoring of weight and vital signs, including checking for refeeding syndrome with regular haematology and biochemistry, must continue until stabilisation and regular nutrition are achieved and weight gain begins. Alternatively admission to a specialised service can occur.

The effects of starvation and under-nutrition

Patients like Emma, who present with excessive food restriction and under-nutrition over an extended period of time, exhibit typical symptoms and behaviours that are a consequence of starvation and are not secondary to any other condition. This was clearly demonstrated in a seminal study (Keys *et al.* 1950) which was designed to investigate the effects of starvation and refeeding on healthy adults but which also helped to explain the abnormal behaviours observed in patients with eating disorders. Physically and psychologically healthy males, conscientious objectors in World War II, were subjected to food restriction until they had lost 25 per cent of pre-morbid body weight over a six-month period, then re-fed for three months. Medical status, haematology and biochemistry, body composition, behaviour and psychological state, eating patterns and mood changes were studied for twelve months from initial assessment.

Cognitive changes observed after weight loss included decreased concentration, poor judgement and apathy. Subjects developed an intense preoccupation with food, recipes and cooking; they hoarded food, made unusual food mixtures, used salt and spices excessively and dramatically increased their coffee and tea consumption, and some developed binge eating and vomiting during refeeding. During the food restriction and weight loss stage, the subjects also became increasingly uninterested in sex and physical activity, most experiencing significant deterioration in mood, with 20 per cent experiencing severe depression. Irritability, anger and anxiety were also common, mood and behavioural changes persisting throughout refeeding and being slow to reverse. These young men did not start out by having an eating disorder, but developed mood and behavioural changes similar to those exhibited by Emma.

> Emma was always checking I did the exact recipe so that she knew her calorie intake. She went through a stage of wanting desperately to help in the kitchen; she would cook food but never eat it. I also had the problem of buying food for the rest of the family and children, which Emma would binge on. I was actually hiding food in our bedroom. I must say food has been horrendous for me; always trying to please everyone until we all started on the vegetarian recipes. I guess we were all on a diet.
>
> Emma's mother

Patients usually develop abnormal eating behaviours to facilitate their food restriction, which become very entrenched (Beumont et al. 1988; Windauer et al. 1993) and are often fiercely defended. All family members may become involved in or be affected by the behaviours, examples of which include:

- Abnormal timing of meals and snacks so as to avoid family meals
- Avoidance of specific foods, particularly foods perceived to be high in energy or 'fattening'
- Binge eating
- Involvement in food preparation, collecting recipes and menus and insisting that others eat but rarely eating with them
- Compensatory purging and exercise

- Difficulty estimating portion size
- Disproportionate time spent thinking (and talking) about food
- Inability to identify hunger or satiety
- Using inappropriate food combinations
- Hiding or disposing of meals
- Chewing food then spitting it out
- Using inappropriate food utensils
- Poor food variety
- Reduced spontaneity and flexibility with food
- Abnormal speed of eating
- Unusual rigidity and rituals around food
- 'Debiting' food intake, e.g. food intake rationed according to exercise
- Excessive use of condiments, e.g. salt, pepper, chilli, soy sauce, vinegar
- Filling up on bulky low-energy foods or calorie-free fluids
- Cutting food into very small pieces before eating
- Hoarding food and non-food items
- Repeated re-heating of food and fluids

Referral to a dietitian

Suitably skilled and experienced dietitians are key members of the eating disorders treatment team (ADA 2006; Wakefield and Williams 2009). Their role includes providing detailed assessment of a patient's nutritional status and abnormal eating behaviours, and assessment of the risk of refeeding syndrome with appropriate dietary prescription (Wakefield and Williams 2009). Dietitians should always work as part of a multidisciplinary team (ADA 2006; Thomas 2000; Wakefield and Williams 2009) and their relationship with the patient is often pivotal in bringing about major shifts in motivation and collaborative behaviour (Herrin 2003). Education of other team members in nutritional principles and basic science is another important role, along with teaching patients and families about normal nutrition and working out how best to achieve this. It is usually advisable in the outpatient situation for the dietitian to do the weighing of the patient, with communication to the other treatment team members.

Where there is no dietitian, the general practitioner, physician, paediatrician or psychiatrist, assisted perhaps by a practice nurse, will need to take over the last two tasks as well as nutritional assessment, as described later. The skills required for nutritional management in eating disorders are somewhat different from those appropriate to other areas of dietetic practice in that patients are usually younger and need to be given permission to eat more, to enjoy their food and settle for 'good enough' eating and normal weight. Discussion of normal weight ranges, average weight ranges and weight appropriate for the patient can be tiger territory. All treatment team members must tackle this and be in frequent communication to ensure a united approach, with each delivering the same message.

Nutritional assessment

> So I guess there wasn't enough supervision or communal eating. I had to concentrate on me at the time as I had breast cancer and that obscured my view. I had the operation, came home and suddenly realised I was looking at a skeleton. We took Emma to the GP who did some blood tests. She had had glandular fever so I may have written her weight loss off as that.
>
> Emma's mother

In patients like Emma who present with signs of disordered eating it is important to assess nutritional status in four key areas: anthropometry; biochemistry; clinical symptoms; and dietary behaviours. Early recognition of an eating disorder by the GP and prompt referral to specialist clinicians will ensure appropriate intervention. Emma's mother and GP were initially both distracted from her real diagnosis by her glandular fever and the mother's own health issues. Emma's eating disorder had become very entrenched by the time she saw specialist clinicians for treatment.

Anthropometry

An adult patient's weight and height should be measured and their body mass index (BMI) calculated, to give an assessment of whether they are underweight, overweight or within the healthy weight range (WHO 1995), bearing in mind that BMI is an imperfect guide and less useful in males and females who exercise heavily. If the patient is significantly underweight, which for adults means having a BMI of 17.5 or less, this fulfils DSM-IV diagnostic criteria for anorexia nervosa (APA 2000). Patients with bulimia nervosa or binge eating disorder will present as either slightly underweight, within the normal weight range or overweight, so other signs of malnutrition, binge eating or purging must be sought (APA 2000). A child or adolescent presenting with a suspected eating disorder should also be weighed and measured, but BMI charts are less appropriate in younger patients than growth charts or BMI percentile charts (National Center for Health Statistics 2000). Anthropometric information needs to be set in the context of the individual's recent medical and weight history, desired weight and frequency of self-weighing in addition to their preoccupation with food and fears of weight gain. Clinicians should be aware that excessive exercise results in a high muscle mass and very low body fat, which may mask a BMI that should be lower than it appears, and an underlying eating disorder.

Biochemistry

Biochemical tests required at initial assessment include sodium, potassium, phosphate and blood glucose levels, with serum and urine osmolality to assess hydration, specific gravity of urine being a simple and useful measure in this regard. Haematology and ECG should also be performed along with amylase and liver function tests. Abnormally low levels of magnesium, phosphate and potassium, with normal hydration, can indicate an acute state of malnutrition (Brooks and Melnik 1995; Kohn *et al.* 1998; Solomon and Kirby 1990) and a risk of developing refeeding syndrome. Potassium is likely to be low if the patient is purging, and must be replaced, while low sodium can be related to exercise and/or compulsive water drinking and will usually improve if these behaviours can be contained.

Clinical observations

Weight loss, low body temperature, pulse rate and blood pressure with exaggerated postural responses, cold extremities and poor peripheral circulation may be accompanied by dehydration, which can occur in the absence of obvious weight loss if fluid intake is abruptly curtailed. Clinical signs of dehydration include poor skin turgor (skin hanging in loose folds), brown dry tongue, halitosis, dull sunken eyes, and an elevated or normal pulse rate which in an emaciated patient is more alarming than the usual bradycardia. The younger the patient the more likely this is to constitute a medical emergency.

Constipation occurs frequently in patients with eating disorders (Zipfel *et al.* 2006). It can develop as a result of excessive food restriction, inadequate fluid intake, poor muscle tone of bowel and pelvic floor, and laxative abuse. Patients with anorexia nervosa usually experience delayed gastric emptying and slower peristalsis (Robinson *et al.* 1998; Waldholtz and Andersen 1990), which they may describe as gastric bloating and discomfort after meals. Loss of dental enamel, calluses on hands, a sore throat, bloodshot eyes and enlarged salivary glands are clinical indicators of vomiting.

Amenorrhea is also a common symptom in eating disorders and, if prolonged, increases the patient's risk of developing osteoporosis. Excessive dieting or exercise, or both, result in body fat levels dropping, with subsequent falls in oestrogen production. Adequate oestrogen is essential for regular menstruation and bone strength. In males, weight loss results in lower testosterone production, with reduced libido, bone mineral density and muscle mass.

Dietary assessment

It is essential to ask patients with a possible eating disorder about their daily food intake, to assess the nutritional adequacy of their diet. Exclusion of key food groups, such as carbohydrates (bread, pasta, potato and rice), protein (meat, fish, dairy, eggs), fats (any oils or spread) and calcium-rich foods (dairy and fortified soy) is indicative of under-nutrition.

Eating disordered patients often ingest excessive quantities of raw fruits and vegetables (Rock and Yager 1987) to fill up on and to suppress appetite, along with excessive amounts of condiments, chewing gum, diet or low-calorie foods, salt and artificial sweeteners. This should be discouraged as it prevents intake of more nutritious foods.

> Emma's cousin, who she admired, was vegetarian, so that's how I accepted it. At first she ate vegetarian meals with eggs and cheese when we had meat, so I thought that was just Emma. Food also became a huge problem with me trying to cook 'healthy food' on her request. She was given a vegetarian cookbook and we cooked meals from it. They were healthy meals but probably not enough for growing teenagers.
>
> Emma's mother

An association between vegetarianism and dietary restraint has been demonstrated in eating disorder patients (O'Connor *et al.* 1987; Sullivan and Damani 2000), with rates of vegetarianism reported at 50 per cent (Bakan *et al.* 1993). Patients report that a vegetarian diet is a socially acceptable way to reduce calorie and fat intake, and becoming vegetarian may provide an alibi to dietary restriction. Vegetarianism should be regarded with suspicion in young adults, particularly if the family is not also vegetarian, and if associated with other warning signs of restrictive dietary behaviour.

Excessive food restriction often leads to episodes of binge eating, although patients are usually more secretive about this aspect of their eating disorder. If the clinician suspects bulimic behaviours, it is appropriate to ask direct questions about binge eating and subsequent compensatory behaviours, such as laxative abuse and self-induced vomiting. Family members often will have noticed signs of purging, such as empty laxative packets, or the state of the bathroom, and will bring these to the clinician's attention.

> Neighbours brought in an abundance of food when I got home from the hospital and Emma began to eat a lot, regaining some weight for a while. I thought 'thank God, we're over that', until I discovered she was bingeing and purging. Emma would go to school without breakfast, didn't take lunch, and was desperate to eat dinner early. She would eat masses of food at dinner, crying and saying: 'I don't feel full'. She'd disappear after meals. I tried to talk to her about it but I mostly watched and worried. She didn't want to talk about it.
>
> Emma's mother

Assessment of fluid intake

Questions should be asked about the quantity and type of fluids consumed, plus motivation for excessive or restrictive drinking. It was demonstrated that fluid intake was disordered in the majority of patients in an inpatient sample, with only 15 per cent drinking in the recommended range and most choosing excessive quantities of calorie-free fluids such as water, tea, coffee, and diet cola (Hart *et al.* 2005). Reasons given by patients for drinking excessively were related to eating disorder behaviours, such as to aid vomiting, feeling full and to decrease appetite (Hart *et al.*, in press). Some patients, particularly younger patients, restricted their fluid intake to avoid fullness, to feel in control and to maintain a sense of feeling empty. Excessive caffeine intake in patients with objective binge eating and vomiting was to stimulate metabolism, boost energy levels, and aid purging (Hart *et al.*, 2011).

Refeeding syndrome

The refeeding syndrome describes disturbances in electrolyte, vitamin, mineral, bone and muscle homeostasis that may occur upon refeeding an emaciated patient (Brooks and Melnik 1995; Solomon and Kirby 1990). Patients sometimes induce this syndrome by eating large amounts of easily ingested carbohydrates such as sweets in order to avoid specialised hospitalisation, or it can be caused by infusion of dextrose solutions in emergency wards. The clinical features are confusion, chest pain and heart failure. The syndrome is a medical emergency requiring gradual balanced re-nutrition, mineral (phosphate and magnesium), electrolyte and thiamine replacement, with cardiac and electrolyte monitoring (Brooks and Melnik 1995; Solomon and Kirby 1990). Blood levels of phosphate and thiamine levels can fall when phosphate-containing intermediaries and metabolic cofactors are utilised upon initiation of refeeding. Medical risk is high with recent rapid weight loss and low BMI (usually 14 or less), low serum phosphate, magnesium, potassium, glucose and zinc, high serum urea levels and prolonged QTc interval (Kohn *et al.* 1998).

Nutritional intervention

Nutritional intervention (NI) involves a number of strategies to assist patients with eating disorders in the recovery process. These include:

1   Assessment and provision of advice for appropriate healthy weight range and management of the rate of weight gain. Recommended weight gain is 0.5 kg/week in an outpatient or day-patient setting and 0.5-1.0 kg/week for inpatients (Gowers *et al.* 2004). Recommended BMI is at least 20 kg/m^2 in patients older than 18 and a BMI of 19 kg/m^2 for younger patients.
2   Advising on normal eating patterns, such as: thinking about what normal or 'good enough' eating really means rather than some idealised view of the perfect diet; eating for enjoyment as well as health; developing spontaneous and flexible eating behaviours rather than rigid inflexible habits; and

developing sensitivity to cues for eating that most people follow, such as appetite, time of day, social situation and visual appeal (Beumont *et al.* 1988; Williams and O'Connor 2000).

3   Providing accurate nutritional information and assisting patients to make connections between the amount and variety of food they eat and their state of health and energy (Williams and O'Connor 2000).

4   Structuring and planning meals, including a written outline of several 'model' days for patients and carers, which include recommended daily amounts of nutrients, energy, and 'forbidden' foods. Support for carers to formulate healthy appropriate guidelines for family meals (Herrin 1999; Williams and O'Connor 2000).

5   Limiting the number of foods that patients may refuse to eat, with likes and dislikes clearly identified and differentiated from eating disordered aversions and feared foods (Huse and Lucas 1983). Patients commonly request long lists of foods that they don't want to eat because of self-diagnosed allergies or intolerances, such as bloating from wheat or milk products. Food intolerances should be endorsed only when medically indicated, rather than from self-reported histories (Hart *et al.* 2008).

6   Advising on fluid intake, such as the amount and types of drinks structured within a meal plan. This will help to regulate intake and reduce the impact excessive fluid intake may have on suppressing appetite and preventing intake of more appropriate food. Education should also be provided about fluid losses from frequent vomiting increasing the need for additional fluid. Patients who restrict their fluid intake should be guided to include adequate fluids and educated about the dangers of dehydration (Hart *et al.*, 2011).

7   Behavioural strategies that can be encouraged include using a food intake diary, eating at an appropriate pace, eating with others where possible (Herrin 1999; O'Connor *et al.* 1988; Salvy and McCargar 2002) and developing a hierarchy of foods/eating situations previously avoided from least anxiety-provoking to most anxiety-provoking, with graded exposure to these foods (Ashley and Crino 2010).

8   Teaching practical and social eating skills with advice on meal preparation and cooking, and learning about eating in its social context (Ashley and Crino 2010; Cockfield and Philpot 2009; Merriman 1996).

Challenges of nutritional intervention

Conducting meaningful counselling sessions with a starving patient is difficult. Techniques that encourage eating and weight gain usually provoke anxiety and resistance to change (Omizo and Oda 1988), and the person suggesting an increase in food intake is viewed with fear and mistrust (Woo 1986). Patients may become more emotionally disturbed as (a) eating disorder coping strategies are removed and (b) they become more aware of the underlying issues (Williams and O'Connor 2000); change may be accompanied by marked anxiety (Krey *et al.* 1989). The clinician must be aware of these difficulties and remain non-judgemental in dealing with dietary non-compliance and manipulative behaviours (Woo 1986), such as falsification of weight, which can be difficult to detect. It is important for the clinician not to over-react to such behaviours, but rather to recognise them as part of the disorder of eating and encourage collaboration in improving the situation. Nevertheless a high index of suspicion should be maintained, particularly if the patient does not look to be gaining the weight indicated by the scales. Clinical impression, investigations and corroborative evidence from other team and family members are essential.

Conclusion

Food intake and nutritional status are fundamental factors in the development and diagnoses of eating disorders. Addressing and correcting these is the major challenge in treatment and recovery, and all clinicians involved in treating patients with eating disorders need to have some understanding of nutritional and dietetic principles, with access to multidisciplinary services including a dietitian. General practitioners, physicians, paediatricians and psychiatrists often face the greatest difficulties with this aspect of treatment. This is particularly so when consultation with a specialised dietitian or admission to a specialised treatment service cannot be organised easily or quickly. Holding the fort becomes crucial and we hope this chapter provides practical assistance with this daunting task.

References

American Dietetic Association (ADA) (2006) 'Position of the American Dietetic Association: Nutrition intervention in the treatment of anorexia nervosa, bulimia nervosa, and other eating disorders', *J Am Diet Assoc* 106, 12: 2073–82.

American Psychiatric Association (APA) (2000) *DSM-IV-TR: Diagnostic and Statistical Manual of Mental Disorders,* 4th edn (text revision), Washington, DC: American Psychiatric Press.

Ashley, M. and Crino, N. (2010) 'A novel approach to treating eating disorders in a day-hospital treatment program', *Nutr Diet* 67: 155–9.

Bakan, R., Birmingham, C. L., Aeberhardt, L., and Goldner, E. M. (1993) 'Dietary zinc intake of vegetarian and nonvegetarian patients with anorexia nervosa', *Int J Eat Disord* 13, 2: 229–33.

Beumont, P. J., O'Connor, M., Touyz, S. W., and Williams, H. (eds) (1988) 'Nutritional counselling in the treatment of anorexia and bulimia nervosa', in P. J. Beumont, M. O'Connor, S. W. Touyz and H. Williams (eds), *Handbook of Eating Disorders, Part 1* (pp. 349–56), Amsterdam: Elsevier Biomedical Press.

Brooks, M. J. and Melnik, G. (1995) 'The refeeding syndrome: An approach to understanding its complications and preventing its occurrence', *Pharmacotherapy* 15: 713–26.

Cockfield, A., and Philpot, U. (2009) 'Managing anorexia from a dietitian's perspective', *Proceedings of the Nutrition Society* 68: 281–8.

Gowers,, S., Pilling, S., Treasure, J., Fairburn, C., Palmer, B., Bell, L., *et al.* (2004) *Eating Disorders: Core Interventions in the Treatment and Management of Anorexia Nervosa, Bulimia Nervosa and Related Eating Disorders. Clinical Guideline 9.* London: National Institute for Clinical Excellence.

Hart, S., Abraham, S., Luscombe, G., and Russell, J. (2005) 'Fluid intake in patients with eating disorders', *Int J Eat Disord* 38, 1: 55–9.

Hart, S., Abraham, S., Luscombe, G., and Russell, J. (2008) 'Eating disorder management in hospital patients: Current practice among dietitians in Australia', *Nutr Diet* 65: 16–22.

Hart, S., Abraham, S., Franklin, R. C., and Russell, J. (2011) 'The reason why eating disorder patients drink', *Eur Eat Disord Rev,* 19, 2:121–128. Article first published online: 8 Oct 2010, DOI: 10.1002/erv.1051.

Hebebrand, J., Muller, T. D., Holtkamp, K., and Herpertz-Dahlmann, B. (2007) 'The role of leptin in anorexia nervosa: Clinical implications', *Mol Psychiatry* 12, 1: 23–35.

Herrin, M. (1999) 'Balancing the scales: Nutritional guidelines for women with eating disorders', *AWHONN Lifelines* 3: 26–34.

Herrin, M. (2003) *Nutrition Counseling in the Treatment of Eating Disorders,* 2nd edn, New York: Brunner-Routledge.

Huse, D. M. and Lucas, A. R. (1983) 'Dietary treatment of anorexia nervosa', *J Am Diet Assoc* 83: 687–90.

Johnson, W. G., Jarrell, M. P., Chupurdia, K. M., and Williamson, D. A. (1994) 'Repeated binge/purge cycles in bulimia nervosa: Role of glucose and insulin', *Int J Eat Disord* 15, 4: 331–41.

Keys, A., Brozek, J., Henschel, A., Mickelsen, O., and Taylor, H. L. (1950) *The Biology of Human Starvation*, Minneapolis: University of Minnesota Press.

Kohn, M. R., Golden, N. H., and Shenker, I. R. (1998) 'Cardiac arrest and delirium: Presentations of the refeeding syndrome in severely malnourished adolescents with anorexia nervosa', *J Adoles Health* 22: 239–43.

Krey, S. H., Palmer, K., and Porcelli, K. A. (1989) 'Eating disorders: The clinical dietician's changing role', *J Am Diet Assoc* 89: 41–3.

Merriman, S. H. (1996) 'Nutrition education in the treatment of eating disorders: A suggested 10 session course', *J Hum Nutr Diet* 9: 377–80.

National Center for Health Statistics, in collaboration with the National Center for Chronic Disease and Health Promotion (2000) *CDC Growth Charts.* Online. Available: http://www.cdc.gov/growthcharts (accessed 25 September 2010).

O'Connor, M. A., Touyz, S. W., Dunn, S. M., and Beumont, P. J. (1987) 'Vegetarianism in anorexia nervosa? A review of 116 consecutive cases', *Med J Aust* 147: 540–2.

O'Connor, M., Touyz, S., and Beumont, P. (1988) 'Nutritional management and dietary counselling in bulimia nervosa: Some preliminary observations', *Int J Eat Disord* 7: 657–62.

Omizo, S. A. and Oda, E. A. (1988) 'Anorexia nervosa: Psychological considerations for nutrition counselling', *J Am Diet Assoc* 88: 49–51.

Robinson, P. H., Clarke, M., and Barrett, J. (1998) 'Determinants of delayed gastric emptying in anorexia nervosa and bulimia nervosa', *Gut* 29: 458–64.

Rock, C. and Yager, J. (1987) 'Nutrition and eating disorders: A primer for clinicians', *Int J Eat Disord* 6: 267–80.

Russell, J., Hooper, M., and Hunt, G. (1996) 'Insulin response in bulimia nervosa as a maker of nutritional depletion', *Int J Eat Disord* 20, 3: 307–13.

Russell, J., Baur, L. A., Beumont, P. J., Byrnes, S., Gross, G., Touyz, S., Abraham, S., and Zipfel, S. (2001) 'Altered energy metabolism in anorexia nervosa', *Psychoneuroendocrinology* 26: 51–63.

Salvy, S. J. and McCargar, L. (2002) 'Nutritional interventions for individuals with bulimia nervosa', *Eat Weight Disord* 7: 258–67.

Solomon, S. M. and Kirby, D. F. (1990) 'The refeeding syndrome: A review', *JPEN* 14: 90–7.

Sullivan, V. and Damani, S. (2000) 'Vegetarianism and eating disorders – partners in crime?', *Eur Eat Disord Rev* 8: 263–6.

Tchanturia, K., Anderluh, M. B., Morris, R. G., Rabe-Hesketh, S., Collier, D. A., Sanchez, P., and Treasure, J. L. (2004) 'Cognitive flexibility in anorexia nervosa and bulimia nervosa', *J Int Neuropsychol Soc* 10: 513–20.

Thomas, D. (2000) 'The dietician's role in the treatment of eating disorders', *Nutr Bull* 25: 55–60.

Wakefield, A. and Williams, H. (2009) *Practice Recommendations for the Nutritional Management of Anorexia Nervosa in Adults*, Deakin, ACT: Dietetic Association Australia. Online. Available: http://www.daa.asn.au/files/DINER/Anorexia%20Nervosa_Final.pdf (accessed 25 September 2010).

Waldholtz, B. D. and Andersen, A. E. (1990) 'Gastrointestinal symptoms in anorexia nervosa: A prospective study', *Gastroenterology* 98: 1415–19.

WHO (1995) *Physical Status: The Use and Interpretation of Anthropometry* (WHO Technical Report Series No. 854), Geneva: WHO.

Williams, H. and O'Connor, M. (2000) 'Dietetics and nutrition', in D. Gaskill and F. Sanders (eds), *The Encultured Body: Policy Implications for Healthy Body Image and Disordered Eating Behaviours*, Vol. 1 (pp. 126–31), Brisbane: Queensland University of Technology.

Windauer, U., Lennerts, W., Talbot, P., Touyz, S. W., and Beumont, P. J. (1993) 'How well are "cured" anorexia nervosa patients? An investigation of 16 weight-recovered anorexic patients', *Br J Psychiatry* 163: 195–200.

Woo, L. M. H. (1986) 'Diet counseling: Treatment of anorexia nervosa and bulimia', *Top Clin Nutr* 1: 73–84.

Zipfel, S., Sammett, I., Rapps, N., Herzog, W., Herpertz, S., and Martens, U. (2006) 'Gastrointestinal disturbances in eating disorders: Clinical and neurobiological aspects', *Auton Neurosci* 129: 99–106.

Chapter 9

Pharmacotherapy of eating disorders

Leora David, Allegra Broft and B. Timothy Walsh

Anorexia nervosa

Case study

My daughter Estée, age 13, developed anorexia nervosa two years ago. Estée is the youngest of three daughters and we live in a rural setting. My husband and I own and run a business. Before developing AN, Estée was a delightful, totally well-behaved girl, perfectionistic and with a tendency to be a worrier. Initially, we observed changes in her eating pattern and mood: she began turning down previously enjoyed foods such as ice cream and chocolate, isolated herself from family members, began nightly jogs, and developed uncharacteristically irritable moods. We wondered if these behavioural changes were due to her transfer to a new school after her best friend moved house. Over five months, Estée's weight fell to a medically unsafe range. After several unsuccessful attempts at seeking help from general practitioners, Estée was admitted to hospital for four weeks in February 2009, which improved her weight slightly, and by which time the AN diagnosis was clear.

Suzanne (mother)

The search for an effective pharmacological treatment for anorexia nervosa (AN) began in the early 1960s with the development of a combined chlorpromazine and insulin treatment aimed at facilitating weight restoration. In a 1966 publication, Dally and Sargant reported that chlorpromazine, a first-generation antipsychotic, 'which lessens the patient's fear of and resistance to eating' leads to an increased rate of weight gain as compared to standard inpatient methods of bedrest and elevated caloric intake (Dally and Sargant 1966: 793). Since 1966, a range of drugs, primarily antidepressants and antipsychotics, have been investigated as potential treatments for AN. However, despite the optimistic tone of the Dally and

Sargant report, fifty years later, an effective pharmacological treatment for AN has yet to be conclusively demonstrated. At this time, there is a strong consensus that non-pharmacologic interventions, and not medications, remain the cornerstone of treatment for AN.

Nonetheless, clinicians at times consider medications as a part of the treatment plan for AN. This chapter discusses research on medication strategies tested to date.

Antidepressants

Based on the hypothesis that the depressive and anxious features often seen in AN might suggest a common aetiological pathway with depression, and therefore a common treatment approach, antidepressants have become a target in eating disorders treatment research. Antidepressants have been evaluated in several randomized, placebo-controlled trials, in the contexts of weight restoration and relapse prevention, with minimal to no success in alleviating eating disorder symptoms or facilitating the weight restoration process (Claudino *et al.* 2006).

Selective serotonin reuptake inhibitors (SSRIs), which act by indirectly increasing the amount of serotonin in the synaptic cleft, have been investigated as a possible treatment for AN in part due to evidence suggesting dysregulation of serotonergic pathways in the brains of underweight and weight-restored patients with AN (Kaye *et al.* 2005).

Nevertheless, fluoxetine, an SSRI with demonstrated efficacy in other eating disorders, was not found to have an advantage over placebo when combined with a structured behavioural inpatient programme aimed at normalizing eating and weight (Attia *et al.* 1998). One surprising and noteworthy aspect of this finding was that besides conferring no additional benefit on normalization of eating and weight, there was no added improvement in mood and/or anxiety symptoms. Fluoxetine has also been studied as an aid in preventing relapse; however, the largest trial assessing the use of fluoxetine in a weight-restored population found no evidence of benefit (Walsh *et al.* 2006). Other SSRIs, including citalopram and sertraline, have also failed to promote weight gain as compared with placebo, albeit in non-randomized trials (Fassino *et al.* 2002; Santonastaso *et al.* 2001).

Other antidepressant medications have been studied, without promising results. Tricyclic antidepressants (TCAs) were initially of interest in the treatment of AN, due in part to weight gain that may occur as a side effect. However, these too seem to lack efficacy in weight restoration. For example, when compared with placebo, neither amitriptyline nor clomipramine helped patients to gain weight (Biederman *et al.* 1985; Lacey and Crisp 1980). These older medications can also be associated with adverse side effects, including antimuscarinic and anticholinergic effects ranging from dry mouth and constipation to impaired memory, and potentially dangerous cardiac effects. Bupropion is an antidepressant with a unique mechanism of action (favouring action on dopaminergic and noradrenergic systems), and may have one of the more favourable side-effect profiles among antidepressants. However, a study among patients with eating disorders (specifically, bulimia nervosa (BN)), found a relatively high rate of seizures with use of bupropion (Horne *et al.* 1988), and it is currently relatively contraindicated for use in AN as well as BN.

One most common question that arises in treating patients with AN is whether an antidepressant/anti-anxiety medication such as an SSRI may be appropriate in the treatment. The overall negative findings in antidepressant treatment trials means there is minimal evidence at this time to support their use in AN, even if the primary goal of use is to address associated mood and/or anxiety symptoms. Because the semi-starvation state itself (without coexisting AN) can cause mood and anxiety symptoms, the standard treatment recommendation is for the patient to first undergo nutritional rehabilitation, and to delay evaluation for antidepressant medications such as SSRIs until the patient achieves and maintains weight in a medically stable range (usually above 90 per cent of ideal body weight). Medication treatment for associated mood and/or anxiety symptoms may be appropriate if such symptoms persist in the face of significant weight restoration.

Antipsychotics

Antipsychotics were the first class of drugs to be systematically investigated as potential treatments for AN. It was hypothesized that the distorted thoughts and behaviours surrounding eating and body image in patients with AN were similar in origin to the delusions of patients with schizophrenia or other psychotic disorders (Kruger and Kennedy 2000).

As mentioned above, chlorpromazine, a first-generation antipsychotic (FGA), was the first pharmacological intervention to be studied in the treatment of AN, without much success (Dally and Sargant 1966). While other FGAs, including pimozide and sulpiride, were studied in the early 1980s (Kruger and Kennedy 2000), the interest in first-generation antipsychotics has largely been replaced by an interest in second-generation antipsychotics (SGAs) as a potential treatment for AN, due in part to their more benign side-effect profile.

There is preliminary evidence that SGAs may be beneficial in treatment of underweight patients with AN (McKnight and Park 2010). Of these, olanzapine has been the most frequently studied, with promising initial results. In one randomized controlled trial, patients taking olanzapine achieved more rapid weight gain and exhibited fewer obsessional symptoms than patients taking placebo (Bissada *et al.* 2008). Indeed, olanzapine may be the best candidate in the literature at this time for treatment of acute AN, but larger, controlled trials are needed to assess its potential risks and benefits more thoroughly. Other SGAs have been studied less extensively in non-placebo controlled trials, including amisulpride and quetiapine (McKnight and Park 2010). Further study of this class of medications, particularly olanzapine, may be useful in developing pharmacological interventions for AN.

Other medications

The potential efficacy of other classes of medications has had limited exploration. Some agents that have been studied include lithium carbonate, zinc, tetrahydrocannabinol, naltrexone, clonidine, recombinant growth hormone, metoclopramide, domperidone, and cisapride (Steffen *et al.* 2006). Many of these medications have been investigated because they target systems thought to play a role in the aetiology and maintenance of AN, or because they are known to promote weight gain in normal-weight populations. None is used in the treatment of AN at this time, or is supported for use by existing treatment research.

After her initial hospitalization, Estée was entered into a Maudsley-based treatment at a privately run eating disorders clinic. Psychiatric care was not available in this setting, though a local paediatrician provided a prescription for olanzapine, for 'anxiety over eating, and the need to exercise constantly'. Olanzapine was given initially on an as-needed basis. It appeared to help Estée stay slightly calmer, and later was made a daily medication. Maudsley treatment continued for three to four months. One month into treatment, suicidal thoughts and multiple forms of self-injury emerged. An episode of head-banging at the outpatient clinic led to discharge from that setting's care, and we sought formal psychiatric consultation. Fluoxetine was prescribed at a dose of 20 mg per day in July 2009 as a result of this evaluation, with minimal follow-up from the prescribing psychiatrist. We noticed no improvement in eating disorder symptoms or mood and fluoxetine was discontinued when suicidal thoughts seemed to worsen.

Estée had several psychiatric hospitalizations during the latter half of 2009 due to imminent potential for significant self-harm as well as for continued underweight. During this time, she tried several other medications for anxiety and agitation, including clonazepam and diazepam. We noted that clonazepam worsened her agitation and tendency towards self-harm. Diazepam was more successful.

More recently, Estée's weight has stabilized in a medically appropriate weight range, above 90 per cent of ideal body weight. She receives 5 mg of olanzapine twice daily, with additional dosing as needed for agitation. A low dose of sertraline has been added recently, on an outpatient basis, to alleviate ongoing mood symptoms, and we are waiting to see if this will benefit her. Our primary goal and priority for Estée at present is to maintain her weight in the medically appropriate range.

Suzanne (mother)

Conclusion

Despite more medication trials for the treatment of AN, little has changed since Dally and Sargant first published their report in 1966. There are no widely studied and accepted pharmacological interventions for AN, and methodological limitations have prevented an accurate understanding of drug efficacy. For example, many medication studies in AN have occurred in the context of structured behavioural treatments that are known to lead to weight gain independent of medication. Therefore, potential benefits of these medications in a circumstance where a structured treatment programme is unavailable, or the patient is not willing to participate, are less clear (although several studies of SSRIs in outpatients have not shown benefit). Other limitations of medication trials in AN include small sample sizes and high attrition rates, further limiting generalizability of trial results.

Meanwhile, individual clinicians are left to decide on the use of medications in AN treatment. Estée's story illustrates the trial and error process that often characterizes medication use for AN patients. Estée tried different medications: importantly, largely *in conjunction with* an evidence-based psychotherapy treatment (Maudsley) for her illness. Her paediatrician initially prescribed olanzapine, which she and her family believed led her to be calmer. This treatment response may be consistent with evidence suggesting that olanzapine decreases AN-related obsessionality among patients with AN (Bissada *et al.* 2008). Estée's doctors also tried two SSRIs: fluoxetine, when acutely underweight, and sertraline, upon weight restoration.

As discussed, the lack of efficacy of fluoxetine during the acute phase of her illness is not surprising looking at treatment research literature to date. Further, besides the lack of evidence in support of fluoxetine's use during acute AN, additional specific issues must be noted when considering starting this class of medication in children and adolescents: notably, data which suggests worsening of suicidal behaviour in a very small number of children and young adults treated with an SSRI. Estée's experience illustrates the importance of close monitoring by a doctor whenever medications are prescribed. On the other hand, Estée's doctor's decision to initiate a trial of sertraline during the weight-restored phase of her recovery may have been a reasonable intervention at this time, to target residual mood and anxiety symptoms not resolved by nutritional restoration to a weight range above 90 per cent of ideal body weight.

Overall, while treatment literature for AN does not suggest medication offers substantial benefits, Estée's story illustrates the value of a flexible treatment approach, and the need for a multidisciplinary treatment team in which psychosocial forms of treatment play a primary role.

Bulimia nervosa

Case study: Andrea

I am a 26-year-old woman with a ten-year history of bulimia nervosa and a nearly lifelong history of mild depression. I have been in psychotherapy for several years, with steady improvements in my mood and functioning. The psychotherapy treatment has helped me understand why my eating disorder evolved, and has helped me make positive changes. I decided on a career change from the entertainment industry to teaching, which was more fulfilling; I also felt this change lessened competitive feelings over shape and weight that I harboured towards women in my former industry. Despite these changes, the psychotherapy treatment did not specifically target my bulimic behaviours and my binge eating and vomiting persisted on a near-daily basis.

Andrea

In contrast to the lack of effective pharmacological interventions for the treatment of AN, the binge eating and purging symptoms associated with BN have been shown to be responsive to medication treatments. In particular, the Federal Drug Administration (FDA) in the United States has approved fluoxetine for use in treatment of BN. Additionally, other pharmacological interventions have been studied, and many appear helpful in alleviating the disordered eating behaviours and attitudes of BN. However, because medications do not often lead to complete abstinence from binge eating and purging, pharmacological treatments for BN should usually be considered in combination with other forms of therapy.

Antidepressants

As with AN, the rationale for the use of antidepressants in the treatment of BN initially centred on the observation that these patients often exhibit mood and anxiety disturbances in addition to disordered eating behaviours. This association prompted a series of trials aimed at determining the clinical utility of antidepressants in BN, resulting in a fairly consistent body of evidence for the efficacy of antidepressants in managing this disorder.

As mentioned above, fluoxetine has been demonstrated to be effective in reducing eating disorder symptomatology and is currently the only FDA-approved medication for BN. Six randomized controlled trials have examined the efficacy of fluoxetine as compared with placebo. With the exception of one study with inpatients who were receiving concurrent psychotherapy, improvements in binge eating, purging, and eating-related attitudes were consistently reported (Shapiro *et al.* 2007). The optimal dose of fluoxetine for treating BN is 60 mg/

day, greater than the typical antidepressant dose of 20 mg/day (Fluoxetine Bulimia Nervosa Collaborative Study Group 1992). Fluoxetine has also been shown to be effective in a population of patients who responded poorly to therapy (CBT or IPT) (Walsh *et al.* 2000), and may be useful in preventing relapse following initial recovery (Romano *et al.* 2002). Interestingly, fluoxetine's mechanism of action in BN appears independent of its effect on mood (Goldstein *et al.* 1999). Based on these positive findings, fluoxetine is often considered to be a first line of treatment for BN.

Although there are fewer trials examining the efficacy of other antidepressants in BN, preliminary evidence is largely positive. The SSRI, sertraline, for example, led to a significant reduction in binge eating and purging episodes in an outpatient population as compared to placebo (Milano *et al.* 2004). Fluvoxamine, another SSRI, may decrease the likelihood of relapse following inpatient psychotherapy (Fichter *et al.* 1996). Other classes of antidepressants have also been studied and found to be effective, including the TCAs, imipramine and desipramine, and the monoamine oxidase inhibitors phenelzine and isocarboxazid (American Psychiatric Association 2006). However, because these medications can be associated with adverse side effects and strict dietary requirements, they are rarely used as a first line of BN treatment.

The antidepressant bupropion has been studied but, as mentioned previously, is not recommended for use in BN due to the high rate of grand mal seizures (Steffen *et al.* 2006). In clinical practice, therefore, SSRIs tend to be favoured due to their more benign side-effect profile and a more extensive body of research supporting their use in BN.

Other medications

Besides the more commonly used antidepressants, other agents have been found effective in decreasing the episodes of binge eating and vomiting, in a small number of trials. Topiramate, an anticonvulsant, has been shown to lead to a decrease in the frequency of binge eating, at least in the short term (Arbaizar *et al.* 2008). Other medications with evidence of efficacy include: ondansetron, typically used as an anti-emetic in patients undergoing chemotherapy; flutamide, an androgen antagonist; and trazodone (Shapiro *et al.* 2007). Finally, some medications have been evaluated for use in BN without conclusive positive findings, including reboxetine, D-fenfluramine, lithium carbonate, phenytoin and naltrexone (Steffen *et al.* 2006). It is unclear whether any of these compounds constitute effective interventions for patients with BN.

My general practitioner prescribed medications for my depression over the years, including sertraline, fluoxetine, and venlafaxine. I found the fluoxetine to be most effective and took 20 mg daily for two years. This was at least moderately helpful for mood symptoms but did not seem to ease my bulimic behaviours. My therapist prompted me to see a psychiatrist with eating disorders expertise. After evaluation, the psychiatrist recommended increasing fluoxetine to 60 mg daily. The psychiatrist also recommended a nutritional consultation, and short-term specialized CBT for BN at a nearby eating disorders clinic.

I discussed this possibility with my therapist, and began a twenty-session CBT treatment, while continuing my previous psychotherapy treatment. Within a short time after starting the CBT, and relatively concurrent with the medication increase, I was able to cease binge eating and purging behaviours.

Andrea

Conclusion

Based on the current body of research, fluoxetine remains the only FDA-approved intervention for BN. There is also preliminary evidence for the efficacy of other medications, with SSRIs usually recommended as a first approach. For Andrea, fluoxetine seemed most helpful, especially after her dosage was increased to 60 mg daily. However, even when medications help ease BN symptoms, they may not lead to complete remission on their own. For this reason, the psychiatrist's recommendation of a course of CBT in addition to the medication change likely contributed to Andrea's success. Long term, however, Andrea's prognosis is unclear, as long-term outcome of medication treatment for BN has not been extensively studied.

Eating Disorders Not Otherwise Specified (ED-NOS)

The third category of eating disorders listed in DSM-IV, Eating Disorders Not Otherwise Specified (ED-NOS), encompasses those patients with sub-threshold AN or BN, as well as patients with other forms of clinically significant eating disorder symptoms. A growing body of research is aimed at understanding and treating particular subgroups of ED-NOS, including Binge Eating Disorder (BED), night eating syndrome (NES), and purging disorder (PD).

BED is characterized by binge eating in the absence of compensatory behaviours and is often associated with obesity. While evidence is limited, three classes of medications have been studied for treating this disorder and, in general, have been found to be associated with short-term reductions in the frequency of binge eating episodes (Stefano *et al.* 2008).

Among antidepressants, SSRIs have been most extensively studied, and many have been found helpful, including fluoxetine, sertraline, citalopram, fluvoxamine, and escitalopram (American Psychiatric Association 2006). The anti-obesity medication, sibutramine, also appears useful in treating BED (Wilfley *et al.* 2008), but side effects require close monitoring (Padwal and Majumdar 2007). In particular, concerns about the cardiovascular side effects of sibutramine have led to withdrawal of approval in some countries. The anti-epileptic medications topiramate and zonisamide may also benefit patients with BED (Steffen *et al.* 2006) but these have cognitive and other side effects.

Night eating syndrome, characterized by a delay of normal circadian rhythms leading to night-time eating and insomnia, is also associated with obesity. Evidence points to SSRIs as a useful first-line treatment for night eating syndrome, with sertraline the most extensively studied (O'Reardon *et al.* 2005). Finally, though speculative, SSRIs such as fluoxetine may help treat purging disorder, characterized by frequent purging in the absence of binge eating (Keel *et al.* 2005), based on its similarity to BN. To date, no randomized controlled medication trials for the treatment of purging disorder have been published.

Conclusion

As this review of evidence for the use of pharmacological interventions in eating disorders demonstrates, we have much to learn. For patients with BN, good evidence supports the use of fluoxetine and other SSRIs. While the treatment literature is less clear for patients with AN, medications may be helpful in individual cases, and may depend on the treatment phase. Overall, there is ample reason to hope that treatments for eating disorders will improve as we learn more about the populations affected and refine current interventions. It is hoped that additional studies, for example, of olanzapine, will clarify the utility of medication for AN and other eating disorders.

References

American Psychiatric Association (APA) (2006) 'Treatment of Patients With Eating Disorders', 3rd edn, *Am J Psychiatry* 136: 4–54.

Arbaizar, B., Gomez-Acebo, I., and Llorca, J. (2008) 'Efficacy of Topiramate in Bulimia Nervosa and Binge-Eating Disorder: A Systematic Review', *Gen Hosp Psychiatry* 30: 471–5.

Attia, E., Haiman, C., Walsh, B. T., and Flater, S. R. (1998) 'Does Fluoxetine Augment the Inpatient Treatment of Anorexia Nervosa?', *Am J Psychiatry* 155: 548–51.

Biederman, J., Herzog, D. B., Rivinus, T. M., Harper, G. P., Ferber, R. A., Rosenbaum, J. F., Harmatz, J. S., Tondorf, R., Orsulak, P. J., and Schildkraut, J. J. (1985) 'Amitriptyline in the Treatment of Anorexia Nervosa: A Double-Blind, Placebo-Controlled Study', *J Clin Psychopharmacol* 5: 10–16.

Bissada, H., Tasca, G. A., Barber, A. M., and Bradwejn, J. (2008) 'Olanzapine in the Treatment of Low Body Weight and Obsessive Thinking in Women With Anorexia Nervosa: A Randomized, Double-Blind, Placebo-Controlled Trial', *Am J Psychiatry* 165: 1281–8.

Claudino, A. M., Hay, P., Lima, M. S., Bacaltchuk, J., Schmidt, U., and Treasure, J. (2006) 'Antidepressants for Anorexia Nervosa', *Cochrane Database Syst Rev*: CD004365.

Dally, P. and Sargant, W. (1966) 'Treatment and Outcome of Anorexia Nervosa', *Br Med J* 2: 793–5.

Fassino, S., Leombruni, P., Daga, G., Brustolin, A., Migliaretti, G., Cavallo, F., and Rovera, G. (2002) 'Efficacy of Citalopram in Anorexia Nervosa: A Pilot Study', *Eur Neuropsychopharmacol* 12: 453–9.

Fichter, M. M., Kruger, R., Rief, W., Holland, R., and Dohne, J. (1996) 'Fluvoxamine in Prevention of Relapse in Bulimia Nervosa: Effects on Eating-Specific Psychopathology', *J Clin Psychopharmacol* 16: 9–18.

Fluoxetine Bulimia Nervosa Collaborative Study Group (1992) 'Fluoxetine in the Treatment of Bulimia Nervosa. A Multicenter, Placebo-Controlled, Double-Blind Trial', *Arch Gen Psychiatry* 49: 139–47.

Goldstein, D. J., Wilson, M. G., Ascroft, R. C., and Al-Banna, M. (1999) 'Effectiveness of Fluoxetine Therapy in Bulimia Nervosa Regardless of Comorbid Depression', *Int J Eat Disord* 25: 19–27.

Horne, R. L., Ferguson, J. M., Pope, H. G. Jr., Hudson, J. I., Lineberry, C. G., Ascher, J., and Cato, A. (1988) 'Treatment of Bulimia with Bupropion: A Multicenter Controlled Trial', *J Clin Psychiatry* 49: 262–6.

Kaye, W. H., Frank, G. K., Bailer, U. F., Henry, S. E., Meltzer, C. C., Price, J. C., Mathis, C. A., and Wagner, A. (2005) 'Serotonin Alterations in Anorexia and Bulimia Nervosa: New Insights from Imaging Studies', *Physiol Behav* 85: 73–81.

Keel, P. K., Haedt, A., and Edler, C. (2005) 'Purging Disorder: An Ominous Variant of Bulimia Nervosa?' *Int J Eat Disord* 38: 191–9.

Kruger, S. and Kennedy, S. H. (2000) 'Psychopharmacotherapy of Anorexia Nervosa, Bulimia Nervosa and Binge-Eating Disorder', *J Psychiatry Neurosci* 25: 497–508.

Lacey, J. H. and Crisp, A. H. (1980) 'Hunger, Food Intake and Weight: The Impact of Clomipramine on a Refeeding Anorexia Nervosa Population', *Postgrad Med J* 56 (Suppl. 1): 79–85.

McKnight, R. F. and Park, R. J. (2010) 'Atypical Antipsychotics and Anorexia Nervosa: A Review', *Eur Eat Disord Rev* 18: 10–21.

Milano, W., Petrella, C., Sabatino, C., and Capasso, A. (2004) 'Treatment of Bulimia Nervosa with Sertraline: A Randomized Controlled Trial', *Adv Ther* 21: 232–7.

O'Reardon, J. P., Peshek, A., and Allison, K. C. (2005) 'Night Eating Syndrome: Diagnosis, Epidemiology and Management', *CNS Drug Reviews* 19: 997–1008.

Padwal, R. S., and Majumdar, S. R. (2007) 'Drug Treatments for Obesity: Orlistat, Sibutramine, and Rimonabant', *The Lancet* 369: 71–7.

Romano, S. J., Halmi, K. A., Sarkar, N. P., Koke, S. C., and Lee, J. S. (2002) 'A Placebo-Controlled Study of Fluoxetine in Continued Treatment of Bulimia Nervosa After Successful Acute Fluoxetine Treatment', *Am J Psychiatry* 159: 96–102.

Santonastaso, P., Friederici, S., and Favaro, A. (2001) 'Sertraline in the Treatment of Restricting Anorexia Nervosa: An Open Controlled Trial', *J Child Adolesc Psychopharmacol* 11: 143–50.

Shapiro, J. R., Berkman, N. D., Brownley, K. A., Sedway, J. A., Lohr, K. N., and Bulik, C. M. (2007) 'Bulimia Nervosa Treatment: A Systematic Review of Randomized Controlled Trials', *Int J Eat Disord* 40: 321–36.

Stefano, S. C., Bacaltchuk, J., Blay, S. L., and Appolinario, J. C. (2008) 'Antidepressants in Short-Term Treatment of Binge Eating Disorder: Systematic Review and Meta-Analysis', *Eat Behav* 9: 129–36.

Steffen, K. J., Roerig, J. L., Mitchell, J. E., and Uppala, S. (2006) 'Emerging Drugs for Eating Disorder Treatment', *Expert Opin Emerg Drugs* 11: 315–36.

Walsh, B. T., Agras, W. S., Devlin, M. J., Fairburn, C. G., Wilson, G. T., Kahn, C., and Chally, M. K. (2000) 'Fluoxetine for Bulimia Nervosa Following Poor Response to Psychotherapy', *Am J Psychiatry* 157: 1332–4.

Walsh, B. T., Kaplan, A. S., Attia, E., Olmsted, M., Parides, M., Carter, J. C., Pike, K. M., Devlin, M. J., Woodside, B., Roberto, C. A., and Rockert, W. (2006) 'Fluoxetine After Weight Restoration in Anorexia Nervosa: A Randomized Controlled Trial', *JAMA* 295: 2605–12.

Wilfley, D. E., Crow, S. J., Hudson, J. I., Mitchell, J. E., Berkowitz, R. I., Blakesley, V., and Walsh, B. T. (2008) 'Efficacy of Sibutramine for the Treatment of Binge Eating Disorder: A Randomized Multicenter Placebo-Controlled Double-Blind Study', *Am J Psychiatry* 165: 51–8.

Chapter 10

Psychotherapies in eating disorders

Tracey D. Wade and Hunna J. Watson

Psychotherapies that have been evaluated with randomised controlled trials (RCTs) are the focus of this chapter. For adults with anorexia nervosa (AN) the consensus is that specialist care should include nutritional rehabilitation and weight restoration, in addition to psychotherapy. Among children and adolescents with AN, family-based interventions that collaboratively address the eating disorder have been the most evaluated and supported. Cognitive behaviour therapy (CBT) is indicated as the treatment of choice for adults with bulimia nervosa (BN). Interpersonal psychotherapy (IPT) is a viable alternative but may take longer to improve symptoms. For children/adolescents with BN, psychotherapies with supporting evidence include CBT-based approaches and family-based treatment that directly targets symptoms. Binge eating disorder (BED) can be treated with CBT of a less intensive variety than is required for BN.

Primary care professionals have an essential role in the treatment of eating disorders, providing initiation and coordination of specialist care, and monitoring and treatment of medical complications.

> **Case study: Susan**
>
> I am 19 years old and developed AN four years ago. My parents have both worked full-time for most of my life. Nothing remarkable happened in my life until I turned 15. During the summer holidays of that year I broke up a relationship with a possessive boyfriend who threatened to kill himself if I broke off the relationship. He subsequently took an overdose but survived. This event made me feel that a retreat from sexuality would be a good thing and simplify life. My parents were busy and unavailable at this time and I remember thinking: 'I won't eat and I hope people notice'.
>
> Susan

Susan started to increase exercise, cut out snacks, and decrease intake at meals. By age 16, she had decreased her body mass index (BMI) from 23.7 to 16.2, and she spent two months in hospital getting nasogastric refeeding. At age 17 she maintained her BMI at 19.3 with the help of her mother who encouraged her to eat, but she refused further professional help. At 18 years Susan left home, and within twelve months her BMI was 15.7. She had presented for help on one occasion to a non-specialist counsellor whom she found to be unsympathetic. Susan was becoming concerned about her condition as she didn't want to get old and still have AN.

Case study: Melanie

I am a 26-year-old working in the health profession, and I have an eight-year history of BN. My illness started when my first serious relationship with a boy broke up. To feel better about myself I started dieting and losing weight, and received many positive comments about my appearance. Within six months I began an extremely restrictive diet, often not eating during the day until the evening meal. Soon after this, I started binge eating during the evening, and then during the day. I then started inducing vomiting in an effort to prevent weight gain from the binge eating. At times I was bingeing and vomiting six times a day. The course of my symptoms has fluctuated over time, improving when life is going well, but worsening when stressful life events occur, especially those related to significant relationships. I have been too embarrassed to seek treatment, but have now asked my general practitioner to refer me to someone for help, as my eating is interfering with my ability to work and socialise.

Melanie

Overview

As the case studies illustrate, getting appropriate psychotherapeutic help for an eating disorder can be more difficult than for other psychological disorders. First, the person is typically ambivalent if not resistant to the idea of seeking treatment, due to shame and embarrassment or having overvalued beliefs about the importance of body shape and weight goals. Second, finding specialists who can offer a long-term and effective service can be difficult. Third, the person may start and drop out of treatment on several occasions, due to ambivalence about change.

Given these difficulties, it is not surprising that many different psychotherapeutic approaches are tried for eating disorders. However, relatively few of these approaches have been rigorously evaluated. The focus of the current chapter is to provide an overview of those psychotherapies that have been evaluated using the best-practice methodology, namely RCTs, where the psychotherapy is compared to another condition, which could be a 'no treatment' condition, or, as is typical for AN, some other credible psychotherapy. Across the eating disorders, we provide tables summarising the *number* of RCTs (one trial = low, 2–4 = moderate, and five or more = high) and the *magnitude of effect* at follow-up (none = no beneficial effect; low = slight beneficial effect; moderate = moderate beneficial effect; substantial = substantial and persistent effect). In order to inform these tables, reviews of treatment studies and reports from individual treatment studies have been accessed from 2004 onwards for this purpose. Overall, thirty-five reviews and 116 possible RCTs pertaining to treatment were published over this time – further information on the methodology and a full list of the references are contained in Watson *et al.* (2010).

Anorexia nervosa

Children and adolescents

Relatively few psychotherapeutic approaches have been evaluated for children and adolescents. As shown in Table 10.1, family-based therapies are the most evaluated and supported by the evidence, with the Maudsley family-based

Table 10.1 Summary of the strength of evidence for different psychotherapeutic approaches for anorexia nervosa

Treatment approach	Degree to which evaluated	Magnitude of effect
Anorexia nervosa – children and adolescents		
Cognitive behaviour therapy	Low	Moderate
Ego-oriented therapy	Low	Moderate
Maudsley family-based treatment	High	Substantial
Inpatient psychiatric treatment	Low	Moderate
Specialised outpatient treatment	Low	Moderate
Anorexia nervosa – adults		
Behavioural therapy	Low	Low
Cognitive analytic therapy	Low	Low
Cognitive behaviour therapy	High	Low
Maudsley family-based treatment	Low	Low
Family therapy (non-Maudsley therapy)	Low	Low
Focal psychoanalytic therapy	Low	Low
Interpersonal psychotherapy	Low	None
Refeeding	Low	Low
Specialist supportive clinical management	Low	Low

treatment (FBT) being the most researched. FBT is markedly different from traditional family therapy. This therapy views the eating disorder symptoms as a complex interaction of aetiologic factors, where unhelpful family communications and relationships are seen to be a consequence of the illness, and the family is viewed as an essential resource to aid in the individual's recovery. In the first phase of treatment, the exclusive focus is on refeeding, where parents are charged with taking control over this process. Two subsequent phases are included, namely transferring control over eating back to the young person and addressing psychosocial and other issues such as comorbidity and family relationships.

Eisler and colleagues (2000) compared a one-year programme of conjoint family therapy to separated family therapy in forty outpatients with AN. The total patient group experienced an average 13 kg weight gain, and significant improvement in weight, bulimic symptoms, obsessionality, eating disorder attitudes and behaviours, self-esteem, and mood. Conjoint family therapy was superior to separated family therapy in improving traits related to eating disorders, mood, obessionality, and psychosocial functioning. A recent study showed good maintenance of gains at four-year follow-up for the entire group where 89 per cent of participants had a healthy body weight and 91 per cent of postmenarcheal females had menstrual return (Lock *et al.* 2006).

FBT has been compared to individual approaches, namely CBT (Ball and Mitchell 2004) and ego-oriented therapy (Robin *et al.* 1994). CBT programmes aim to alter unhelpful thinking processes and behaviours that maintain eating disorders, and directly address behaviours such as excessive dietary restriction, laxative and diuretic misuse, purging, and over-exercising, with an emphasis on improving nutritional health. They may address additional factors implicated in the maintenance of AN, such as low self-esteem, perfectionism, poor interpersonal functioning, and difficulties with emotion regulation. Ego-oriented therapy focuses on building coping skills, on developing one's identity (i.e. beyond the pursuit of thinness), and on addressing interpersonal issues regarding physical, social, and emotional maturation. With respect to CBT, 78 per cent of completers in each group had a good outcome at the end of treatment. At twelve-month follow-up, 80 per cent of the FBT group and 69 per cent of the ego-oriented therapy group were at or above target weight and 93 per cent of the FBT and 80 per cent of the ego-oriented therapy participants had resumed or commenced menses.

More recently a comparison between FBT and ego-oriented therapy (renamed adolescent-focused individual therapy) has been conducted by James Lock and colleagues (2010). While there was no difference between the groups at the end of treatment with respect to full remission, FBT was significantly superior in this respect at six- and twelve-month follow-up. However, given that over the follow-up period both groups made similar gains in body mass index and eating psychopathology, it was concluded that individual therapy was a good alternative where FBT is not possible.

In summary, while inpatient treatment for adolescents can be indicated for acute medical concerns, the data to date support the use of outpatient treatment using FBT. If such an approach had been used with Susan, the course of her illness might have been shorter and nasogastric refeeding might have been avoided. However, further research is required to compare FBT to other credible therapies and to investigate FBT effectiveness among those with a longer duration of illness (i.e. more than three years).

Adults

As shown in Table 10.1, the research relating to adults is less conclusive, with a high dropout rate a major impediment to progress. With the exception of CBT, only one RCT exists for each different psychotherapeutic approach. A significant difference between active treatments was shown by Pike and colleagues (2003), where patients who were weight-restored during inpatient treatment and then received CBT over one year post-discharge did better than people offered nutritional counselling in the post-discharge period. In terms of relapse risk reduction, only 22 per cent relapsed with CBT versus 53 per cent with nutritional counselling, and significantly more patients who received CBT met criteria for a good outcome.

Another significant difference was shown for the use of refeeding (Rigaud *et al.* 2007), where eighty-one individuals with AN undergoing standard psychiatric treatment (dietary treatment, behaviour therapy, psychotherapy, and self-help group sessions) were randomised to eight weeks of refeeding or treatment-as-usual control. At post-treatment, those in the refeeding group achieved superior weight gain, gain in fat-free mass, and total energy intake compared to treatment-as-usual. After discharge, the relapse-free period was significantly higher in refed versus treatment-as-usual patients.

Recent interest has been shown in specialist supportive clinical management, shown to be significantly superior to IPT and CBT, where good outcome was attained by 0 per cent in IPT, 5 per cent in CBT, and 25 per cent in specialist supportive clinical management at the end of the twenty-week treatment phase (McIntosh *et al.* 2005). However, as with all the studies described here that show significant differences between different conditions, replication is required before these approaches can be confidently recommended as treatments of choice.

In conclusion, in the face of such outcomes, it is important to understand that weight restoration alone does not substantially alter the natural course of AN, necessitating consideration of other approaches including psychotherapy. Second, specialist treatment is significantly better than no treatment. In an early study with adolescent and young adult females, Crisp and colleagues (1991) established that various psychotherapies (group, individual, inpatient) were superior to no treatment, with no differences between the active treatments, albeit inpatient treatment was associated with a higher level of dropout. As summarised by Hay and Claudino (2010: 471): 'There is consensus on the need for specialist care that includes nutritional rehabilitation and weight restoration in addition to psychotherapy.'

Bulimia nervosa

Adolescents

While older adolescents are routinely entered into adult treatment studies for BN, only two studies focus solely on adolescents with BN, making it difficult to identify a preferred approach, as shown in Table 10.2. A comparison between CBT guided self-care and FBT (Schmidt *et al.* 2007) showed that at six months, bingeing had undergone a significantly greater reduction in the guided self-care group. While this difference disappeared at twelve months, the conclusion was that CBT guided self-care has the slight advantage of offering a more rapid reduction of bingeing, lower cost, and greater acceptability for adolescents with BN or subclinical BN. A second study (Le Grange *et al.* 2007) supported the use of FBT adapted for BN, whereby binge-and-purge abstinence was significantly higher for those treated with FBT compared to supportive psychotherapy at post-treatment (39 per cent versus 18 per cent) and six-month follow-up (29 per cent versus 10 per cent).

Adults

As can be seen in Table 10.2, CBT and related approaches have been the most examined and supported treatment for BN. In a review of RCT data, Hay and colleagues (2004) reported a significant effect favouring CBT over wait-list or no-treatment on a variety of indicators, and comparisons of CBT with other psychotherapies revealed significant differences favouring CBT on abstinence rate with no differences on bulimic symptoms, general psychiatric symptoms, or psychosocial/interpersonal functioning. Shapiro and colleagues (2007) summarised twelve trials and found that CBT performed better than exposure therapy, supportive therapy, nutritional counselling, and nondirective psychodynamic treatment. CBT performed similarly to IPT in one study at one-year follow-up, but was associated with a faster rate of improvement from pretreatment to endpoint.

Given this body of research, some specific recommendations can be made with respect to the use of psychotherapy with BN, as recommended by the National Institute for Clinical Excellence guidelines (2004). First, guided self-help based on a CBT approach is considered a front-line treatment. Second, for those who require more intensive treatment, a specialist therapist can offer CBT. A study by Fairburn and colleagues (2009) suggests that CBT-enhanced (focused), which focuses on eating- and weight-related behaviours and cognitions, can be used, or, for those people who have pronounced problems with clinical perfectionism, low self-esteem, interpersonal difficulties or mood intolerance, CBT-enhanced (broad) can be used, which additionally focuses on the identified problematic issue. Across the whole sample, at endpoint 53 per cent of all patients with BN and 61 per cent at follow-up had a global eating disorder psychopathology score less than one standard deviation above the community mean. Third, if CBT is not

Table 10.2 Summary of the strength of evidence for different psychotherapeutic approaches for bulimia nervosa

Treatment approach	Degree to which evaluated	Magnitude of effect
Bulimia nervosa – adolescents		
Cognitive behaviour therapy guided self-help	Low	Moderate
Maudsley family-based treatment	Low	Moderate
Bulimia nervosa – adults		
Active light	Low	None
Cognitive behaviour therapy	High	Substantial
Cognitive behaviour therapy guided self-help	Moderate	Substantial
Cognitive behaviour therapy pure self-help	Moderate	Low
Cognitive behaviour therapy + antidepressant medication	Moderate	Moderate
Cognitive behaviour therapy pure self-help + antidepressant medication	Moderate	Moderate
Crisis intervention	Low	None
Dialetical behaviour therapy	Low	Moderate
Guided imagery	Low	Moderate
Interpersonal psychotherapy	Moderate	Substantial
Multimodal day programme	Low	Moderate
Multimodal inpatient programme	Low	Moderate
Nutritional management	Low	Low
Repetitive transcranial magnetic stimulation	Low	None
Stress management	Low	Low

Note: Pure self-help refers to providing the client with a self-help book and guided self-help refers to provision of the self-help book and a limited number of sessions (e.g. six to eight) with a therapist to help guide the person through the book and the associated homework assignments.

indicated for some reason then IPT is a viable alternative, as long as the client is aware that it takes longer to lead to significant improvement than CBT. IPT may be particularly useful for a client such as Melanie in our case study, where deterioration in eating is triggered by interpersonal events. Use of antidepressant medication is also an option, as outlined in the preceding chapter, 'Pharmacotherapy of eating disorders'.

With both AN and BN, where the disordered eating does not quite meet the diagnostic criteria for an eating disorder it is recommended that the clinician follow the guidelines on the treatment of the eating problem that most closely resembles the patient's eating disorder (National Institute for Clinical Excellence 2004: 5).

Binge eating disorder

BED tends to have a later onset, usually around the mid-twenties, and so treatment approaches have been examined with adults only. In general, BED is best treated the same way as BN, where 'less intensive and non-specialist CBT is likely to be efficacious, combined where appropriate with weight management strategies, either behavioural or pharmacologic' (Hay and Claudino 2010: 471). BED is often comorbid with overweight and obesity, and Table 10.3 indicates that behavioural weight loss approaches may be an effective non-pharmacologic weight management strategy. In such interventions strict dieting and an ideal weight goal are discouraged – instead the emphasis is on healthy and balanced eating, a pattern of moderate and consistent dietary restraint, and an achievable, realistic, healthy weight range. This approach will not conflict with the goal of decreasing the frequency of binge eating – unlike some weight management strategies which over-emphasise dietary restriction and specific weight goals, which are well-established triggers for bingeing.

Table 10.3 Summary of the strength of evidence for different psychotherapeutic approaches for binge eating disorder

Treatment approach	Degree to which evaluated	Magnitude of effect
Binge eating disorder in adults		
Behavioural weight loss	Moderate	Moderate
Behavioural weight loss guided self-help	Low	Low
Behavioural weight loss + antidepressant medication	Low	Moderate
Behavioural weight loss + cognitive behaviour therapy	Low	Moderate
Behavioural weight loss + cognitive behaviour therapy + antidepressant medication	Low	Moderate
Cognitive behaviour therapy	High	Substantial
Cognitive behaviour therapy guided self-help	Moderate	Moderate
Cognitive behaviour therapy pure self-help	Moderate	Moderate
Cognitive behaviour therapy + anticonvulsant medication	Low	Moderate
Cognitive behaviour therapy + antidepressant medication	Moderate	Low
Cognitive behaviour therapy guided self-help + obesity medication	Low	Moderate, Low for +OM
Cognitive behaviour therapy pure self-help + motivational interviewing	Low	Moderate
Virtual-reality-based therapy	Low	Low

Treatment guidelines

- American Psychiatric Association (APA) (2006) *Practice Guidelines for the Treatment of Patients with Eating Disorders*, 3rd edn, Washington, DC: American Psychiatric Association.
- National Institute for Clinical Excellence (2004) *Eating Disorders: Core Interventions in the Treatment and Management of Anorexia Nervosa, Bulimia Nervosa and Related Eating Disorders. Clinical Guideline 9*, London: NICE.

Evidence-based treatment manuals

- Cooper, M., Todd, G., and Wells, A. (2009) *Treating Bulimia Nervosa and Binge Eating: An Integrated Metacognitive and Cognitive Therapy Manual*, London: Routledge.
- Fairburn, C.G. (2008) *Cognitive Behavior Therapy and Eating Disorders*, New York: Guilford Press. A transdiagnostic approach developed for use with adults with all types of eating disorders.
- Grilo, C.M. and Mitchell, J.E. (2010) *The Treatment of Eating Disorders: A Clinical Handbook*, New York: Guilford Press. This edited book contains eleven 'mini-manuals' covering treatments for AN, BN and BED.
- Le Grange, D. and Lock, J. (2007) *Treating Bulimia in Adolescents: A Family-Based Approach*, New York: Guilford Press.
- Lock, J., Le Grange, D., Agras, S., and Dare, C. (2002) *Treatment Manual for Anorexia Nervosa: A Family-Based Approach*, New York: Guilford Press.
- Waller, G., Cordery, H., Corstorphine, E., Hinrichsen, H., Lawson, R., Mountford, V., and Russell, K. (2007) *Cognitive Behavioural Therapy for Eating Disorders. A Comprehensive Treatment Guide*, Cambridge: Cambridge University Press.

Evidence-based self-help books

- Cooper, M., Todd, G., and Wells, A. (2000) *Bulimia Nervosa: A Cognitive Therapy Programme for Clients*, London: Jessica Kingsley.
- Cooper, P.J. (1993) *Bulimia Nervosa and Binge Eating: A Guide to Recovery*, London: Robinson.
- Fairburn, C.G. (1995) *Overcoming Binge Eating*, New York: Guilford Press.
- Schmidt, U. and Treasure, J. (1993) *Getting Better Bit(e) by Bit(e): A Survival Kit for Sufferers of Bulimia Nervosa and Binge Eating Disorders*, Hove: Brunner-Routledge.

Evidence-based books for carers

- Lock, J. and Le Grange, D. (2005) *Help Your Teenager Beat an Eating Disorder*, New York: Guilford Press.

- Treasure, J., Smith, G., and Crane, A. (2007) *Skills Based Learning for Caring for a Loved One with an Eating Disorder: The New Maudsley Method*, London: Routledge.

References

Ball, J. and Mitchell, P. (2004) 'A randomized controlled study of cognitive behavior therapy and behavioral therapy for anorexia nervosa patients', *Eat Disord* 12: 303–14.

Crisp, A.H., Norton, K., Gowers, S., Halek, C., Bowyer, C., Yeldham, D., Levett, G., and Bhat, A. (1991) 'A controlled study of the effect of therapies aimed at adolescent and family psychopathology in anorexia nervosa', *Br J Psychiatry* 159: 325–33.

Eisler, I., Dare, C., Hodes, M., Russell, G., Dodge, E., and Le Grange, D. (2000) 'Family therapy for adolescent anorexia nervosa: The results of a controlled comparison of two family interventions', *J Child Psychol Psychiatry* 41: 727–36.

Fairburn, C.G., Cooper, Z., Doll, H.A., O'Connor, M.E., Bohn, K., Hawker, D.M., Wales, J.A., and Palmer, R.L. (2009) 'Transdiagnostic cognitive-behavioral therapy for patients with eating disorders: A two-site trial with 60-week follow-up', *Am J Psychiatry* 166: 311–19.

*Hay, P.J., and Claudino, A. de M. (2010) 'Evidence-based treatment for the eating disorders', in W.S. Agras (ed.) *The Oxford Handbook of Eating Disorders* (pp. 452–79), New York: Oxford University Press.

*Hay, P.J., Bacaltchuk, J., Stefano, S., and Kasahyap, P. (2004) 'Psychological treatments for bulimia nervosa and binging', *Cochrane Database of Systematic Reviews* 3: CD000562. DOI: 10.1002/14651858.CD000562.pub2.

Le Grange, D., Crosby, R.D., Rathouz, P.J., and Leventhal, B.L. (2007) 'A randomized controlled comparison of family-based treatment and supportive psychotherapy for adolescent bulimia nervosa', *Arch Gen Psychiatry* 64: 1049–56.

Lock, J., Couturier, J., and Agras, S. (2006) 'Comparison of long-term outcomes in adolescents with anorexia nervosa treated with family therapy', *J Am Acad Child Adolesc Psychiatry* 45: 666–72.

Lock, J., Le Grange D., Agras, W.S., Moye, A., Bryson, S.W., and Jo, B. (2010) 'Randomized clinical trial comparing family-based treatment with adolescent-focused individual therapy for anorexia nervosa', *Arch Gen Psychiatry* 67: 1025–1032.

McIntosh, V., Jordan, J., Carter, F., Luty, S., McKenzie, J., Bulik, C., Framptom, C.M., and Joyce, P.R. (2005) 'Three psychotherapies for anorexia nervosa: A randomized controlled trial', *Am J Psychiatry* 162: 741–7.

National Institute for Clinical Excellence (NICE) (2004) *Eating Disorders: Core Interventions in the Treatment and Management of Anorexia Nervosa, Bulimia Nervosa and Related Eating Disorders. Clinical Guideline 9*, London: NICE.

Pike, K.M., Walsh, B.T., Vitousek, K., Wilson, G.T., and Bauer, J. (2003) 'Cognitive behavior therapy in the posthospitalization treatment of anorexia nervosa', *Am J Psychiatry* 160: 2046–9.

Rigaud, D., Brondel, L., Poupard, A.T., Talonneau, I., and Brun, J.M. (2007) 'A randomized trial on the efficacy of a 2-month tube refeeding regimen in anorexia nervosa: A 1-year follow-up study', *Clin Nutr* 26: 421–9.

Robin, A.L., Siegel, P.T., Koepke, T., Moye, A.W., and Tice, S. (1994) 'Family therapy versus individual therapy for adolescent females with anorexia nervosa', *J Dev Behav Pediatr* 15: 111–16.

Schmidt, U., Lee, S., Beecham, J., Perkins, S., Treasure, J., Yi, I., Winn, S., Robinson, P., Murphy, R., Keville, S., Johnson-Sabine, E., Jenkins, M., Frost, S., Didge, L., Berelowitz, M., and Eisler, I. (2007) 'A randomized controlled trial of family therapy and cognitive behavior therapy guided self-care for adolescents with bulimia nervosa and related disorders', *Am J Psychiatry* 164: 591–8.

*Shapiro, J.R., Berkman, N.D., Brownley, K.A., Sedway, J.A., Lohr, K.N., and Bulik, C.M. (2007) 'Bulimia nervosa treatment: A systematic review of randomized controlled trials', *Int J Eat Disord* 40: 321–36.

*Watson, H.J., Elphick, R., Dreher, C., Steele, A., and Wilksch, S. (2010) *Eating Disorders Prevention and Management: An Evidence Review.* Prepared for the Commonwealth Department of Health and Ageing by the Butterfly Foundation on behalf of the National Eating Disorders Collaboration Project.

*Reviews of treatments

Chapter 11

Families as an integral part of the treatment team

Treatment culture and standard of care challenges

Renee Rienecke Hoste, Angela Celio Doyle and Daniel Le Grange

---

Case study

My 24-year-old daughter is recovering from anorexia. When her eating disorder appeared twelve years ago we sought the best, most reputable, treatment available. This included several extended inpatient stays. Our family was largely excluded, except for participation in infrequent 'family' therapy sessions in which the aetiology of our daughter's eating disorder was explored. The suggestion was that some pathology within the family was to blame.

Leslie

History of the family in eating disorder treatment

The role of the family in the onset, development, and maintenance of eating disorders has a long and often negative history. Although families were not initially blamed for causing the illnesses, even the earliest description of treatment for anorexia nervosa (AN) involved removing the patient from the parental home (Morton 1694). This approach to treatment continued almost 200 years later, as described by Louis-Victor Marcé in 1860:

> This hypochondriacal delirium, then, cannot be advantageously encountered so long as the subjects remain in the midst of their own family and their habitual circle ... It is therefore indispensable to change the habitation and surrounding circumstances, and to entrust the patients to the care of strangers.
>
> (Marcé 1860: 265)

Sir William Gull, who coined the term 'anorexia nervosa' in 1873, also believed that 'patients should be fed at regular intervals and surrounded by persons who would have moral control over them; relations and friends being generally the worst attendants' (Gull 1874: 26). Contemporaries of Gull suggested that patients with AN '*must be removed entirely from their usual domestic surroundings, involving, as they always do, much that is unwholesome for the patient and tending directly to foster perversion of the ego*' (Silverman 1997: 5). Jean-Martin Charcot had perhaps one of the more direct and damning statements in regard to the role of the family in treatment:

> Admission to the hospital enabled me to effect … the absence of the father and mother, who had themselves become very nervous, and whose presence would … prevent any effective treatment … it is necessary to separate growing and adult children from their father and mother whose influence, as experience shows, is especially pernicious.
>
> (Charcot 1888: 15–17)

These early physicians clearly felt that patients would benefit from being separated from their family members during the treatment process (an approach that would later come to be colloquially known as 'parentectomy'), but often stopped short of identifying families as the cause of the illness. By the early 1900s, however, a British physician reported that 'unhappy or ill-conducted homes, sometimes with "spoiling" by foolish parents, were largely to blame' for the development of AN in several of his patients (Ryle 1936: 895). During the 1960s and 1970s, seminal works by influential theorists suggested that eating disorders were driven by desires for autonomy, independence, and separation from one's parents (Bruch 1962; Selvini Palazzoli 1974), and that families of individuals with AN were characterized by enmeshment, overprotectiveness, rigidity, and lack of conflict resolution (Minuchin *et al.* 1975, 1978). Rather than excluding parents from treatment, these theorists believed parents should be involved in treatment to change the problematic patterns of interaction that led to the eating disorder's development. Unfortunately, this also contributed to treatment providers attributing disordered eating to familial psychopathology, resulting in parents experiencing much blame and guilt.

However, research has not supported the existence of an 'anorexogenic' family (Dare *et al.* 1994), putting into question the assumption that familial psychopathology is necessary for an eating disorder to develop. In fact, research has generally not confirmed that family functioning is a specific risk factor for eating disorders (Jacobi *et al.* 2004). Eating disorders are complex illnesses with sociocultural, psychological, and genetic components, all of which may need to be present for an eating disorder to develop. Problematic family interactions, such as parental criticism about shape and weight, may contribute to the development of an eating disorder (Fairburn *et al.* 1997), but are likely to be one piece of the puzzle rather than the sole cause of the illness.

Clinical efforts have also contributed to a paradigm shift in which families are beginning to be regarded as a resource during treatment, rather than an obstacle. Work at the Maudsley Hospital in London has perhaps been the most influential in this regard. The development of family-based treatment (sometimes referred to as the 'Maudsley method or approach'), and growing empirical support for its efficacy, have shown that involving parents in the treatment of their eating disordered child can lead to a positive outcome. It also suggests that problematic family interactions may develop as a result of living with someone with an eating disorder. Although the role of parents in the aetiology of eating disorders is unclear, what is clear is that living with an eating disordered individual has a profound impact on all family members. The eating disordered individual may gradually become the focus of the family (Nielsen and Bara-Carril 2003) and medical complications associated with the illness can be a tremendous emotional and financial burden. Unsurprisingly, families presenting for treatment may appear 'dysfunctional', but the idea that this dysfunction followed development of the eating disorder, rather than caused development of the eating disorder, is becoming more widely accepted (Lacey and Price 2004; Le Grange and Eisler 2008; Nielsen and Bara-Carril 2003).

Families are now seen as integral to the treatment of children and adolescents with eating disorders. In a recent position paper, the Academy for Eating Disorders stated: 'families should be involved routinely in the treatment of most young people with an eating disorder' (Le Grange et al. 2010: 4). Family-based treatment has been shown to be effective in the treatment of adolescent AN (Eisler et al. 2000; Le Grange et al. 1992; Lock et al. 2006; Robin et al. 1999; Russell et al. 1987) and there is evidence that it is effective for adolescents with bulimia nervosa (Le Grange et al. 2007). This treatment approach will be reviewed next.

Family-based treatment for anorexia nervosa

Family-based treatment (FBT) is an outpatient treatment consisting of 15–20 sessions over six to 12 months. Unlike many psychotherapeutic approaches, FBT does not assume to know the cause of the eating disorder, and there is little emphasis on trying to uncover possible contributing factors. Because of the serious medical and psychological consequences of AN, the goals of this symptom-focused treatment are to rapidly restore a child to physical health and minimize the impact of AN on the child's developmental trajectory. In contrast to historical views on the role of the family in treatment, FBT utilizes the family as the primary resource in the recovery process (Lock et al. 2001).

In the first of three phases of treatment, parents are provided with psychoeducation about the nature of AN. It is explained that the ego-syntonic nature of the illness generally prevents sufferers from appreciating the danger they are in and willingly making changes to reverse their state of starvation. Thus, parents are asked to temporarily take charge of their child's eating until the AN has loosened its grip and the child is able to once again make these decisions on his or her own. At the same time, the therapist aligns the patient with his or her siblings, placing the siblings in a supportive role and leaving the task of weight restoration solely to the parents. The resistance often encountered by parents during the weight restoration process can be quite difficult. Throughout treatment the therapist emphasizes the importance of maintaining a non-blaming stance toward the patient and helping the parents remember that their child is not in control of the eating disordered behaviours.

Families are ready to move into the second phase of treatment when the patient is nearing his or her ideal body weight and resistance to parental control over eating has decreased. During this phase, parents gradually hand back control over eating to their child. The extent of responsibility returned to the child will depend largely on the child's age and on the eating habits that were typical of the family prior to the onset of the eating disorder.

The third phase begins when the child has reached a healthy weight and the eating disorder symptoms have largely subsided. With the eating disorder no longer impeding the patient's development, the focus shifts to a discussion of ways in which parents can support their child through the developmental challenges of adolescence that lie ahead.

Family-based treatment for bulimia nervosa

Family-based treatment for bulimia nervosa (BN) comprises three similar phases. Instead of focusing on weight restoration, however, parents are encouraged to help their child regulate his or her eating and reduce binge eating and purging. FBT for BN tends to take a more collaborative approach, with the adolescent patient working with the parents to change eating disordered behaviour. This approach is possible in part because BN is often experienced as ego-dystonic and thus the adolescent is more motivated to change.

The medical and psychological comorbidities that often accompany both AN and BN necessitate a team approach to treatment, with a therapist to guide FBT, a physician to monitor medical stability and, if necessary, a psychiatrist to manage psychotropic medications. Unfortunately, although FBT is a potentially life-saving treatment option, many families are not receiving this treatment.

Empirically supported treatments

Families deserve to know more about evidence-based care. My daughter lost twelve years of her life – most of her childhood – to misinformed treatment. Many treatment providers still subscribe to outdated notions about this disease.

Not until recently, after ten years of disordered eating and seven inpatient stays at five different facilities, did we learn about Maudsley. It made sense to us. My husband is a scientist and I'm a science teacher. The method was based on scientific data and seemed more reasonable than

> other models. With the Maudsley method, our daughter was not expected to come up with the motivation to get better and/or search for some event in her past that made her get sick. My husband and I were able to be an active part of her treatment.
>
> Leslie

The use of empirically supported treatments (ESTs) is gaining attention. Ethical considerations suggest that patients deserve to have access to treatment approaches that have been shown to be effective. Although additional studies are needed, family-based treatment currently has the strongest empirical support for adolescents under the age of 18 who have had AN for less than three years (Fisher *et al.* 2010; Keel and Haedt 2008; Lock and Le Grange 2005). Fewer data are available to support any one approach in the treatment of BN, but FBT and cognitive behavioural therapy show early promise in the literature (Le Grange *et al.* 2007; Schmidt *et al.* 2007).

Unfortunately there are several barriers to practitioners utilizing FBT and other ESTs in actual clinical practice. First, FBT is different from more typical psychotherapeutic treatment in that it first and foremost emphasizes the medical crisis of AN and focuses on rapid weight restoration before attending to psychosocial concerns. Second, many therapists have not received training in FBT, as formal training opportunities for FBT were limited until several years ago.

Therapist manuals are available for AN (Lock *et al.* 2001) and BN (Le Grange and Lock 2007), which allow practitioners to learn the approaches on their own. Also, the Training Institute for Child and Adolescent Eating Disorders provides therapists with the opportunity to become fully trained and certified in FBT. Several training workshops are required as part of the certification process and experienced therapists provide thorough supervision prior to granting of full certification (details: www.train2treat4ed.com).

Incomplete knowledge of or misconceptions about ESTs may dissuade therapists from using an approach or parents from seeking that particular treatment. For example, misconceptions of FBT include the belief that it involves 'force feeding'; that its focus is weight restoration, ignoring the psychological needs of the patient; that FBT is not appropriate for older adolescents; and that certain families (e.g. single parents) are unable to use this approach effectively. Even therapists trained in FBT may encounter resistance from misinformed treatment providers also involved in the patient's care, making the requisite team approach quite challenging. These misconceptions are damaging, and public and professional education may help to assuage worries that a particular EST will not work or, worse, is harmful. Parent-led advocacy groups and education organizations, such as www.maudsleyparents.org and www.effectivechildtherapy.com, are helping to raise awareness.

Other treatments for eating disorders that include parents in the therapeutic process are being evaluated and may accumulate empirical support. For instance, Adolescent Focused Therapy (also referred to as Ego-Oriented Individual Therapy) has demonstrated good outcomes in two randomized controlled trials (Lock *et al.*, 2010; Robin *et al.* 1999). While the treatment is focused on individual meetings with the adolescent, one-quarter of the sessions are reserved for parent meetings. Additionally, in a current randomized controlled trial at the University of Chicago and Stanford University evaluating cognitive behavioural therapy for adolescents with BN, parental involvement is expected.

Conclusion

It's hard not to be embittered by the damage we suffered as a family. Most difficult to reconcile is the ineffective treatment our daughter endured and the time lost before we found the Maudsley method. As our daughter became re-nourished we were amazed at how her eating disordered behaviours peeled away, her depression lifted and her anxiety disappeared. Today she is happy and healthy! I continue to be stunned by the transformation. She suffered from AN for more than a decade, was considered 'chronic' and unlikely to recover. We tried many types of treatment, but the only thing that worked was full nutrition. I encourage parents to focus on this. Expect that your child's eating disorder will argue convincingly against your involvement, but stay the course. Your child is more likely to cooperate if you have a good therapist for support, and recovery does not have to be protracted.

Leslie

The tide is turning. Parents are increasingly recognized as an integral and positive element of recovery from an eating disorder. We hope that increased opportunities for training in FBT, continued emphasis on provision of empirically supported treatments, and correction of misconceptions about FBT and the family's role in therapy will open the door to the provision of more effective and timely treatments for individuals suffering from these debilitating illnesses.

References

Bruch, H. (1962) 'Perceptual and Conceptual Disturbances in Anorexia Nervosa', *Psychosom Med* 24: 187–94.

Charcot, J. M. (1888) *Clinical Lectures on Certain Diseases of the Nervous System*, Detroit, MI: George S. Davis.

Dare, C., Le Grange, D., Eisler, I., and Rutherford, J. (1994) 'Redefining the Psychosomatic Family: The Pre-Treatment Family Process in 26 Eating Disorder Families', *Int J Eat Disord* 16: 211–26.

Eisler, I., Dare, C., Hodes, M., Russell, G., Dodge, E., and Le Grange, D. (2000) 'Family Therapy for Adolescent Anorexia Nervosa: The Results of a Controlled Comparison of Two Family Interventions', *J Child Psychol Psychiatry* 41: 727–36.

Fairburn, C. G., Welch, S. L., Doll, H. A., Davies, B. A., and O'Connor, M. E. (1997) 'Risk Factors for Bulimia Nervosa: A Community-Based Case-Control Study', *Arch Gen Psychiatry* 54: 509–17.

Fisher, C. A., Hetrick, S. E., and Rushford, N. (2010) 'Family Therapy for Anorexia Nervosa', *Cochrane Database Syst Rev* 4: CD004780.

Gull, W. W. (1874) 'Anorexia Nervosa (Apepsia Hysterica, Anorexia Hysterica)', *Trans Clin Soc Lond* 7: 22–8.

Jacobi, C., Hayward, C., de Zwaan, M., Kraemer, H. C., and Agras, W. S. (2004) 'Coming to Terms with Risk Factors for Eating Disorders: Application of Risk Terminology and Suggestions for a General Taxonomy', *Psychol Bull* 130: 19–65.

Keel, P. K. and Haedt, A. (2008) 'Evidence-Based Psychosocial Treatments for Eating Problems and Eating Disorders', *J Clin Child Adolesc Psychol* 37: 39–61.

Lacey, J. H. and Price, C. (2004) 'Disturbed Families, or Families Disturbed?', *Br J Psychiatry* 184: 195–6.

Le Grange, D. and Eisler, I. (2008) 'Family Interventions in Adolescent Anorexia Nervosa', *Child Adolesc Psychiatr Clin N Am* 18: 159–73.

Le Grange, D. and Lock, J. (2007) *Treating Bulimia in Adolescents: A Family-Based Approach*, New York: Guilford Press.

Le Grange, D., Eisler, I., Dare, C., and Russell, G. F. (1992) 'Evaluation of Family Treatments in Adolescent Anorexia Nervosa: A Pilot Study', *Int J Eat Disord* 12: 347–57.

Le Grange, D., Crosby, R. D., Rathouz, P. J., and Leventhal, B. L. (2007) 'A Randomized Controlled Comparison of Family-Based Treatment and Supportive Psychotherapy for Adolescent Bulimia Nervosa', *Arch Gen Psychiatry* 64: 1049–56.

Le Grange, D., Lock, J., Loeb, K., and Nicholls, D. (2010) 'Academy for Eating Disorders Position Paper: The Role of the Family in Eating Disorders', *Int J Eat Disord* 43: 1–5.

Lock, J. and Le Grange, D. (2005) 'Family-Based Treatment of Eating Disorders', *Int J Eat Disord* 37: S64–7.

Lock, J., Le Grange, D., Agras, W. S., and Dare, C. (2001) *Treatment Manual for Anorexia Nervosa: A Family-Based Approach*, New York: Guilford Press.

Lock, J., Couturier, J., and Agras, W. S. (2006) 'Comparison of Long Term Outcomes in Adolescents Treated with Family Therapy', *J Am Acad Child Adolesc Psychiatry* 45: 666–72.

Lock, J., Le Grange, D., Agras, W. S., Moye, A., Bryson, S., and Jo, B. (2010) 'Randomized Clinical Trial Comparing Family-Based Treatment to Adolescent-Focused Individual Therapy for Adolescents with Anorexia Nervosa', *Arch Gen Psychiatry*, 67: 1025–1032.

Marcé, L. V. (1860) 'On a Form of Hypochondriacal Delirium Occurring Consecutive to Dyspepsia, and Characterized by Refusal of Food', *Journal of Psychological Medicine and Mental Pathology* 13: 264–6.

Minuchin, S., Baker, B. L., Rosman, B. L., Liebman, R., Milman, L., and Todd, T. C. (1975) 'A Conceptual Model of Psychosomatic Illness in Children: Family Organization and Family Therapy', *Arch Gen Psychiatry* 32: 1031–8.

Minuchin, S., Rosman, B. L., and Baker, B. L. (1978) *Psychosomatic Families: Anorexia Nervosa in Context*, Cambridge, MA: Harvard University Press.

Morton, R. (1694) *Phthisiologia, or, a Treatise of Consumptions*, London: Smith and Walford.

Nielsen, S. and Bara-Carril, N. (2003) 'Family, Burden of Care and Social Consequences', in J. Treasure, U. Schmidt, and E. van Furth (eds) *Handbook of Eating Disorders*, 2nd edn, Chichester: John Wiley & Sons.

Robin, A. L., Siegel, P. T., Moye, A. W., Gilroy, M., Dennis, A. B., and Sikand, A. (1999) 'A Controlled Comparison of Family versus Individual Therapy for Adolescents with Anorexia Nervosa', *J Am Acad Child Adolesc Psychiatry* 38: 1482–9.

Russell, G. F., Szmukler, G. I., Dare, C., and Eisler, I. (1987) 'An Evaluation of Family Therapy in Anorexia Nervosa and Bulimia Nervosa', *Arch Gen Psychiatry* 44: 1047–56.

Ryle, J. A. (1936) 'Anorexia Nervosa', *Lancet* ii: 893–9.

Schmidt, U., Lee, S., Beecham, J., Perkins, S., Treasure, J., Yi, I., Winn, S., Robinson, P., Murphy, R., Keville, S., Johnson-Sabine, E., Jenkins, M., Frost, S., Dodge, L., Berelowitz, M., and Eisler, I. (2007) 'A Randomized Controlled Trial of Family Therapy and Cognitive Behaviour Therapy Guided Self-Care for Adolescents with Bulimia Nervosa and Related Disorders', *Am J Psychiatry* 164: 591–8.

Selvini Palazzoli, M. P. (1974) *Self-Starvation*, London: Chaucer.

Silverman, J. A. (1997) 'Anorexia Nervosa: Historical Perspective on Treatment', in D. M. Garner and P. E. Garfinkel (eds) *Handbook of Treatment for Eating Disorders*, New York: Guilford Press.

Chapter 12

Effectively engaging the family in treatment

Stephanie Milstein and Carrie Arnold

Case study

When I became acutely ill with anorexia nervosa at the age of 20, I couldn't understand why my friends and family were worried. I felt fine. More than that, I felt good. Sure, I was freezing, even in the muggy summer heat and had a nasty habit of blacking out almost every time I stood up. The hair on my head was falling out in chunks, and simultaneously sprouting over my face and stomach. Yet I could exercise for hours a day. I was acing my advanced science courses at college. And I looked in the mirror and saw a normal-looking person. In fact, I could stand to lose ten more pounds. Looking back, I realize my health and future were in serious jeopardy. If my parents hadn't insisted I receive inpatient treatment, I probably would have died. Yet upon discharge from the hospital or residential treatment programme, my parents were invariably advised to stand back – I needed to exert control over my food and my life, and they would hinder my recovery.

Carrie

What makes recovery difficult?

Carrie's experience will illustrate that while every eating disorder case must be individually assessed, there are critical, fundamental ingredients which can assist adolescents or young adults, and their families, through an effective journey towards recovery.

Unfortunately, as with Carrie, many families have repeated negative experiences prior to finding effective treatment. They are often told to back off, and wait for insight and motivation. Consequently, they feel powerless.

Family-based treatment (FBT)

The family-based treatment approach offers beneficial concepts that can be integrated into any treatment approach for anorexia nervosa (AN) in adolescents. This mobilization of the family and the patient as a team sets this approach apart from other treatment plans.

Initial sessions and early recovery stance

The first meeting lays the foundation for treatment: a positive initial contact is critical. Carrie's parents were told to stand back, at great detriment to their daughter's health.

The goal for the first few treatment sessions with a family is to put them at ease while thoroughly assessing their individual situation, also empowering them with family strengths and resources. The family, as well as the patient, needs to believe the provider working with them is capable of getting them through this process.

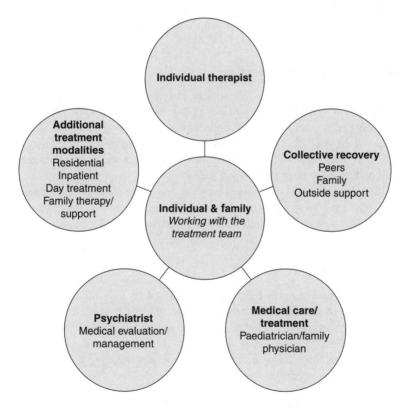

Figure 12.1 Recipe for success: it takes a team!

While parents and families do not cause eating disorders, their involvement in treatment is essential. Lock and le Grange (2005: 55) address the role of the therapist in coaching parents in the following way: 'We believe you are a key ingredient to your child's success in fighting the eating disorder ... it's our job, to alleviate any anxiety or guilt that is keeping you from contributing to your child's return to health.'

It takes a team

A comprehensive team approach empowers parents, patients, and providers to work together. The eating disorder feeds off the sufferer; it employs their intelligence, skill, and determination or wilfulness to maintain control over them. Therefore, the smarter, the more wilful and skilful the patient, the more sophisticated the eating disorder. Team communication and collaboration are essential to prevent confusion and misunderstandings and to reinforce a unified message.

Patients and family members need to sign releases of information at the onset of treatment that allow all team members to collaborate. This needs to be a non-negotiable term of treatment. Resistance towards authorizing ongoing family involvement in treatment needs to be addressed to avoid impeding progress.

Doing what is most effective

Utilization of evidence-based treatment provided by licensed and certified providers is essential; however, not everything works for everyone. If something is working, keep doing it; if not, collaborate with your team, re-evaluate and examine alternatives. Recovery is filled with challenges for the patient, their family, and the treatment team; however, the overall theme is that the team will prevail and together beat the eating disorder.

Burnout can occur and this is where the team approach is most beneficial. Everyone needs to work together all the way through. There are no shortcuts. Have a plan for discussing titration and decreasing the frequency of appointments, based on progress, to prevent patient dropout with initial improvement.

Honesty is imperative

Be upfront and honest regarding the goals of treatment, to build trust and validate the seriousness of the situation and illness. It is also helpful to indicate, if appropriate, that outpatient treatment may not be sufficient and a more aggressive level of care, that is, inpatient or residential treatment, may be necessary to medically/psychiatrically stabilize the patient. Identifying and discussing criteria for remaining at the current level of care versus initiating a higher level of care can be helpful.

Self-care is essential

Team members must make time for self-care and maintain effective and professional boundaries and limits. They can maintain momentum and enhance motivation by providing encouragement, positive reinforcement, optimism, and support to each other as well as to the patient and family. Importantly, providers need to find creative means of utilizing support and engaging in self-care and to role-model this to parents and family members to help them replenish themselves, who, in turn, will be encouraged to do the same with the patient.

Externalize the eating disorder

The therapist and other recovery team members must remember that the illness does not represent who the patient is, but that the illness has taken over the patient. 'This strategy is key in maintaining engagement with the adolescent while attacking AN. Failure to achieve this separation can increase resistance to the treatment on the patient's part' (Lock *et al*. 2001: 52). The goal is to empower the patient, their family and the team to jointly combat the eating disorder. This can be challenging since the eating disorder tends to employ cognitive distortions such as dichotomous (all or none) thinking.

Barriers/complicating factors

A baffling aspect of AN is that sufferers, no matter how desperate their physical and/ or psychological illness, can often function at baseline or even at extraordinary levels in their daily lives in areas unrelated to their personal health, weight, shape, appearance and eating. Note how Carrie could exercise for hours a day, despite eating extremely little. Furthermore, this study concluded that symptoms once thought to be primary features of AN were actually symptoms of starvation. This reinforces the need to first and foremost address weight and nutritional restoration in recovery.

The patient is often unaware of or denies the illness since they may truly not feel ill and, consequently, may interpret their own behaviours and thoughts as normal. This emotional state is referred to as being anosognosic. This is not a choice or conscious denial, but a feature of brain dysfunction, and is dangerous on many levels. Carrie did not see herself as emaciated, but rather as someone who could lose more weight.

Eating disorder symptoms are also frequently experienced as being egosyntonic, therefore making treatment more difficult. AN is described as egosyntonic because patients view their symptoms as congruent with their own values. Combined with perfectionism tendencies, drive towards thinness, rigid thinking patterns and difficulties with set-shifting and different defence mechanisms, this can complicate treatment.

Conclusion

Components to introduce at treatment onset and reinforce throughout the recovery process include the following:

- Recovery comes first and must be top priority.
- Food is medicine. The prescription is full nutrition, weight restoration and/or abstinence from compensatory behaviours.

- Don't negotiate with the eating disorder.
- Family is viewed as a resource.
- The parents'/caretakers' job is to plan and provide and supervise feeding. The patient's job is to eat and utilize skills and support.
- Eating disorders are serious and life-threatening and do not 'just go away'.
- Parents don't cause eating disorders and patients are not to blame for their eating disorder.
- Eating disorders are brain disorders, not a choice or means of seeking attention.

References

Lock, J. and Le Grange, D. (2005) *Help Your Teenager Beat an Eating Disorder*, New York: Guilford Press.

Lock, J., Le Grange, D., Agras, W.S., and Dare, C. (2001) *Treatment Manual for Anorexia Nervosa: A Family Based Approach*, New York: Guilford Press.

Chapter 13

Involving carers: a skills-based learning approach

Elizabeth Goddard, Simone Raenker and
Janet Treasure

Case study: Katie

Katie is 29, a medical researcher. Her sister Marlene, age 28, developed anorexia at age 13.

I was 15 when I noticed Marlene brushing her teeth excessively. Marlene had become secretive, wore long-sleeved clothes and was very thin. When a friend confided Marlene was cutting herself, I confronted my sister who admitted she had been excessively weighing herself and making herself vomit for several months. A meticulous diary documented her habits.

Our family initially participated in a family counselling service via our GP. The few group sessions were a disaster. Upset and confused, my parents and I did not understand why Marlene was deliberately hurting herself. After blaming ourselves for her behaviour, we ended up crying and directing accusatory comments at each other. Marlene ceased individual counselling after a few sessions. Until eighteen months ago, her life was a vicious cycle of bulimia nervosa (BN), anorexia nervosa (AN) and obsessive compulsive disorder (OCD), with weight loss and gain cycles, alongside brief sojourns with various counsellors, psychologists and psychiatrists.

The anorexia has been devastating for our family, though its impact has been eased through participation in a carer project (a study for carers of people with eating disorders at the Institute of Psychiatry, King's College, London).

Katie

The carer project that Katie refers to involved a skills-based training approach in a self-help format. Katie and her mum took part in this project twelve years after Marlene was first diagnosed with AN. They were given a skills-based learning book (Treasure *et al.* 2007) supplemented with a set of DVDs.

My mother and I participated in skills-based training which has been enormously helpful, providing us with practical skills to care for Marlene. It challenged previous ways we dealt with her illness.

Even Dad began to read the coping skills material. Talking openly about Marlene's illness for the first time was a big step for our family and each member began changing the ways we dealt with and reacted to certain situations. The down-to-earth, practical nature of the skills' training, which placed the family at the heart of helping eating disorder patients, and didn't blame the family, was inspirational.

I grieve for the loss of my family but am quietly optimistic. I understand challenges and relapses will continue and that Marlene may not fully recover. However, if she is happy and healthy most of the time, I will feel our family has all worked together to help achieve this.

Katie

The approach to carers

The collaborative care skills training approach is a philosophy with an accompanying set of skills and techniques that any carer (professional and lay), in various settings, can implement with the aim of achieving change in their situation (Treasure *et al.* 2010). Although partners are included in this model, their specific role is discussed in Chapter 16 and therefore will not be discussed separately here.

Carers are a resource in the treatment process and can be helped to implement some of the same skills as professionals in the home. Carers have more contact with the patient and can help by reinforcing effective change talk (the first stage in change, change talk, is for the patient to be able to voice the desire, need, reason or ability to change). Teaching carers skills in how to elicit change talk and positively reinforce it by teaching the skills of motivational interviewing (MI) is a key part of the intervention. Furthermore, carers can provide a warm and compassionate milieu which is a more effective backdrop to change. Kindness and compassion rather than overprotection or criticism and hostility can foster self-esteem and optimise the sense that the patient has the ability, with support if needed, to change. Helping carers regulate their own emotional reactions is another key component of this intervention.

Impact on family members and close others

Without intervention, family life begins to revolve around the eating disorder (ED) and relationships change (Sepulveda *et al.* 2009; Whitney and Eisler 2005). Automatic assumptions and misconceptions about the illness can lead to guilt, shame, and desperation. Caring for someone with an ED is distressing (Whitney *et al.* 2005) and carers often show high, sometimes clinical, levels of anxiety, depression, and caregiving burden (Zabala *et al.* 2009). Although mothers' level of distress appears greater than fathers' on objective measures (Kyriacou *et al.* 2008), fathers express great concern and anxiety concerning the patient and often feel better placed to react in a less emotionally driven way (Raenker *et al.* 2011). Also, the marital relationship between carers can become strained as they cope with the ED effects on themselves and their family (Latzer *et al.* 2009).

Unaffected siblings can be positive role models to the patient (Honey *et al.* 2006) but a qualitative study reveals that siblings feel burdened as mediators in the parent–child relationship of their affected sibling (Dimitropoulos *et al.* 2009). Although some noted that they became closer to their siblings, they also discussed the adverse effects of the illness on the sibling–sibling relationship and their sense of responsibility (Dimitropoulos *et al* 2009).

> The anorexia has been devastating for our family …. Until the onset of the eating disorder Marlene and I had a close relationship.
>
> Katie

Responding to the needs of carers

The need to maintain confidentiality within the clinical setting is often used as an excuse not to consider the needs of carers or offer support (Graap *et al.* 2008; Haigh and Treasure 2003; Treasure *et al.* 2001; Whitney *et al.* 2005; Winn *et al.* 2007; Zabala *et al.* 2009). However, interventions have been developed to address their needs and reduce their level of distress, self-blame and burden. Studies are promising, suggesting carers benefit from additional support (Goddard *et al.*, in press; Sepulveda *et al.* 2008a, 2008b; Uehara *et al.* 2001). Furthermore, several studies suggest that by providing carers with additional support and skills training we may be able to positively influence those who have an eating disorder (Goddard *et al.* 2010; Goddard *et al.*, in press; Uehara *et al.* 2001). The skills training approach therefore has multiple aims: (1) to improve the well-being of carers, and (2) to enable carers to use their skills in a positive way to impact the ED.

> Following the caregiver workshops we are close again and Marlene trusts me … I let her know I'm not perfect either, and confide when I make an error or forget to do something … I'm now in a healthier relationship where I'm learning not to insist on taking care of everything. I'm learning to let people make their own mistakes – this is a big change from my previous attitude of wanting to save the world.
>
> Katie

Theoretical underpinning of the collaborative care skills training approach

Maintenance factors are those that may promote the illness *once it has already started*. Of critical importance to the work with carers and family members are the interpersonal maintaining factors whereby responses of close others aggravate the ED symptoms (Schmidt and Treasure 2006). By interrupting these maintenance factors we may interrupt the course of the illness and promote recovery.

The inadvertently perpetuating role of certain carers' behaviour and interactions – for example, expressed emotion (criticism, hostility and overprotection) – can adversely affect therapeutic engagement and response. This model has been elaborated by recognising how families can accommodate to and enable ED symptoms by participating in behaviours relating to maladaptive emotional regulation strategies and extreme cognitive styles (Sepulveda *et al.* 2009). These elements are hypothesised to have a subsidiary negative effect on the person with the ED.

> I learnt my previous attempts to help Marlene had not been particularly constructive or helpful – though done with the best intentions – and there were better and more consistent ways to help her.
>
> Katie

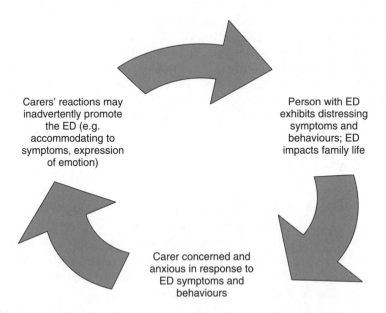

Figure 13.1 A model depicting the cycle of unhelpful interaction patterns between carer and individual with an eating disorder.

Responses to the illness

Below is a model that describes how carers can get trapped into a cycle of behaviour and emotional responses that can inadvertently perpetuate the illness.

In our model, carers' complex responses to the illness can be considered along two continuums: directive – non-directive; over-emotional – unemotional. The skills training intervention helps carers find a balance. Expressed emotion (EE) refers to some of these responses and is a way of conceptualising the interactions carers have with the patient. Two aspects of EE are emotional over-involvement and criticism/hostility, which are natural responses driven by stress, frustration and helplessness caused by the ED. Research suggests that patients experiencing various different illnesses, including EDs, suffer from a higher relapse rate if carers exhibit higher levels of EE, particularly if they also spend a lot of time together (Butzlaff and Hooley 1998; Hooley 2007; van Furth *et al.* 1996).

The collaborative care skills training approach uses animal analogies to convey different response patterns to carers. This can help carers identify areas where they would like to try a different approach. Carers may have their own 'default' style of caring or responding to the illness (perhaps because of their own temperament or coping style) and often go into different 'modes' at different times. Our research suggests that the skills training approach helps to reduce carers' distress, and also that the observed reduction in carers' expressed emotion and accommodation and enabling behaviours is associated with symptomatic improvement in the patient with the ED (Goddard *et al.*, in press).

> Animal metaphors helped define what care they gave – my mother discovered she was a jellyfish, being strongly into self-blame, and my father learnt he was an ostrich, not wanting to acknowledge the illness. I thought I was a bit of each.
>
> Katie

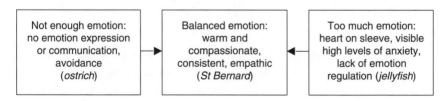

Figure 13.2 Emotional regulation: striking the right balance.

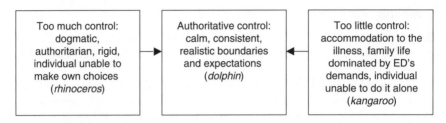

Figure 13.3 Direction – a consistent and calm approach to setting boundaries.

Katie highlights her parents' initial responses:

I tried to break the news gently to our parents, while at the same time protecting Marlene from their initial horrified reaction. Our father never acknowledged that Marlene was properly ill ('pull yourself together'; 'eating is fundamental so just do it') [*rhinoceros*] and avoided discussing her illness [*ostrich*], though underneath he was worried sick. Our mother cried a lot and blamed herself [*jellyfish*]; her feelings of guilt would continue for the next fourteen years.

I was billed as the over-achieving older sister and tried to hold the fort, supporting and organising everyone, ignoring my own emotions [*ostrich*]. Result: none of our responses were helpful and Marlene's anorexia thrived.

Katie

Emotional regulation

The *jellyfish* describes a carer's response when they have difficulty regulating their own stress and anxiety and become over-emotional. The patient with the ED may start to 'mirror' these emotions. They may become more anxious or upset if an overly anxious carer expresses high levels of distress and anxiety. This can make the patient feel more guilty about their illness, exacerbating feelings of low self-worth (Treasure *et al.* 2007, 2010). This over-emotionality in a household or between people can lead to exhaustion, but when a carer can manage their own stress and anxiety they model self-care and compassion to the patient. A mother, Pam, recognised her anxiety was hindering her daughter Sarah's recovery and had the confidence to seek therapeutic support for herself.

For five years it's been a slow process of gradual recovery. My anxiety remains; I still feel panic at times although through therapy, I've learnt coping mechanisms. Therapy has helped me take the stigma and shame out of it for Sarah. I've new purpose in life and have learnt to listen. Sarah

> has learnt coping mechanisms and is kinder to herself. She has much grit.
> I'm glad when she says: 'Mum, back off' and 'Mum, go away'. Because when
> her illness reared she was a little girl in great need.
>
> Pam

On the other hand, carers can struggle to cope with the complex emotions, behaviours and changing relationships resulting from the ED, and may bury their heads in the sand like an *ostrich*. By not acknowledging the illness and its effects on oneself and the family, the illness thrives. Moreover, the patient may misinterpret this reaction and feel their struggles are not sufficiently valid to be discussed. The cycle then continues; the illness takes a stronger hold as the patient's self-esteem plummets, and the ED becomes a solace. A carer may have ostrich tendencies if they try to carry on as 'normal', as if they are not affected by the illness and can cope with everything. Pam and Katie reflect on their ostrich tendencies:

> As a family we're more self-reflective now about our own issues and
> demons and ask how can we expect/ask Sarah to deal with her illness if
> we stick our heads in the sand ourselves.
>
> Pam

> A second revelation was about myself in relation to others. I had thought
> I was being good by being strong but learnt the best behaviour and being
> perfect was not always the answer.
>
> Katie

Carers can break this cycle of over- or under-emotionality by regulating their own emotions and expressing them in a calm, honest, emotionally intelligent way, like a *St Bernard*. It is almost as if a carer becomes the emotion regulator for the patient. A St Bernard is consistent and persistent in its care. By remaining calm and compassionate throughout times of high stress and anxiety, a carer shows the patient these distressing emotions can be tolerated. A St Bernard can express warmth and love in the face of anger, tantrums and insults. By adopting the 'St Bernard approach' carers provide a safe environment where patients can express emotions without fear of reprisal. An important aspect is for carers to model good self-care themselves, which can have repercussions for the patient.

> Amazing things can happen as a result of attending skills-based work-shops. The lessons kick-started my mother attending yoga classes with Marlene and my father, almost unbelievably, has started guitar lessons. He has three guitars – he bought them a long time ago but did not play them. He has suffered depression. But now, in his fifties, he is taking lessons. Last but not least, Marlene is talking about enrolling for nursing studies.
>
> Katie

Direction versus guidance

In response to the stress and frustration provoked by the illness, carers can turn to logic and pragmatism. A *rhinoceros* attempts to persuade the person that their behaviour is irrational and the cons of the illness far outweigh the benefits. This approach inevitably leads to frustration and conflict. Where patients are often ambivalent towards change (Treasure and Ward 1997), logical persuasion to engage in change is met with resistance. Arguments and a stressful home environment facilitate ED symptoms as the patient retreats further into the safety of the ED.

Carers can also become critical in their frustration and despair. This constant, persistent attempt to change another's behaviour can be interpreted as critical and irritating, like a *terrier*. Importantly, research suggests the sensitivity of people with EDs to threat and an anxious disposition means they may be particularly sensitive to this criticism and negative feedback (Harrison *et al.* 2010). Katie notes that a supportive family environment is necessary for the ED to be overcome.

> My experience is an ED sufferer can eventually work through their prob-lems to become better if friends and family provide a supportive, loving, consistent, non-judgemental environment.
>
> Katie

At the other end of the spectrum, a *kangaroo* carer is a protector. This type of caring is a way of shielding the patient from harm (e.g. negative feedback) so that they avoid stress or anxiety. A carer who responds in this way, again propelled by anxiety or fear of the repercussions, can become over-involved and take responsibility from the patient. In the long run, this encourages dependence and anxiety as the individual does not feel a sense of mastery (Wood *et al.* 2003). Carers may also find themselves caught in the 'reassurance trap', driving miles to find the 'right' food, or altering their own healthy exercise routines. This response pattern can be too permissive, accommodating and enabling the illness so that symptoms become more entrenched (Sepulveda *et al.* 2009).

Recognition of our behaviour and emotional response was exactly what we needed. If Marlene said 'do I look fat in this?' we learnt to say 'I don't think that is a helpful thing to talk about right now, Marlene'. More than a decade had passed since my sister developed AN and this skills-based training was a revelation. Our family learnt about the importance of eating meals at the table together, making time for this even when parents both worked. Our parents began to say 'Marlene, having dinner every night together is now non-negotiable', and encouraged her involvement in food preparation. Our family became supportive in a tangible way.

Katie

Carers can find a balance, represented by the *dolphin*. This is a carer who is consistently supportive and compassionate but firm in setting boundaries. A dolphin is like a lifebelt, providing support when needed but nudging and guiding the patient towards independence, encouraging decision-making, resilience development and a sense of mastery.

A mother, Veronica, was an 'over-carer' who took a leap of faith.

With my changes in attitude and behaviour, Henrietta quickly got into recovery ....As her mother I had wanted to do everything. But helping a child recover from an ED is about setting and recognising the boundaries and being open to guidance.

When Henrietta rang and said she planned to commit suicide I said that was her problem, and she would have to deal with it, and said 'goodbye'. I felt dreadful but I had learnt and recognised that nothing I could say would prevent every single solitary thing from happening and fearing it might happen – I was devastated saying what I did but I had to rise to this challenge for the sake of Henrietta's recovery. Half an hour later Henrietta called back and asked what I was doing at the weekend as though nothing had happened.

The point is, from that moment progress was made. The key was that I had digested the lessons of setting boundaries and taking a less hands-on approach. As a mother it was very difficult to step back. No one likes seeing anyone sick ... Henrietta chose to live. I was very relieved to receive her phone call confirming this.

Veronica

Understanding behaviour traps: functional analysis

Carers are helped to consider 'functional analysis' to explore how they might trigger or respond in an unhelpful way to difficult behaviours. A functional analysis has three parts: Antecedent, Behaviour, and Consequence (ABC). A carer can break down their responses to ED behaviour in this way. For example, see Figure 13.4.

Through this reflection, carers can recognise the cycle that enables the eating disorder to thrive. Consider the next example in Figure 13.5.

Some behaviour change will be more difficult than others. To increase the likelihood of success and to ensure the patient feels supported, conversations may need to take place outside the immediate 'hot' environment – for example, meals.

Antecedent	Behaviour	Consequence
Rigidity around meal times	Arranging family life to fit in with rigid meal time demands (*kangaroo*)	Short term: no confrontation, peaceful meal times Long term: reinforces rigidity of individual, behaviours become more entrenched

Figure 13.4 ABC – kangaroo response.

Antecedent	Behaviour	Consequence
Rigidity around meal times	Compassion towards anxiety felt at a change in routine, supportive and calm yet firm that the meal time will be different today (*dolphin*)	Short term: high anxiety; argument; refusal to comply; possibly willing to give it a go Long term: individual able to cope with flexible meal times through practice and with support

Figure 13.5 ABC – the dolphin.

Antecedent	Behaviour	Consequence
Internal triggers: e.g. anxiety around food, fear of losing control External triggers: e.g. criticism, teasing	Rigidity around meal times	Positive: feeling of safeness, being in control, soothing Negative: criticism from others, cause of stress in the household

Figure 13.6 ABC to understand loved one's behaviour.

Negotiating plans in advance and negotiating reasonable expectations are important.

Functional analyses can also be used to help understand the triggers of the patient's behaviours. They may have their own internal triggers, or outside events may trigger a response.

Encouraging behaviour change

A model of behaviour change can be a helpful tool for carers in assessing (a) how they feel about change, and (b) how their loved one feels about change. Prochaska's Transtheoretical Model of Change (Prochaska and Velicer 1997) describes the different stages people go through before committing to behaviour change. The cycle emphasises that people are fluid in their thoughts about change and these alter on a daily, if not hourly, basis. This model suggests that change may be a circle for a while but gradually it becomes a spiral as more knowledge and skills are mastered and the revolutions gradually stop. It also indicates how interventions may need to be adjusted to the stage of change – for example, a carer/therapist voicing change talk in the pre-contemplation stage of ambivalence will only provide opportunity for the patient to counter with anti-change talk.

Verbalising a commitment to change is likely to be an important predictor of behaviour change (Amrheim *et al.* 2003: Rollnick *et al.* 2008). Therefore, to get someone to move towards change, a carer, in essence, needs to encourage them to argue the case *for* change and commit to it out loud. Although difficult, carers can help the patient do this. This model can also be used to demonstrate that progress around the spiral can be driven by recognising the importance of and improving confidence in change.

Communication techniques: motivational interviewing

The skills training programme teaches the principles of motivational interviewing (MI) as a communication tool for carers to use with their loved ones (Rollnick *et al.* 2008; Treasure *et al.* 2007). MI is a language used to promote change. The ethos of MI is empathetic, compassionate and non-judgemental. Once the communication channels are opened, carers can work and talk in a collaborative, open and honest manner with the person with an ED to elicit change. Finding the right balance of emotional expression (*St Bernard*) and consistent, balanced support (*dolphin*) is the platform from which calm, compassionate and caring communication can evolve, where the patient feels safe to disclose his/her feelings, and to test expression and regulation of emotion. Once commitment to change is achieved, carers can encourage other behaviour change strategies, such as goal setting and behavioural experiments.

Conclusion

Working with carers is an important, if not crucial, aspect to the care of people with EDs across all ages. A family and close network can become closer and more resilient because of these shared experiences and the deepening intimacy and trust that can develop from successful collaboration. Veronica shares her experience:

I consider myself lucky when I reflect on my daughters' eating disorders and this is because of the positive impact they have had on our family relationships. I never had this intimacy with my parents. The relationship with my three children has improved because we dealt with the eating disorders as a family. The fundamental strength of our relationships has been brought about by our journey. I have watched some families destroy themselves. We never know what will happen in life but if we build on it, good things happen. Today I run a carers' support group and carers' workshops, sit on a carers' forum, carers' steering groups and study groups, all in mental health. I also beat the drum for carers in raising awareness with professionals through public speaking engagements. I could not do this work if I had remained an obsessive helper. Accepting the need for boundaries has given me strength.

The same that happened to my family has happened to others and I try to draw on my lessons as a carer in helping parents. I suggest they start by making small changes that they feel safe with. Carers see change as being large and threatening. But they can cope with something small, like saying to their child: 'I am sorry (but) I am not listening to this conversation again today' and walk away. For me, this worked and I have seen many people change. By learning coping skills, relationships with children improve – families go from desperate to great fun.

… It comes back to a leap of faith and understanding that what we have been doing does not help and we need to make changes. If something is not working, change it.

Veronica

Note

The New Maudsley Method and the Maudsley Approach – they are different

The New Maudsley Method differs from the original Maudsley Approach model. The Maudsley Approach – developed and used in the Random Controlled Trial (RCT) started in 1979 – is a behaviourally focused, manualized family therapy for adolescents with AN. The New Maudsley Method comprises strategies to support adult carers in helping their adult offspring manage their recovery. It is designed for adults with an eating disorder or people with a severe and enduring illness. The theory and practical guidelines behind the New Maudsley Method are covered in two books, one primarily for families (Treasure J. *et al.* 2007) and another for professionals (Treasure J. *et al.* 2010).

References

Amrheim, P. C., Miller, W. R., Yahne, C. E., Palmer, M., and Fulcher, L. (2003) 'Client commitment language during motivational interviewing predicts drug use outcomes', *J Consult Clini Psychol* 71: 862–78.

Butzlaff, R. L. and Hooley, J. M. (1998) 'Expressed emotion and psychiatric relapse: A meta-analysis', *Arch Gen Psychiatry* 55: 547–52.

Dimitropoulos, G., Klopfer, K., Lazar, L., and Schacter, R. (2009) 'Caring for a sibling with anorexia nervosa: A qualitative study', *Eur Eat Disord Rev* 17: 350–65.

Goddard, E., Macdonald, P., and Treasure, J. (2010) 'An examination of the impact of the Maudsley Collaborative Care Skills Training Workshops on patients with anorexia nervosa: A qualitative study', *Eur Eat Disord Rev*, n/a. doi: 10.1002/erv. 1042.

Goddard, E., Macdonald, P., Sepulveda, A. R., Naumann, U., Landau, S., Schmidt, U., and Treasure, J. (in press) 'Testing an interpersonal model of anorexia nervosa: A randomised controlled trial using self help materials', *Br J Psychiatry*.

Graap, H., Bleich, S., Herbst, F., Scherzinger, C., Trostmann, Y., Wancata, J., and de Zwaan, M. (2008) 'The needs of carers: A comparison between eating disorders and schizophrenia', *Soc Psychiatry Psychiatr Epidemiol* 43: 800–7.

Haigh, R. and Treasure, J. (2003) 'Investigating the needs of carers in the area of eating disorders: Development of the carer's needs assessment measure (CaNAM)', *Eur Eat Disord Rev* 11: 125–41.

Harrison, A., Sullivan, S., Tchanturia, K., and Treasure, J. (2010) 'Emotional functioning in eating disorders: attentional bias, emotion recognition and emotion regulation', *Psychol Med* 40: 1887–97.

Honey, A., Clarke, S., Halse, C., Kohn, M., and Madden, S. (2006) 'The influence of siblings on the experience of anorexia nervosa for adolescent girls', *Eur Eat Disord Rev* 14: 315–22.

Hooley, J. M. (2007) 'Expressed emotion and relapse of psychopathology', *Annu Rev Clin Psychol* 3: 329–52.

Kyriacou, O., Treasure, J., and Schmidt, U. (2008) 'Understanding how parents cope with living with someone with anorexia nervosa: Modelling the factors that are associated with carer distress', *Int J Eat Disord* 41: 233–42.

Latzer, Y., Lavee, Y., and Gal, S. (2009) 'Marital and parent-child relationships in families with daughters who have eating disorders', *J Fam Issues* 30: 1201–20.

Prochaska, J. M. and Velicer, W. F. (1997) 'The transtheoretical model of health behavior', *Am J Health Promot* 12: 38–48.

Raenker, S., Schmidt, U., *et al.* (2011) 'Caregiving experience and needs of fathers of people with an eating disorder' (submitted).

Rollnick, S., Miller, W. R., and Butler, C. C. (2008) *Motivational Interviewing in Health Care*, New York: Guilford Press.

Schmidt, U. and Treasure, J. (2006) 'Anorexia nervosa: Valued and visible. A cognitive-interpersonal maintenance model and its implications for research and practice', *Br J Clin Psychol* 45: 343–66.

Sepulveda, A. R., Lopez, C., Macdonald, P., and Treasure, J. (2008a) 'Feasibility and acceptability of DVD and telephone coaching-based skills training for carers of people with an eating disorder', *Int J Eat Disord* 41: 318–25.

Sepulveda, A. R., Lopez, C., Todd, G., Whitaker, W., and Treasure, J. (2008b) 'An examination of the impact of the Maudsley eating disorder collaborative care skills workshops on the well-being of carers: A pilot study', *Soc Psychiatry Psychiatr Epidemiol* 43: 584–91.

Sepulveda, A. R., Kyriacou, O., and Treasure, J. (2009) 'Development and validation of the Accommodation and Enabling Scale for Eating Disorders (AESED) for caregivers in eating disorders', *BMC Health Services Research* 9: 171.

Treasure, J. and Ward, A. (1997) 'A practical guide to the use of motivational interviewing in anorexia nervosa', *Eur Eat Disord Rev* 5: 102–14.

Treasure, J., Murphy, T., Szmukler, G., Todd, G., Gavan, K., and Joyce, J. (2001) 'The experience of caregiving for severe mental illness: A comparison between anorexia nervosa and psychosis', *Soc Psychiatry Psychiatr Epidemiol* 36: 343–7.

Treasure, J., Smith, G., and Crane, A. (2007) *Skills-Based Learning for Caring for a Loved One with an Eating Disorder: The New Maudsley Method*, London: Routledge.

Treasure, J., Macdonald, P., and Schmidt, U. (eds) (2010) *The Clinician's Guide to Collaborative Care in Eating Disorders*, London: Routledge.

Uehara, T., Kawashima, Y., Goto, M., Tasaki, S. I., and Someya, T. (2001) 'Psychoeducation for the families of patients with eating disorders and changes in expressed emotion: A preliminary study', *Compr Psychiatry* 42: 132–8.

van Furth, E. F., van Strien, D. C., Martina, L. M. L., van Son, M. J. M., Hendrickx, J. J. P., and van Engeland, H. (1996) 'Expressed emotion and the prediction of outcome in adolescent eating disorders', *Int J Eat Disord* 20: 19–31.

Whitney, J. and Eisler, I. (2005) 'Theoretical and empirical models around caring for someone with an eating disorder: The reorganization of family life and inter-personal maintenance factors', *J Ment Health* 14: 575–85.

Whitney, J., Murray, J., Gavan, K., Todd, G., Whitaker, W., and Treasure, J. (2005) 'Experience of caring for someone with anorexia nervosa: Qualitative study', *Br J Psychiatry* 187: 444–9.

Winn, S., Perkins, S., Walwyn, R., Schmidt, U., Eisler, I., Treasure, J., Berelowitz, M., Dodge, L., Frost, S., Jenkins, M., Johnson-Sabine, E., Keville, S., Murphy, R., Robinson, P., and Yi, I. (2007) 'Predictors of mental health problems and negative caregiving experiences in carers of adolescents with bulimia nervosa', *Int J Eat Disord* 40: 171–8.

Wood, J. J., McLeod, B. D., Sigman, M., Hwang, W., and Chu, B. (2003) 'Parenting and childhood anxiety: Theory, empirical findings, and future directions', *J Child Psychol Psychiatry* 44: 134–51.

Zabala, M., Macdonald, P., and Treasure, J. (2009) 'Appraisal of caregiving burden, expressed emotion and psychological distress in families of people with eating disorders: A systematic review', *Eur Eat Disord Rev* 17: 338–49.

Chapter 14

The therapeutic alliance in cognitive behavioural therapy for adults with eating disorders

Jane Evans and Glenn Waller

Our aim here is to consider the role of the therapeutic alliance within cognitive behaviour therapy (CBT) for treatment of eating disorders (part of the 'how it is done' element of therapy). It is not our intention to go into much detail regarding the technology of CBT itself (the 'what is done' element), as that is well detailed elsewhere (e.g. Fairburn 2008; Waller *et al.* 2007). However, we do provide a brief introduction to the topic, in order to make the rest of this chapter meaningful to those who work in other modalities. CBT is a psychotherapy which is based on the principle that unhealthy patterns of cognition/thinking can result in emotional, behavioural and physiological problems that will maintain the negative thinking pattern, creating a vicious cycle. For example, an individual who thinks 'I am only worthwhile if I am slim' is likely to feel anxious and depressed and to restrict her or his food intake, resulting in starvation. In turn, that restrictive behaviour can lead to less stable mood, more concrete beliefs about the importance of body size, and bulimic behaviours. Evidence-based approaches (e.g. Fairburn 2008) focus initially (and often mainly) on the role of these maintaining factors and how to modify them in order to escape from the eating disorder. As with CBT for other disorders, this approach to the eating disorders stresses the importance of early behavioural change (e.g. exposure to feared foods; behavioural experiments) and biological stabilization, followed by a greater emphasis on cognitive and emotional factors (e.g. cognitive challenges; surveys).

The final point to make before considering the therapeutic relationship in CBT for the eating disorders is why this matters. The simplest answer is that CBT has the best and fastest impact of all psychological therapies with the majority of adults with eating disorders (Fairburn and Harrison 2003; Fairburn *et al.* 2009; National Institute for Clinical Excellence 2004). It is also developing its evidence base with more restrictive eating disorders (e.g. Fairburn and Dalle Grave 2008) and with younger cases (e.g. Pretorius *et al.* 2009). To ensure that the greatest number of sufferers get the best possible care, CBT needs to be delivered with due attention to both the 'what' and the 'how'.

While the role of the therapeutic relationship is not ignored either in CBT in general (e.g. Gilbert and Leahy 2007) or in CBT for the eating disorders (e.g. Fairburn 2008; Waller *et al.* 2007), it is often assumed to be ignored in this field.

Therefore, in this chapter we will address issues in the therapeutic alliance that the clinician should consider when undertaking CBT for eating disorders. Our own work is primarily the delivery of CBT with adults and older adolescents, so our focus is on this age group in this chapter, but we believe the same broad principles apply in working with younger cases and parents. We begin with a case (treated by JE), to illustrate our points.

Case study: Sarah

I was 18 or 19 when my eating disorder developed. I was in my first year at university in England and the rest of my family had moved abroad several years previously. The eldest of a large family, I have always been competitive and perfectionist, felt inferior to my pretty best friends and felt quite insignificant. Another factor was the summer holiday when I went to stay with my family. I was quite desperate to 'fit in' and get to know some of the locals. I felt like a foreigner and they seemed to judge people by their appearance. As a rather hyper-sensitive person, any comments went straight to my heart and made me feel unconfident. Then, one guy said he liked me, and later raped me. I felt ashamed, dirty and stupid and guilty for getting into that situation. In hindsight, I think I wanted to be rid of my old self and started shrinking myself, and imposed very strict discipline on my eating and exercise with strong willpower. My little diet soon became a more punishing regime. When I returned to university I started running every morning and evening, hardly eating and focusing on my work. I guess I was trying to forget myself and was missing my family.

The anorexia helped me to control how I felt, and numb any sense of sadness and anger. It enabled me to control at least what I thought was myself, because I understood I could not control the outside circumstances. But the more I controlled what I ate and lost weight, the harder it became to see anything rationally.

I lost a lot of weight, and although at first people said: 'Oh you look really good', it's a fine line between looking good and healthy, and looking ill. When my housemates pleaded with me to seek help, I saw a [doctor], who referred me to the university counsellor who said I was depressed, prescribed Prozac, and told me to eat five Mars bars daily, which didn't help. Although I didn't want help then, believing I had no problem; I just wanted to please my housemates. I didn't take the Prozac. I carried on and said: 'No thank you, I'm fine'.

Sarah

For the next few years, Sarah received no support, but her condition continued to deteriorate. After university, she moved to France, and her BMI dropped to 13.6. She was admitted to a general psychiatric unit, where she received six months' inpatient treatment, being given 'privileges' (e.g. a book, her own clothes, or a half-hour walk with a nurse) for each kilogram she gained until she reached the target BMI of 18. She received no therapy during this time and received no follow-up. Her condition slowly deteriorated after she left hospital. Over the next seven years she half-heartedly sought treatment several times, but was never convinced she wanted to change. She then saw a psychodynamic therapist for two years intermittently, alongside seeing a dietitian. The therapy focused on discussing her emotional states, but Sarah was unable to make any changes to her eating or weight. Plans made with her dietitian were never put into practice.

> At this point, Sarah was referred to our specialist eating disorders service and began CBT treatment for her eating disorder. By now, she had been suffering from anorexia nervosa for fifteen years. Her body mass index (BMI) was 15.2. For the first few months of treatment, Sarah seemed engaged. She was compliant with completing food diaries and with being weighed each week, and was motivated. However, this was translating into only minimal weight gain, and little meaningful change in her eating behaviours. Around this time, she fractured her femur and hit rock bottom, losing the weight she had gained (and more). Through discussion in supervision, I concluded that although my instinct was to provide Sarah with more empathy and compassion, I needed to get firmer to help her find her way out of the anorexia nervosa. This process will be described throughout the chapter.
>
> Jane E.

Our clinical experience

We begin with the assumption that there are many different stances when deciding what makes an effective therapeutic alliance for working with eating disorders. These stances are likely to be affected by our personality, experience, gender, and age. For example, one of us (GW) is widely regarded as being relatively firm and 'boundaried' about therapy tasks, while the other (JE) is generally seen as nicer and more empathic. These are common themes in our supervision, although we each recognize that the 'stern/nice' balance can shift from patient to patient according to the patient's nature, their eating disorder and our response to them.

We have learned in supervision (GW is JE's supervisor, and GW is supervised by another peer) that we can take this dialectic of apparently opposing stances ('stern' and 'nice'), and arrive at a synthesis that facilitates treatment. This balanced approach has been labelled as a 'judicious blend of empathy and firmness' (Wilson *et al.* 1997: 82). While we do not ignore the importance of being judicious in reaching the right blend, we will refer to this approach as 'firm empathy' in this chapter. Our experience is that reaching such a synthesis is usually the product of discussing the pros and cons of different courses of action in directing treatment, combining firmness and empathy in a way that preserves the structure and direction that underpin CBT without losing the therapeutic bond. Indeed, the evidence from our clinic is that the CBT team achieves a very strong therapeutic alliance with our patient group (Waller *et al.*, in press). Of course, the key is always to ensure the patient benefits from treatment to the maximum possible degree, so we aim to back this stance with evidence that our patients are getting better (e.g. improvement in attitudes and symptoms; low attrition rates).

The evidence base

Cognitive behavioural therapy (CBT) is the psychotherapeutic approach with the best evidence base when working with eating disorders (e.g. Fairburn and Harrison 2003). However, while we continue to increase the proportion of patients who benefit from treatments, there is a long way to go. Even the best available approaches are only moderately effective (e.g. Fairburn and Harrison 2003). Should CBT respond to the common charge that it does not make full use of the therapeutic alliance as a tool in helping individuals to overcome their eating disorders?

Definition of the therapeutic alliance

Both Fairburn (2008) and Waller *et al.* (2007) describe the need for a collaborative working relationship in CBT for the eating disorders. While that relationship has many definitions, Bordin (1979) provides a particularly helpful one, using the term 'the working alliance'. That alliance comprises three parts – the establishment of shared *goals* between patient and clinician, acceptance of the *tasks* that each needs to perform, and the attachment *bond* between the two individuals. This is obviously a relationship where different perspectives might have different impacts on treatment outcome, so both patient and therapist perspectives need to be considered.

Of course, it can be argued that the therapeutic alliance already does receive attention within CBT, with discussion in many core texts from its earliest days (e.g. Beck *et al.* 1979). CBT generally treats an effective working alliance as valuable because it facilitates the action of the technological elements of this approach (e.g. exposure, behavioural activation, cognitive challenges, behavioural experiments, skills training, surveys), rather than being useful as a therapeutic tool in its own right. In the case of CBT for the eating disorders, where there is evidence of the importance of behavioural change from very early on, it can even be argued that the therapeutic activity results in the establishment of a good working alliance (e.g. Safer and Hugo 2006). There is some evidence in support of this proposal in CBT for depression, where sudden improvements in symptoms are associated with subsequent and maintained improvements in the therapeutic alliance (Tang and DeRubeis 1999).

What is the evidence that the therapeutic alliance plays a role in therapy outcomes?

The therapeutic alliance is commonly referred to as a key element of treatment. There is evidence of an association between the working alliance and therapy outcomes, but that effect is only moderate (e.g. Hardy *et al.* 2007; Horvath and Symonds 1991; Martin *et al.* 2000). Some conclude that the therapeutic alliance is the strongest contributor to treatment outcomes (e.g. Luborsky *et al.* 2002), while others conclude that the 'technological' elements of therapy have an effect that surpasses the generic therapeutic alliance effect (e.g. Rounsaville and Carroll 2002). It appears inappropriate to conclude that therapy alliance effects are the same for all therapies and disorders (e.g. Beutler 2002; Chambless 2002). In particular, Crits-Cristoph *et al.* (1991) have shown that the impact of therapist effects differs across therapies and therapists, with the working alliance being central in unstructured psychological therapies but not in structured therapies such as CBT. Perhaps the best conclusion is that empathy, genuineness and warmth are 'necessary but not sufficient to produce an optimum therapeutic effect' (Beck *et al.* 1979: 45).

Relevance to the eating disorders

Despite clinical suggestions that the therapeutic alliance is important in different psychotherapeutic approaches to working with eating disorders (e.g. Miller and Mizes 2000), there is little evidence this is so. One alternative possibility is that the sufferer is more likely to develop a positive therapeutic alliance as a *result* of early therapeutic gains, enhancing motivation and optimism (Safer and Hugo 2006). Given the lack of empirical evidence, we will focus on our clinical experience of what is helpful when using CBT with individual cases.

First steps – instilling hope

Obviously, the low motivation common in eating disorder patients is likely to significantly influence the therapeutic alliance, whatever the therapy used. Even if they want to change, many patients will doubt they can do so, given their past experiences of their disorder and failed therapies. Therefore, part of our role is to help prevent our patients from falling into this trap of helplessness. Expressing hope about the usefulness of therapy is an important factor in engaging patients (e.g. Russell and Shirk 1998) and can enhance outcomes (e.g. Safren *et al.* 1997). To do this, we aim to balance being realistic and optimistic about the possibility that any patient can benefit or recover. We present evidence on the outcomes of

CBT for eating disorders (based on both research studies and local outcomes). We also stress that the more work patients put in (and the more we stick to CBT principles, including individualization of treatment), the higher the likelihood they will get better. Thus, the patient can develop a sense of agency in their recovery. This approach helps the patient to feel heard and understood, with obvious positive implications for the therapeutic alliance.

We push for early behavioural change (e.g. introducing dietary structure) because it is critical in enhancing the patient's (and clinician's) levels of hope, and hence the therapeutic alliance. Many sufferers come to us with a long treatment history in different settings using different modalities, and considered 'lost causes'. However, with a little bit of 'naïve optimism' on our part ('Well, I see no reason why you should have less chance of getting better than anyone else who comes here ...'), balanced with empathy ('... despite the fact that you have had a lousy time and lots of things have kept your eating problem going ...') and firmness ('... but there is no way round the core tasks of therapy if you want to get better'), those patients have gone on to make a full recovery. So, the message is that it is always worth being hopeful, whether you are a clinician or a sufferer.

> With Sarah, it was vital that I held on to the naïve optimism that we have described here. She had been suffering for a long time and had experienced various treatments, none of which had enabled her to move forward from her eating disorder. During that first stage of treatment, it could be argued that my optimism and empathy were a little too strong and that I was less firm than I might have been, in that I was always hoping this was the week we would see behaviours begin to change. That balance might have held us back for longer. However, it can equally be argued that it was necessary to start with the stance that I did (with the aim of moving to a more effective balance with firmness), as the risk of Sarah disengaging in a state of helplessness was likely to be high, and she needed to know that I believed it was possible for her to recover.
>
> Jane E.

Balancing empathy and firmness as we progress through treatment

As CBT progresses, we use the therapeutic alliance to assist as we aim to maintain and develop the key early behavioural changes (e.g. adding content to food intake). The aim is to balance empathy and firmness at all times, rather than to see these as conflicting or sequential elements. The balance itself might shift across the course of therapy, but there is never a point where either element is sufficient on its own or better than the other.

To be able to empathize with the patient's position, we aim to formulate their eating problems in an individualized way. Through understanding the patient's unique set of experiences, beliefs and actions, we are able to make sense of and validate their experience (e.g. Lynch *et al.* 2006). If patients feel understood, they are more likely to accept the need for change. That empathy needs to be maintained when the patient finds the tasks of therapy demanding, but it cannot be allowed to prevent us maintaining appropriate firmness (e.g. when maintaining pressure to challenge and test the effectiveness of their maladaptive coping strategies). Young *et al.* (2003: 93) state that clinicians are often: '*so empathic that they do not push patients to face reality, or they are too confrontational and cause patients to feel defensive and misunderstood*'. The clinician's constant challenge is to hold both positions in mind throughout the therapy process – to push for change, while empathizing with how difficult this can be for the patient.

Although early behaviour change is critical in CBT for eating disorders, clinicians can be tempted to avoid pushing for such change until there is a solid working alliance (e.g. to reduce the perceived risk of dropout). Thus, we potentially have a Catch-22 situation – waiting for a strong and trusting alliance before pushing for behavioural change, but running the risk that such an alliance is less likely to develop if the patient has not experienced behavioural change. We overcome this potential trap by being honest from the beginning of therapy about both the potential for change and the work needed to achieve it. The clinician needs to be authoritative (an expert, with useful knowledge to impart) rather than authoritarian (giving instruction and expecting compliance). Importantly, when the patient holds a positive perception of the clinician, this assists therapy in a range of ways (McNeil *et al.* 1987; Waddington 2002).

In short, with CBT, there is no value in being supportive without pressing for change. The combination of firmness and empathy is needed from the start, but the amount of pressure to assert along the way must be carefully considered. We suggest discussing the need for behavioural change from early on, while being clear that you understand this will be a highly anxious time and giving the patient permission to express concerns about the therapy process.

In Sarah's case, I did not push hard enough for behavioural change early on. Not until the crisis of her broken hip and her hitting rock bottom did I realize the importance of applying pressure on her to decide about making real, meaningful and measurable behavioural change. At this point, the therapeutic alliance was strong enough that Sarah was able to respond positively. In keeping with the point above, I have no way of knowing whether Sarah would have dropped out of treatment if I had taken this approach earlier. It might have been too early for Sarah to have trusted me enough to support her in taking this risk and facing the anxiety associated with weight gain. Alternatively, we might have been able to make progress much earlier, while strengthening the alliance (and Sarah's physical condition) more swiftly.

Jane E.

The role of collaboration in facilitating risk-taking

Collaboration is fundamental to the therapeutic alliance within CBT, providing common goals, and enabling patients to explore and test the evidence (Beck and Young 1985). Therefore, we approach each therapy task as a learning experience both for the patient and for ourselves. Inherent to this approach, we have to accept our beliefs might be wrong (e.g. the patient might be right about caloric needs). If clinicians find it hard to accept being proved wrong, they will have trouble building a collaborative relationship, where learning and change are a mutual venture.

A key issue in such collaboration is the pace at which we encourage the patient to move forward. Each behavioural change that we and our patients try out has to involve a manageable level of risk – eliciting enough anxiety that the patient can learn from the outcome, yet not so much that the patient is unable to carry out the change or immediately retreats from it. The anxiety that patients can tolerate differs across individuals, so collaboration over setting the pace of change is critical (as long as the patient and clinician do not enter into a mutual 'delusion' that change is happening or about to happen when it clearly is not from any objective standpoint).

This 'delusion' might have been partially occurring early in Sarah's treatment. We developed the analogy of her dipping her toe in the water, but never actually getting in. Therefore, she was experiencing the cold (behavioural change) as aversive and running from it, without being able to adjust to the temperature and discovering it wasn't that bad after all.

Jane E.

Who is in control?

The issue of control is particularly pertinent in the eating disorders. Fairburn (2008: 27) concludes, '*if they feel they are being controlled, coerced or misled, patients will resist change*'. It is therefore imperative that the patient feels part of a truly collaborative process and not that they are having something done to them. Importantly, we include the need for control in the individual's case formulation, so the issue can be discussed openly and honestly. In this way, any potential control-based conflicts within the therapeutic alliance and obstacles to therapy can be predicted and avoided or resolved. So who is in control? The most effective answer is that control over defeating the illness rests with the patient and the clinician in collaboration.

> The control was handed to Sarah by offering choices. The options were we either:
>
> - start working on meaningful weight gain with clear targets;
> - consider an inpatient stay for weight gain; or
> - end therapy (following a few brief sessions of preparation for managing a more limited life with the eating disorder).
>
> Jane E.

This approach had a positive outcome with Sarah.

> The boundaries put down by my therapist were helpful – I think I needed them. Although unpleasant at times, it was necessary. Without that discipline, I could have continued to drift and float and so I needed the push. I didn't want to waste any more time. I realized I needed to work much harder at the weight gain – that I hadn't been trying hard enough. I'd only been taking baby steps. I desperately didn't want to be an inpatient again – I wanted to carry on living my life.
>
> Sarah

Modelling compassion in the therapeutic alliance

It is a mistake to assume the careful balance between firmness and empathy is simply an excuse for pushing for more behavioural change. Given how commonly one sees difficulties with low self-esteem, self-criticism and sensitivity to 'failure' in patients with eating disorders, the balance with empathy is crucial. If we are not firm enough, sufferers will struggle to make meaningful behavioural change; if we are not empathic enough, we risk the patient taking away the message they have failed through not achieving each agreed goal. Such a sense of failure in therapy means the patient is likely to use familiar behavioural means (restriction/bingeing/purging/exercising) as their coping strategy for managing the consequent emotions. It is important we are aware of this risk and set up exposure, behavioural experiments or other tasks as 'win–win' situations. Each such task is a learning experience. If the patient achieves a goal, this is great; if they do not, what useful things can we extract from the experience, to problem-solve and facilitate progress?

To achieve this 'win–win' outcome in CBT, the clinician should model a non-critical and non-punitive stance. We should be honest, supportive, encouraging and compassionate. This stance allows therapy sessions to be a place where the patient feels safe enough to test expressing fears, anxieties, disappointments, anger and other emotional states that have previously been avoided and blocked out, because we provide an environment free of criticism. However, the clinician is not the only person in the room who could be critical of the patient – many patients are immediately and strongly critical of themselves. It is important that we help patients to give themselves praise for doing things well, while also recognizing what needs further work and finding appropriate ways to achieve this. We aim to help patients to develop this approach to shift the negative bias in their thinking, finding a more compassionate 'self–self' talk to challenge their internal critic. A useful strategy is to ask patients to describe the characteristics of the teacher who helped them learn most in the past. Common features that emerge include being nurturing, kind, supportive, knowledgeable, and firm. We aim to portray these characteristics ourselves, but also to help the patient adopt some of these characteristics in their dialogues with themselves, to give them the best chance of recovery.

Sarah decided to continue with therapy and to work on weight gain. This approach enabled her to accept that the journey has often been a process of 'two steps forward, one step back'. She has been able to problem-solve each time she has hit an obstacle, and move on from it, rather than cata-strophizing, criticizing herself and giving up. From the start she had been quick to condemn herself in the face of adversity. I hoped to model to Sarah that she could be kinder to herself, and that this might help her to continue her hard work rather than blaming herself and therefore want-ing to give up. Over time and as her weight has increased, it has become easier for her to challenge her internal critic.

However, in order for Sarah to make meaningful progress in developing self-compassion, it became apparent that it was necessary for us to work on the rape. It was necessary for a strong therapeutic alliance to have been established for this work to take place, so that Sarah was able to trust me enough to feel safe. Sarah had made a number of appraisals about the assault that had resulted in much self-blame and guilt. It was necessary for us to work through the memory in order to re-appraise what had occurred and shift the blame to the perpetrator. This enabled Sarah to then be able to show more compassion to herself and to feel more deserving of being well and having a fulfilled life.

Jane E.

When things go wrong

It is important to use the alliance to address problems in therapy – either when they emerge or in advance. Again, the 'firm empathy' approach is central, with its underlying themes of honesty and transparency. For example, when a patient such as Sarah is stuck, making no therapeutic progress, we need to point this out and provide realistic choices for where to go next (including options such as staying ill, rather than taking active steps towards change). In short, the working alliance importantly is one where the patient has the expectation from early on that they are responsible for change, and can see the clinician is both optimistic and realistic about the possibility of such change.

Conclusion

This chapter has explicitly addressed the role of the therapeutic alliance in CBT for eating disorders – an issue often only implicitly considered. The stance we find most effective is one of 'firm empathy' – balancing the demands of this approach with the need to ensure the patient feels understood and valued. This approach can only work if based on honesty, transparency and the assumption that the patient is his or her own therapist (while the clinician is a coach, helping the patient to get the best results from CBT). We hope no one who reads this chapter will believe they can ignore the therapeutic alliance when working in a CBT framework. It cannot be treated as trivial or as something to do mechanically; it must be tailored to the needs and strengths of each patient. For example, the approach might need to be adapted where the patient (or indeed the clinician) has dependent traits.

So, does this approach work? Perhaps the best evidence is the way in which our patients respond by leaving their eating disorder behind. Therefore, let us finish by returning to Sarah, as an example of the outcome of a firm, empathic stance in CBT:

Following the implementation of this firmer approach, Sarah began to gain weight, reaching a BMI of 18 at the time of writing (and increasing). The journey has not been smooth, and often Sarah's anxiety has resulted in her becoming stuck again. But through utilizing much of what has been outlined in this chapter, Sarah has been able to make the choice to continue with weight gain and work towards recovery. Alongside this weight gain, she has begun to accept and experience her emotional states rather than using restriction as a means of blocking them out. She has learned to be much kinder to herself and no longer feels like someone observing life, but is someone now experiencing it. There is a way to go, and we need to review targets and goals constantly. Therefore, I need to apply firm empathy to support Sarah in her continued journey towards recovery.

Jane E.

The final words belong to Sarah. They reflect how far she has come in terms of being kind to herself while continuing to advance towards recovery.

The main thing that made me want to get my life back was love. I think I wanted to be alive to love and help people. If I had carried on the way I was, maybe I wouldn't last that long. Now I want to be alive, and accept the gift that we have been given.

Sarah

References

Beck, A. and Young, J. (1985) 'Depression', in D. Barlow (ed.) *Clinical Handbook of Psychological Disorders* (pp. 206–44), New York: Guilford Press.

Beck, A. T., Rush, A. J., Shaw, B. F., and Emery, G. (1979) *Cognitive Therapy of Depression*, New York: Guilford Press.

Beutler, L. E. (2002) 'The dodo bird is extinct', *Clin Psychol Sci Pract* 9: 30–4.

Bordin, E. S. (1979) 'The generalizability of the psychoanalytic concept of the working alliance', *Psychother: Theory, Res Pract* 16: 252–60.

Chambless, D. L. (2002) 'Beware the dodo bird: The dangers of overgeneralization', *Clin Psychol Sci Pract* 9: 13–16.

Crits-Christoph, P., Baranackie, K., Kurcias, J. S., Beck, A. T., Carroll, K., Perry, K., Luborsky, L., McLellan, A. T., Woody, G. E., Thompson, L., Gallagher, D., and Zitrin, C. (1991) 'Meta-analysis of therapist effects in psychotherapy outcome studies', *Psychother Res* 1: 81–91.

Fairburn, C. (2008) *Cognitive Behaviour Therapy and Eating Disorders*, New York: Guilford Press.

Fairburn, C. G. and Dalle Grave, R. (2008) 'Enhanced CBT (CBT-E) for anorexia nervosa: Preliminary results from Oxford and Verona', paper presented at the Eating Disorders Research Society, Montreal, September.

Fairburn, C. G. and Harrison, P. J. (2003) 'Eating disorders', *The Lancet* 361: 407–16.

Fairburn, C. G., Cooper, Z., Doll, H. A., O'Connor, M. E., Bohn, K., Hawker, D. M., Wales, J. A., and Palmer, R. L. (2009) 'Transdiagnostic cognitive-behavioral therapy for patients with eating disorders: A two-site trial with 60-week follow-up', *Am J Psychiatry* 166: 311–19.

Gilbert, P. and Leahy, R. L. (eds) (2007) *The Therapeutic Relationship in the Cognitive Behavioral Psychotherapies*, London: Routledge.

Hardy, G. E., Cahill, J., and Barkham, M. (2007) 'Models of the therapeutic relationship and prediction of outcome: A research perspective', in P. Gilbert and R. L. Leahy (eds) *The Therapeutic Relationship in the Cognitive Behavioural Psychotherapies*, London: Routledge.

Horvath, A. O. and Symonds, B. D. (1991) 'Relation between working alliance and outcome in psychotherapy: A meta-analysis', *J Counsel Psychol* 38: 139–49.

Luborsky, L., Rosenthal, R., Diguer, L., Andrusyna, T. P., Berman, J. S., Levitt, J. T., Seligman, D. A., and Krause, E. D. (2002) 'The dodo bird verdict is alive and well – mostly', *Clin Psychol Sci Pract* 9: 2–12.

Lynch, T. R., Chapman, A. L., Rosenthal, M. Z., Kuo, J. R., and Linehan, M. M. (2006) 'Mechanisms of change in dialectical behavior therapy: Theoretical and empirical observations', *J Clin Psychol* 62: 459–80.

Martin, D. J., Garske, J. P., and Davis, M. K. (2000) 'Relation of the therapeutic alliance with outcome and other variables: A meta-analytic review', *J Consult Clin Psychol* 68: 438–50.

McNeil, B., May, R., and Lee, V. (1987) 'Perceptions of counselor source characteristics by premature and successful terminators', *J Counsel Psychol* 34: 86–9.

Miller, K. J. and Mizes, J. S. (eds) (2000) *Comparative Treatments of Eating Disorders*, New York: Free Association Books.

National Institute for Clinical Excellence (NICE) (2004) *Eating Disorders: Core Interventions in the Treatment and Management of Anorexia Nervosa, Bulimia Nervosa and Related Eating Disorders*, London: British Psychological Society.

Pretorius, N., Arcelus, J., Beecham, J., Dawson, H., Doherty, F., Eisler, I., Gallagher, C., Gowers, S., Isaacs, G., Johnson-Sabine, E., Jones, A., Newell, C., Morris, J., Palmer, R., Richards, L., Ringwood, S., Rivera, E., Rowlands, L., Simic, M., Treasure, J., Waller, G., Williams, C., Yi, I., Yoshioka, M., and Schmidt, U. (2009) 'Cognitive-behavioural therapy for adolescents with bulimia nervosa: The acceptability and effectiveness of internet-based delivery', *Behav Res Ther* 47: 729–36.

Rounsaville, B. J. and Carroll, K. M. (2002) 'Commentary on dodo bird revisited: Why aren't we all dodos yet?', *Clin Psychol Sci Pract* 9: 17–20.

Russell, R. L. and Shirk, S. R. (1998) 'Child psychotherapy process research', *Adv Clin Child Psychol* 20: 93–124.

Safer, D. L. and Hugo, E. M. (2006) 'Designing a control for a behavioral group therapy', *Behav Ther* 37: 120–30.

Safren, S. A., Heimberg, R. G., and Juster, H. R. (1997) 'Client expectations and their relationship to pretreatment symptomatology and outcome of cognitive-behavioral group treatment for social phobia', *J Consult Clin Psychol* 65: 694–8.

Tang, T. Z. and DeRubeis, R. J. (1999) 'Sudden gains and critical sessions in cognitive-behavioral therapy for depression', *J Consult Clin Psychol* 67: 894–904.

Waddington, L. (2002) 'The therapy relationship in cognitive therapy: A review', *Behav Cogn Psychother* 30: 179–91.

Waller, G., Corstorphine, E., Cordery, H., Hinrichsen, H., Lawson, R., Mountford, V., and Russell, K. (2007) *Cognitive-Behavioural Therapy for the Eating Disorders', A comprehensive Treatment Guide*, Cambridge: Cambridge University Press.

Waller, G., Evans, J., and Stringer, H. (in press). The therapeutic alliance in the early part of cognitive-behavioral therapy for the eating disorders', *Int J. Eat Disord.*

Wilson, G. T., Fairburn, C. G., and Agras, W. S. (1997) 'Cognitive behavioral therapy for bulimia nervosa', in D. M. Garner, and P. E. Garfinkel (eds) *Handbook of Treatment for Eating Disorders*, New York: Guilford Press.

Young, J. E., Klosko, J. S., and Weishaar, M. E. (2003) *Schema Therapy: A Practitioner's Guide*, New York: Guilford Press.

Chapter 15

Integrating dialectical behaviour therapy and family-based treatment for multidiagnostic adolescent patients

Anita Federici and Lucene Wisniewski

Case study: Maria

We had a long prodrome up to the development of my daughter Maria's anorexia. She had a sad winter the year she turned 14 with difficulties at home and at school. She didn't tell anyone what was happening at school, but she suddenly began to behave in an unpredictable and angry way. I didn't understand why until I found evidence that she may be cutting herself. It was a scary time. I did not know but during this time she began to purge in an effort to lose weight. High school started and she joined the cross-country team. She started to be unnaturally terrified of getting fat and wouldn't eat favourite foods. The weight loss happened so fast I was stunned. I would ask Maria to eat more food and she would reluctantly take a few bites. An adolescent medicine specialist diagnosed anorexia and referred us to a therapist who said Maria needed to eat three meals and two snacks per day. Meals were very difficult as Maria often beat her head against the floor while eating, or tried to run from the house. She was irritable and emotionally labile. She started scratching herself. She became suicidal and was admitted to the hospital seven times, twice to gain weight and stop purging but mostly due to suicidal ideation around the time of her menses. Maria was getting distraught, her anger increased and she remained deeply depressed, sleeping much of the day and unable to concentrate on anything. Residential care was recommended but I felt the problem was the treatment approach, not our family. I wasn't encouraged to participate in her care – the team put her in charge. We began to seek other treatment options ... we wanted to bring our family together to fight this illness.

Ann

What is dialectical behaviour therapy (DBT)?

DBT is a comprehensive outpatient treatment originally designed to target recurrent suicidal and self-injurious behaviours (e.g. cutting, burning, etc.) in adult women suffering from borderline personality disorder (BPD) (Linehan 1993). BPD is characterized by pervasive emotion regulation deficits, interpersonal difficulties, fears of abandonment, identity disturbances, impulsivity, and/or chronic suicidal and self-injurious behaviours (American Psychiatric Association 2000; see Miller *et al.* (2008) for a review of diagnosing BPD in adolescent patients). DBT is an integrative treatment that blends the change-based strategies of cognitive behavioural therapy (e.g. self-monitoring, psychoeducation, behavioural assessment, challenging maladaptive thoughts, exposure to feared situations) with Eastern philosophies and acceptance-based approaches (Linehan 1993). In addition, DBT emphasizes the importance of the therapeutic relationship and pays particular attention to emotion regulation deficits as they relate to impulsive and self-destructive behaviours. Within the DBT model, self-destructive behaviours (e.g. purging, self-injury, etc.) are viewed as the patient's best attempt (although maladaptive) to cope with painful emotions. Without the skills to tolerate or manage overwhelming feelings, some patients use symptoms as a way to suppress or escape from their internal experiences (Chapman *et al.* 2006). As a whole, DBT is designed to teach patients more adaptive ways of coping with emotions and interpersonal situations without engaging in maladaptive, and potentially life-threatening, behaviours.

The biosocial theory: how emotion dysregulation develops

As noted, DBT is based on an emotion regulation model and treatment is guided by the biosocial theory. While research in this area is growing, the biosocial theory suggests that deficits in the ability to adaptively regulate emotions are due to the interaction between a biological vulnerability and an invalidating environment (Linehan 1993). Biologically, researchers believe some people are naturally more sensitive to their emotions from birth (e.g. they may respond to situations with more intense emotions and take longer to 'return to baseline' after getting activated). According to this theory, these biological vulnerabilities are exacerbated when repeatedly paired with an '*invalidating environment*'. Invalidating environments are those that dismiss or punish an individual's emotional experiences. Such environments communicate that an individual and his/her emotions are unacceptable, overly intense, or otherwise inappropriate. Invalidating responses to strong emotions (1) communicate that one's internal experiences and feelings are problematic and (2) fail to teach an individual how to manage emotion more effectively. As a result, individuals may respond by avoiding feelings altogether, which ultimately means they never learn how to understand and express themselves skilfully.

Basic structure of DBT: the modes of treatment

The overarching emphasis in DBT is on the continuing assessment and treatment of targeted behaviours in the context of patient–therapist collaboration.

To manage multiple problem behaviours efficiently and effectively, DBT sessions are organized around a '*treatment hierarchy*'. The hierarchy dictates, in order of importance, which problem behaviours take precedence, as follows: (1) life-threatening behaviours, (2) behaviours that interfere with receiving treatment, and (3) quality-of-life-interfering behaviours. In standard DBT, treatment is typically provided over a twelve-month period and involves four components:

- **Individual therapy** – Patients meet once per week with a DBT-trained therapist to decrease crisis and therapy-interfering behaviours, develop clear treatment and life goals, improve quality of life, and reinforce newly learned DBT skills.
- **Group skills training** – Skills groups, typically offered once per week, are designed to help patients develop a range of adaptive coping skills including emotion regulation, distress tolerance, interpersonal effectiveness, and mindfulness.
- **Telephone skills coaching** – The purpose of between-session phone contact is to help patients generalize skills to their real-world environments when difficult situations arise. Phone coaching involves a brief (e.g. ten-minute) phone conversation on skills which might help in a given moment.
- **Therapist consultation team** – In a full DBT programme, all therapists are active members of a weekly consultation team. At this meeting therapists get support, coaching and guidance to ensure they can offer quality treatment and remain true to the DBT model.

Why do we need new treatment approaches for adolescent eating disorders?

Family-based treatments (FBT) appear to have the greatest impact on adolescents suffering from an eating disorder (ED) (e.g. Lock *et al.* 2001). Approximately two-thirds of adolescent patients with a primary diagnosis of AN are recovered after completing FBT and up to 90 per cent of those are fully weight-recovered at five-year follow-up (Eisler *et al.* 2000). Despite these promising findings, not all patients respond effectively to standard treatment approaches. Data evaluating predictors of treatment outcome and dropout in adolescents participating in FBT are limited. There are data, however, to suggest that adolescent patients with moderate to severe ED symptoms, particularly those with comorbid Axis I disorders, greater emotional dysregulation (e.g. suicidal/self-injurious behaviours, problems with anger) and/or those with personality disorder features (e.g. borderline personality disorder), may represent a form of the illness that practitioners consider 'difficult to treat' (Le Grange *et al.* 2008; Lock *et al.* 2006).

Although there are no 'easy' cases in ED treatment, the combination of an ED with other psychological illnesses presents a greater clinical challenge. We have observed this in our own clinic. While many adolescent patients respond positively to standard FBT, we have been increasingly challenged by a subgroup of patients and their families who (a) fail to adequately connect with the treatment team, (b) do not demonstrate clinically meaningful changes over time, and/or (c) whose complex and varied clinical presentations make FBT untenable at times. With respect to these cases, our FBT team struggled to apply the treatment in the context of recurrent suicidal/self-injurious behaviour, explosive and often uncontrollable angry outbursts, and/or substantial resistance to treatment goals. The difficulty in engaging this particular subgroup of patients in standard FBT often resulted in our clinicians (and the families they treat) feeling ineffective and burned out.

Why integrate DBT into standard family-based treatment?

> A new therapist suggested Maria needed adolescent DBT due to her ongoing problems with suicidal ideation, self-injury and emotional chaos. On learning about it I realized immediately this was made for her!
>
> Ann

In response to the need for innovative clinical interventions for multidiagnostic adolescents with an ED, we are exploring the feasibility and acceptability of an integrated FBT/DBT approach. Based on our clinical experience and the growing literature on the effectiveness of DBT-based approaches for 'difficult to treat' patients, we have been experimenting with ways to combine what we know to be effective in family-based care for an ED with what is indicated for the treatment of emotion dysregulation, including treatment of those with recurrent suicidal behaviour and/or BPD.

It has been suggested that FBT (a treatment focused on parental control) and DBT (a treatment based on collaboration with the patient) are incompatible. We do not agree. We have found DBT to be a useful adjunct to FBT both in terms of the clinical framework and in treatment planning when there is a history of self-injurious or suicidal behaviours.

> Our plan was to work on Maria's eating disorder in family-based (Maudsley) therapy and for her to work on her other problems with the DBT therapist. This was a bit groundbreaking, as DBT generally required no other therapists involved. But our psychiatrist talked to the DBT therapist and they worked out a plan which has worked very well.
>
> Ann

Our treatment conceptualization has been that all adolescent patients start out receiving standard FBT, as this treatment carries the most empirical support. We consider adding full DBT (e.g. individual therapy, skills groups, telephone coaching) when:

- The child has a history of recurrent suicidal and/or self-injurious thinking and behaviour (as Maria is described).
- The child presents with significant emotional dysregulation.
- There is a high degree of criticism by parents in (and beyond) the FBT sessions (increase in invalidating environment).

In our clinic, we have structured treatment to maximize exposure to emotion regulation concepts and skills to both facilitate compliance with FBT and further reduce maladaptive behaviours. In this model, our more complex adolescent patients meet one-on-one with an individual DBT therapist weekly in addition to regular (e.g. weekly/biweekly) FBT sessions. We have found that the integration of the two approaches has been very helpful to both patients and their families. The individual therapist does not directly address meal planning and weight gain (this is done with the family therapist); the emphasis is instead on helping patients tolerate and skilfully manage the painful and distressing emotions that arise as a response to food exposure and weight gain. DBT therapists implement both acceptance (e.g. normalizing emotions, validating the difficulty in making the changes outlined in FBT) and change strategies (e.g. behaviour chain analyses, exposure protocols, skill coaching) in an effort to help patients manage treatment more adaptively.

In addition to the promising research findings described above, our rationale for integrating DBT with FBT is based on the following.

DBT provides structure for managing multiple high-risk behaviours

Specifically, DBT has the capacity to potentiate FBT in cases where there is significant emotion dysregulation and especially a history of self-injury or suicidality (Rathus and Miller 2002). We have experienced parents having difficulty setting limits around food with their teenager when these particular circumstances exist. Likewise, we have encountered many adolescent patients who have indicated that they have not disclosed various high-risk behaviours (e.g. self-injury) in standard FBT for fear of being misunderstood or judged. Standard family-based treatments for EDs do not include specific protocols for managing comorbid suicidal/self-injurious behaviours and/or BPD features; thus they are often not systematically discussed or tracked over the course of treatment. Without a clear understanding of the function of recurrent suicidal and self-injurious behaviours and strategies for managing them, such situations create greater chaos with little change.

DBT was specifically designed, and is fundamentally structured, to address life-threatening behaviours (Linehan 1993). Families and patients are oriented to the *treatment hierarchy*, which creates a system, and a non-judgemental space, to discuss and treat self-destructive behaviours. Any behaviour that places a patient at imminent risk of dying is considered top priority in DBT; this includes suicidal and self-injurious behaviours as well as ED symptoms that cause life-threatening conditions (e.g. bradycardia, heart arrhythmias, electrolyte imbalances; see Wisniewski *et al.* (2007)). In our case example, Maria's severe food restriction and purging behaviours were considered life-threatening due to her medical instability.

> Maria's food and weight considerations were made to be medical decisions to be taken care of with FBT .... Her [individual] therapist works with her on learning to regulate her emotions without hurting herself.
>
> Ann

Likewise, in our centre, the family works together in FBT to help the child gain medical stability. Concurrently, the child works with an individual DBT therapist to 'radically accept' the current treatment plan, decrease target behaviours, build motivation and commitment to treatment goals, and use DBT skills to better communicate needs within the family context. Individual therapy begins with a review of the diary card, completed daily by patients and used to track emotions and behaviours that arise during the week. Any life-threatening urges/behaviours are targeted directly with the use of detailed behaviour chain analyses (see Linehan (1993) and Wisniewski *et al.* (2007) for examples of diary cards and behaviour chain worksheets).

DBT emphasizes emotional processing and affect regulation

As discussed, DBT is based on an emotion regulation model; thus, each mode of DBT (e.g, individual treatment, skills training, telephone coaching, consultation team) seeks to enhance the patient's ability to more accurately identify, and adaptively tolerate, a variety of emotional experiences. This is especially important for individuals with an ED, particularly those who demonstrate an impaired ability to identify, describe, and express emotion.

> During the group sessions I would learn how much effort it was for Maria to regulate her emotions in specific situations. Before the DBT group, I just saw what was on the surface.
>
> Ann

Some data suggest ED relapse is greater when emotion regulation deficits persist within the individual and their external environment. For example, some adult patients have reported that ongoing emotion regulation deficits were strongly related to relapse (Federici and Kaplan 2007). Additionally, adolescent patients are more likely to have a poor treatment outcome if the family environment is characterized by high expressed emotion (e.g. hostility, anxious over-involvement, criticism/intolerance; Treasure *et al.* 2008). In FBT, where the overarching emphasis is on weight gain and ongoing meal planning, our clinical experience has been that patients with multiple diagnoses (e.g. an eating disorder and post-traumatic stress disorder) require greater attention to regulating emotion and tolerating distress.

> We worked hard to get Maria's calories up to about 1,600 calories per day and her weight plateaued, though by this point she was extremely depressed and I think the lack of weight loss that week triggered her first suicidal thoughts ... she was irritable and emotionally labile. She started scratching herself. Self-injury increased during this time. She became suicidal every month when her period returned and she was admitted to the hospital three more times, mostly due to suicidal ideation.
>
> Ann

In our experience, DBT has been a valuable addition to standard FBT given the emphasis on discussing and targeting problematic emotional responses and related behaviours within a non-judgemental framework. DBT offers families a skill-based language with which they can address problematic episodes. For example, an adolescent may experience distress and become dysregulated when her parents require her to eat a feared food (e.g. a cheeseburger) at dinner. DBT's focus on acceptance and validation – '*it makes sense that you are feeling distressed AND you still have to eat it*' – as well as language around skill use to manage emotions – '*what distress tolerance skills can you use to calm yourself down so you can eat the cheeseburger?*' – helps families reduce emotional escalation and problem-solve more effectively.

DBT helps to decrease blame and increase collaboration

Family therapy for a child or a teen's ED is difficult work. Parents often describe feeling afraid and at fault for their child's illness, and patients often report feeling shameful and anxious about telling parents and/or therapists about their suicidal and/or self-injurious behaviours. When treating multidiagnostic adolescents in FBT, families may feel stuck and frustrated with the slow, or lack of, progress in treatment. In our experience, DBT has helped decrease tension and polarization between patients and their parents. In this model, patients and their families are oriented to the *biosocial theory* (as described above) in an effort to cultivate a compassionate understanding of the factors that prompt and/or maintain symptoms, including those that occur within (e.g. high criticism) and beyond (e.g. unrealistic cultural standards regarding beauty) the family unit. Parents learn that their child's emotionality stems from a biological vulnerability *and* that their child's needs for validation may be different from those of other family members. Likewise, patients learn that their parents are doing their best, given their emotions and past learning histories.

> The very first [assumption] is that everyone is doing the best they can, but that everyone needs to do better. It's funny but that little statement was so helpful to me – whenever Maria was needing tons of support, I could remind myself that she was doing the best that she could ... and since that wasn't enough, she needed me to step up and do the rest for her. Even this one session did a lot for our family. It united us as a team ... and she has more patience with us as she realizes we are also doing the best we can.
>
> Ann

Ultimately, DBT teaches families to find the validity in the other's response. Rather than searching for who is 'right' and who is 'wrong', the emphasis in DBT is on finding a synthesis or a 'middle ground' between two (seemingly) opposite views (Linehan 1993). We have found that this has worked well with families who feel they are 'at war' with their child's eating disorder. As Maria's mother tells us about the DBT/FBT integration: 'There is no criticism of our family or individual members, just ideas for how to do better working toward our own goals.' For example, we often work to help families find a synthesis between the needs of the patient ('I want my parents to stop policing me around my meal plan') and the needs of the parents ('we want our daughter to stop starving herself'). From a DBT perspective, the needs of both parties are valid. One way we have managed this using the FBT/DBT model is to have the families work on ways to validate each other while setting caring limits, while the adolescent patient works in individual DBT to become more skilful, and often earn back trust from their parents. In these cases, the collaborative spirit of DBT establishes a language and a method for patients and families to work on goals together. As Maria's mother explains: 'Both Maudsley and DBT incorporate parents to help the child improve. This has been a great help to us.'

DBT pays specific attention to motivation and commitment issues

Many adolescents suffering from an ED are ambivalent about change (Zaitsoff and Taylor 2009). In DBT, the unique and ongoing balance between acceptance and change-based strategies helps to reduce ambivalence and increase commitment to treatment goals. Often, and even in the presence of life-threatening ED behaviours that parents are managing in FBT, the DBT therapist works on building motivation for change based on what the patient is able and willing to work on in a given moment. For example, while a teenager may not be in agreement with her parents' goal that she eats more, she may, however, be interested in finding a way to get out of treatment. In this scenario, the individual DBT therapist might help the patient to (a) non-judgementally accept themselves and the reality of their current situation (e.g. that their mother and father have needs and are fearful for the patient's life) and (b) work on ways to create a situation in which the need for intensive treatment would be decreased (e.g. eliminate life-threatening behaviours, enhance communication with parents, etc.). We have found, as patients learn more effective skills to meet their needs (e.g. emotion regulation, interpersonal effectiveness), motivation increases.

DBT focuses on concrete generalizable skills

In our centre DBT skills are taught to all adolescents and parents while they are in FBT. While FBT alone may be able to help patients become nutritionally stable and receive exposure to the things they fear most (food), DBT skills can help provide the adolescent, and their family, with more effective ways to manage the emotions that arise around food and eating.

> The weekly (DBT) groups have helped us learn how to regulate emotions, get through a crisis, improve interpersonal skills and stop black and white thinking. When this all started, Maria didn't have many coping skills, so when a programme or therapist told her to use her coping skills, it wasn't possible because her coping skills were purging and not eating!
>
> Ann

Teaching families how to use DBT skills has been invaluable. While patients learn how to better identify their emotions and adaptively solve problems without symptoms, parents learn how to help their children be more effective and apply skills across a variety of situations. Equipped with a common language around emotion and a concrete 'tool box' of skills, families work together toward more effective communication and less emotional reactivity. Much as Maria's mother describes below, we have found that teaching families how to validate one another, respond to suicidal crises, and reinforce adaptive behaviour has had an exceptional and positive impact on treatment outcome.

> Much information is passed to us in the groups and we have homework and a manual to refresh our memories between sessions. We all learn the same things. In the weekly groups, I see how Maria is applying her skills. Because

> we all go together, I have more understanding and insight into what my daughter's challenges are and how she is reacting to them. In the group, she also sees that we are working hard to help her most effectively. So, the DBT group keeps us all working together with a common set of instructions. That's been really great. It's given us a feeling of working together, rather than working at cross-purposes.
>
> Ann

Our families (and patients) in the FBT/DBT model have also informed us that the various DBT components (telephone skills coaching, individual therapy, and the weekly skills training groups) have significantly helped them generalize the skills learned in treatment to the broader life context. We believe that this generalization is a key factor in the positive treatment outcomes we are observing.

Is there any evidence for the use of DBT for complex EDs?

We want to be clear that the model of incorporating DBT adjunctively to FBT is a novel and, as yet, untested treatment approach. Data show that DBT significantly decreases suicidal and self-injurious behaviours in adult patients with BPD (Linehan *et al.* 2006) and adolescents with BPD traits (Rathus and Miller 2002). Due to these compelling findings, DBT has evolved into an exciting and promising treatment for a range of complex emotional disorders, including EDs. Data from several studies have shown that modified DBT interventions (e.g. stand-alone skills training, individual DBT) are effective in reducing binge eating and purging behaviours in adults (e.g. Safer *et al.* 2001) and adolescents (Safer and Jo 2010) suffering from mild to moderate EDs. However, researchers and clinicians continue to be interested in the application of DBT for individuals with complex and severe ED presentations like Maria's. Our group's preliminary evidence suggests DBT may be an effective intervention for multidiagnostic adult ED patients when blended with standard ED interventions (Ben-Porath *et al.* 2009a, 2009b). Furthermore, two small studies (Chen *et al.* 2008; Palmer *et al.* 2003) on adult ED patients with comorbid BPD have shown that integrating DBT with standard ED interventions results in significantly fewer suicidal, self-injurious and ED behaviours, as well as number of days admitted to hospital.

Conclusions

We have described a novel approach to treating complex, multidiagnostic adolescent patients with an ED using a blended DBT/FBT model. We propose that DBT treatment can be a useful adjunct to FBT when the child presents with significant emotional dysregulation, suicidal or self-injurious behaviours, and/or has not responded adequately to FBT alone. We are in the process of systematically evaluating the feasibility and acceptability of this innovative approach. Future research should be conducted to empirically evaluate this model and to assess for whom it is appropriate.

References

American Psychiatric Association (APA) (2000) *DSM-IV-TR: Diagnostic and Statistical Manual of Mental Disorder*, 4th edn (Text Revision), Washington, DC: American Psychiatric Press.

Ben-Porath, D., Wisniewski, L., and Warren, M. (2009a) 'Differential Response to Dialectical Behaviour Therapy Adapted for Eating Disordered Patients with and without a Comorbid Borderline Personality Diagnosis', *Eat Disord* 17: 225–41.

Ben-Porath, D., Wisniewski, L., and Warren, M. (2009b) 'Outcomes of a DBT Day Treatment Program for Eating Disorders: Clinical and Statistical Significance', *J Contemp Psychother* 40: 115–23.

Chapman, A. L., Gratz, K. L., and Brown, M. Z. (2006) 'Solving the Puzzle of Deliberate Self-Harm: The Experiential Avoidance Model', *Behav Res Ther* 44: 371–94.

Chen, E. Y., Matthews, L., Allan, C., Kuo, J. R., and Linehan, M. M. (2008) 'Dialectical Behaviour Therapy for Patients with Binge-Eating Disorder or Bulimia Nervosa and Borderline Personality Disorder', *Int J Eat Disord* 41: 505–12.

Eisler, I., Dare, C., Hodes, M., Russell, G., Dodge, E., and Le Grange, D. (2000) 'Family Therapy for Adolescent Anorexia Nervosa: The Results of a Controlled Comparison of Two Family Interventions', *J Child Psychol Psychiatry* 41: 727–36.

Federici, A. and Kaplan, A. S. (2007) 'The Patient's Account of Relapse and Recovery in Anorexia Nervosa: A Qualitative Study', *Eur Eat Disord Rev* 26: 1–10.

Le Grange, D., Crosby, R., and Lock, J. (2008) 'Predictors and Moderators of Outcome in Family-Based Treatment for Adolescent Bulimia Nervosa', *J Am Acad Child Adolesc Psychiatry* 47, 4: 464–70.

Linehan, M. M. (1993) *Cognitive Behavioural Treatment of Borderline Personality Disorder*, New York: Guilford Press.

Linehan, M. M., Comtois, K. A., Murray, A. M., Brown, M. Z., Gallop, R. J., Heard, H. L., *et al.* (2006) 'Two-Year Randomized Trial and Follow-Up of Dialectical Behaviour Therapy vs Therapy by Experts for Suicidal Behaviours and Borderline Personality Disorder', *Arch Gen Psychiatry* 63: 757–66.

Lock, J., Le Grange, D., Agras, W. S., and Dare, C. (2001) *Treatment Manual for Anorexia Nervosa: A Family-Based Approach*, New York: Guilford Press.

Lock, J., Couturier, J., Bryson, S., and Agras, S. (2006) 'Predictors of Dropout and Remission in Family Therapy for Adolescent Anorexia Nervosa in a Randomized Clinical Trial', *Int J Eat Disord* 39, 8: 639–47.

Miller, A., Muehlenkampb, J. J., and Jacobson, C. M. (2008) 'Fact or Fiction: Diagnosing Borderline Personality Disorder in Adolescents', *Clin Psychol Rev* 28, 6: 969–81.

Palmer, R. L., Birchall, H., Damani, S., Gatward, N., McGrain, L., and Parker, L. (2003) 'A Dialectical Behaviour Therapy Program for People with an Eating Disorder and Borderline Personality Disorder: Description and Outcome', *Int J Eat Disord* 33: 281–6.

Rathus, J. H. and Miller, A. L. (2002) 'Dialectical Behaviour Therapy Adapted for Suicidal Adolescents', *Suicide Life-Threat Behav* 32, 2: 146–57.

Safer, D. L. and Jo, B. (2010) 'Outcome from a Randomized Controlled Trial of Group Therapy for Binge Eating Disorder: Comparing Dialectical Behaviour Therapy Adapted for Binge Eating to an Active Comparison Group Therapy', *Behav Ther* 41, 1: 106–20.

Safer, D. L. Telch, C. F., and Agras, W. S. (2001) 'Dialectical Behaviour Therapy for Bulimia Nervosa', *Am J Psychiatry* 158: 632–4.

Treasure, J., Sepulveda, A. R., MacDonald, P., Whitaker, W., Lopez, C., Zabala, M., Kyriacou, O., and Todd, G. (2008) 'Interpersonal Maintaining Factors in Eating Disorders: Skill Sharing Interventions for Carers', *Inte J Child and Adolesc Health* 1, 4: 331–8.

Wisniewski, L., Safer, D. L. and Chen, E. (2007) 'DBT for Patients with Eating Disorders', in L. Dimeff and K. Koerner (eds) *Dialectical Behaviour Therapy in Clinical Practice: Applications across Disorders and Settings*, New York: Guilford Press.

Zaitsoff, S. L. and Taylor, A. (2009), 'Factors Related to Motivation for Change in Adolescents with Eating Disorders', *Eur Eat Disord Rev* 16: 227–33.

Chapter 16

Couples therapy for anorexia nervosa

Cynthia M. Bulik, Donald H. Baucom and
Jennifer S. Kirby

Case study: Duncan

Nadia did not have an eating disorder when we met. She moved to England from Spain to learn English, and was working as a pharmacist. The eating disorder came on gradually. The main reason was probably Nadia feeling depressed about her job. Nadia had little support, much responsibility and little appreciation of her hard work.

Gradually her feelings of depression and isolation merged with feelings about food and body image. Loneliness and self-doubt came first and remained the underlying source of the problems. Nadia is clever, beautiful, kind, and loving. She is very focused and works hard to achieve things, sometimes concentrating so much she blocks out everything else. I think Nadia felt trapped in her job, by the mortgage on our new house, in a foreign country. Suddenly she was trapped in a life she had never expected, and felt lost.

Nadia began to cut out foods. She went from semi-skimmed milk, to fully skimmed to mixing milk and water, to water. No dressing on salads, no butter on toast. No treats. It was so gradual and mixed with other feelings, and difficulties at work, that I didn't notice immediately. I tried to support and listen to her worries about work, hoping she would feel happier.

Looking back, I wish we had help earlier. But Nadia wanted me to support and be there for her, not to drag her to some psychologist. By now she was only eating cereals, lettuce, and tomatoes. She was terribly depressed and skinny, crying every night, never smiling or laughing and rarely chatting.

She was obsessed with exercising, particularly cycling and swimming. I wanted to help, so I stopped doing things by myself, so I could be there for Nadia, thinking otherwise she might not cope. At the same time, I didn't share my own feelings or worries. Nadia needed help, not me. Guidance on how to best help her would have been helpful at this time.

Being an adult, Nadia had difficulty accepting my suggestions or comments. She said: 'You are not my father', 'You are my boyfriend, just support me and love me, don't tell me what to do.' Her words hurt, especially as I was already doing everything I could to be a caring, loving boyfriend. At the same time, I am glad that I was there for Nadia, and that we went through this together; our relationship is definitely stronger now.

The worst time was when Nadia completely shut me out, denying her illness. I fielded questions from family and friends to protect her and this was tiring. I turned to self-help carer books but Nadia said: 'Don't pretend you are a professional' or 'What's that then, page 46 of the book?' and 'Speak to me like my boyfriend, not a doctor.' It would have been helpful for me to share these difficult moments with others.

The turning point came when Nadia changed her job and started a Masters. Suddenly she mixed with people with similar ambitions and interests. She had something to enjoy and look forward to each day and I heard her laugh for the first time in eighteen months. Eventually, Nadia acknowledged she was not well physically. She saw a consultant psychiatrist and was an inpatient for five weeks on a private eating disorder ward. I felt relieved and scared.

The hospital's support and resources helped Nadia immensely but her own will and desire inspired her recovery. She eventually admitted she was unable to restore the weight alone. Afterwards, Nadia's mother lived with us for several months and, despite Nadia's occasional resistance, took charge of the meals.

Nadia is now completing a PhD and is fit, healthy and happy. But for a long while after she was better, I felt tired and down – like an elastic band stretched to the limit and prone to snapping easily. I had less patience, and became angrier more quickly. I attended a special group for carers at the hospital, but it was poorly attended, and badly run, so I stopped going. I needed help to return to my old self, but there was nothing. It was like, okay, Nadia is better, everything is fine. The experience left me feeling numb, and I needed re-energizing.

I remain short on patience. Yoga has helped, and holidays too! The carer must look after their self, otherwise, it becomes hard to care for somebody else. We still have a few food issues. I want to talk to someone about this, rather than risk it deteriorating.

Duncan

Engaging partners in the treatment of anorexia nervosa in adults

As Duncan's case vividly illustrates, AN exists within a social context. Anorexia affects relationships, and relationships affect the course of anorexia. Although engaging the family in the treatment of adolescents is critical, typically we still treat adults with AN primarily via individual therapy. Often partners are desperate to help, but feel impotent and directionless when it comes to helping their loved one.

What do we know about the treatment of anorexia nervosa in adults?

Despite the fact that AN is a serious disorder, with high medical and psychiatric comorbidity (Hudson *et al.* 2007), high relapse (Kaplan *et al.* 2008), and one of the highest mortality rates of any psychiatric disorder (Birmingham *et al.* 2005; Sullivan 1995), the evidence base for treatment for adults remains limited. Preliminary evidence suggests that cognitive-behavioural therapy (CBT) may be effective in preventing relapse after weight restoration (Pike *et al.* 2003), and that specialist supportive-clinical management may be more effective than interpersonal psychotherapy (IPT), with CBT holding a middle position (McIntosh *et al.* 2005, 2006). Why do we know so little? First, given the fairly low population base rate of AN, small single-site studies cannot recruit sufficiently large samples to draw meaningful conclusions. Second, dropout is unacceptably high (average dropout around 50 per cent) – probably reflecting ambivalence about treatment (Halmi 2008; Le Grange and Loeb 2007).

Whereas with some disorders, patients long to have their painful symptoms taken away (e.g. phobias, depression), in AN, patients cling desperately to their low weight and are deeply fearful of giving up their disorder. From that vantage point, the patient and therapist may feel on opposite sides rather than working together towards a common therapeutic goal. Yet we have not found effective approaches to keep adults with AN in therapy and to create the sense of cooperation and teamwork necessary to help decrease their anxiety about recovery and weight restoration.

We are more effective at treating adolescents (Le Grange and Loeb 2007) in part because families can play a central role in keeping their child in treatment, can toe the hard line if need be, and be a supportive buffer during recovery. What can we learn from our successes with youth (Russell *et al.* 1987) to improve our outcomes for adults with AN? How can we leverage the families of adults to improve motivation, decrease ambivalence, and enhance recovery from this potentially life-threatening illness? These questions prompted our development of a couple-based intervention for adults with AN.

The importance of relationships in anorexia nervosa

As Duncan's story illustrates, people with AN do enter relationships, proving old stereotypes untrue (Brinch *et al.* 1988; Bulik *et al.* 1999). In fact, most adults presenting for treatment for AN are in relationships. More importantly, patients emphasize the centrality of relationships in the recovery process. A group of seventy women who had been treated ten years earlier listed having a supportive partner as the main factor contributing to their recovery (Tozzi *et al.* 2003). If relationships are so important, we asked, why aren't we focusing on them more in treating our adult patients?

Marital adjustment/distress in individuals with anorexia nervosa

We also know from studies of other disorders that a distressed, critical, or hostile relationship can interfere with recovery and worsen the course of illness. Negative relationships are a source of stress and predict relapse (Hooley and Hiller 2001). Many adults with eating disorders report relationship difficulties, and marital distress is common when one spouse has an eating disorder (Franzen and Gerlinghoff 1997; Hodes *et al.* 1997; Van Buren and Williamson 1988). In a small case series (Woodside and Shekter-Wolfson 1990), seven patients were separated or divorced, and three reported experiencing significant marital difficulties. Of eleven mothers with eating disorders, ten reported significant marital distress (Timini and Robinson 1996). Although samples were small, distress was common. It was unclear whether marital distress existed before the eating disorder, or whether the eating disorder resulted in additional distress. Regardless of the order of occurrence, these findings contributed to our perception that helping partners to develop an appropriately supportive stance may be a valuable addition to the standard treatment of adults with anorexia.

Communication in couples with anorexia nervosa

As in Duncan's case, communication can become crippled between partners when one member has AN. Without guidelines, partners are often unclear how to talk about the eating disorder with the patient. Effective communication forms the basis of support, and support is extremely valuable in the recovery process. The two fundamental categories of support – instrumental and emotional — both rely on effective communication (Cutrona *et al.* 1990). Communication is the most consistent predictor of long-term relationship functioning (Karney and Bradbury 1995). A small study compared patients with eating disorders and their partners with maritally distressed and non-distressed couples while engaging in a conflictual and non-conflictual conversation. The eating disorder couples engaged in more negative non-verbal communication than the non-distressed couples, but less than the distressed couples (Van den Broucke *et al.* 1995). They also employed fewer constructive communication skills than the non-distressed couples. Anorexia nervosa is a deeply secretive and often lonely disorder, yet effective communication is critical for couples to be able to address the disorder at all. Specifically targeting communication is vital to any treatment for AN that includes the partner.

Sexual functioning in couples with anorexia nervosa

Healthy sexual functioning is important for relationship quality in general, but for individuals with AN it takes on added complexities as distorted body image, body dissatisfaction, and shame, central features of the disorder (Grabhorn *et al.* 2005; Gupta *et al.* 1995; Seeger *et al.* 2002), can impact both affection and sexual functioning. Over 80 per cent of patients with AN report primary or secondary difficulties in their sexual relationship (Raboch and Faltus 1991). Decreased sexual desire (66.9 per cent) and increased sexual anxiety (59.2 per cent) are common in women with eating disorders (Pinheiro *et al.* 2009). Approximately 40 per cent of a mixed eating disorder sample reported sexual discord (Morgan *et al.* 1995). In a study of more than 200 patients with eating disorders and their partners, patient ratings of their relationship functioning generally were less favourable than spouse ratings on affection, cohesion, sexuality, and identity (analogous to self-esteem) (Woodside *et al.* 2000).

Sexual concerns wax and wane together with various features of anorexia. Sexual satisfaction is inversely related to degree of caloric restriction (Wiederman *et al.* 1996). Unsurprisingly, the greater the weight loss, the lower the sexual enjoyment (Beumont *et al.* 1981), and libido tends to re-emerge with weight restoration (Morgan *et al.* 1999). Couples in which one partner has AN vary tremendously in the nature of their sexual relationship. Addressing affection, intimacy, and sexuality in the treatment of adults with AN highlights not only an important component of relationship functioning, but also core features of the eating disorder, namely body image concerns, within the context of an intimate relationship.

Caregiver experiences and relationships

Duncan vividly illustrates the bewildering world of a partner dealing with AN – not knowing whether to be gentle or firm, to remain silent or to speak up, to sacrifice one's own health for the well-being of the partner. These are all common dilemmas.

Our understanding of caregiving in AN stems primarily from research on parents. Overall, those in caring roles report greater burden than those caring for a relative with bulimia (Santonastaso *et al.* 1997), and poorer general health and even greater caregiving challenges than carers of people with schizophrenia (Treasure *et al.* 2001). Common themes include the 'loss' of the person and the relationship that was there before the illness struck, the pervasive negative impact of the eating disorder on the family, struggling with difficult eating-related behaviours, the dependent nature of patients, and the stigma, shame, and guilt associated with eating disorders (Treasure *et al.* 2001). Parents often report distress, guilt, and helplessness (Whitney *et al.* 2005). Partners report similar feelings coupled with additional domains such as the impact on children and social functioning. Our couple-based intervention aims to transform the relationship into a source of effective support and a tool for change. To develop this intervention, we drew from couple-based cognitive-behavioural therapy.

Cognitive-behavioural couple therapy (CBCT)

Cognitive-behavioural couple therapy (CBCT) is a widely used therapeutic approach that targets relationship functioning by teaching partners communication and problem-solving skills, helping to enhance understanding of relationship interactions, and addressing emotions in an adaptive manner (Baucom and Epstein 1990). By acknowledging that individual psychopathology occurs in an interpersonal context, CBCT is effective when one partner is suffering a psychiatric illness. Effective intervention includes working within an individual's natural social environment to optimize change. Given that partners form a core component of one's natural environment, intervening on a couple level promotes and maintains needed changes for the individual. Typically, partners are willing and eager to help when their loved one is suffering, but fear inadvertently making matters worse. Thus, one goal of the therapy is to assist the partner with developing a plan and increasing confidence in being helpful.

Three couple-based strategies exist: (1) partner-assisted interventions, (2) disorder-specific interventions, and (3) general couple therapy (Baucom et al. 1998). Partner-assisted interventions enlist the partner as a surrogate therapist or coach and may include homework assignments with which the partner may help outside of the session. The relationship is not the focus of change; rather, the partner helps the patient make individual changes. In disorder-specific interventions, the relationship is targeted, but only in relation to the patient's own difficulties. The treatment focuses 'on the ways in which a couple interacts or addresses situations related to the individual's disorder that might contribute to the maintenance or exacerbation of the disorder' (Baucom et al. 1998: 63). In general couple therapy, the primary focus is on marital distress with the intent of relationship improvement assisting with the individual's disorder.

What is UCAN?

UCAN (Uniting Couples in the treatment of Anorexia Nervosa) is based on the perspective that although one member of the couple has anorexia, the disorder occurs in an interpersonal context. For patients who are married or have a committed partner, this partner is a central part of that social environment which can contribute to the alleviation, maintenance, and/or exacerbation of the eating disorder. Our intervention helps the couple work together as an effective team to approach the eating disorder.

The UCAN model

Figure 16.1 presents the UCAN model. The minimization of relationship distress and building of relationship enhancement skills are posited to decrease negative,

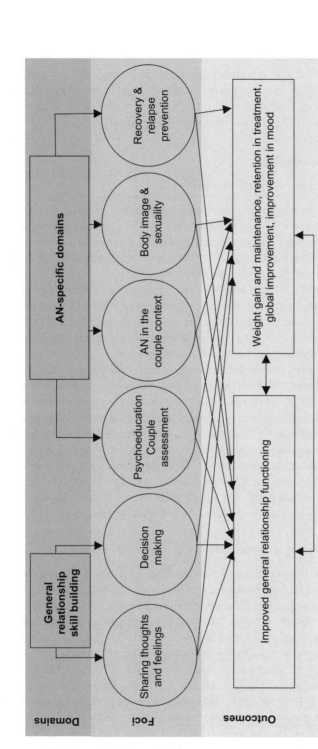

Figure 16.1 Effects of UCAN on anorexia nervosa and general relationship functioning.

critical relationship functioning which can serve as a broad-based, chronic stressor associated with slips and relapses. Intervention in these areas not only impacts general functioning, but also provides additional skills for addressing anorexia-specific concerns. Likewise, AN is a stressor on most relationships and, as AN improves, the overall relationship is likely to benefit too.

UCAN session content

Phase one: creating a foundation for later work

Despite having a strong and satisfying relationship, Duncan and his partner, Nadia, did not know how to address Nadia's AN as a couple, and particularly struggled attempting to communicate about it. Because this is a common experience, a fundamental goal of UCAN is to help couples build a supportive foundation for addressing AN effectively as a team.

Phase one of UCAN focuses on three goals: (1) understanding the couple's experience of anorexia; (2) providing psychoeducation about AN and the recovery process; and (3) teaching the couple effective communication skills. UCAN begins with a thorough assessment of the couple's relationship history, both partners' experience of anorexia, and how AN has influenced and been influenced by the couple's relationship. The psychoeducation component focuses on AN symptoms and associated comorbidities, biological and environmental risk factors, and the recovery process. By presenting this psychoeducation to both members of the couple, UCAN aims to provide a comprehensive and shared understanding of AN to help foster teamwork. This teamwork is further cultivated through teaching essential communication and problem-solving skills that are instrumental in successful couple-based interventions. Through didactic instruction and extensive in- and out-of-session practice, the couple learn how to express thoughts and feelings, listen responsively, and solve problems/make decisions as a team. This approach equips the couple to address issues central to anorexia.

Phase two: addressing anorexia nervosa within a couples context

A fundamental treatment goal for individuals with AN is the resumption of a healthy body weight and development of healthy eating behaviours (e.g. avoidance of restricting and purging). As the patient addresses these treatment goals in individual therapy, phase two of UCAN concurrently helps the couple develop an effective support system for this individual work. The second phase begins by guiding the couple in considering features of AN they find most challenging, and employing their communication skills in responding to these challenges more effectively as a team. For example, Duncan and Nadia would have been encouraged to consider how Duncan can support Nadia in eating meals without adopting a role of strict monitor or commenting inappropriately on what she has not eaten or 'should' be eating. By discussing eating in a way that promotes recovery, the couple can develop more positive interactions around eating within their relationship, which could contribute to Nadia's development of healthier eating and help Duncan feel useful and purposeful. This same approach would be applied to other AN features Nadia may experience such as excessive exercise, purging or restricting. In this way, both partners would clearly understand Duncan's role in Nadia's treatment and recovery, and Duncan's experience of confusion and helplessness would be notably decreased.

Phase two of UCAN broadens the focus to body image and sexual issues. The couple are encouraged to use their communication skills in discussing body image issues and countering problematic interaction patterns. This begins with an in-session conversation in which the patient shares their experience of body image with the partner. Body image distortions and body dissatisfaction can be two of the most puzzling features of AN for the partner, so it is important that the couple have the opportunity to increase understanding and empathy for one another's body image experiences. The partner is also encouraged to discuss their own body image challenges. The couple can then employ their decision-making skills to develop more effective ways of interacting around body image within their relationship. With Duncan and Nadia, such conversations would help to counter avoidance of Nadia's body image issues.

The body image work is a natural entrée into the couple's physical relationship. Phase two concludes with consideration of how the couple's physical relationship can impact and be impacted by the patient's experience of negative body image and the eating disorder more broadly. The couple are encouraged to consider challenges within their physical relationship more broadly and relative to the AN more specifically. Because couples vary widely in their physical and sexual relationships, UCAN is tailored to the couple's current level of functioning and assists them in developing healthier patterns within their physical relationship that reflect the patient's current experience of AN and body image more specifically.

Phase three: relapse prevention and termination

The final phase of UCAN focuses on relapse prevention and the couple's next steps. The couple are presented with psychoeducation on recovery and relapse prevention and the therapist helps them develop effective responses. The treatment concludes with a review of the UCAN experience and a consideration of how the couple need to continue working together against anorexia. Phase three of UCAN would have helped Duncan and Nadia identify how to remain united in recovery by helping Duncan to be supportive without becoming 'Nadia's therapist'.

Thus, UCAN addresses multiple aspects of AN from a couple perspective, leveraging the patient's key relationship in a variety of ways to address the eating disorder. By integrating UCAN into a broader intervention for anorexia, we acknowledge the critical role that a committed partner can play in recovery from AN and anticipate that it will lead to more favourable and lasting treatment gains.

UCAN in the room

UCAN is being tested for individuals who are in committed relationships and are living together. Patients and partners can be of any sex or sexual orientation. UCAN is designed to be an augmentation therapy. Unlike family-based treatments for adolescent anorexia, partners are not asked to take responsibility for monitoring patient weight and eating. The developmentally appropriate approach avoids power imbalances that could emerge if the partner is in a position of complete authority. The UCAN therapist works with each couple to tailor the optimal stance of the partner with reference to the eating disorder. Close collaboration with an individual therapist, a dietitian, and a treating psychiatrist enables UCAN to focus primarily on working with the couple towards recovery.

Discussion

Testing is ongoing and early indications are that UCAN has the potential to change the standard of practice for adults with anorexia. A major strength may be assisting with retention in treatment. Whereas UCAN will continue to evolve, we believe that any mindful inclusion of partners in treatment acknowledges that AN exists on both the personal and interpersonal level and represents an important advance in improving outcomes of this complex and often lethal disorder.

References

Baucom, D. H. and Epstein, N. (1990) *Cognitive-Behavioural Marital Therapy*, New York: Brunner/Mazel.

Baucom, D. H., Shoham, V., Mueser, K. T., Daiuto, A. D., and Stickle, T. R. (1998) 'Empirically Supported Couple and Family Interventions for Marital Distress and Adult Mental Health Problems', *J Consult Clin Psychol* 66: 53–88.

Beumont, P., Abraham, S., and Simson, K. (1981) 'The Psychosexual Histories of Adolescent Girls and Young Women with Anorexia Nervosa', *Psychol Med* 11: 131–40.

Birmingham, C., Su, J., Hlynsky, J., Goldner, E., and Gao, M. (2005) 'The Mortality Rate from Anorexia Nervosa', *Int J Eat Disord* 38: 143–6.

Brinch, M., Isager, T., and Tolstrup, K. (1988) 'Anorexia Nervosa and Motherhood: Reproduction Pattern and Mothering Behaviour of 50 Women', *Acta Psychiatr Scand* 77: 611–17.

Bulik, C., Sullivan, P., Fear, J., Pickering, A., and Dawn, A. (1999) 'Fertility and Reproduction in Women with Anorexia Nervosa: A Controlled Study', *J Clin Psychiatry* 2: 130–5.

Cutrona, C. E., Cohen, B., and Igram, S. (1990) 'Contextual Determinants of the Perceived Supportiveness of Helping Behaviours', *J Soc Pers Relat* 7: 553–62.

Franzen, U. and Gerlinghoff, M. (1997) 'Parenting by Patients with Eating Disorders: Experiences with a Mother-Child Group', *Eat Disord* 5: 5–14.

Grabhorn, R., Stenner, H., Kaufbold, J., Overbeck, G., and Stangier, U. (2005) 'Shame and Social Anxiety in Anorexia and Bulimia Nervosa', *Z Psychosom Med Psychother* 51: 179–93.

Gupta, M., Gupta, A., Schork, N., and Watteel, G. (1995) 'Perceived Touch Deprivation and Body Image: Some Observations Among Eating Disordered and Non-Clinical Subjects', *J Psychosom Res* 39: 459–64.

Halmi, K. A. (2008) 'The Perplexities of Conducting Randomized, Double-Blind, Placebo-Controlled Treatment Trials in Anorexia Nervosa Patients', *Am J Psychiatry* 165: 1227–8.

Hodes, M., Timini, S., and Robinson, P. (1997) 'Children of Mothers with Eating Disorders: A Preliminary Study', *Eur Eat Disord Rev* 5: 11–24.

Hooley, J. M. and Hiller, J. B. (2001) 'Family Relationships and Major Mental Disorder: Risk Factors and Preventive Strategies', in B. R. Sarason and S. Duck (eds) *Personal Relationships: Implications for Clinical and Community Psychology* (pp. 61–87), New York: John Wiley.

Hudson, J. I., Hiripi, E., Pope, H. G. Jr., and Kessler, R. C. (2007) 'The Prevalence and Correlates of Eating Disorders in the National Comorbidity Survey Replication', *Biol Psychiatry* 61: 348–58.

Kaplan, A. S., Walsh, B. T., Olmsted, M., Attia, E., Carter, J. C., Devlin, M. J., Pike, K. M., Woodside, B., Rockert, W., Roberto, C. A., and Parides, M. (2008) 'The Slippery Slope: Prediction of Successful Weight Maintenance in Anorexia Nervosa', *Psychol Med* 39, 6: 1037–45.

Karney, B. R. and Bradbury, T. N. (1995) 'The Longitudinal Course of Marital Quality and Stability: A Review of Theory, Methods, and Research', *Psychol Bull* 118: 3–34.

Le Grange, D. and Loeb, K. (2007) 'Early Identification and Treatment of Eating Disorders: Prodrome to Syndrome', *Early Interv Psychiatry* 1: 27–39.

McIntosh, V., Jordan, J., Carter, F., Luty, S., McKenzie, J., Bulik, C., Frampton, C., and Joyce, P. (2005) 'Three Psychotherapies for Anorexia Nervosa: A Randomized Controlled Trial', *Am J Psychiatry* 162: 741–7.

McIntosh, V. V., Jordan, J., Luty, S. E., Carter, F. A., McKenzie, J. M., Bulik, C. M., and Joyce, P. R. (2006) 'Specialist Supportive Clinical Management for Anorexia Nervosa', *Int J Eat Disord* 39: 625–32.

Morgan, C. D., Wiederman, M. W., and Pryor, T. L. (1995) 'Sexual Functioning and Attitudes of Eating-Disordered Women: A Follow-Up Study', *J Sex Marital Ther* 21: 67–77.

Morgan, J. F., Lacey, J. H., and Reid, F. (1999) 'Anorexia Nervosa: Changes in Sexuality During Weight Restoration', *Psychosom Med* 61: 541–5.

Pike, K., Walsh, B., Vitousek, K., Wilson, G., and Bauer, J. (2003) 'Cognitive Behaviour Therapy in the Posthospitalization Treatment of Anorexia Nervosa', *Am J Psychiatry* 160: 2046–9.

Pinheiro, A. P., Raney, T. J., Thornton, L. M., Fichter, M. M., Berrettini, W. H., Goldman, D., Halmi, K. A., Kaplan, A. S., Strober, M., Treasure, J., Woodside, D. B., Kaye, W. H., and Bulik, C. M. (2009) 'Sexual Functioning in Women with Eating Disorders', *Int J Eat Disord* 43, 2: 123–9.

Raboch, J. and Faltus, F. (1991) 'Sexuality of Women with Anorexia Nervosa', *Acta Psychiatr Scand* 84: 9–11.

Russell, G. F. M., Szmukler, G. I., Dare, C., and Eisler, I. (1987) 'An Evaluation of Family Therapy in Anorexia and Bulimia Nervosa', *Arch Gen Psychiatry* 44: 1047–56.

Santonastaso, P., Saccon, D., and Favaro, A. (1997) 'Burden and Psychiatric Symptoms on Key Relatives of Patients with Eating Disorders: A Preliminary Study', *Eat Weight Disord* 2: 44–8.

Seeger, G., Braus, D. F., Ruf, M., Goldberger, U., and Schmidt, M. H. (2002) 'Body Image Distortion Reveals Amygdala Activation in Patients with Anorexia Nervosa: A Functional Magnetic Resonance Imaging Study', *Neurosci Lett* 326: 25–8.

Sullivan, P. F. (1995) 'Mortality in Anorexia Nervosa', *Am J Psychiatry* 152: 1073–4.

Timini, S. and Robinson, P. (1996) 'Disturbances in Children of Patients with Eating Disorders', *Eur Eat Disord Rev* 4: 183–8.

Tozzi, F., Sullivan, P. F., Fear, J. L., McKenzie, J., and Bulik, C. M. (2003) 'Causes and Recovery in Anorexia Nervosa: The Patient's Perspective', *Int J Eat Disord* 33: 143–54.

Treasure, J., Murphy, T., Szmukler, G., Todd, G., Gavan, K., and Joyce, J. (2001) 'The Experience of Caregiving for Severe Mental Illness: A Comparison Between Anorexia Nervosa and Psychosis', *Soc Psychiatry Psychiatr Epidemiol* 36: 343–7.

Van Buren, D. J. and Williamson, D. A. (1988) 'Marital Relationships and Conflict Resolution Skills of Bulimics', *Int J Eat Disord* 7: 735–41.

Van den Broucke, S., Vandereycken, W., and Vertommen, H. (1995) 'Marital Intimacy in Patients with an Eating Disorder: A Controlled Self-Report Study', *Br J Clin Psychol* 34, 1: 67–78.

Whitney, J., Murray, J., Gavan, K., Todd, G., Whitaker, W., and Treasure, J. (2005) 'Experience of Caring for Someone with Anorexia Nervosa: Qualitative Study', *Br J Psychiatry* 187: 444–9.

Wiederman, M. W., Pryor, T., and Morgan, C. D. (1996) 'The Sexual Experience of Women Diagnosed with Anorexia Nervosa or Bulimia Nervosa', *Int J Eat Disord* 19: 109–18.

Woodside, D. and Shekter-Wolfson, L. (1990) 'Parenting by Patients with Anorexia Nervosa and Bulimia Nervosa', *Int J Eat Disord* 9: 303–9.

Woodside, D. B., Lackstrom, J. B., and Shekter-Wolfson, L. (2000) 'Marriage in Eating Disorders Comparisons Between Patients and Spouses and Changes Over the Course of Treatment', *J Psychosom Res* 49: 165–8.

Chapter 17

Relapse prevention

Marion P. Olmsted, Jacqueline C. Carter and Kathleen M. Pike

Case study

From age 11, I restricted food intake as I didn't feel good enough no matter what my achievements. In my twenties, through cognitive behaviour therapy (CBT), I began changing worthless thoughts of myself, to deserving thoughts. This was like the lifting of a veil and, after years of resisting therapy, I wanted to recover.

My independence felt amazing and I entered a first, real, loving relationship. This clover patch period of my life lasted about three years. Then triggers went off. Big time.

First my mother – my devoted prime carer throughout my long illness – required a leg amputation. I felt guilty. Mum had given up much for me and now this had happened to her.

Then my best friend, Jess, died of leukaemia and a friend, Aimee, died at age 20 from anorexia.

With this sadness I became vulnerable and anorexia took hold again. To top it off, my dad, who has suffered lifetime anxiety, was diagnosed with a chronic illness. I felt guilty because I was too unwell to stay at home and care for my parents.

These four major events occurred within twelve months and the 'A' snuck up. I felt ashamed. I thought I was past being obsessed by weight and food. But while busy helping my parents, Jess and Aimee, I missed some meals. This was easy to do, as I had not developed a sense of hunger.

After losing a little weight, I did not feel good admitting this to myself but it calmed my anxiety. This is what it does.

I was helping others with appointments, thinking I should grab something to eat, and I would not. Initially I remembered to eat something before bedtime. I would think 'I have to eat'. I did try. Really try. I wanted to appear I was okay, and not let people down; these were my thoughts as I picked up the rules of eating the same food, at the same time, every day; I had to do things by certain times; these thoughts returned quickly. I thought I was quelling my anxiety but I was feeding it. Anorexia is very sneaky.

Amazing how my 'A' triggers popped back so quickly. My psychiatrist likens it to a waterfall. The nearer I get to the fall, the faster I go.

Two years later I am making slow progress and this time when I recover I will have lifelines in place. In a way I am glad the relapse happened with those big triggers because now I know:

(a) I must eat three meals and three snacks every day. The minute I let go I will relapse.

(b) Maintain my support group – my psychiatrist – and behaviour with the CBT positive thoughts replacing negative thoughts. Constant support with positive self-talk helps to deflect the 'A' mindset.

(c) Surround myself with positive affirmations in my home.

(d) Be honest with others and myself. I could have avoided the distress of the past two years if I had reached out immediately, instead of thinking: 'I will upset my family if I tell them'. They are a lot more upset now.

(e) Constant vigilance is necessary.

Reaching out is vital the moment the first 'A' thought appears. NOW I would immediately reach out and say: 'Hey, I need help' before the 'A' takes off.

Learning about my illness helps me understand and accept that I have not let others or myself down by relapsing. I must not feel guilty.

Above all, I know now I must not skip a meal, to avoid my brain getting in starvation mode. A relapse can set in quickly. Like I said, less than six weeks.

Jennifer (age 38)

Review of the research on relapse in eating disorders

How common is relapse?

A range of estimates of relapse rates in eating disorders has been reported depending upon the definitions of relapse used, the length of follow-up, and the methodologies employed. For anorexia nervosa (AN), rates of relapse ranging from 9 to 65 per cent following weight restoration have been reported (e.g. Carter *et al.* 2004; Eckert *et al.* 1995; Eisler *et al.* 1997; Keel *et al.* 2005; Pike *et al.* 2003; Strober *et al.* 1997; Walsh *et al.* 2006), with rates of relapse tending to be lower in adolescent samples than among adults. For bulimia nervosa (BN), relapse rates ranging from 30 to 63 per cent have been reported (e.g. Field *et al.* 1997; Grilo *et al.* 2007; Herzog *et al.* 1999; Keel *et al.* 2005; Olmsted *et al.*1994, 2005; Pyle *et al.* 1990; Richard *et al.* 2005). Studies that have examined the timing of relapse reveal that the risk of relapse is highest during the first four to twelve months post-treatment (e.g. Carter *et al.* 2004; Kordy *et al.* 2002; McFarlane *et al.* 2008; Olmsted *et al.* 1994). This suggests that relapse prevention efforts should be most intensive for the first year immediately following acute treatment and amelioration of behavioural symptoms.

What predictors of relapse have been identified?

Knowledge of factors that predict relapse following successful initial treatment of the eating disorder may suggest important targets for relapse prevention interventions. Some studies have identified demographic and clinical features that are predictive of relapse in AN, including older age at presentation (Deter and Herzog 1994); higher number of previous hospitalizations (Treat *et al.* 2008); and higher pre-treatment purge frequency (Deter and Herzog 1994). Olmsted and colleagues (1994) found that younger age and higher vomiting frequency at intake were associated with a higher risk of relapse in BN. In a transdiagnostic sample consisting of AN, BN and eating disorder not otherwise specified (EDNOS), McFarlane and colleagues (2008) found that more severe pre-treatment dietary restriction predicted relapse following day hospital treatment. Taken together, these study outcomes suggest that patients with more severe or chronic eating disorders at presentation may be at a higher risk of relapse, and intensive relapse prevention treatment may be particularly important for these patients. One study found that higher levels of obsessive-compulsive symptoms were associated with higher risk of relapse in AN (Carter *et al.* 2004), suggesting that effectively treating comorbid obsessive-compulsive symptomatology in AN may be important in order to reduce the risk of relapse.

Several studies have identified treatment process variables that predict relapse. A lower rate of weight gain during treatment has been shown to be associated with relapse at follow-up in AN (Castro *et al.* 2004; Steinhausen *et al.* 2009; Treat *et al.* 2008). Slower adherence to the prescribed meal plan during day hospital treatment predicted relapse at follow-up in another study based on a mixed eating disorder sample (McFarlane *et al.* 2008). Rapid response in terms of cessation of bingeing and vomiting in patients with BN treated in a day hospital was associated with a much lower rate of relapse over the following two years, in comparison to patients who responded more slowly to treatment (Olmsted *et al.* 1996). Similarly, Halmi and colleagues (2002: 1107) found that BN patients who had maintained abstinence from binge eating and purging for a longer time during CBT were less likely to relapse. These findings suggest that patients who make slower progress during acute treatment are more prone to relapse later. This may reflect ambivalence about change and/or reduced time available to address the issues that emerge after symptom control has occurred.

A number of studies have identified areas of vulnerability that persist after acute treatment that are associated with relapse. Higher residual weight concern in AN (Carter *et al.* 2004), greater body image disturbance (Freeman *et al.* 1985; Keel *et al.* 2005) and higher weight-based self-esteem (McFarlane *et al.* 2008) in mixed AN/BN samples predict relapse. These results suggest that interventions aimed at reducing overconcern about weight, decreasing body image disturbance, and broadening sources of self-worth may be important targets for relapse prevention efforts. Second, lower motivation to stay well at the end of treatment has been shown to predict relapse in both AN and BN (Castro-Fornieles *et al.* 2007; Halmi *et al.* 2002). This suggests a continued focus on motivational enhancement strategies during relapse prevention treatment may be important. Finally, the persistence of residual symptoms at the end of a course of acute treatment is associated with relapse. In one study of BN, Olmsted and colleagues (1994) found that higher vomiting frequencies and higher levels of dietary restraint at post-treatment were associated with a higher risk of relapse. Similarly, McFarlane and colleagues (2008) found that higher residual binge/purge symptoms at post-treatment predicted relapse. For AN, excessive exercise aimed at weight control (Carter *et al.* 2004; Steinhausen *et al.* 2009; Strober *et al.* 1997) and even a small amount of weight loss (Kaplan *et al.* 2009) during the initial few weeks immediately following completion of acute treatment are predictive of relapse. These findings reinforce the importance of obtaining symptom abstinence to promote long-term recovery. Overall, important targets for relapse prevention interventions include body image, self-esteem, motivation to stay well, and complete control of behavioural symptoms.

Jennifer noted the short time it took to move from coping and maintaining wellness to full relapse:

> I had lost a few kgs and felt better; and thought: 'I am probably better off without that weight'; this was the 'A' taking over again. I was overwhelmed it could come back so strongly and the behaviours return so easily. This happened in less than six weeks.
>
> Jennifer

This clinical account underscores the importance of identifying early indicators of risk with patients when they are still in acute treatment and helping them anticipate and respond adaptively when such events occur.

Are there evidence-based relapse prevention treatments?

To our knowledge, only five published controlled studies have examined relapse prevention treatments for AN. Eisler and colleagues (1997) found no difference in the rates of relapse at five-year follow-up among twenty-one AN patients who were randomly assigned to receive either family therapy or individual supportive therapy for one year following weight restoration in a hospital-based programme. Pike and colleagues (2003) conducted a randomized study evaluating CBT for thirty-three weight-restored adults with AN. In this study, the CBT group achieved a better outcome in terms of relapse rates compared to the comparison group which received supportive nutritional counselling. Carter and colleagues (2009) recently conducted a non-randomized clinical trial comparing CBT (n = 46) and maintenance treatment as usual (MTAU) (n = 42) for weight-restored adults with AN. At one year, 35 per cent of the CBT group and 66 per cent of the MTAU group had relapsed (Carter *et al.* 2009: 205). The results of the two medication studies were inconsistent. Kaye and colleagues (2001) reported that the antidepressant medication fluoxetine was superior to placebo in preventing relapse in a randomized double-blind trial of thirty-five AN patients. However, Walsh and colleagues (2006) found no benefit from fluoxetine in preventing relapse following weight restoration in a double-blind, placebo-controlled randomized trial of ninety-three AN patients who were also receiving individual CBT.

Few controlled studies have examined relapse prevention interventions for BN. One study offered additional CBT sessions to prevent relapse to successful responders to CBT for BN (Mitchell *et al.* 2004). These patients were instructed to contact their therapist for up to eight booster sessions over the seventeen-week follow-up, at no charge, if they felt at risk of relapse. Although some patients experienced problems and relapsed, none contacted the clinic for booster sessions (Mitchell *et al.* 2004: 553). The researchers concluded that a more structured relapse prevention programme may be more effective. Two pilot studies of a text messaging-based aftercare intervention for BN had mixed results (Bauer *et al.* 2003; Robinson *et al.* 2006). Finally, Fichter and colleagues (1996) demonstrated that the antidepressant medication fluvoxamine was helpful in preventing relapse in a double-blind, placebo-controlled study of seventy-two patients with BN who had successfully completed inpatient treatment.

Although there is little research evidence regarding effective relapse prevention treatment, the most support exists for CBT. Pharmacotherapy, especially for coexisting problems, should be considered on an individual basis. Of utmost importance is the provision of planned treatment and support focused on maintaining recovery.

Pathways to relapse

As Jennifer illustrates, maintaining wellness requires considerable effort, vigilance and being prepared. A framework for this vigilance is provided by helping the patient to explore potential pathways and identify those that need changing or close monitoring.

Social and occupational environment

Some occupations and social networks focus strongly on food, dieting and/or controlling weight. Friends, family members and colleagues at work may intentionally or unintentionally provide a fertile environment for growth of eating disordered thoughts or behaviours.

Other environmental aspects include stress level, social support and illness-related habitual responses to specific environmental cues. These can relate to the physical environment or interpersonal situations, that generally led to food restriction or other symptoms previously. After identifying triggers for illness behaviours, decisions can be made on handling each situation; this might mean deciding not to return to a specific job or social group, or involve a series of deliberate exposures to the situation with a plan to prevent the triggered illness response.

Lifestyle and self-care

Recovery can be conceptualized as a delicate flower that requires daily care to foster its growth. Maintaining a healthy schedule with respect to regular meals, adequate sleep and a balance of work and leisure activities is essential. Although meticulous self-care may benefit most people, the potential costs in recovery are much higher.

> It does not have to be a big event that brings you undone. When overtired, overstressed or overwhelmed the AN thoughts can creep in. When there is a stressful period – or a very happy period – it's easy to get caught up in the moment, and let basic things go, like a snack, and the AN can creep back. It distracts us from ourselves and this is how it can sneak in while we are focusing on helping others. We have to look after ourselves first.
>
> Jennifer

Function of the eating disorder

Understanding the function served by the eating disorder and developing an alternative means of meeting this need are essential tasks for ongoing wellness. Some benefits provided by the eating disorder may be apparent, while others may be more difficult to identify. Many patients can acknowledge that the eating disorder may have distracted them from other concerns, helped them manage or avoid emotions, suppressed memories, or provided an effective means of self-soothing. Other common functions include feeling protected from failure, maturity or sexuality, lowering expectations or perceived expectations from others, eliciting care or attention from others, providing equilibrium in the family system, forming the basis of the patient's identity or self-concept, providing a measure of self-worth or accomplishment, and anxiety reduction. Jennifer noted that her anxiety increased when her weight and eating improved:

> And I still had panic attacks – it was almost like they replaced the weight and food part of the 'A' for that time.
>
> Jennifer

Tolerating the discomfort involved in managing life without the protective coat of the eating disorder is a huge challenge. While the longer-term solution includes skill building and re-evaluation of core beliefs, in the shorter term it is helpful for the patient to be forewarned and to have a coping plan in place. She must move forward in a 'reinforcement vacuum' while slowly and gradually learning other methods of self-soothing and meeting her needs.

Beliefs and expectations

The misconception that amelioration of visible behavioural symptoms indicates that recovery has occurred is common among eating disorder patients and their family and friends.

> My psychiatrist thought I was recovered and coping brilliantly; I did not want anyone else to know that I had backslidden a bit. Because I was no longer the emaciated skeleton I was at 28 years of age, I was meant to be 100 per cent recovered. I couldn't tell my family, friends and partner that I was not.
>
> Jennifer

Education and information about the process of recovery and risk factors for relapse is essential to combat the patient's understandable wish to return to a normal (unsheltered) life and the wish of others to believe the eating disorder has been overcome. The most consistent predictors of relapse, based on available research, are the signs of an incomplete recovery; these include residual symptoms or the quick return of weight control efforts, body image concerns, and the belief that one's value as a person is related to weight or shape. A full recovery takes time and effort.

Preventing relapse

Exposure and response prevention

Exposure and response prevention is a recognized method of reducing the power of a specific cue or situation to elicit a habitual, or in this case illness-related, response. It is also an important part of CBT focused on relapse prevention. During the acute phase of treatment, the exposures may initially focus on phobic or binge foods and extend to identified high-risk situations. In the relapse prevention phase of treatment, once initial symptom control has been achieved, the focus may broaden to include mood states, physical states, unstructured time, challenging social situations, stressful interpersonal communications and self-critical thoughts. Exposure to many of these potential triggers can be either anticipated or deliberately arranged. This allows the patient to plan the exposure and the strategies and supports to resist engaging in illness behaviours. As part of the reintegration of normal life activities, it is also helpful to develop the ability to identify unexpected challenging situations, problem-solve and develop a plan.

A big hurdle in working toward recovery during the relapse prevention phase is accepting the need for ongoing exposure tasks and careful planning. This may require the patient to challenge thoughts (her own and/or those of others) that she has spent enough time and energy on treatment and should now be able to manage on her own.

Addressing the functions served by the eating disorder

The eating disorder may serve several functions and each may mark an assemblage of needs, worries, information deficits, beliefs and skill gaps. Working through these issues involves validating the patient's needs, providing educational information about needs and how they can be met, testing unhelpful beliefs with behavioural experiments, shifting beliefs with cognitive restructuring, and developing skills to manage life without an eating disorder. This may include anxiety and/or stress management, problem solving, assertiveness training, relaxation training, learning how to make friends and develop relationships, balancing 'shoulds' and 'wants', and managing coexisting illnesses or the sequelae of trauma.

Another case study, Claire, provides a simple example. Claire noticed her parents were very attentive, coaxing her to eat and taking her to appointments when she was acutely ill with AN. As she gained weight and looked healthier, she worried she would not get enough care and attention if well. Claire's therapist helped her identify that a need to be cared for is normal and reasonable. Together they explored methods for self-care and self-nurturing and discussed what care and attention might realistically be expected from others in the context of good health. Claire developed a behavioural experiment to test her assumption that her parents would not have time for her outside of her illness. This involved inviting them to see a movie at a mutually convenient time. The positive results of this experiment were incorporated into the cognitive restructuring emphasized in this phase of therapy. Broader exploration of Claire's social functioning revealed she had few friends and felt awkward with people her age. Plans were made to help her develop her communication skills and learn how to build friendships.

Body image, weight concern and weight-based self-esteem

Ongoing shape and weight concerns and weight-based self-esteem have been linked to relapse. For some patients the challenge is to accept their weight or shape, while for others allowing their body to function without being controlled is the bigger issue. It is useful to directly address the more concrete discomfort with the body along with any self-critical thoughts or symptomatic behaviours such as body checking or avoidance, ill-fitting clothing, frequent weighing, or difficulty choosing clothing for the day. These can all be addressed with CBT and this work, which often starts in initial acute treatment protocols, needs to continue into the maintenance phase of treatment and often for an extended period.

Support from family and friends

Well-informed family and friends can assist the recovery process by keeping expectations appropriate, providing practical support and celebrating daily successes in moving forward. Most importantly, they can provide a safe place for the patient to check emerging thoughts or behaviours that may indicate the eating disorder is trying to 'sneak back in'.

Conclusion

Relapse is common in eating disorders and appears to be more common among those who are more severely ill, respond more slowly or less completely to initial treatments, or return too soon to behaviours, environments or situations that have contributed to or supported the eating disorder in the past. The common misconception that weight restoration and control of behavioural symptoms are sufficient to warrant a return to daily routines and the demands of normal life has tended to minimize the important role of maintenance therapy and the considerable ongoing work and effort involved in preventing relapse.

> Weight restoration is important but is only part of recovery. You have to be weight restored to take in the other treatments and they require ongoing maintenance.
>
> Jennifer

Eating disorder knowledge has advanced to the point where we can focus on developing long-term wellness maintenance approaches. These may be ideally informed by the integration of research findings and the insight of patients like Jennifer who have recovered and relapsed. Significant research is needed to establish the most effective approaches.

References

Bauer, S., Percevic, R., Okon, E., Meerman, R., and Kordy, H. (2003) 'Use of text messaging in the aftercare of patients with bulimia nervosa', *Eur Eat Disord Rev* 11: 279–90.

Carter, J. C., Blackmore, E., Sutandar-Pinnock, K., and Woodside, D. B. (2004) 'Relapse in anorexia nervosa: A survival analysis', *Psychol Med* 34: 671–9.

Carter, J. C., McFarlane, T. L., Bewell, C. V., Olmsted, M. P., Woodside, D. B., Kaplan, A. S., and Crosby, R. (2009) 'Maintenance treatment for anorexia nervosa: Cognitive behavior therapy versus treatment as usual', *Int J Eat Disord* 42: 202–7.

Castro, J., Gila, A., Puig, J., Rodriguez, S., and Toro, J. (2004) 'Predictors of rehospitalization after total weight recovery in adolescents with anorexia nervosa', *Int J Eat Disord* 36: 22–30.

Castro-Fornieles, J., Casulà, V., Saura, B., Martínez, E., Lazaro, L., Vila, M., Plana, M. T., and Toro, J. (2007) 'Predictors of weight maintenance after hospital discharge in adolescent anorexia nervosa', *Int J Eat Disord* 40, 2: 129–35.

Deter, H. C. and Herzog, W. (1994) 'Anorexia nervosa in a long-term perspective: Results of the Heidelberg-Mannheim study', *Psychosom Med* 56, 1: 20–7.

Eckert, E. D., Halmi, K. A., Marchi, P., Grove, W., and Crosby, R. (1995) 'Ten-year follow-up of anorexia nervosa: Clinical course and outcome', *Psychol Med* 25, 1: 143–56.

Eisler, I., Dare, C., Russell, G. F., Szmukler, G., Le Grange, D., and Dodge, E. (1997) 'Family and individual therapy in AN: A 5-year follow-up', *Arch Gen Psychiatry* 54: 1025–30.

Fichter, M. M., Krüger, R., Rief, W., Holland, R., and Döhne, J. (1996) 'Fluvoxamine in prevention of relapse in bulimia nervosa: Effects on eating-specific psychopathology', *J Clin Psychopharmacol* 16, 1: 9–18.

Field, A. E., Herzog, D. B., Keller, M. B., West, J., Nussbaum, K., and Colditz, G. A. (1997) 'Distinguishing recovery from remission in a cohort of bulimic women: How should asymptomatic periods be described?', *J Clin Epidemiol* 50, 12: 1339–45.

Freeman, R. J., Beach, B., Davis, R., and Solyom, L. (1985) 'The prediction of relapse in bulimia nervosa', *J Psychiatr Res* 19: 349–53.

Grilo, C. M., Pagano, M. E., Skodol, A. E., Sanislow, C. A., McGlashan, T. H., Gunderson, J. G., and Stout, R. L. (2007) 'Natural course of bulimia nervosa and of eating disorder not otherwise specified: 5-year prospective study of remissions, relapses, and the effects of personality disorder psychopathology', *J Clin Psychiatry* 68, 5: 738–46.

Halmi, K. A., Agras, W. S., Mitchell, J., Wilson, G. T., Crow, S., Bryson, S. W., and Kraemer, H. (2002) 'Relapse predictors of patients with bulimia nervosa who achieved abstinence through cognitive behavioral therapy', *Arch Gen Psychiatry* 59: 1105–9.

Herzog, D. B., Dorer, D. J., Keel, P. K., Selwyn, S. E., Ekeblad, E. R., Flores, A. T., Greenwood, D. N., Burwell, R. A., and Keller, M. B. (1999) 'Recovery and relapse in anorexia and bulimia nervosa: A 7.5-year follow-up study', *J Am Acad Child Adolesc Psychiatry* 38, 7: 829–37.

Kaplan, A. S., Walsh, B. T., Olmsted, M., Attia, E., Carter, J. C., Devlin, M. J., Pike, K. M., Woodside, B., Rockert, W., Roberto, C. A., and Parides, M. (2009) 'The slippery slope: Prediction of successful weight maintenance in anorexia nervosa', *Psychol Med* 39, 6: 1037–45.

Kaye, W. H., Nagata, T., Weltzin, T. E., Hsu, L. K., Sokol, M. S., McConaha, C., Plotnicov, K. H., Weise, J., and Deep, D. (2001) 'Double-blind placebo-controlled administration of fluoxetine in restricting- and restricting-purging-type AN', *Biol Psychiatry* 49: 644–52.

Keel, P. K., Dorer, D. J., Franko, D. L., Jackson, S. C., and Herzog, D. B. (2005) 'Postremission predictors of relapse in women with eating disorders', *Am J Psychiatry* 162, 12: 2263–8.

Kordy, H., Kramer, B., Palmer, R. L., Papezova, H., Pellet, J., Richard, M., and Treasure, J. (2002) 'Remission, recovery, relapse, and recurrence in eating disorders: Conceptualization and illustration of a validation strategy', *J Clin Psychol* 58: 833–46.

McFarlane, T., Olmsted, M. P., and Trottier, K. (2008) 'Timing and prediction of relapse in a transdiagnostic eating disorder sample', *Int J Eat Disord* 41: 587–93.

Mitchell, J. E., Agras, W. S., Wilson, G. T., Halmi, K., Kraemer, H., and Crow, S. (2004) 'A trial of a relapse prevention strategy in women with bulimia nervosa who respond to cognitive-behavior therapy', *Int J Eat Disord* 35, 4: 549–55.

Olmsted, M. P., Kaplan, A. S., and Rockert, W. (1994) 'Rate and prediction of relapse in bulimia nervosa', *Am J Psychiatry* 151: 738–43.

Olmsted, M. P., Kaplan, A. S., Rockert, W., and Jacobsen, M. (1996) 'Rapid responders to treatment of bulimia nervosa', *Int J Eat Disord* 19: 279–85.

Olmsted, M. P., Kaplan, A. S., and Rockert, W. (2005) 'Defining remission and relapse in bulimia nervosa', *Int J Eat Disord* 38: 1–7.

Pike, K. M., Walsh, B. T., Vitousek, K., Wilson, G. T., and Bauer, J. (2003) 'Cognitive behavior therapy in the posthospitalization treatment of AN', *Am J Psychiatry* 160: 2046–9.

Pyle, R. L., Mitchell, J. E., Eckert, E. D., Hatsukami, D., Pomeroy, C., and Zimmerman, R. (1990) 'Maintenance treatment and 6-month outcome for bulimic patients who respond to initial treatment', *Am J Psychiatry* 147: 871–5.

Richard, M., Bauer, S., and Kordy, H. (2005) 'Relapse in anorexia and bulimia nervosa: A 2.5-year follow-up study', *Eur Eat Disord Rev* 13: 180–90.

Robinson, S., Perkins, S., Bauer, S., Hammond, N., Treasure, J., and Schmidt, U. (2006) 'Aftercare intervention through text messaging in the treatment of bulimia nervosa – feasibility pilot', *Int J Eat Disord* 39, 8: 633–8.

Steinhausen, H. C., Grigoroiu-Serbanescu, M., Bovadjieva, S., Neumärker, K. J., and Metzke, C. W. (2009) 'The relevance of body weight in the medium-term to long-term course of adolescent anorexia nervosa: Findings from a multisite study', *Int J Eat Disord* 42, 1: 19–25.

Strober, M., Freeman, R., and Morrell, W. (1997) 'The long-term course of severe anorexia nervosa in adolescents: Survival analysis of recovery, relapse, and outcome predictors over 10–15 years in a prospective study', *Int J Eat Disord* 22: 339–60.

Treat, T. A., McCabe, E. B., Gaskill, J. A., and Marcus, M. D. (2008) 'Treatment of anorexia nervosa in a specialty care continuum', *Int J Eat Disord* 41, 6: 564–72.

Walsh, B. T., Kaplan, A. S., Attia, E., Olmsted, M., Parides, M., Carter, J. C., Pike, K. M., Devlin, M. J., Woodside, B., Roberto, C. A., and Rockert, W. (2006) 'Fluoxetine after weight restoration in AN: A randomized controlled trial', *J Am Med Assoc* 295: 2605–12.

Part 3

Clinical presentations
of subgroups

Introduction

Eric van Furth

The number of stumbling blocks along the road to recovery for both sufferer and clinician are many. On a societal level service availability (where can I get help?) is limited, as well as service accessibility due to waiting lists or demands set by treatment professionals (for example, minimum body mass index (BMI) for entry to a programme). In many countries service affordability or insurance reimbursement is also limited. On an individual level and in part due to the nature of eating disorders, on average, it takes an individual 4.2 years to recognize and acknowledge her disorder (patient delay). In our Dutch system, where the general practitioner serves as the gatekeeper to specialized care, doctor delay is 1.1 years on average (de la Rie *et al.* 2006). This may be attributed to the difficulty of diagnosing eating disorders and to a lack of training on eating disorders in many GPs. Also, patients often don't present their complaints and symptoms openly or they explicitly don't want to be referred for treatment. As a result only 50 per cent of sufferers with anorexia nervosa and approximately one in three sufferers with bulimia nervosa are detected in primary care (Keski-Rahkonen *et al.* 2007, 2009). Part 3 is devoted to specific subgroups of eating disorder sufferers, their barriers to care and specific needs in diagnosis and treatment.

Peter Doyle, Angela Smyth and Daniel Le Grange (Chapter 18) focus on the differences and commonalities between childhood and adult eating disorders. They remind us that the 'treatments for adult and adolescent patients differ because of the myriad of varying durations of illness and differing developmental stages'. Consequently, we always need to apply the available empirical evidence to the individual's circumstances and wishes to establish a mutually agreed upon treatment plan.

Sloane Madden (Chapter 19) discusses the difficulties of recognizing and diagnosing early onset eating disorders. He draws attention to a study which 'confirmed the presence of anorexia-like illnesses in children as young as 5 years'. Madden also addresses the poor match between the DSM criteria and the clinical symptoms of children and adolescents. This chapter also reveals a dearth of knowledge about binge eating disorder in children.

Julie O'Toole (Chapter 20) presents an experience-based approach to food phobia in children. This relatively straightforward method clearly begs for empirical support. The lack of treatment for these children – Beau and his parents had flown '3,000 miles across country to our clinic' – struck me as tragic.

Angélica Claudino and Christina Morgan (Chapter 21) provide a clear overview of binge eating disorder (BED). Our body of knowledge on this new (?) disorder is slowly growing, but there is much we still don't know. For example, it struck me how little we know about the eating and compensatory behaviour of people with BED.

Stefanie Gilbert (Chapter 22) looks at eating disorders in African American women. Her conclusion that 'it is important that therapists evaluate the impact of patients' acculturation, racial identity, and history of trauma on their body image and eating behaviours' is an important message for all ethnic groups around the world.

Jorunn Sundgot-Borgen and Solfrid Bratland-Sanda (Chapter 23) address the specifics of eating disorders and athletes. They explore the two-edged sword of exercise and emphasize early identification and management of eating disorders in athletes. The next challenge in this group is the prevention of eating disorders by collaborating with local and national sports federations.

It cannot be a coincidence that the last chapter, by John Morgan, is on males with eating disorders (Chapter 24). We know so little about boys and men with an eating disorder and should be careful to draw any firm conclusions. The author rightly points out that men are an under-diagnosed and under-treated group. The 'contradictory drive towards both leanness and muscularity' may help disguise the eating disorder and 'personal and social stigma' forms an extra barrier to treatment.

References

de la Rie, S.M., Noordenbos, G., Donker, M., and Van Furth, E.F. (2006) 'Evaluating treatment of eating disorders from the patient's perspective', *Int J Eat Disord* 39: 667–76.

Keski-Rahkonen, A., Hoek, H.W., Susser, E.S., Linna, M.S., Sihvola, E., Raevuori, A., Bulik, C.M., Kaprio, J., and Rissanen, A. (2007) 'Epidemiology and course of anorexia nervosa in the community', *Am J Psychiatry* 164: 1259–65.

Keski-Rahkonen, A., Hoek, H.W., Linna, M.S., Raevuori, A., Sihvola, E., Bulik, C.M., Rissanen, A., and Kaprio, J. (2009) 'Incidence and outcomes of bulimia nervosa: A nationwide population-based study', *Psychol Med* 39: 823–31.

Chapter 18

Childhood and adulthood: when do eating disorders start and do treatments differ?

Peter M. Doyle, Angela Smyth and Daniel Le Grange

Age of onset

Eating disorders are more often diagnosed in females than in males and typically have their onset in mid- to late adolescence (Hudson *et al.* 2007; Lucas *et al.* 1991). However, it is not uncommon for children and early adolescents to present for treatment of an eating disorder (see Chapter 19, 'Recognising and diagnosing early onset eating disorders'). Such cases can be challenging diagnostically, as some eating disorder aspects overlap with normal child development (Watkins and Lask 2009). For example, a clinician familiar with developmental stages would not expect an 11-year-old girl to necessarily be menstruating. However, according to the Diagnostic and Statistical Manual of Mental Disorders (DSM-IV-TR), a diagnostic criterion for anorexia nervosa (AN) is the absence of menses (American Psychiatric Association 2000). The clinician must try to ascertain whether the 11-year-old patient has prevented onset of menses by maintaining a low, unhealthy weight or is simply not developmentally ready to menstruate.

The cognitive symptoms of an eating disorder can also be difficult to measure, with some children unable to grasp abstract concepts like 'self-evaluation'. Again, the clinician has the difficult task of determining whether the child is purposefully denying certain cognitive symptoms, endorsing or denying symptoms based on a misunderstanding of questions posed, or truly does not have eating disordered cognitions. In these cases, obtaining collateral information from parents and caregivers can be helpful.

A small body of literature does report the emergence of eating disorders in middle-aged women with no prior history of an eating disorder (Beck *et al.* 1996; Cumella and Kally 2008). Given the dearth of published literature on this phenomenon, however, more systematic investigation is necessary before definitive statements can be made about the frequency of this type of presentation.

Case studies

Tara

Tara, 16, has a six-month history of bulimia nervosa (BN), binge-purge subtype. She presented for evaluation of an eating disorder after her mother noticed empty fast-food containers and discarded candy wrappers under her bed.

> Besides food disappearing from the kitchen, I was concerned that Tara was staying too long in the bathroom with the water running, including taking two or three showers daily. I remember her becoming a 'picky eater' about six months ago. She began cutting out more and more foods from her regular diet and talking a lot about her weight and a desire to lose weight. Tara began exercising more often, was watching exercise videos and doing sit-ups in her room at night. In the weeks immediately preceding our presentation, I noticed food was being eaten more quickly and my pantry was empty by mid-week. Although not initially suspicious, that's when I checked to see if Tara was taking food into her bedroom. When confronted, Tara admitted she had been binge eating at night when everyone was asleep. However, she denied self-induced vomiting. She was reluctant to engage in treatment, but I insisted we seek professional advice.
>
> Tara's mother

Rhonda

Rhonda, 49, has a thirty-five-year history of anorexia nervosa (AN), restricting subtype. When she first presented for treatment in our clinic ten years ago, she had been battling AN for many years.

> My eating disorder developed in my teens, but I did not seek treatment until in my twenties. My attempts at recovery had some success, but my eating disorder symptoms would return and again cause me to restrict my caloric intake and lose weight. Despite this struggle, I graduated college, took a job in an administrative position and have remained gainfully employed.
>
> Rhonda

Do treatments differ?

For the clinician treating a patient with an eating disorder, the age at which the illness began is not as critical as the age at which the patient presents for treatment. Obviously, clinicians can only treat those who present for treatment. The patient's age at presentation will guide many of the clinician's decisions about treatment. These age-related treatment decisions are influenced by two main patient factors that can differ greatly between adult and adolescent patients: duration of illness and developmental stage.

With the acknowledgement that no two eating disorder cases are the same, some general statements apply to most adolescent and adult cases seen in an eating disorders clinic. The first is that adults will usually present having had a longer duration of illness. Adult patients who present for treatment often report battling their illness for many years or even decades, considerably longer than the average adolescent case.

Along with this longer duration, many clinicians report that their adult patients show greater stability in their symptom profiles and less migration between diagnoses. However, this is an empirical question and research has already found diagnostic migration in adults with eating disorders (Eddy *et al.* 2008). The question of diagnostic stability is further complicated because diagnostic categories from DSM-IV-TR do not consistently map onto clinical presentations seen in child and adolescent eating disorder patients. In fact, some authors suggest that future editions of DSM specifically examine the possibility of using different diagnostic categories for children and adolescents (Eddy *et al.* 2010).

Unfortunately, longer duration of illness and stability of symptoms also mean the eating disorder is more likely to have infiltrated many aspects of an adult patient's life. Change is difficult when addressing any long-standing habit or behavioural pattern. When a patient has been binge eating and purging at a set frequency for many years, breaking this pattern can be more difficult than breaking the binge/purge 'habits' of an adolescent who has been ill with BN for only a few months. The adult patient's self-identity has formed over many years and may be firmly grounded to include 'eating disorder patient' as one of its main descriptors. Although treatment efforts may aim at improving eating disorder symptoms, treatment for many adult patients will take a more palliative care approach. Medical complications from years of starvation, vomiting, laxative abuse, and other eating disorder behaviours can be irreversible. Treatment in these instances is often designed to minimize the patient's physical deterioration rather than achieve full resolution of their eating disorder symptoms. In adult AN patients, the optimal goal will be weight restoration to a pre-morbid weight. However, as children and adolescents are still growing, goal weights can become a moving target. Typically, goal weights for adolescents with AN are based not on the pre-morbid weight of the patient, but on sex and height norms for the patient's age group.

The other patient factor that will guide the treatment approach is the developmental stage of the patient. Children and adolescents live with parents, guardians, or other caregivers who can play an important role in many aspects of treatment. Parental involvement usually begins with the initial referral for treatment.

Tara's parents were involved in her treatment all along, initially in a primary role. They were asked to make food choices for all of Tara's meals, to eat with Tara at every meal (to help her prevent binge eating) and stay with her for at least one hour following meals (to prevent possible self-induced vomiting). As her symptoms diminished, Tara was asked to become more involved in making food choices and eventually began to eat without monitoring. Within six months, her binge eating stopped and she was not engaging in compensatory behaviours such as self-induced vomiting or excessive exercising. Tara's parents watched her personality return to the way she was before her eating disorder and were delighted when their daughter began eagerly talking about attending college after high school graduation.

Unlike adults, children and adolescents rarely self-refer for treatment. As Tara's case illustrates, typically a parent or caregiver sets up the initial treatment appointment and provides further instrumental support by transporting and accompanying the patient to their appointment. Utilizing the parental involvement and support can aid treatment efforts. Adult patients are autonomous, however, and may not accept this type of parental involvement.

Treatment for adults

When adult eating disorder symptoms are sufficiently impairing or life-threatening, inpatient hospitalization is necessary. However, due to limited resources and high costs, the goal of inpatient treatment is to stabilize the patient medically and psychologically sufficiently to allow for discharge to a less intensive treatment setting. This may be a step-down approach to a partial hospitalization programme (PHP) or an intensive outpatient programme (IOP). The PHP and IOP options, while less intensive and less costly than inpatient programmes, still require a high level of staff resources and patient or third-party payer expense. Ultimately, treatment providers seek to have eating disorder patients managed through outpatient psychotherapy.

Outcomes of outpatient psychotherapy for eating disorders vary greatly. In the United Kingdom, the National Institute for Clinical Excellence (NICE 2004) surveyed professionals across different mental health disciplines and reviewed the published literature to assign grades for various outpatient therapies. Letter grades of 'A' (treatments with strong clinical and randomized-control research support) down to 'C' (treatments with the support of expert clinicians, but lacking empirical study or support) were assigned. Cognitive behaviour therapy was given a grade of 'A' when used to treat adults with BN (CBT-BN) and binge eating disorder (CBT-BED). Interpersonal psychotherapy for BN and BED also has good empirical and clinical support, as does modified dialectical behaviour therapy for BED. No treatments for adults with AN earned a NICE grade above 'C'.

Rhonda's extreme caloric restriction sometimes impacted her memory and attention, causing problems for her at work when she failed to finish tasks or did them incorrectly. However, her perfectionist tendencies and drive also made her a valuable asset and enabled her to keep her job.

Although Rhonda managed to maintain steady employment, the eating disorder heavily affected her social life. Once close with her parents and siblings, she became increasingly estranged from them. Arguments about her weight and eating habits led family members to present Rhonda with ultimatums to enter treatment 'or else'. When these treatment efforts did not produce changes in her eating disordered behaviour, Rhonda's frustrated family insisted she was 'choosing to stay sick'. To avoid the inevitable confrontations and arguments, Rhonda spent less time with her family. She now sees her parents only at the holidays and her sister less often.

During her long illness, Rhonda has been hospitalized several times due to medical problems related to her eating disorder (abnormal electrolyte levels, cardiac arrhythmias, and kidney failure). She also suffers from osteoporosis, a result of decades spent without menstruating. She sees a psychologist for individual psychotherapy, a nephrologist for kidney failure and an internist for general medical care.

Unlike treatments for children and adolescents, which often involve family members or other caregivers, adults with eating disorders are usually seen alone, either in one-to-one therapy or in a group setting where the other group members share diagnoses. This is true for clinical as well as practical reasons. First, many adults have moved from their childhood homes and the practicality of bringing together family members for weekly treatment is too burdensome. In Rhonda's case, there was the added complication of emotional (as well as physical) distance between the patient and her family. Family members may see a more treatment-refractory patient as continuing their eating disorder by choice rather than suffering an illness that has taken over their life. Friends and family may express disappointment or anger, blaming the patient for the continuation of the disorder and its impact on the family system. Patients with eating disorders show decreased quality of life compared to non-eating disordered samples (de la Rie *et al.* 2005).

Treatment for children and adolescents

Relatively few randomized controlled trials have investigated efficacious treatments for children and adolescents with eating disorders (Le Grange and Lock 2005). As a result, guidelines are lacking and clinicians often use the same treatments that they use with adult patients. Some of these approaches transition well from adult populations to child and adolescent populations. CBT-BN has been found efficacious in a case series of young people aged 12–18 (Lock 2005; Schapman-Williams *et al.* 2006), and a guided self-care form of CBT also shows promise for adolescents (Schmidt *et al.* 2007). For adolescent AN, the most empirical support exists for a manualized intervention called family-based treatment for AN (FBT-AN; Lock and Le Grange 2001; Lock *et al.* 2001), commonly referred to as the Maudsley approach, which utilizes the parents and other caregivers in treatment, charging them with the initial task of restoring the patient's weight. As treatment progresses, control over decisions about food, eating, and exercise is slowly returned to the patient, to the extent that the control is developmentally appropriate given the patient's age. Case series have demonstrated that this approach is feasible and effective (Le Grange *et al.* 2005) and that treatment teams other than the developers can learn and implement the treatment well (Loeb *et al.* 2007). FBT-AN seems to work as well with younger children as with adolescents (Lock *et al.* 2006).

Other treatments, such as psychodynamic and cognitive therapies, have also been studied for adolescents with AN (Bowers *et al.* 1996; Jeammet and Chabert 1998; Robin *et al.* 1999), but only ego-oriented psychotherapy has been included in randomized controlled trials. Statements about how these interventions compare with FBT-AN would be speculative pending further research.

NICE guidelines (2004) recommend family involvement for children and adolescents with eating disorders, and other authors conclude that family interventions are effective for adolescents with AN (Le Grange and Lock 2005). The treatments outlined above demonstrate better relative efficacy than treatments for adult patients, perhaps because multiple family members are involved in the patient's recovery. Despite the success of FBT with children and adolescent patients, this approach does not naturally cross over into work with adults with AN. However, innovative research is ongoing using a family-based approach with adults (Bulik *et al.*, 2011; Chen *et al.*, 2010).

Conclusion

Eating disorders most often have their onset during middle and late adolescence, but can begin earlier and later, possibly even in middle age. Diagnosing eating disorders in young children can be difficult because of the overlap between normal pre-pubertal development and the physical symptoms of an eating problem. Treatments for adult and adolescent patients differ because of the myriad of varying durations of illness and differing developmental stages. Adult patients tend to present themselves for treatment and may not have built-in support networks available to assist their recovery. Children and adolescents often have parents or other caregivers whose care helps combat the eating disorder. As a result, studies examining treatment outcome find that prognoses are better for children and adolescents, especially those patients with a short duration of illness.

References

American Psychiatric Association (APA) (2000) *DSM-IV-TR: Diagnostic and Statistical Manual of Mental Disorders*, 4th edn (Text Revision), Washington, DC: American Psychiatric Press.

Beck, D., Casper, R., and Andersen, A. (1996) 'Truly Late Onset of Eating Disorders: A Study of 11 Cases Averaging 60 Years of Age at Presentation', *Int J Eat Disord* 20, 4: 389–95.

Bowers, W.A., Evans, K., and Van Cleve, L. (1996) 'Treatment of Adolescent Eating Disorders', in M.A. Reinecke, F.M. Dattilio and A. Freeman (eds) *Cognitive Therapy*

With Children and Adolescents: A Casebook for Clinical Practice (pp. 227–50), New York: Guilford Press.

Bulik, C.M., Baucom, D.H., Kirby, J.S., and Pisetsky, E. (2011) 'Uniting Couples (in the Treatment of) Anorexia Nervosa (UCAN)', *Int J Eat Disord* 44, 1: 19–28.

Chen, E.Y., Le Grange, D., Celio Doyle, A., Zaitsoff, S., Doyle, P., Roehrig, J.P., and Washington, B. (2010) 'Case Series of Family-Based Therapy for Weight Restoration in Young Adults With Anorexia Nervosa', *J Contemp Psychother* 40, 4: 219–224.

Cumella, E.J. and Kally, Z. (2008) 'Profile of 50 Women with Midlife-Onset Eating Disorders', *Eat Disord* 16, 3: 193–203.

de la Rie, S.M., Noordenbos, G., and van Furth, E.F. (2005) 'Quality of Life and Eating Disorders', *Qual Life Res* 14, 6: 1511–22.

Eddy, K.T., Dorer, D.J., Franko, D.L., Tahilani, K., Thompson-Brenner, H., and Herzog, D.B. (2008) 'Diagnostic Crossover in Anorexia Nervosa and Bulimia Nervosa: Implications for DSM-V', *Am J Psychiatry* 165, 2: 245–50.

Eddy, K.T., Le Grange, D., Crosby, R.D., Hoste, R.R., Doyle, A.C., Smyth, A., and Herzog, D.B. (2010) 'Diagnostic Classification of Eating Disorders in Children and Adolescents: How Does DSM-IV-TR Compare to Empirically-Derived Categories?', *J Am Acad Child Adolesc Psychiatry* 49, 3: 277–87.

Hudson, J.I., Hiripi, E., Pope, H.G., and Kessler, R.C. (2007) 'The Prevalence and Correlates of Eating Disorders in the National Comorbidity Survey Replication', *Biol Psychiatry* 61, 3: 348–58.

Jeammet, P. and Chabert, C. (1998) 'A Psychoanalytic Approach to Eating Disorders: The Role of Dependency', in A.H. Esman (ed.) *Adolescent Psychiatry: Developmental and Clinical Studies,* Vol. 22 (pp. 59–84), Mahwah, NJ: Analytic Press.

Le Grange, D. and Lock, J. (2005) 'The Dearth of Psychological Treatment Studies for Anorexia Nervosa', *Int J Eat Disord* 37, 2: 79–91.

Le Grange, D., Binford, R., and Loeb, K.L. (2005) 'Manualized Family-Based Treatment for Anorexia Nervosa: A Case Series', *J Am Acad Child Adolesc Psychiatry* 44: 41–6.

Lock, J. (2005) 'Adjusting Cognitive Behavior Therapy for Adolescents with Bulimia Nervosa: Results of a Case Series', *Am J Psychother* 59, 3: 267–81.

Lock, J. and Le Grange, D. (2001) 'Can Family Based Treatment of Anorexia Nervosa Be Manualized?', *J Psychother Pract Res* 10, 4: 253–61.

Lock, J., Le Grange, D., Agras, W.S., and Dare, C. (2001) *Treatment Manual for Anorexia Nervosa: A Family-Based Approach*, New York: Guilford Press.

Lock, J., Le Grange, D., Forsberg, S., and Hewell, K. (2006) 'Is Family Therapy Useful for Treating Children with Anorexia Nervosa? Results of a Case Series', *J Am Acad Child Adolesc Psychiatry* 45, 11: 1323–8.

Loeb, K.L., Walsh, B.T., Lock, J., Le Grange, D., Jones, J., Marcus, S., Weaver, J., and Dobrow, I. (2007) 'Open Trial of Family-Based Treatment for Full and Partial Anorexia Nervosa in Adolescence: Evidence of Successful Dissemination', *J Am Acad Child Adolesc Psychiatry* 46, 7: 792–800.

Lucas, A.R., Beard, C.M., and O'Fallon, W.M. (1991) '50-Year Trends in the Incidence of Anorexia Nervosa in Rochester, Minn: A Population-Based Study', *Am J Psychiatry* 148, 7: 917–29.

National Institute for Clinical Excellence (NICE) (2004) *Eating Disorders: Core Interventions in the Treatment and Management of Anorexia Nervosa, Bulimia Nervosa and Related Eating Disorders, Clinical Guideline No. 9*, London: NICE. Online. Available: www.nice.org.uk/guidance/CG9 (accessed 26 August 2010).

Robin, A.L., Siegel, P.T., Moye, A.W., Gilroy, M., Dennis, A.B., and Sikand, A. (1999) 'A Controlled Comparison of Family versus Individual Therapy for Adolescents with Anorexia Nervosa', *J Am Acad Child Adolesc Psychiatry* 38, 12: 1482–9.

Schapman-Williams, A.M., Lock, J., and Couturier, J. (2006) 'Cognitive-Behavioral Therapy for Adolescents with Binge Eating Syndromes: A Case Series', *Int J Eat Disord* 39, 3: 252–5.

Schmidt, U., Lee, S., Beecham, J., Perkins, S., Treasure, J., Yi, I., Winn, S., Robinson, P., Murphy, R., Keville, S., Johnson-Sabine, E., Jenkins, M., Frost, S., Dodge, L., Berelowitz, M., and Eisler, I. (2007) 'A Randomized Controlled Trial of Family Therapy and Cognitive-Behavioral Guided Self-Care for Adolescents with Bulimia Nervosa or Related Disorders', *Am J Psychiatry* 164, 4: 591–8.

Watkins, B. and Lask, B. (2009) 'Defining Eating Disorders in Children', in L. Smolak and K. J. Thompson (eds) *Body Image, Eating Disorders, and Obesity in Youth: Assessment, Prevention, and Treatment*, 2nd edn (pp. 35–46), Washington, DC: American Psychological Association.

Chapter 19

Recognising and diagnosing early onset eating disorders

Sloane Madden

Case study: Stephanie

Stephanie developed anorexia nervosa (AN) at 11 years of age and is undergoing treatment using the Maudsley approach.

Stephanie developed AN in fifth grade. I first noticed her developing a strict routine around school, dance, study, chores and healthy eating. Meals were not finished, water was requested rather than milk and lunches were coming home half-eaten. Despite this, Stephanie exhibited few eating disorder symptoms; she wasn't over-exercising or hiding or refusing food. In fact weight loss was the only symptom until one day we were walking and she felt faint.

Within a week I approached our general practitioner who advised to bring Stephanie in for a 'chat'. This discussion focused on healthy eating though, of course, Stephanie knew all she was being told and more. Visits during the next six weeks revealed rapid weight loss with food consumption notably more difficult. Eventually my husband insisted on a referral to a specialist. Our general practitioner who, by her own admission, was completely out of her depth researched adolescent eating issues and directed us to a paediatrician and hospital specialising in family-based treatment (FBT).

I'm glad that rather than excuse Stephanie's behaviour, I insisted on an assessment by a qualified practitioner. I learnt that early intervention has a big influence on treatment outcome. Without FBT I doubt Stephanie would have survived. We could not reason with her and struggled to make her eat.

When Stephanie was developing AN, she became clingy and was at my side a lot. She stopped playing with friends, was obsessed with achieving the best in her studies and dance and became inflexible with plans. She was only animated when shopping for food, preparing food or watching TV cooking shows. She aimed to be a world-class chef and looked up training opportunities and menus. As this made her happy we encouraged her culinary interest. When Stephanie was diagnosed with AN, I felt robbed, like the previous months sharing her dream had been a lie and the illness somehow had sucked me in.

We attempted FBT following our first visit with the clinician; it was hell. Two days after our second appointment, Stephanie was admitted to hospital via emergency suffering low heart rate, low blood pressure and dehydration. The naso-gastric tube saved her life and, after six long weeks, where the staff never gave up or let me give up, she was finally able to eat a full meal.

Stephanie accepted the naso-gastric tube willingly and immediately her vitals began to improve. She left hospital seven weeks later, the day before her twelfth birthday; she had gained 8 kg and had been off the naso-gastric tube for only a week. To see her eat was like a miracle. Our clinician said he would get our daughter back and we trusted him and he has kept his word. To hear Stephanie laugh and share her feelings again, to see her impulsively skip, are pleasures I feared may have gone forever.

Ten months on, Stephanie is eating six meals a day and has regained her lost weight plus the weight she should have gained during her illness (13 kg in six months). This has given us much hope. She has some way to go and maintains an interest in supermarkets but I'm trying to limit this.

Stephanie's mother

Eating disorders and children

Eating disorders occur in young children but research has been limited. This lack of information and awareness means eating disorders in children are frequently unrecognised and their potential seriousness underestimated. This problem is highlighted in one of only a few published studies of early onset eating disorders which noted that at the time of first diagnosis, 51 per cent of children had life-threatening complications of their disorder including bradycardia (low heart rate), hypotension (low blood pressure) and hypothermia (Madden *et al.* 2009). This chapter will look at the types of eating disorders seen in children aged 7 to 12 years, their occurrence rate, how they present and their complications.

This chapter will not look at feeding disorders but rather at the common eating disorder presentations in this age group including anorexia nervosa (AN), food avoidant emotional disorder, food phobia and functional dysphagia.

Frequency of eating disorders in children

Lifetime prevalence rates for AN in women range from 1.4 to 2 per cent and with the inclusion of partial syndrome AN are as high as 4.3 per cent (Wade *et al.* 2006). Lifetime prevalence of bulimia nervosa (BN) ranges from 4 to 7 per cent of women (Schmidt *et al.* 2007). While eating disorders are most commonly thought to develop in adolescence, few epidemiological studies have focused on adolescents and only three population-based studies have focused exclusively on children (Pinhas *et al.* 2008). This limits our ability to describe the scale of the problem and to clearly define eating problem types seen in children. Of studies that have focused on children, incidence rates for AN are approximately one-third of those seen in adolescents and adults (Madden *et al.* 2009).

In their community-based study Lewinsohn *et al.* (2000) found that lifetime prevalence rates for eating disorders in adolescent females were similar to those in adults, with full syndrome AN or BN affecting 2.3 per cent, and partial syndrome AN or BN affecting a further 2.8 per cent, with full or partial syndrome BN not seen before 12 years of age. Interestingly, when a sub-sample of adolescents was followed into adulthood new cases of AN were extremely rare while BN continued to present at similar rates to those seen in late adolescence.

These findings indicate that AN most commonly has its onset in late adolescence, with up to a quarter of all presentations first occurring in childhood. BN on the other hand primarily presents in late adolescence and early adulthood, with only rare presentations in younger age groups. This, however, may be changing, with recent evidence pointing to both an increase in the rates of eating disorders in children and a decrease in the age of onset in AN (Nicholls *et al.* 2008).

What do eating disorders in children look like?

The few studies that have looked at eating disorders in children suggest that children, like Stephanie, are less likely to report fear of weight gain and fatness (Lask and Bryant-Waugh 1992), more likely to deny the severity of their illness (Fisher *et al.* 2001), more likely to present with non-specific somatic symptoms (Blitzer *et al.* 1961) and more likely to be diagnosed with eating disorder not otherwise specified (EDNOS). They are also less likely to be diagnosed with BN, more likely to be male, less likely to report vomiting or laxative abuse, to have lost weight more rapidly and to have a lower percentage ideal body weight than older individuals with eating disorders (Peebles *et al.* 2006).

More recently the first prospective study of early onset eating disorders has highlighted more specific and worrying issues in this group. This study, which asked paediatricians and child psychiatrists around Australia to report all suspected cases of eating disorders in children aged 12 years and under, confirmed the presence of anorexia-like illnesses in children as young as 5 years. No cases of BN were reported and one in four cases were males. Vomiting was rarely seen and while somatising, denial of severity of illness and denial of body image concerns were all reported, these symptoms tended to cluster in the same patients. A latent class analysis revealed that 79 per cent of patients in this group presented with classic symptoms of AN including severe food restriction, over-exercise, abnormal body image and fear of fatness. The remaining 21 per cent fell into a group commonly known as food avoidant emotional disorder, to be described later in the chapter (Madden *et al.* 2009).

Of concern, however were high rates of hospitalisation, life-threatening medical complications, psychiatric comorbidity and poor correlation with current diagnostic schema. In this study of children at the point of first presentation with an eating disorder, 79 per cent required hospitalisation, 51 per cent had life-threatening medical complications of their illness, 62 per cent had comorbid psychiatric illnesses including depression, anxiety and obsessive compulsive disorder and 30 per cent were taking psychotropic medications. Children had been symptomatic for an average of six months before their initial presentation and had lost an average of 6.3 kg (Madden *et al.* 2009). While 6 kg may not seem a lot of weight for those used to treating adults, in an 8-year-old girl this equates to more than 25 per cent of average weight. Two subsequent, as yet unpublished, studies from Canada and the United Kingdom recorded lower levels of hospitalisation in this age group, of 50 per cent and 44 per cent respectively (Pinhas *et al.* 2008).

Finally, the study demonstrated the poor correlation between current diagnostic criteria for eating disorders and eating disorder presentations in children. Only 32 per cent of children met DSM-IV (American Psychiatric Association 1994) diagnostic criteria for AN despite 79 per cent presenting with psychological symptoms and behaviours typical of the disorder. While two-thirds of patients presented with both psychological symptoms required for a diagnosis of AN (fear of weight gain and abnormal body image) less than 45 per cent met weight criteria for a diagnosis of AN despite the previously reported high rates of medical complications and hospitalisation.

Developmentally appropriate diagnosis

As with all psychiatric disorders, eating disorder presentations vary according to the developmental capacity of affected individuals. Besides differences in psychological and social development, physical development is a vital consideration.

Current DSM-IV criteria for AN require a refusal to maintain body weight at or above a minimally normal weight for age and height (a body mass index (BMI) of less than 17.5 kg/m²) or a failure to make minimum expected weight gains when AN develops during early childhood or adolescence. Individuals suffering from AN maintain an intense fear of gaining weight or becoming fat, even though they are underweight, and have a distorted perception of their body weight and shape. These criteria, however, may not accurately reflect the clinical features in children like Stephanie for several reasons. Compared with adults, children have limited expressive language capacity, less ability to think in an abstract fashion and less awareness of emotions (WCEDCA 2007). Additionally, the variable nature of normal growth in children undermines the utility of weight-based cut-offs in diagnosis. These differences may manifest in numerous ways including the following:

- Children may be unable to express distress in terms of body shape and weight but may instead describe somatic symptoms such as abdominal pain.
- Young children may not report fear of weight gain while at a low weight but may do so only when weight is restored to a more healthy level.
- Young children may be reluctant to confide their symptoms to adults for fear of censure.
- The presence of amenorrhea is an important diagnostic feature for AN in post-menarchal girls but may be a developmentally inappropriate criterion in young girls, in whom a history of delay in onset of puberty may be important.
- The DSM-IV criteria specify that weight should be less than 85 per cent of expected weight for height; however, this may lead to an underestimate of the severity of low weight in younger children in whom linear growth has also been affected (WCEDCA 2007).

To address these perceived deficiencies several groups have suggested modified diagnostic criteria for AN in children and adolescents and the addition of some child-specific diagnoses. Most prominent among these groups has been the Great Ormond Street (GOS) group in the UK which has proposed the GOS criteria (Nicholls *et al.* 2000).

As with DSM-IV criteria for AN the GOS criteria focus on weight and eating abnormalities. However, unlike DSM-IV, the GOS criteria allow for diagnosis to be made on the basis of behaviour or psychological distortions rather than expressed psychological concerns alone. In particular, the GOS criteria allows a diagnosis of AN on the basis of determined food avoidance and weight loss, or failure to gain weight in the absence of any physical or mental illness, in addition to any two of the following: preoccupation with body weight, preoccupation with energy intake, distorted body image, fear of fatness, self-induced vomiting, extensive exercising, or laxative abuse (Nicholls *et al.* 2000). This focus on behaviour, as well as reported concerns, allows for diagnosis in younger children unable or unwilling to express their distress in terms of weight and shape concerns. In a review of 114 consecutive patients admitted for medical resuscitation at the Children's Hospital at Westmead, a large paediatric teaching hospital in Australia, 87 per cent of children met GOS criteria for AN while only 67 per cent met DSM-IV criteria (Madden and Byrne 2005).

Food avoidant emotional disorder

The term food avoidant emotional disorder (FAED) was first used in the 1980s to describe children with significant weight loss resulting from dietary restriction in the absence of weight and shape concerns and underlying organic illness (Bryant-Waugh 2000; Higgs *et al.* 1989). In this disorder, children frequently presented with non-specific medical complaints, including abdominal pain, lethargy and nausea, that were seen by the family as responsible for weight loss, in addition to emotional problems, such as school avoidance, obsessional behaviour and depression (Nicholls *et al.* 2000). Such children were noted to deny weight and shape concerns and to lack behaviours typically seen in AN including vomiting, excessive exercise, laxative abuse and avoidance of high-calorie foods.

Three recent studies in Australia, Canada and the United Kingdom have highlighted the relative importance of FAED in children. In these prospective studies of first presentation eating disorders in children aged between 5 and 12 years inclusive, latent class analysis identified two common presentations consistent with both AN and FAED. Over 32 per cent of the 469 children identified fell into the FAED group. These children differed from those in the AN group in that they were less likely to be concerned about their weight or shape, did not have abnormal body image, were less likely to exercise or vomit, and were more likely to deny the severity of their illness and to present with somatic complaints. Interestingly, as a group they were no more likely than the AN group to have comorbid psychiatric illness or emotional distress (Pinhas *et al.* 2008).

While many children with FAED come to treatment due to malnutrition complications, the lack of weight and shape concerns raises issues of late or missed diagnosis and appropriateness of current treatment interventions. It will be important to clarify if this group of children is distinctly different from those with AN or whether they respond to existing treatments and face similar outcomes. In particular, is this group an early developmental presentation of AN or a distinct disorder?

References

American Psychiatric Association (APA) (1994) *Diagnostic and Statistical Manual of Mental Disorders*, 4th edn, Washington, DC: American Psychiatric Press.

Blitzer, J., Rollins, N., and Blackwell, A. (1961) 'Children who starve themselves: Anorexia nervosa', *Psychosom Med* 23, 5: 369–83.

Bryant-Waugh, R. (2000) 'Overview of the eating disorders', in B. Lask and R. Bryant-Waugh (eds) *Anorexia Nervosa and Related Eating Disorders in Childhood and Adolescence*, 2nd edn, Hove: Psychology Press.

Fisher, M., Schneider, M., Burns, J., Symons, H., and Mandel, F. S. (2001) 'Differences between adolescents and young adults at presentation to an eating disorders program', *J Adolesc Health* 28, 3: 222–7.

Higgs, J., Goodyear, I., and Birch, J. (1989) 'Anorexia nervosa and food avoidance emotional disorder', *Arch Dis Child* 64: 346–51.

Lask, B. and Bryant-Waugh, R. (1992) 'Early-onset anorexia nervosa and related eating disorders', *J Child Psychol Psychiatry* 33, 1: 281–300.

Lewinsohn, P.M., Striegel-Moore, R.H., and Seeley, J.R. (2000) 'Epidemiology and natural course of eating disorders in young women from adolescence to young adulthood', *J Am Acad Child Adolesc Psychiatry* 39, 10: 1284–92.

Madden, S. and Byrne, S. (2005) 'An observational study of patients admitted to the Eating Disorder Unit at The Children's Hospital at Westmead between July 1997 and March 2004', presented at the 7th London International Conference on Eating Disorders, London, April.

Madden, S., Morris, A., Zurynski, Y., Kohn, M., and Elliot, E. (2009) 'The burden of eating disorders in children aged 5–13 years in Australia', *Med J Aust* 190, 8: 410–16.

Nicholls, D., Chater, R., and Lask, B. (2000) 'Children into DSM don't go: A comparison of classification systems for eating disorders in childhood and early adolescence', *Int J Eat Disord* 28, 3: 317–24.

Nicholls, D., Lynn, R., Viner, R., Pinhas, L., and Madden, S. (2008) 'Eating disorders in children: Are the numbers really increasing?', presented at the Royal College of Psychiatry's Child and Adolescent Faculty Residential Conference, Liverpool, September.

Peebles, R., Wilson, J.L., and Lock, J.D. (2006) 'How do children with eating disorders differ from adolescents with eating disorders at initial evaluation?', *J Adoles Health* 39, 6: 800–5.

Pinhas, L., Madden, S., Katzman, D.K., Lynne, R., Morris, A., and Nicholls, D. (2008) 'Restrictive eating disorders in children: Global findings from the International Network of Paediatric Surveillance Units', presented at 'Bridging Science and Practice: Prospects and Challenges', International Conference on Eating Disorders, Seattle, WA, May.

Schmidt, U., Lee, S., Beecham, J., Perkins, S., Treasure, J., Yi, I., Winn, S., Robinson, P., Murphy, R., Keville, S., Johnson-Sabine, E., Jenkins, M., Frost, S., Dodge, L., Berelowitz, M., and Eisler, I. (2007) 'A randomized controlled trial of family therapy and cognitive behavior therapy guided self-care for adolescents with bulimia nervosa and related disorders', *Am J Psychiatry* 164, 4: 591–8.

Wade, T.D., Bergin, J.L., Tiggemann, M., Bulik, C.M., and Fairburn, C.G. (2006) 'Prevalence and long-term course of lifetime eating disorders in an adult Australian twin cohort', *Aust New Zeal J Psychiatry* 40, 2: 121–8.

Workgroup for Classification of Eating Disorders in Children and Adolescents (WCEDCA) (2007) 'Classification of child and adolescent eating disturbances', *Int J Eat Disord* 40 (suppl): S117–22.

Chapter 20

Food phobia of childhood

Julie O'Toole

Case study

Beauregard, 'Beau', is an adorable 6-year-old boy from Alabama with close cropped blonde hair and cowboy boots. He loves animals, his daddy's motorcycle, rides horses and hopes to learn to hunt with a rifle, like his uncles. Beau is in the first grade and just learning to read. He has been raised to be polite, always answering 'yes, Ma'am' and 'yes, Sir' to adults when they speak to him. Beau's parents are divorced, but their houses are not far apart and he goes back and forth depending on which parent's work schedule allows them to care for him.

Beau was at his father's house eating chicken, mashed potatoes and cooked peas when it happened. Chicken and mashed potatoes were his favourite foods and he stuffed his mouth with as much as he could. He tried to swallow, but choked. At first he didn't panic, but when the whole lot seemed like it might go down at once, he jumped up and ran to the bathroom to spit the food out.

Beau returned to the table, but sat quietly and didn't eat any more. His dad and older brothers were busy arguing politics and no one really noticed. From that moment, Beau declined to eat another bite. When asked why not, he insisted there was a chicken bone 'stuck in his throat'.

By day three of no food, only juice, Beau's father was alarmed. The local doctor, to be safe, ordered X-rays of Beau's throat and neck, which were normal. An ear, nose and throat doctor checked to see if there was anything stuck. There was nothing. At this point the doctor, who felt Beau was acting out for attention, advised Beau's dad to 'stop the juice and let him go hungry until he was ready to eat'. But Beau's dad was reluctant to stop the only nourishment Beau would accept and continued the juice.

Two days later when Beau's dad called the doctor back, he was advised to take Beau to a psychologist who worked with the doctor. Beau saw the psychologist, but was unable to explain 'why' he would not eat. At this point, much as he hated crying, Beau cried and cried. His dad was advised to deprive him of toys and television until he agreed to at least try to eat.

When we saw Beau, three weeks after the choking incident, he had lost six pounds and was refusing to drink. His dad, an ironworker, had sought leave from his job and flown with Beau 3,000 miles across country to our clinic.

Little Beau was a charmer, with his Southern politeness and his cowboy boots, but he insisted he could not eat or drink. We inserted a naso-gastric tube and began the medication (olanzapine), which made him sleepy. His father stayed at his side, which we encouraged because night time in hospital can be terrifying for small children.

For ten days we did nothing but refeed Beau, play with him and encourage his father. Then, hearing that Beau had loved bananas before he got ill, we started with mashed bananas. He was afraid.

'I'm so scared, Miss Julie', Beau kept saying. We held his hand and talked about how we were his doctors and would not let him choke. He closed his eyes and took a few tentative nibbles. His eyes lit up with joy when the banana went down without incident. One of our gentlest and most soft-spoken team members now took over from the doctors and quietly helped Beau advance what he would eat. We removed the tube and transferred him to our day treatment unit to prove to ourselves that he would be able to eat in a social setting. Three days later, proud of himself and raising his thin little arms above his head in victory with every new food, we put Beau and his dad on the plane to return to Alabama.

What do we know about food phobia and its treatment?

Food phobia of childhood, primarily reported in pre- or early pubertal children, was first described using this term by Bryan Lask (paediatric psychiatrist) and Rachel Bryant-Waugh (clinical psychologist) in the early 1990s following their work at Great Ormond Street Children's Hospital in London (Lask and Bryant-Waugh 2004). Apart from a few articles on children with a specific phobia involving food, such as that by Matthew Nock of Yale University (Nock 2002) and another by Singer *et al.* (1992), food phobia has received little discussion in paediatric literature except under the general term 'dysphagia' where it is likely to come to the attention primarily of paediatric gastroenterologists and otolaryngologists. This condition has also been referred to as 'functional dysphagia', although 'food phobia' is more intuitive and accurate since it does not always involve swallowing difficulties as such.

From a parent's point of view, food phobia is the sudden onset of refusal to swallow solid food in a developmentally normal child who previously ate well. A choking episode often precedes it, as we saw with Beau, although some children may not actually choke, but may have witnessed choking in another. Rarely, this refusal to eat is preceded by vomiting, and the reason the child gives for refusing food has to do with their 'fear of vomiting'. Even more rarely, a child may insist they will no longer eat because of fear of abdominal pain or stomach pain. Either way, in its severest forms the child will not eat, drink or even swallow their own saliva. In the latter case, they will spit out their saliva constantly, which is not only worrisome to their family, but can quickly lead to dehydration.

Children with food phobia do not share the body dysmorphism or fear of fatness that children with AN or BN express but Beau was distressed by his inability to please his father by eating, and scared that he would 'waste away and die'. In Beau's family history, several members suffered from panic attacks and anxiety, as we commonly find in the extended family of children with food phobia.

A spectrum of severity of illness and response to treatment seems likely in children with food phobia, ranging from those whose symptoms resolve at home after a few days, through to those who respond to outpatient psychological interventions and finally to those whose symptoms have proven intractable to outpatient interventions and who are losing weight and/or becoming dehydrated, like Beau.

Talking, cajoling, bribing, threatening and praising (such as suggested by Beau's paediatrician and psychologist) have no effect on food phobia in those cases severe enough to come to medical attention. So how can they be treated and how long does it take?

Children like Beau can be successfully treated, although treatment is challenging for the whole family since it must start in the hospital. The critical initial step is securing access to the child's gastrointestinal tract in order to deliver adequate calories and fluids to reverse the dehydration and malnutrition. This is done with placement of a naso-gastric tube and the use of liquid feeds. Besides allowing control of the infusion of nutrition, this also allows stepping away from exposing the child to demands that they eat while adjusting to hospital and treatment staff, and learning they will not be punished for not eating.

In our programme, no food is offered during the first week in hospital. This time is used to quietly restore the child physically and encourage the parents to play and have fun with their child. During this week no one talks about food. Meanwhile we begin the administration of olanzapine (Zyprexa®), an atypical antipsychotic, at the low dose of 2.5 mg at bedtime, and gradually increase the dose to 7.5 mg, a level at which we begin to see remission of anxiety and delusional fears surrounding food. Once we reach 7.5 mg/day and the patient is comfortable with staff, we ask the parents to tell us the child's favourite *solid* food and we begin with that.

Refeeding a terrified child with food phobia takes much patience, confidence and reassurance on the part of the initiating team member (in our case a physician), but as soon as the child has swallowed any solid food, we remove the naso-gastric tube and rapidly advance the meals. Once a child is able to 'bite, chew, swallow' we can reassure parents the problem has been taken care of, and the child is put on a tapering dose of olanzapine over three to four weeks and returned home. To date our nearly uniform experience is that symptoms do not recur.

References

Lask, B. and Bryant-Waugh, R. (2004) *Eating Disorders: A Parent's Guide*, rev. edn, New York: Brunner Routledge.

Nock, M. K. (2002) 'A multiple-baseline evaluation of the treatment of food phobia in a young boy', *J Behav Ther Exp Psychiatry* 33: 217–25.

Singer, L. T., Ambuel, B., Wade, S., and Jaffe, A. C. (1992) 'Cognitive-behavioral treatment of health-impairing food phobias in children', *J Am Acad Child Adolesc Psychiatry* 31: 847–52.

Chapter 21

Unravelling binge eating disorder

Angélica M. Claudino and Christina M. Morgan

Case study

> When in her early forties in 2008, Chevese Turner's struggle with loss of control and episodes of overeating since childhood motivated her to found and become chief executive officer of the Binge Eating Disorder Association (BEDA).
>
> In spite of quite frequent binge eating symptoms throughout childhood, Chevese exhibited a normal weight until she was 10 years old, when her paediatrician expressed concerns to her parents. She was bullied at school and her mother, who also had eating problems, began monitoring Chevese's weight and food intake, even dieting with her, with little success, and the scales began to determine how Chevese felt about herself. During her teenage years and early adulthood, family problems (financial difficulties and parental divorce) had emotional impact on Chevese and contributed to increased anxiety and depressive symptoms, engagement in risky and impulsive behaviours (such as substance abuse) as well as worsening of binge eating and weight gain, which led her to reach a body mass index (BMI) in the border range to severe obesity by age 22. Chevese, realizing her global functioning was compromised, with social isolation and academic difficulties, first sought help:
>
> My mental health deteriorated and my waistline expanded until, in great despair, I found a weight management programme and with a therapist, began to work on underlying issues related to my eating binges. At the time, binge eating disorder was not mentioned as a diagnosis, and I was confused about whether I had an eating disorder or a lack of will-power.
>
> Chevese

How did the concept of binge eating disorder emerge?

In eating disorder literature, binge eating refers to a specific form of overeating. Disturbed patterns of eating such as gorging are age-old, but were incorporated as symptoms of eating disorders (EDs) only in the second half of the twentieth century. This eating behaviour was initially observed in people starving with anorexia nervosa (AN) and was later considered the core symptom of bulimia nervosa (BN), which is currently defined by the presence of recurrent episodes of binge eating followed by inappropriate compensatory methods to avoid weight gain (APA 1994).

Since 1950 it has been known that binge eating 'not' followed by inadequate compensatory weight control methods is common among obese people (Stunkard 1959), and according to DSM-IV (APA 1994), these individuals should be classified as having an eating disorder not otherwise specified (EDNOS). This category is designed for disorders of clinical severity that cause distress and impairment and that are not specified within the two broad eating disorder diagnostic classes, namely AN and BN (Fairburn and Bohn 2005). EDNOS are the most prevalent eating disorders found in clinical practice and include, for instance, individuals who regularly purge but do not binge eat, individuals who meet criteria for AN but continue to menstruate or maintain their weight above the minimum required for this diagnosis, and individuals who meet criteria for BN, but binge eat less than twice weekly (APA 1994).

Increased interest in the subgroup of individuals with EDNOS who recurrently binge but do not compensate emerged in the late 1980s/early 1990s. Since then, studies have consistently shown that recurrent binge eating is associated with great distress and psychopathology as well as excess weight (Grilo *et al.* 2009). Based on these evidences, provisional criteria for binge eating disorder (BED) were proposed in DSM-IV (APA 1994) and includes four main criteria: the presence of recurrent binge eating, associated features of control, marked distress regarding binge eating and a frequency of binge eating occurring at least two days a week during the previous six months, and finally and importantly, the binge eating should not be linked to any kind of compensatory method, such as purging. Ongoing work has been critically revising the status of BED diagnosis and its criteria (Wonderlich *et al.* 2009) for possible inclusion in DSM-V (APA n.d.).

How is binge eating defined?

During this initial period ... binges were whatever was accessible when an adult was not looking. Often, it was handfuls of candy, crackers, ice-cream cones (without ice-cream), pretzels or chips.... It was very brief, usually over five to ten minutes. Longer if I had a sizeable stash and was left alone.... I stopped when I ran out of food, was caught eating when not permitted or when I began to feel sick.

Chevese

As Chevese describes, binge eating refers to discrete episodes of uncontrolled overeating, usually involving foods that are high in carbohydrates and fat. These episodes are officially defined in DSM-IV, criterion A (APA 1994), by a temporal aspect (discrete period of time), an objective, quantifiable aspect (the amount of food) and a subjective aspect (experience of lack of control) (Wolfe *et al.* 2009).

Episodes of binge eating are classified as objective (OBE), when they involve the consumption of an 'objectively large' amount of food, or subjective (SBE), when the amount of food is 'perceived as large' but not considered so by the examiner (Fairburn and Cooper 1993). Although BED diagnosis requires the occurrence of OBEs, it is common for patients with BED to report both OBEs and SBEs.

Considerations when assessing a binge episode

Size of self-reported binge episodes can vary dramatically on average caloric intake per episode (30–4931 Kcal) (Wolfe *et al.* 2009). Thus, the examiner and not the patient should decide whether the amount of food consumed is unambiguously large. When classifying an episode, the examiner must ask for a description of typical episodes and consider the circumstances (occasion, place, time of day, hours since last meal). The type or caloric content of the foods involved is not relevant (Fairburn and Cooper 1993).

Loss of control (LOC) refers to the individual subjective experience and can be inferred only through the patient's description of how they feel. Chevese expresses feeling out of control when she says she stopped eating only when she ran out of food or began to feel sick. Others may state: 'I couldn't resist it', 'Once I started, I had to eat the whole packet'. Perceived loss of control over eating, irrespective of the amount of food consumed, has been considered a core feature of binge eating as patients with BED have been found to identify binge episodes more by feelings of LOC than by amount eaten (Telch *et al.* 1998). LOC has also been correlated with psychological distress, ED psychopathology, and functional impairment (Elder *et al.* 2008). However, size may be of particular importance as a risk for weight gain and is also related to impairment (Guss *et al.* 2002).

Features commonly associated with binge eating

The second criterion required for BED diagnosis is the presence of at least three additional features commonly associated with loss of control over eating. A person with BED may eat at a faster rate, not only during binge episodes but also when not binge eating (Yanovski *et al.* 1992). These features may be linked to appetite regulation abnormalities suggesting the need for disturbed satiety mechanisms in binge eaters to be further investigated (Latner and Clyne 2008; Walsh and Boudreau 2003).

> My deep-seated guilt about my secret eating binges produced much anxiety and depression ... I was ashamed I could not keep myself away from food ...
>
> Chevese

Finally, binges tend to occur in secret due to feelings of shame and guilt. The experience of recurrent binge eating can be distressing, and marked distress associated with eating behaviour is considered for BED diagnosis (criterion C).

How often do binges occur in BED?

The frequency requirement of binge eating occurring at least two days a week for the diagnosis of BED remains under debate. The proposed criteria for BED recommend counting the 'binge days' instead of 'binge episodes' because eating patterns of BED patients may be more chaotic, binges can last longer and are not terminated by compensatory behaviours (e.g. purging) as in BN (Wilson and Sysko 2009: 605).

The twice-a-week frequency of binges threshold in use (criteria D) is more controversial because there seems to be no marked difference between patients meeting full criteria for BED and those with sub-threshold BED (less than twice a week frequency) in a broad range of eating- and weight-related characteristics, as well as in associated psychopathology (Wilson and Sysko 2009).

Finally, recurrent binge eating must be present for at least six months for a diagnosis of BED. This requirement is in line with Chevese's life-long report and with findings from community studies showing BED has a stable course and may last longer than eight years (Hudson *et al.* 2007). Nevertheless, future developments of BED diagnosis may consider reducing the mean duration of symptoms to three months, to keep in line with BN criteria (Wilson and Sysko 2009).

By definition, patients with BED should not present regular use of inappropriate compensatory behaviours or complete criteria for other EDs. However, many patients report infrequent purging behaviours (Basdevant *et al.* 1995).

Weight, shape and body dissatisfaction in BED

> We also worked to improve my body image ... I began to accept what I see in the mirror by focusing on me as a person and not me as defined by my size ...
>
> Chevese

Overvaluation of weight and shape refers to an excessive influence of these aspects on self-evaluation, and is a core cognitive feature across EDs. Despite findings that ED psychopathology is less intense in BED than in BN (Crow *et al.* 2002), high levels of weight and shape concerns and body dissatisfaction do occur in BED, and may be as high as in BN (Crow *et al.* 2002) and greater than in obese non-bingers (Wilfley *et al.* 2000b). Furthermore, higher degrees of weight and shape concerns are associated with greater levels of psychopathology (Grilo *et al.* 2008), and may predict response to treatment in BED (Masheb and Grilo 2008). Though not a current diagnostic criterion in BED, these aspects link BED to other EDs.

Distinguishing obese BED patients from obese people

Obese binge eaters are distinguishable from obese non-binge eaters in several dimensions. In terms of eating behaviour, obese binge eaters eat more than obese non-binge eaters in laboratory settings and in weekly reports of food intake (Yanovksi *et al.* 1992). BED obese patients also have higher ED psychopathology, as mentioned above (Wilfley *et al.* 2000b), and body image distress is considered a distinct feature of EDs that differentiates BED from simple obesity.

BED patients also have greater levels of psychiatric symptoms and disorders, particularly in the depressive spectrums (Wilfley *et al.* 2000a). Studies report high lifetime rates of psychiatric disorders in BED (about 75 per cent), with mood and anxiety disorders and substance abuse the most common (Grilo *et al.* 2009; Hudson *et al.* 2007). Chevese describes symptoms in all these areas. Furthermore, studies have revealed that the severity of binge eating rather than the degree of obesity accounts for the association between binge eating and psychiatric morbidity (Telch and Agras 1994). Thus, BED is not only a behaviour that a subgroup of obese people may show, but it seems to be associated with increased psychopathology, and research suggests that obese people with BED can be distinguished from people without. BED does not occur only in obese people; normal-weight people may have BED, although less often.

How many people are affected by BED?

I assumed this diagnosis meant others struggled too but a search through eating disorder groups revealed very few. Either I was a rare sufferer or binge eating disorder was severely under-diagnosed and -discussed.

Chevese

Research on BED epidemiology is limited. Community-based studies have yielded prevalence rates of 1 to 3 per cent for BED (Hay 1998; Hudson *et al.* 2007), with some studies reporting nearly equal proportions for males and females (Grucza *et al.* 2007), which is clearly different from gender ratios in other EDs. BED has been shown to affect an ethnically more diverse group than AN and BN, with similar rates among black and white women (Striegel-Moore and Franko 2003). BED is more frequent among overweight and obese people (Hay 1998) than in normal-weight people, with approximately 65 per cent of those with BED affected by obesity (Striegel-Moore *et al.* 2001).

A longitudinal study of the natural history of ED from a community sample of adolescent girls, reported a cumulative eight-year incidence of 5 per cent (Stice *et al.* 2009).

Risk factors for BED

I struggled as a child with the stigma of being overweight. I was teased and bullied despite being well liked by my peers and teachers.

I felt ashamed I could not keep myself away from food and yet knew that during tumultuous family times and the normal stresses of everyday life it was the only thing that allowed me to escape and simultaneously calm me.

Chevese

Binge eating disorder is believed to result from a combination of factors interacting at different stages of development. Originally, it was believed the causes of binge eating in BED would conform to the model proposed for BN, in which dietary restraint has a central role. In the restraint model, the adoption of a cognitively restrained eating style renders the patient vulnerable to eating disinhibition and compensatory binge eating whenever cognitive control is disrupted (Stice *et al.* 2002).

As demonstrated by Chevese, the dietary-restraint model is not sufficient to explain binge eating in BED. Since childhood she struggled with uncontrolled urges to eat and increasing weight before any attempts at dieting. She mentions the calming effects of food and eating in response to stressful situations such as parental conflict and school-related stress.

Indeed, binge eating has often been associated with depression and negative mood and several researchers have posited its occurrence as an attempt at affect-regulation in some people (Stice *et al.* 2002) as it provides transitory comfort and distraction from aversive emotions. This effect may be enhanced by the concomitant presence of dietary restraint (dietary restraint/negative affect model) (Telch and Agras 1996).

Two case-control studies have examined background risk factors for BED (Fairburn *et al.* 1998; Striegel-Moore *et al.* 2005). These studies found BED to be consistently associated with two classes of risk factors: general risk factors for any psychiatric disorder, such as parental problems, childhood sexual and physical abuse, family conflict, parental eating problems and mood and substance disorders, which seem to interact with risk factors that are specific for eating pathology, such as childhood obesity and negative comments from family about shape, weight or eating. In addition, specific criticism related to shape and weight may render the person particularly vulnerable to development of BED (Pike *et al.* 2006).

Finally, preliminary evidence from family studies suggests familiarity influences the development of BED, as relatives of those with BED are more likely to have a lifetime history of BED, even when obesity is controlled (Hudson *et al.* 2006).

The onset of BED

Most people with BED present for treatment in adulthood, although research has shown BED may begin during late adolescence (Tanofsky-Kraff *et al.* 2007). Based on dietary restraint and dietary restraint/negative mood models, two pathways have been described leading to BED development: either dieting precedes development of binge eating behaviour or binge eating appears before dieting attempts (Grilo and Masheb 2000). As mentioned previously, Chevese belongs to the second group, although she was only diagnosed with BED in her thirties.

Binge eating behaviours in children

> Sometime between the ages of 5 and 7, I discovered the power of food. I discovered I wanted more of it than I was permitted to have, that it was a restricted temptation, and that I thought about it a lot.
>
> Chevese

Chevese is not a rare example of binge eating occurring since childhood. Prevalence rates in young children range from 2 to 10 per cent in community samples and among overweight children rates are greater, with 15–30 per cent reporting binge eating or loss of control eating (LOC) (Tanofsky-Kraff *et al.* 2004), suggesting that, as in adults, these behaviours are associated with obesity.

When studying childhood overeating, researchers have focused on LOC rather than objective binge eating due to limitations in defining 'large amount of food' in growing children. LOC eating in children is associated with other disordered eating symptoms and may be associated with poorer psychosocial functioning and psychiatric symptoms (Morgan *et al.* 2002).

Approaching BED in treatment

Chevese first sought treatment for her eating and weight problems when 22 years old. Despite not having her condition diagnosed, cognitive-behavioural therapy was helpful as an initial approach and she managed to lose some weight and to 'have a new outlook and tools for living', which helped her resume university, marry and have children. She slowly regained weight and, when facing another challenging period of life, reached her highest weight. She continued to seek help, and being finally diagnosed with BED helped her feel able to address her condition. However, weight gain remained a problem and she submitted herself to an unsuccessful lap-band surgery.

> I realized this band around my stomach would not solve my food problems ...
> I would need to continue seeing a treatment team.
>
> Chevese

Treatment of BED is complex, and includes management of three main areas: (a) disordered eating (binge eating) and dysfunctional cognitions such as over-concern with weight and shape; (b) associated psychopathology; and (c) weight problems (when present). Treatment of obesity is a major challenge on its own, and not the focus here. BED management is usually delivered on an outpatient basis.

Practice recommendations stress the importance of specialized care being offered to ED patients, but this is not always available (APA 2006). Thus, those who present low levels of symptoms and no significant functional impact may try less intensive care, in a stepped-care approach. This may include pure (without aid of a mental health professional) or guided self-help interventions, mostly based on CBT for BED and designed to eliminate binge eating (Wilson *et al.* 2000). Self-help interventions are cost-effective and do not require ED-specialized professionals, and thus are suitable as a first approach. These interventions have proven effective in reducing binge eating and ED psychopathology in the short term (Vocks *et al.* 2010: 213). Most often, however, specialized interventions are necessary. Chevese illustrates the importance of continued access to care.

Effective treatments in BED

> I assembled my team to include a psychologist, nutritionist, and several complementary practitioners and worked with a combination of cognitive-behavioural, dialectical-behavioural, and interpersonal-behavioural therapy. We addressed my relationships, unmet emotional needs, and how to listen to my body. We worked to improve my body image.
>
> Chevese

Psychological interventions modified to target BED issues, such as CBT, interpersonal psychotherapy (IPT) and dialectical-behavioural therapy (DBT), are the main treatment options for BED. CBT is considered the first choice (APA 2006) as it shows large effects in reducing binge eating (Vocks *et al.* 2010: 213) and promoting binge abstinence (cessation of binge eating) in the short run, with effects that may last for longer periods (Wilfley *et al.* 2002). However, BED-specific psychological interventions do not lead to significant weight loss in general (Vocks *et al.* 2010: 213). Whether binge eating has a negative impact on weight-loss treatment, and should be addressed first or not, remains controversial. Binge abstinence has been associated with greater weight loss in treatments for BED, either psychological (Wilfley *et al.* 2002) or pharmacological (Devlin *et al.* 2005), and binge remission seems to last longer when BED-specific approaches (CBT or IPT) are offered (Wilson *et al.* 2010). However, behavioural weight-loss management has shown positive results in promoting weight loss and binge reductions in uncontrolled studies (Vocks *et al.* 2010: 205) and in controlled trials, though only in the short run (Wilson *et al.* 2010). Chevese's story strongly illustrates the importance of treating eating symptoms and focusing on positive aspects of life, besides weight.

Pharmacological interventions can also be useful in the treatment of BED. A meta-analytical study on the efficacy of pharmacological interventions supported a moderate effectiveness of several drugs (including antidepressants, anticonvulsants and obesity drugs) in reducing binge frequency and promoting binge remission in the short term (Vocks *et al.* 2010: 214). Practice guidelines recommend treatment with antidepressants (mainly serotonin selective reuptake inhibitors – SSRIs) as an alternative initial approach when psychotherapy is either unavailable or unacceptable. Doses of SSRIs used to target binge episodes are usually higher than recommended to treat depression (e.g. fluoxetine 60 mg/day) (APA 2006: 1114). Anti-obesity agents (e.g. sibutramine, orlistat) or drugs associated with weight loss (e.g. topiramate, zonisamide, atomoxetine) have shown greater rates of binge remission than SSRIs (compared to placebo) in studies, and when used in association with CBT or behavioural weight loss they might increase weight loss (Treasure *et al.* 2010: 589). Despite potential advantages of combined interventions, the risk–benefit balance of drug use is uncertain, as are the long-term effects after short-term medication use (Treasure *et al.* 2010: 589).

Prognosis

After thirty-five years I have perfected bingeing as a coping mechanism. The difference now is that I recognize the binges. Certain foods, situations, and people can contribute to a binge's internal swell. But the quantity is less and I catch myself mid-binge. I am patient with myself; I cannot be perfect and one binge does not mean I have failed miserably.

Chevese

Little is known on the prognosis of BED. In one longitudinal study where patients were hospitalized for treatment, a diagnosis of an ED was still present in nearly 33 per cent of the individuals twelve years later, and about 36 per cent were obese (BMI over 30 kg/m^2) (Fichter *et al.* 2008). Community studies have described an intermittent course for BED, with relapses and remissions (Fairburn *et al.* 2000).

Importance of recognizing BED as an eating disorder category

When my new therapist diagnosed 'binge eating disorder', guilt and shame gave way to relief. Suddenly my food preoccupation and overeating had a name and I could address it.

Chevese

Conclusion

Growing evidence supports BED as a distinct ED based on clinical presentation, epidemiological aspects, body mass index and course. There is also evidence to discriminate BED from obesity not linked to binge eating, in eating patterns, general psychopathology, global functioning, and health-related quality of life, independent of weight level. Specific interventions (psychological) for BED have been developed and are effective. Recognition of BED diagnosis may: improve early identification and treatment of cases, enhance self-esteem of sufferers through understanding of disease aspects, increase treatment resources, reduce stigma through education of health professionals and the general population, help in the identification of risk and protective factors, and enable development of preventive measures.

References

American Psychiatric Association (APA) (1994) *Diagnostic and Statistical Manual of Mental Disorders* (DSM-IV), 4th edn, Washington, DC: APA.

American Psychiatric Association (APA) (2006) 'Practice guidelines for the treatment of patients with eating disorders', in *Practice Guidelines for the Treatment of Psychiatric Disorders,* 3rd edn (pp. 1097–222), Arlington, VA: APA.

Basdevant, A., Pouillon, M., Lahlou, N., Le Barzic, M., Brillant, M., and Guy-Grand, B. (1995) 'Prevalence of binge eating disorder in different populations of French women', *Int J Eat Disord* 18, 4: 309–15.

Crow, S.J., Stewart Agras, W., Halmi, K., Mitchell, J.E., and Kraemer, H.C. (2002) 'Full syndromal versus subthreshold anorexia nervosa, bulimia nervosa, and binge eating disorder: A multicenter study', *Int J Eat Disord* 32, 3: 309–18.

Devlin, M.J., Goldfein, J.A., Petkova, E., Jiang, H., Raizman, P.S., Wolk, S., Mayer, L., Carino, J., Bellace, D., Kamenetz, C., Dobrow, I., and Walsh, B.T. (2005) 'Cognitive behavioral therapy and fluoxetine as adjuncts to group behavioral therapy for binge eating disorder', *Obes Res* 13, 6: 1077–88.

Elder, K.A., Paris, M. Jr., Añez, L.M., and Grilo, C.M. (2008) 'Loss of control over eating is associated with eating disorder psychopathology in a community sample of Latinas', *Eat Behav* 9, 4: 501–3.

Fairburn, C.G. and Bohn, K. (2005) 'Eating disorder NOS (EDNOS): An example of the troublesome "not otherwise specified" (NOS) category in DSM-IV', *Behav Res Ther* 43, 6: 691–701.

Fairburn, C.G. and Cooper, Z. (1993) 'The eating disorder examination' (12th edn), in C.G. Fairburn and T.G. Wilson (eds) *Binge Eating: Nature, Assessment, and Treatment*, (pp. 317–60), New York: Guilford Press.

Fairburn, C.G., Doll, H.A., Welch, S.L., Hay, P.J., Davies, B.A., and O'Connor, M.E. (1998) 'Risk factors for binge eating disorder: A community-based, case-control study', *Arch Gen Psychiatry* 55, 5: 425–32.

Fairburn, C.G., Cooper, Z., Doll, H.A., Norman, P., and O'Connor, M. (2000) 'The natural course of bulimia nervosa and binge eating disorder in young women', *Arch Gen Psychiatry* 57, 7: 659–65.

Fichter, M.M., Quadflieg, N., and Hedlund S. (2008) 'Long-term course of binge eating disorder and bulimia nervosa: Relevance for nosology and diagnostic criteria', *Int J Eat Disord* 41, 7: 577–86.

Grilo, C.M. and Masheb, R.M. (2000) 'Onset of dieting vs binge eating in outpatients with binge eating disorder', *Int J Obes Relat Metab Disord* 24, 4: 404–9.

Grilo, C.M., Hrabosky, J.I., White, M.A., Allison, K.C., Stunkard, A.J., and Masheb, R.M. (2008) 'Overvaluation of shape and weight in binge eating disorder and overweight controls: Refinement of a diagnostic construct', *J Abnorm Psychol* 117, 2: 414–19.

Grilo, C.M., White, M.A. and Masheb, R.M. (2009) 'DSM-IV psychiatric disorder comorbidity and its correlates in binge eating disorder', *Int J Eating Disord* 42, 3: 228–34.

Grucza, R.A., Przybeck, T.R., and Cloninger, C.R. (2007) 'Prevalence and correlates of binge eating disorder in a community sample', *Compr Psychiatry* 48, 2: 124–31.

Guss, J.L., Kissileff, H.R., Devlin, M.J., Zimmerli, E., and Walsh, B.T. (2002) 'Binge size increases with body mass index in women with binge eating disorder', *Obes Res* 10, 10: 1021–9.

Hay, P. (1998) 'The epidemiology of eating disorder behaviors: An Australian community-based survey', *Int J Eat Disord* 23, 4: 371–82.

Hudson, J.I., Lalonde, J.K., Berry, J.M., Pindyck, L.J., Bulik, C.M., Crow, S.J., McElroy, S.L., Laird, N.M., Tsuang, M.T., Walsh, B.T., Rosenthal, N.R., and Pope H.G., Jr. (2006) 'Binge eating disorder as a distinct familial phenotype in obese individuals', *Arch Gen Psychiatry* 63, 3: 313–9.

Hudson, J.I., Hiripi, E., Pope H.G. Jr., and Kessler, R.C. (2007) 'The prevalence and correlates of eating disorders in the National Comorbidity Survey Replication', *Biol Psychiatry* 161, 3: 348–58.

Latner, J.D. and Clyne, C. (2008) 'The diagnostic validity of the criteria for binge eating disorder', *Int J Eat Disord* 41, 1: 1–14.

Masheb, R.M. and Grilo, C.M. (2008) 'Prognostic significance of two sub-categorization methods for the treatment of binge eating disorder: Negative affect and overvaluation predict, but do not moderate, specific outcomes', *Behav Res Ther* 46, 4: 428–37.

Morgan, C.M., Yanovski, S.Z., Nguyen, T.T., McDuffie, J., Sebring, N.G., Jorge, M.R., Keil, M., and Yanovski, J.A. (2002) 'Loss of control over eating, adiposity, and psychopathology in overweight children', *Int J Eat Disord* 31, 4: 430–41.

Pike, K.M., Wilfley, D., Hilbert, A., Fairburn, C.G., Dohm, F.A., and Striegel-Moore, R.H. (2006) 'Antecedent life events of binge eating disorder', *Psychiatry Res* 142, 1: 19–29.

Stice, E., Presnell, K., and Spangler, D. (2002) 'Risk factors for binge eating onset in adolescent girls: A 2-year prospective investigation', *Health Psychol* 21, 2: 131–8.

Stice, E., Marti, C.N., Shaw, H., and Jaconis, M. (2009) 'An 8-year longitudinal study of the natural history of threshold, subthreshold, and partial eating disorders from a community sample of adolescents', *J Abnorm Psychol* 118, 3: 587–97.

Striegel-Moore, R.H. and Franko, D.L. (2003) 'Epidemiology of binge eating disorder', *Int J Eat Disord* 34 (suppl): S19–29.

Striegel-Moore, R.H., Cachelin, F.M., Dohm, F.A., Pike, K.M., Wilfley, D.E., and Fairburn, C.G. (2001) 'Comparison of binge eating disorder and bulimia nervosa in a community sample', *Int J Eat Disord* 29, 2: 157–65.

Striegel-Moore, R.H., Fairburn, C.G., Wilfley, D.E., Pike, K.M., Dohm, F.A., and Kraemer, H.C. (2005) 'Toward an understanding of risk factors for binge eating disorder in black and white women: A community-based case-control study', *Psychol Med* 35, 6: 907–17.

Stunkard, A.J. (1959) 'Eating patterns and obesity', *Psychiatr Q* 33: 284–95.

Tanofsky-Kraff, M., Yanovski, S.Z., Wilfley, D.E., Marmarosh, C., Morgan, C.M., and Yanovski, J.A. (2004) 'Eating-disordered behaviors, body fat, and psychopathology in overweight and normal-weight children', *J Consult Clin Psychol* 72, 1: 53–61.

Tanofsky-Kraff, M., Goossens, L., Eddy, K.T., Ringham, R., Goldschmidt, A., Yanovski, S.Z., Braet, C., Marcus, M.D., Wilfley, D.E., Olsen, C., and Yanovski, J.A. (2007) 'A multi-site investigation of binge eating behaviors in children and adolescents', *J Consult Clini Psychol* 75, 6: 901–13.

Telch, C.F. and Agras, W.S. (1994) 'Obesity, binge eating and psychopathology: Are they related?', *Int J Eat Disord* 15, 1: 53–61.

Telch, C.F. and Agras, W.S. (1996) 'Do emotional states influence binge eating in the obese?' *Int J Eat Disord* 20, 3: 271–9.

Telch, C.F., Pratt, E.M., and Niego, S.H. (1998) 'Obese women with binge eating disorder define the term binge', *Int J Eat Disord* 24, 3: 313–17.

Treasure, J., Claudino, A.M., and Zucker, N. (2010) 'Eating disorders', *The Lancet* 375 (9714): 583–93.

Vocks, S., Tuschen-Caffier, B., Pietrowsky, R., Rustenbach, S.J., Kersting, A., and Herpertz, S. (2010) 'Meta-analysis of the effectiveness of psychological and pharmacological treatments for binge eating disorder', *Int J Eat Disord* 43, 3: 205–17.

Walsh, B.T. and Boudreau, G. (2003) 'Laboratory studies of binge eating disorder', *Int J Eat Disord* 34 (suppl): S30–8.

Wilfley, D.E., Friedman, M.A., Dounchis, J.Z., Stein, R.I., Welch, R.R., and Ball, S.A. (2000a) 'Comorbid psychopathology in binge eating disorder: Relation to eating disorder severity at baseline and following treatment', *J Consult Clin Psychol* 68, 4: 641–9.

Wilfley, D.E., Schwartz, M.B., Spurrell, E.B., and Fairburn, C.G. (2000b) 'Using the eating disorder examination to identify the specific psychopathology of binge eating disorder', *Int J Eat Disord* 27, 3: 259–69.

Wilfley, D.E., Welch, R.R., Stein, R.I., Spurrell, E.B., Cohen, L.R., Saelens, B.E., Dounchis, J.Z., Frank, M.A., Wiseman, C.V., and Matt, G.E. (2002) 'A randomized comparison of group cognitive-behavioral therapy and group interpersonal psychotherapy for the treatment of overweight individuals with binge eating disorder', *Arch Gen Psychiatry* 59, 8: 713–21.

Wilson, G.T. and Sysko, R. (2009) 'Frequency of binge eating episodes in bulimia nervosa and binge eating disorder: Diagnostic considerations', *Int J Eat Disord* 42, 7: 603–10.

Wilson, G.T., Vitousek, K.M., and Loeb, K.L. (2000) 'Stepped care treatment for eating disorders', *J Consult Clin Psychol* 68, 4: 564–72.

Wilson, G.T., Wilfley, D.E., Agras, W.S., and Bryson, S.W. (2010) 'Psychological treatments of binge eating disorder', *Arch Gen Psychiatry* 67, 1: 94–101.

Wolfe, B.E., Baker, C.W., Smith, A.T., and Kelly-Weeder, S. (2009) 'Validity and utility of the current definition of binge eating', *Int J Eat Disord* 42, 8: 674–86.

Wonderlich, S.A., Gordon, K.H., Mitchell, J.E., Crosby, R.D., and Engel, S.G. (2009) 'The validity and clinical utility of binge eating disorder', *Int J Eat Disord* 42, 8: 687–705.

Yanovski, S.Z., Leet, M., Yanovski, J.A., Flood, M., Gold, P.W., Kissileff, H.R., and Walsh, B.T. (1992) 'Food selection and intake of obese women with binge eating disorder', *Am J Clin Nutr* 56, 6: 975–80.

Chapter 22

Eating disorders in women of African descent

Stefanie Gilbert

Case study

My family is African American and my father was in the air force when I was a child. We lived on an airport base in a predominately White environment.

My mother was always trying to control her weight. My dad was a stereotype serviceman, a man of few words, expecting us to respond immediately.

At a new school in Grade 10, my skin became beautiful and my body shape was changing, transforming. I thought it would be better if I lost a little more weight. The GIs were noticing me. I bought diet pills over the counter.

In 11th grade, my father retired, and we lived in a community for the first time. This was very difficult, more racist. Our family of eight took up residence in a predominately White community that resisted minorities moving into the county. We might walk down the street and be called a name. I had been looking forward to my senior year and suddenly had these new challenges. At school, children came from families who had been settled for generations; they didn't need new friends. Besides, they were White. Looking back, I probably had mild depression. I wanted to stay in bed on weekends. My problems here were more to do with race than size.

We moved to another part of town, a large African-American community, and I was attracted to this, but I had been raised in a predominately White environment. The Black environment was not what I imagined.

One boy asked: 'Where are you from, Mars?'

I didn't fit their perception of an African-American person.

I finally get where I thought I would feel at home and I am from Mars!

When I got paid I would go to McDonald's and order two cheeseburgers and a chocolate shake. When I wanted to reward myself, I would eat food.

When I started college I heard stories of people throwing up, taking laxatives. By then I'd tried Weight Watchers: I would put weight on, take it off. So I decided to do what others were doing, and began throwing up after stuffing myself silly. I ate what I liked but wanted to be smaller. I would diet, break out and eat, and throw it up.

At 25 or 26, I worked in a [predominantly White environment] and observed that affluent wealthy women had a greater sense of being thin. I was increasingly aware that I was carrying weight. They were slim, and I was using food to soothe myself. I never really found a group that was like myself.

My husband and I had a fresh start, moving away from family support and long-time friends. I was extremely lonely and worked long hours until 11 pm. My little girls were not seeing me. I began to notice my older daughter, in second grade, starting to gain weight. A loaf of special bread, like raisin bread, would disappear in a day. I feel guilty, not being there for her.

I haven't yet got inner contentment. I am not actively dieting but still binge. When my husband would leave the house I would eat a big hunk of chocolate cake and ice-cream. I did this only when he was out. My mother had done this when my father left the house.

Food has been dominant through my life. A year ago, I lost 46 lbs on Weight Watchers, and then started to cheat. On the weigh-in morning, I would do five hours on the mill and not drink. After Weight Watchers, I would eat all the way home. Weight Watchers was not solving my inner problem.

Intellectually, I know food is not a good choice. I love the taste, but it is not making me happy. I will try to ... get the focus off weight loss and be more mindful about my eating. It is hard to let go of weight loss as the primary goal. I am scared; I stopped purging and gained weight. So if I stop weight loss as a goal, will the same thing happen?

My older daughter is overweight at 17, and I worry she will develop my eating disorder and become emotionally addicted to food. I want to step in early.

Mary

At least until the 1990s, researchers assumed that eating disorders affected only White women. Today, it is generally accepted that, although certain eating disorders (i.e. anorexia) are less common among Black women (Hoek *et al.* 2003; Keel and Klump 2003; Striegel-Moore *et al.* 2003), others (i.e. bingeing and purging) are at least as common if not more prevalent among Black women (Marcus *et al.* 2007; Mulholland and Mintz 2001; Striegel-Moore *et al.* 2000; White and Grilo 2005), although not all studies support this (Gray *et al.* 1987; Striegel-Moore *et al.* 2003). Disordered eating in parts of Africa has been documented since the 1980s (for a review, see Gordon 2001). Recent research in South Africa suggests that levels of disordered eating and body shape dissatisfaction are actually higher among South African Black female students than among their Caucasian counterparts (Le Grange *et al.* 1998; Wassenaar *et al.* 2000). Similarly, in a study based in Britain, Reiss (1996) found significantly more disordered eating attitudes and behaviours among African-Caribbean women than among Caucasian women.

Accumulating research supports the idea that eating disorders may be more common among Black girls and women than was previously thought (Moriarty and Harrison 2008). In a recent study of more than 200 women in Tanzania, Eddy *et al.* (2007) found that one-third of the women endorsed disordered eating attitudes, 10 per cent reported bingeing, and 5 per cent reported purging, with nearly 5 per cent reporting significant eating pathology consistent with an eating disorder not otherwise specified diagnosis (American Psychiatric Association 2000).

Existing statistics may underestimate the prevalence of eating disorders among Black women due to ethnic minority women's general distrust of medical professionals and their reluctance to seek help, combined with the tendency of medical professionals to overlook or misdiagnose eating disorders in women of colour (Cachelin *et al.* 2000, 2001). In addition, because the majority of studies are conducted using convenience samples (generally university students), there is little understanding to date of prevalence rates in rural or lower social classes (for a review of methodological problems in this research area, see Gilbert (2003)). Reported cases of eating disorders within South Africa may offer a poor assessment of actual prevalence rates, given the 'legacy of apartheid and the marginalization of health care, particularly aspects of psychiatric care for the black population' (Szabo and Le Grange 2001: 27). White physicians may have overlooked eating disorders in Black women, while Black women there have had little access to adequate health services, leading to underestimates of those affected. In addition, due to poor access to health care as well as traditional beliefs regarding mental health issues, Black women may have turned to traditional healers, rather than physicians, for treatment (Szabo and Le Grange 2001).

Ethnic differences in clinical presentation

While many diagnostic features of eating disorders may be the same regardless of a patient's ethnicity, there may be some ethnic differences in clinical presentation. For example, when compared to their Caucasian counterparts, African-American women who are anorexic are less likely to report body image distortion (Holden and Robinson 1988), while those who binge exhibit lower levels of shape and weight concern (Pike *et al.* 2001), embrace a less stringent definition of ideal body weight (Gray *et al.* 1987), and are more likely to binge than purge (Lokken *et al.* 2008; Pike *et al.* 2001; Striegel-Moore *et al.* 2005), although not all studies support these findings (Atlas *et al.* 2002; Lester and Petrie 1998).

Factors other than body image disturbance may be more central to the development and maintenance of eating pathology in women of African descent. For example, some research indicates disordered eating may stem from feelings of inadequacy (Bagley *et al.* 2003), or reactions to environmental stress (Striegel-Moore *et al.* 2005), rather than from distress surrounding perceptions of being overweight. Researchers examining South African student samples suggest that high levels of eating pathology among Black South African women may represent responses to changing gender roles and identities rather than simply the effects of Westernization (Szabo and Le Grange 2001).

Initially, researchers examining eating disorders in Black women reported associations between higher social class and both body dissatisfaction (Caldwell *et al.* 1997) and disordered eating behaviours (White *et al.* 1985). However, more recent research suggests that lower socioeconomic status may be a risk factor for eating pathology in women of colour. For example, in a community-based study of adult African-American, Hispanic, and White women, financial strain was positively associated with eating disorder symptoms (Marcus *et al.* 2007), with other researchers reporting similar findings (Langer *et al.* 1991). In another study, 10 per cent of low-income African-American girls met diagnostic criteria for an eating disorder (Vander Wal and Thomas 2004).

Body weight is also positively associated with disordered eating attitudes and behaviours in Black women, with higher body weight associated with more disturbed body image and disordered eating behaviours, especially bingeing (Hrabosky and Grilo 2007; Striegel-Moore *et al.* 2000). Given the accumulating evidence linking heavier body weight with binge eating problems, a patient's obesity may be a 'red flag' suggestive of an underlying eating disorder.

Ethnic differences in risk factors for eating disorders

Eating disorders are considered culture-bound syndromes primarily occurring in societies that emphasize a thin female beauty ideal (for reviews, see Gilbert and Thompson 1996; Smolak and Striegel-Moore 2001). Women who move from a non-Westernized country to a Westernized country report greater disordered eating attitudes and behaviours than do their counterparts back home (Furnham and Alibhai 1983; Furukawa 1994; Greenberg *et al.* 2007). These individuals may internalize certain standards and ideals of the dominant Western culture that, in turn, may contribute to increased body dissatisfaction and eating disturbance.

A plethora of research has examined the Western 'culture of thinness' impact (Thompson 1992) on eating disorder development. Evidence supporting this model suggests a strong relationship between society's glorification of a thin body type, particularly for women, and the increasing eating disorder incidence since the 1960s (Stice 2002).

Numerous studies have revealed the strong negative affective impact of thin media images on women's body image and drive for thinness (for a review, see Gilbert *et al.* 2005), but only a few studies have documented the impact of these images on Black girls and women. In a large-scale study of women in Tanzania, Eddy *et al.* (2007) found that exposure to media and Western influences was positively associated with eating disorder symptoms.

Interestingly, Botta (2000) found that White girls who watch a lot of television displayed more disordered eating behaviours than did African-American girls who watched the same amount of television. However, Moriarty and Harrison (2008) found that television exposure positively predicted eating disorder symptoms in both White and Black girls.

Some have argued that Black girls and women may be somewhat buffered from the impact of media images, since most feature White girls and women (Rucker and Cash 1992), and that African-American culture's greater acceptance of a variety of body shapes may be protective (Smolak and Striegel-Moore 2001; Striegel-Moore *et al.* 2005). Studies suggest that African Americans are less cognizant of and more accepting of overweight than Whites (Skelton *et al.* 2006; Villarosa 1994; West *et al.* 2008).

However, girls and women of colour may be vulnerable to negative self-evaluations due to other factors, such as racist beauty ideals. Historically, Western media influences have glorified European features such as straight hair, a straight nose, white or lighter skin, and delicate facial features, rather than the kinky hair texture, darker skin tones and broader facial features more typical of women of African descent (Adkison-Bradley and Lipford-Sanders 2006; Harris and Kuba 1997), thus portraying Black women as 'the antithesis of the American conception of beauty, femininity, and womanhood' (Lipford-Sanders and Bradley 2005: 302). Black women who internalize Western influences and endorse a Eurocentric standard of beauty are at greater risk for developing an eating disorder (Abrams *et al.* 1993; Smolak and Striegel-Moore 2001).

In a comparative analysis of eating disorder symptoms and their correlates in African, Afro-Caribbean, and African-American women at a historically Black university, Gilbert and colleagues (2009) found that internalization of the Western thin ideal of beauty predicted eating pathology for African-American women, but not for the other two groups. The authors suggest that factors other than the Western ideal of beauty (e.g. racism, acculturative stress) may be more important in understanding the development of eating disorders among women from non-Western societies.

Mary's case

Mary's case offers an intimate glimpse into the pathogenesis of binge eating and bulimia in the life of an African-American woman. Its themes can serve as markers for exploration when conducting psychotherapy with ethnic minority women with similar experiences and concerns.

Although Mary wanted to try therapy, she felt a twinge of reluctance, realizing that eradicating her eating disorder would require giving up the 'junk food' she likes to eat during a binge.

As described earlier, Mary grew up on an air force base, in a predominantly White environment. By 11th grade and after several moves, her family settled in an area that was racist. Mary described an uncomfortable sense of awareness of being different from others, even when her family moved to an area of town populated by more Black people. Even then, she felt different, as the Black people criticized her 'White' ways of speaking and behaving.

> I was told I spoke funny and dressed funny – dressed like White people – and was perceived in terms of the stereotype White middle class – I was more like White people in the way I acted, spoke and dressed. So I didn't fit in.
>
> Mary

Research indicates that, for Black women, assimilation to 'White culture' is associated with increased risk for developing an eating disorder (Abrams *et al.* 1993). Whether this is due to confronting 'White' cultural ideals of beauty or other Western cultural standards for achievement and individualism is unclear. However, a reluctance to accept and identify with mainstream culture seems to be protective (Davis *et al.* 1999; Lokken *et al.* 2008).

By virtue of their race and gender, African-American women are members of two low-status groups that carry the dual oppressions of sexism and racism (Talleyrand 2006). In addition to being targeted for her 'White' mannerisms, Mary was also teased about her larger body size. The boy across the street from her home mocked her relentlessly:

> the boy began calling me names, and my heavy sister began calling me 'big fat momma'. The boy referred to me as 'blob'. He was part of a nasty group of kids who joined his name-calling. I tried to respond with kindness. Weathering that, I was a popular student, but suffering with being called 'The Blob' .... I could be walking across the hall and someone would call out: 'Hey, Blob'.
>
> Mary

Research has revealed a strong association between experiences of abuse, bullying, and discrimination and the development of binge eating disorder. Striegel-Moore *et al.* (2002) found that, in both Black and White women with binge eating disorder, rates of sexual abuse, physical abuse and bullying by peers were significantly higher than in healthy comparison women. In another study, Quinlan *et al.* (2009) found that more frequent and upsetting weight-related teasing experiences were associated with worse psychological functioning. Adolescents most distressed by weight-related teasing exhibited lower self-esteem and greater depressive symptoms regardless of how often they experienced the teasing.

For Mary, negative body image evolved in response to teasing related to her size, racism regarding her African-American heritage, and being one of the only Black girls at her school. An uneasy awareness of the differences between her body shape and that of other Caucasian and Asian classmates contributed to a growing sense of body dissatisfaction.

> White people's body shape is different. Many times the younger Caucasians had a slimmer, different body shape. I seemed more round in the hips…. In college, Asian students had smaller body shapes than me. I wanted to eat what I wanted but stay small like them.
>
> Mary

Feeling that she didn't 'fit in', Mary turned to food as a replacement for acceptance and a feeling of community. Food offered nurturance, safety, and comfort when she felt overwhelmingly displaced, isolated, and irrelevant. She symbolically turned to her father, as food was the primary source of comfort and support he offered.

> Now there was no group to hang out with; I did not go out socially with friends or guys. But I could always have a great meal with my family because my dad is a great cook.
>
> Mary

For Mary, food continues to have nostalgic implications, harking back to a childhood in which her father's ability to express love and comfort was conveyed almost exclusively through food:

> In our household my dad expressed his love through cooking … Dad didn't say 'I love you' all the time but always put food on the table…. Food was connected with love.
>
> Mary

In turn, 'you ate what was put before you' communicated acceptance of and appreciation for the 'love' that was offered. For Mary the adult, food remains linked with feelings of love, a legacy of her relationship with her father. Today, the most 'wonderful' gifts her husband gives her are meals he cooks, even though 'he isn't a great cook!'

In Mary's ongoing struggle, food became both battleground and refuge. Bingeing, a behaviour 'inherited' from her mother, became her primary coping mechanism. Mary remembers her mother engaging in this behaviour when her father was out of the house, and describes this as her mother's 'me time'.

> This was her, and now my, private quiet time: watch TV, read a book and eat…. I'm concerned my daughter will do the same.
>
> Mary

In the context of these familial and cultural issues, Mary's eating disorder acquires meaning that can facilitate recovery. Her bingeing can be understood as an understandable coping strategy offering comfort and support when there is little 'me' time.

> I eat as a reward. My pampering is eating. To find another thing that is not tied to food is a challenge.
>
> Mary

In struggling to manage the competing demands of business executive, wife, and mother of two, Mary may have adopted the prevailing mythical 'Black superwoman' ideal that requires that she 'do all' and 'be all' (Trotman 2002). This cultural imperative to portray one's self as a strong survivor has implications for African-American women's emotional and physical health (Greene 1994; Talleyrand 2006).

Mary's therapy has focused on understanding the solace that food offers her, but recognizing, too, that such solace is temporary. Almost immediately after bingeing, Mary is filled with remorse for her behaviour. Although she presented for treatment with a goal of losing weight, an important part of therapy has been re-conceptualizing her treatment goals in terms of better self-care. Clearly, losing weight will benefit her overall physical health. However, unless her goal incorporates the overarching value of self-care, she might turn to other self-destructive behaviours. Understanding how her family of origin may have used food rather than words to communicate and nurture has helped Mary become more assertive, rather than using food to channel her emotions. Identifying compulsive eating as a self-destructive behaviour has enabled her to adopt alternative coping strategies.

Treatment recommendations

A history of teasing, bullying or discrimination may be important to understanding a patient's body image or eating pathology. By exploring early experiences with racism, abuse or teasing, patients can understand the way in which internalization of these traumatic experiences may have contributed to the development of body dissatisfaction and disordered eating. Exploration of cultural conflicts can help to uncover the impact of divergent achievement and beauty ideals on the patient's body image, eating habits, and emotional well-being.

Clinicians can find clues to a patient's feelings about her body in the patient's posture and non-verbal communications. Mary, for example, rarely attends a session in which she doesn't place one of the pillows from the sofa where she is sitting in front of her chest, drawing her arms around it tightly. Discussing this behaviour openly with the therapist, she admitted that she feels ashamed of her body size and wishes to cover it in front of the therapist, who is petite. Discussion of such transference issues can illuminate the impact of self–other comparisons on body image and the development of body shame in relation to obesity. As treatment progresses, therapists can note changes in body language that may indicate improvements in body image and/or a reduction in negative self-comparisons.

Therapists need to be aware of their own countertransference issues related to overweight and obesity or to societal attitudes toward African Americans. For example, therapists may have internalized negative stereotypes about overweight African Americans and may approach patients with anger or uneasiness on a verbal or non-verbal level. It is important for therapists with such concerns to seek supervision to resolve issues such as these which could impair their ability to be effective (Watson 2003).

To date, little has been written about the specific therapeutic needs of Black girls and women with eating disorders, but more attention is being paid to ensure that popular measures are reliable and valid for evaluating eating disorder symptomatology in this population (Bardone-Cone and Boyd 2007; Franko *et al.* 2004). In addition to utilizing these standardized measures, however, it is important for therapists to evaluate the impact of patients' acculturation, racial identity, and history of trauma on their body image and eating behaviours. Understanding the meaningful connotations of food in the patient's life history can help make sense of the disordered eating behaviour and offer a potential pathway towards recovery. By viewing each patient's experience as unique, therapists are best able to understand and treat their patient's eating disorder.

References

Abrams, K.K., Allen, L.R., and Gray, J.J. (1993) 'Disordered Eating Attitudes and Behaviours, Psychological Adjustment, and Ethnic Identity: A Comparison of Black and White Female College Students', *Int J Eat Disord* 14, 1: 49–58.

Adkison-Bradley, C. and Lipford-Sanders, J. (2006) 'Counseling African American Women and Girls', in Courtland C. Lee (ed.) *Multicultural Issues in Counseling: New Approaches to Diversity*, 3rd edn, Alexandria, VA: American Counseling Association.

American Psychiatric Association (APA) (2000) *Diagnostic and Statistical Manual of Mental Disorders*, 4th edn (Text Revision), Washington, DC: American Psychiatric Association.

Atlas, J.G., Smith, G.T., Hohlstein, L.A., McCarthy, D.M., and Kroll, L.S. (2002) 'Similarities and Differences Between Caucasian and African American College Women on Eating and Dieting Expectancies, Bulimic Symptoms, Dietary Restraint, and Disinhibition', *Int J Eat Disord* 32: 326–34.

Bagley, C.A., Character, C.D., and Shelton, L. (2003) 'Eating Disorders Among Urban and Rural African American and European American Women', *Women Ther* 26, 1–2: 57–80.

Bardone-Cone, A. and Boyd, C. (2007) 'Psychometric Properties of Eating Disorder Instruments in Black and White Young Women: Internal Consistency, Temporal Stability, and Validity', *Psychol Assess* 19, 3: 356–62.

Botta, R.A. (2000) 'The Mirror of Television: A Comparison of Black and White Adolescents' Body Image', *J Comm* 50, 3: 144–59.

Cachelin, F.M., Veisel, C., Barzegarnazari, E., and Striegel-Moore, R.H. (2000) 'Disordered Eating, Acculturation, and Treatment Seeking in a Community Sample of Hispanic, Asian, Black, and White Women', *Psychol Women Q* 24, 3: 156–65.

Cachelin, F.M., Rebeck, R., Veisel, C., and Striegel-Moore, R.H. (2001) 'Barriers to Treatment for Eating Disorders Among Ethnically Diverse Women', *Int J Eat Disord* 30, 3: 269–78.

Caldwell, M., Brownell, K., and Wilfley, D. (1997) 'Relationship of Weight, Body Dissatisfaction, and Self-Esteem in African American and White Female Dieters', *Int J Eat Disord* 22, 2: 127–30.

Davis, N.L., Clance, P.R., and Gailis, A.T. (1999) 'Treatment Approaches for Obese and Overweight African American Women: A Consideration of Cultural Dimensions', *Psychother Theor Res Pract Train* 36, 1: 27–35.

Eddy, K.T., Hennessey, M., and Thompson-Brenner, H. (2007) 'Eating Pathology in East African Women: The Role of Media Exposure and Globalization', *J Nerv Ment Dis* 195, 3: 196–202.

Franko, D.L., Striegel-Moore, R.H., Barton, B.A., Schumann, B.C., Garner, D.M., Daniels, S.R., Schreiber, G.B., and Crawford, P.B. (2004) 'Measuring Eating Concerns in Black and White Adolescent Girls', *Int J Eat Disord* 35, 2: 179–89.

Furnham, A. and Alibhai, N. (1983) 'Cross-Cultural Differences in the Perception of Female Body Shapes', *Psychol Med* 13, 4: 829–37.

Furukawa, T. (1994) 'Weight Changes and Eating Attitudes of Japanese Adolescents Under Acculturative Stress: A Prospective Study', *Int J Eat Disord* 15, 1: 71–9.

Gilbert, S. (2003) 'Eating Disorders in Women of Color', *Clin Psychol Sci Pract* 10, 4: 444–55.

Gilbert, S. and Thompson, J.K. (1996) 'Feminist Perspectives of Eating Disorders', *Clin Psychol Sci Pract* 3, 3: 183–202.

Gilbert, S., Keery, H., and Thompson, J.K. (2005) 'The Media's Role in Body Image and Eating Disorders', in E. Cole (ed.) *Featuring Females: Feminist Analyses of Media* (pp. 41–56), Washington, DC: American Psychiatric Association.

Gilbert, S.C., Crump, S., Madhere, S., and Schutz, W. (2009) 'Internalization of the Thin Ideal as a Predictor of Body Dissatisfaction and Disordered Eating in African, African-American, and Afro-Caribbean Female College Students', *J Coll Student Psychother* 23, 3: 196–211.

Gordon, R.A. (2001) 'Eating Disorders East and West: A Culture-Bound Syndrome Unbound', in M. Nasser, M.A. Katzman and R.A. Gordon (eds) *Eating Disorders and Cultures in Transition* (pp. 1–23), New York: Brunner-Routledge.

Gray, J.J., Ford, K., and Kelly, L.M. (1987) 'The Prevalence of Bulimia in a Black College Population', *Int J Eat Disord* 6, 6: 733–40.

Greenberg, L., Cwikel, J., and Mirsky, J. (2007) 'Cultural Correlates of Eating Attitudes: A Comparison Between Native-Born and Immigrant University Students in Israel', *Int J Eat Disord* 40, 1: 51–8.

Greene, B. (1994) 'African American Women', in L. Comas-Diaz and B. Greene (eds) *Women of Color: Integrating Ethnic and Gender Identities in Psychotherapy*, New York: Guilford Press.

Harris, D.J. and Kuba, S.A. (1997) 'Ethnocultural Identity and Eating Disorders in Women of Color', *Prof Psychol Res Pract* 28, 4: 341–7.

Hoek, H.W., van Hoeken, D., and Katzman, M.A. (2003) 'Epidemiology and Cultural Aspects of Eating Disorders: A Review', in M. Maj, K. Halmi, J.J. Lopez-Ibor and N. Sartorius (eds) *Eating Disorders*, Chichester: Wiley.

Holden, N.L. and Robinson, P.H. (1988) 'Anorexia Nervosa and Bulimia Nervosa in British Blacks', *Br J Psychiatry* 152: 544–9.

Hrabosky, J.I. and Grilo, C.M. (2007) 'Body Image and Eating Disordered Behaviour in a Community Sample of Black and Hispanic Women', *Eat Behav* 8, 1: 106–14.

Keel, P.K. and Klump, K.L. (2003) 'Are Eating Disorders Culture-Bound Syndromes? Implications for Conceptualizing Their Etiology', *Psychol Bull* 129, 5: 747–69.

Langer, L., Warheit, G., and Zimmerman, R. (1991) 'Epidemiological Study of Problem Eating Behaviors and Related Attitudes in the General Population', *Addict Behav* 16, 3–4: 167–73.

Le Grange, D., Telch, C.F., and Tibbs, J. (1998) 'Eating Attitudes and Behaviors in 1,435 South African Caucasian and Non-Caucasian College Students', *Am J Psychiatry* 155: 250–4.

Lester, R. and Petrie, T.A. (1998) 'Physical, Psychological, and Societal Correlates of Bulimic Symptomatology Among African American College Women', *J Counsel Psychol* 45: 315–21.

Lipford-Sanders, J. and Bradley, C. (2005) 'Multiple-Lens Paradigm: Evaluating African American Girls and Their Development', *J Counsel Dev* 83, 3: 299–304.

Lokken, K.L., Worthy, S.L., Ferraro, F.R., and Attmann, J. (2008) 'Bulimic Symptoms and Body Image Dissatisfaction in College Women: More Affected by Climate or Race?', *J Psychol* 142, 4: 386–94.

Marcus, M.D., Bromberger, J.T., Wei, H.L., Brown, C., and Kravitz, H.M. (2007) 'Prevalence and Selected Correlates of Eating Disorder Symptoms Among a Multiethnic Community Sample of Midlife Women', *Ann Behav Med* 33, 3: 269–77.

Moriarty, C. and Harrison, K. (2008) 'Television Exposure and Disordered Eating Among Children: A Longitudinal Panel Study', *J Comm* 58, 2: 361–81.

Mulholland, A.M. and Mintz, L.B. (2001) 'Prevalence of Eating Disorders Among African American Women', *J Counsel Psychol* 48, 1: 111–16.

Pike, K.M., Dohm, F.A., Striegel-Moore, R.H., Wilfley, D.E., and Fairburn, C.G. (2001) 'A Comparison of Black and White Women with Binge Eating Disorder', *Am J Psychiatry* 158, 9: 1455–60.

Quinlan, N.P., Hoy, M.B., and Costanzo, P.R. (2009) 'Sticks and Stones: The Effects of Teasing on Psychosocial Functioning in an Overweight Treatment-Seeking Sample', *Soc Dev* 18, 4: 978–1001.

Reiss, D. (1996) 'Abnormal Eating Attitudes and Behaviours in Two Ethnic Groups from a Female British Urban Population', *Psychol Med* 26, 2: 289–9.

Rucker, C. and Cash, T. (1992) 'Body Images, Body-Size Perceptions, and Eating Behaviours Among African-American and White College Women', *Int J Eat Disord* 12, 3: 291–9.

Skelton, J.A., Busey, S.L., and Havens, P.L. (2006) 'Weight and Health Status of Inner City African American Children: Perceptions of Children and Their Parents', *Body Image* 3, 3: 289–93.

Smolak, L. and Striegel-Moore, R.H. (2001) 'Challenging the Myth of the Golden Girl: Ethnicity and Eating Disorders', in R.H. Striegel-Moore and L. Smolak (eds) *Eating Disorders: Innovative Directions in Research and Practice* (pp. 111–32), Washington, DC: American Psychological Association.

Stice, E. (2002) 'Risk and Maintenance Factors for Eating Pathology: A Meta-Analytic Review', *Psychol Bull* 128, 5: 825–48.

Striegel-Moore, R.H., Wilfley, D.E., Pike, K.M., Dohm, F.A., and Fairburn, C.G. (2000) 'Recurrent Binge Eating in Black American Women', *Arch Fam Med* 9, 1: 83–7.

Striegel-Moore, R.H., Dohm, F.A., Pike, K.M., Wilfley, D.E., and Fairburn, C.G. (2002) 'Abuse, Bullying, and Discrimination as Risk Factors for Binge Eating Disorder', *Am J Psychiatry* 159, 11: 1902–7.

Striegel-Moore, R.H., Dohm, F.A., Kraemer, H.C., Taylor, C.B., Daniel, S., Crawford, P.B., and Schreiber, G.B. (2003) 'Eating Disorders in White and Black Women', *Am J Psychiatry* 160, 7: 1326–31.

Striegel-Moore, R.H., Franko, D.L., Thompson, D., Barton, B., Schreiber, G.B., and Daniels, S.R. (2005) 'An Empirical Study of the Typology of Bulimia Nervosa and its Spectrum Variants', *Psychol Med* 35, 11: 1563–72.

Szabo, C.P. and Le Grange, D. (2001) 'Eating Disorders and the Politics of Identity: The South African Experience', in M.A. Katzman and R.A. Gordon (eds) *Eating Disorders and Cultures in Transition* (pp. 24–33), New York: Brunner-Routledge.

Talleyrand, R.M. (2006) 'Potential Stressors Contributing to Eating Disorder Symptoms in African American Women: Implications for Mental Health Counselors', *J Ment Health Counsel* 28, 4: 338–52.

Thompson, J.K. (1992) 'Body Image: Extent of Disturbance, Associated Features, Theoretical Models, Assessment Methodologies, Intervention Strategies, and a Proposal for a DSM-IV Diagnostic Category – Body Image Disorder', in M. Hersen, R.M. Eisler, and P.M. Miller (eds) *Progress in Behaviour Modification* (pp. 3–54), Sycamore, IL: Sycamore Publishing.

Trotman, F.K. (2002) 'Feminist Psychotherapy with Older African American Women', in F.K. Trotman and C.M. Brody (eds) *Psychotherapy and Counseling with Older Women: Cross-Cultural, Family and End-of-Life Issues* (pp. 144–60), New York: Springer Publishing Company.

Vander Wal, J. and Thomas, N. (2004) 'Predictors of Body Image Dissatisfaction and Disturbed Eating Attitudes and Behaviours in African American and Hispanic Girls', *Eat Behav* 5, 4: 291–301.

Villarosa, L. (1994) 'Dangerous Eating', *Essence* 24: 19–21.

Wassenaar, D.R., Le Grange, D., Winship, J., and Lachenicht, L. (2000) 'The Prevalence of Eating Disorder Pathology in a Cross-Ethnic Population of Female Students in South Africa', *Eur Eat Disord Rev* 8: 225–36.

Watson, M.M. (2003) 'Clinical Issues with African-American Women', in J.B. Sanville and E.B. Ruderman (eds) *Therapies with Women in Transition: Toward Relational Perspectives with Today's Women*, Madison, CT: International Universities Press, Inc.

West, D.S., Raczynski, J.M., Phillips, M.M., Bursac, Z., Gauss, C., and Montgomery, B.E. (2008) 'Parental Recognition of Overweight in School-Age Children', *Obesity* 16, 3: 630–6.

White, M.A. and Grilo, C.M. (2005) 'Ethnic Differences in the Prediction of Eating and Body Image Disturbances Among Female Adolescent Psychiatric Inpatients', *Int J Eat Disord* 38, 1: 78–84.

White, W.C., Hudson, L., and Campbell, S.N. (1985) 'Bulimarexia and Black Women: A Brief Report', *Psychother Theor Res Pract Train*, Special Issue: *Psychotherapy with Ethnic Minorities* 22, 2S: 449–50.

Chapter 23

Eating disorders and athletes

Jorunn Sundgot-Borgen and Solfrid Bratland-Sanda

Case study: Kelly

Kelly, 20 years old, is a former elite athlete in the weight-class sport taekwondo. Her first attempt to lose weight occurred at the age of 9 because her coach told her to do so. By the age of 12, the weight-loss regimes became serious, and Kelly developed severe anorexia nervosa (AN). Although her main goal was to compete in the next Olympic Games, her exercise focus changed from performance to weight loss. Several practitioners were suspicious about her eating behaviour, but did not identify it. Instead, they focused on somatic issues such as fatigue and temperature regulation. As an athlete Kelly was automatically assumed to be healthy. Not until the age of 18 was she diagnosed with an eating disorder (ED) and offered treatment. Now, two years later, she receives ongoing outpatient treatment and is again competing at an elite level, this time in cycling (primarily track racing). Recently she has also been diagnosed with Asperger syndrome.

What is so special about sports?

In taekwondo, most athletes starve before weigh-ins and eat a lot after. I realized I was different when I started fearing the feast after weigh-ins. I felt that my teammates would never understand and felt especially isolated at those times. I am a fighter who wants to win and will not let a little obstacle stand in my way.

Kelly

Physical activity is a significant contributor to health, and being physically inactive increases the risk for diseases and mortality (Haskell *et al.* 2007). The benefits of physical activity include physical aspects, such as improved cardiovascular function, lung capacity, digestion, and body composition, as well as psychological variables such as better sleep, mood and self-efficacy (Bouchard *et al.* 2007). However, some hazards are associated with high amounts of competitive sport, such as higher risk for injuries, higher prevalence of exercise-induced asthma, and higher prevalence of disordered eating and eating disorders among athletes compared with non-athletes (Sundgot-Borgen & Torstveit 2004).

For athletes, the body and more specifically body composition and leanness are important performance variables. Many qualities necessary for becoming a champion in sports already predispose the athletes for development of eating disorders. Although the typical athlete has a lean and muscular body, not everyone perceives their own body as optimal for their specific sport (Ravaldi *et al.* 2003). In some cases, such as Kelly's, the coach might want the athlete to diet, and athletes often experience pressure to achieve the 'ideal' body type (Drinkwater *et al.* 2005; Sundgot-Borgen 1994). Thus, in addition to socio-cultural demands placed on males and females to achieve and maintain an ideal body shape, elite athletes are under pressure to improve performance and conform to specific requirements of their sport. Coaches and officials evaluate them almost daily (Nattiv *et al.* 2007; Sundgot-Borgen 1994). These factors may lead to dieting, use of disordered eating behaviours, and development of severe eating disorders, such as AN in Kelly's case.

Body shape and weight are especially important for athletes in leanness sports such as endurance sports (e.g. cross-country running and skiing, cycling, biathlon, triathlon), aesthetic sports (e.g. gymnastics, rhythmic gymnastics, dancing, figure skating), weight-class sports (e.g. martial arts, wrestling, boxing, kick boxing) and gravitation sports (e.g. ski jump, height jump). In addition, some sports have rules that make dieting and weight fluctuation common.

Prevalence of disordered eating and eating disorders

As Kelly says, dieting behaviour prior to competition is common among athletes in weight-class sports. Up to 70 per cent of athletes in such sports report dieting and weight fluctuation (Sundgot-Borgen & Torstveit 2010). The prevalence of eating disorders is higher for both male (8 per cent) and female (22 per cent) athletes compared with non-athletic controls (0.5 and 10 per cent, respectively) (Sundgot-Borgen & Torstveit 2004). Furthermore, clinical eating disorders are more prevalent in sports in which leanness and/or a specific weight are considered important performance factors (47 per cent) compared with non-leanness sports (20 per cent) and non-athletic controls (21 per cent) (Torstveit *et al.* 2008). However, these studies included adult athletes and it is important to note that a recent study did not detect differences between adolescent elite athletes in leanness and non-leanness sports, and the non-athlete control group reported higher prevalence of disordered eating compared with the athletes (Martinsen *et al.* 2010). One possible explanation is that the adolescent elite athletes have not yet been exposed to the demands of the specific sports as much as older athletes (Martinsen *et al.* 2010). Another possible explanation is that weight and/or low fat mass are perceived as equally important for adolescent athletes in, for example, soccer, as for athletes in weight-class sports such as taekwondo.

Exercise and eating disorders: the two-edged sword

> When I am cycling to and from work, it is a form of self-regulation. I need this time away from people to decompress; my life is too stressful without it. [...] When I am on training rides, cycling serves a different purpose. It's not at a leisurely pace and sometimes even painful or difficult. But, I do it because I love it. Pushing myself beyond my limits brings me joy and satisfaction. I don't honestly think there's a better feeling than the feeling I have after climbing a hill I never thought I could, break my own PR, or rise above some other upward bound I have in my head. It feels amazing!
>
> Kelly

A common perception is that people with eating disorders mainly exercise for weight- and appearance-related reasons (American Psychiatric Association 1994). However, physical activity and exercise are complex issues in eating disorders and studies show that weight- and appearance-related reasons are equally important among females with and without eating disorders, and perceived as important regardless of how much exercise is actually performed (Boyd *et al.* 2007; Bratland-Sanda *et al.* 2010a; Vansteelandt *et al.* 2007). This variety of reasons for exercise can also be seen in athletes, even at elite level. For most athletes, the performance and the urge to win are the main goal. For others, training serves as an important way of regulating emotions and affects, and some perceive the weight-regulating effect of exercise as important. Kelly's quote illustrates this complexity of reasons for exercise.

The hazardous edge of the sword is the excessive exercising. Up to 50 per cent and 80 per cent of bulimic and anorectic patients, respectively, exercise excessively (Davis *et al.* 1997). Kelly describes how she used and 'abused' exercise; that there were times when she did not want to exercise but she did not let herself stop. She felt that it was too risky to rest, and she now thinks the exercise was much more compulsive during her AN period. A Swedish study showed that 48 per cent of athletes in individual sports with high physical demands reported one or more incidences of overtraining syndrome (i.e. excessive exercise compared with the restitution status) (Kenttä *et al.* 2001). This overtraining syndrome can occur without the presence of an ED. Eating disordered patients who exercise excessively have more severe ED psychopathology, longer duration of treatment, poorer treatment outcome and higher risk of relapse compared with the non-excessive exercisers (Bratland-Sanda *et al.* 2010b; Brewerton *et al.* 1995; Steinhausen *et al.* 2008; Strober *et al.* 1997). Therefore, it is important to identify and manage excessive exercising among both athletes and non-athletes with eating disorders. Elite athletes can exercise for twenty-six hours or more per week without this being excessive. However, when the motive is punishment or energy expenditure, rather than performance enhancement, it should be considered excessive training.

A healthy volume of exercise should be considered a beneficial treatment supplement. Physical activity seems to enhance life quality, physical fitness, body composition, and bone mineral density in patients with both AN and BN (Carraro *et al.* 1998; Chantler *et al.* 2006; Duesund and Skårderud 2003; Sundgot-Borgen *et al.* 2002). From an affect regulation perspective, the physical activity can also serve as a break from difficult therapy (Beumont *et al.* 1994). However, the physical activity must be appropriately prescribed: type, intensity, duration and frequency should be adjusted to the patient's medical status, nutrition status, body composition and bone mineral density. We therefore recommend that exercise physiologists or comparable professionals be included in the treatment team.

Risk and trigger factors

I started trying to lose weight at the age of 9, in response to a request from my coach. At 12 years of age, I started reading everything about dieting and sought advice from older teammates. Their advice was haphazard and lacking in evidence, but I accepted it as an ultimate truth. I followed their rules and added some irrational ones of my own. I began to lose weight at a rapid pace and realized this was a much easier way to 'win'. I learned early that sporting outcomes are not always predictable; even the best athletes have off-days sometimes. I felt that I could not always ensure victories in the ring, but I could control my weight and it quickly became more important to me than my performance. By the age of 15, I was very underweight and malnourished. I no longer cared whether I won or lost. My athletic performances became inconsistent; sometimes I won big competitions, but more frequently, I was too tired to fight like I used to. My energy was focused on losing more weight. My thoughts revolved around food and exercise.

Kelly

In athletes, eating disorders are caused by multiple factors. The predisposing factors consist of biological/genetic, psychological and socio-cultural factors. Although no prospective controlled studies on athletes and eating disorders have been published, it is suggested that sport-specific risk factors include personality factors, pressure to lose weight leading to restricted eating and/or frequent weight cycling, body dissatisfaction, early start of sport-specific training, injuries, symptoms of overtraining, and the impact of coaching behaviour (Drinkwater *et al.* 2005). The reported sport-specific trigger factors include comments from coaches, teammates or significant others, injury, a sudden increase in amount of exercise, decreased performance level, perceived pressure about a certain weight necessary to enhance performance, frequent dieting, and weight fluctuation. Kelly was exposed to pressure to lose weight at an early age and although she chose the weight class, her coach motivated her.

Consequences

Longer periods with low energy availability, with or without disordered eating, can impair health and physical performance (Nattiv *et al.* 2007). As in non-athletes, medical complications involve the cardiovascular, endocrine, reproductive, gastrointestinal, renal, and central nervous systems (Nattiv *et al.* 2007). In several studies, the negative effects of rapid weight loss (e.g. fasting, dehydration) and longer periods of restricted energy intake on performance, growth, cognitive function and health have been discussed (O'Connor and Caterson 2006). Low energy availability can affect both the menstrual cycle and bone mineral density. Menstrual irregularities can also affect bone mineral density, and these three factors can occur in a cycle called the female athlete triad (Nattiv *et al.* 2007). Finally, menstrual dysfunction has been associated with increased risk for injuries (Drinkwater *et al.* 2005).

Identification and treatment of eating disorders among athletes

One primary care doctor saw me as a teenager for temperature regulation problems, fatigue, weight loss, etc. She asked: 'By the way, how is your eating?' I started to tell her about my extremely rigid eating plan, of which I was very proud. She didn't stick around to hear anything beyond my breakfast (the biggest meal of my day). Sometimes, I think if she had waited and listened a few minutes longer, she may have put the pieces together.

I would like people involved in primary care to remember that eating disorders are not always easy to spot. The sufferers might be winning international tournaments and excelling in other areas of life, but that does not necessarily mean they are fine. Early intervention is important, regardless of weight and appearance. Also, my primary care providers' honesty has been vital to my recovery.

Kelly

Identification of eating disorders among athletes must go beyond focusing on those who meet the diagnostic criteria to include those who have low energy availability and/or are practising pathogenic weight-control behaviours

(Drinkwater *et al.* 2005). It is important to examine behaviour – the physical, emotional and psychological state of the athlete. What Kelly describes is unfortunately very common. Our experience is that when eating disordered athletes seek a consultation with a physician, the usual reasons are fatigue, injuries, overtraining and depressive symptoms. And, as Kelly says, they are considered healthy because they are athletes. It is therefore important that the physician has adequate knowledge about ED symptoms and psychopathology, and asks the athlete about their eating behaviour.

If an athlete has been identified as having disordered eating or is believed to be 'at risk' for abnormal eating behaviour by medical staff, athletic trainer, coaching staff and/or team-members, the athlete should be referred to a sports nutritionist, for nutritional assessment and meal planning. The aim should be to help the athlete understand the nutritional needs for good health and performance. The nutritionist should ask questions to determine whether the athlete has an optimal energy intake or not. If the athlete is not able to improve their intake by guidance, the athlete should be referred to the team physician or general practitioner.

What should the assessment include?

- Detailed medical history review
- Physical examination with:
  - blood tests
  - biochemical test
  - dual X-ray absorptimetry (to determine the percentage of body fat and the bone mineral density)
- Nutrition and fluid intake
- Training and competition motivation, goals and history

Athletes diagnosed with disordered eating, but no other underlying medical disorder, and who are unable or unwilling to follow the eating recommendations made by the nutritionist and/or physician, should be referred to an ED treatment specialist experienced in working with athletes. If the physician and/or ED specialist recommends treatment, the athlete should be considered 'injured' and asked to agree to treatment in order to later be allowed to return to training and competition (Drinkwater *et al.* 2005).

Can the athlete continue with the sport during treatment?

For athletes who agree to treatment, eligibility to continue training while symptomatic should be determined on an individual basis by treatment staff. At the minimum, the athlete should be cleared medically and psychologically, their training/competition should not be used as a means to diet or control their weight, and they should be required to follow a prescribed set of health maintenance criteria. These criteria have to be individualized and generally include, but are not limited to: (a) being in treatment, complying with the treatment plan, and progressing toward therapeutic goals; (b) maintaining a weight of at least 90 per cent of expected weight, and, in accordance with Behnke's theoretical concept of minimal body mass, a body fat greater than 6 per cent for male athletes and greater than 12 per cent for female athletes, or more if prescribed by the treatment team; and (c) eating enough to comply with the treatment plan regarding weight gain or weight maintenance (Drinkwater *et al.* 2005). Sometimes negotiation with athletes is important in areas of energy intake and return to training and competition. However, the ED treatment team always makes the decisions and the athlete's health has priority. For athletes willing to follow the recommended treatment, and include their coach (if athlete and coach have a good relationship) in the treatment and, if appropriate, also the parents, the compliance and prognosis are expected to be good (Nattiv *et al.* 2007).

The athlete may return to competition when the goal weight or body composition is reached and they are mentally prepared and really want to compete. For athletes who refuse treatment, training and competition should be withheld until they agree to participate in treatment (Drinkwater *et al.* 2005).

While re-feeding, Kelly took a break from most types of exercise. This break lasted for two to three months, and she gradually increased the amount of exercise. She checked in frequently with the dietician and the exercise physiologist to ensure she was in a positive energy balance. Kelly considered this very important and her view concurs with our experiences in treatment of eating disordered athletes. Finally, maintaining open lines of communication between coaches and members of the ED team is important. Coaches are in a prime position to monitor athletes' behaviours and reactions. Some coaches may have difficulty discussing sensitive issues related to disordered eating either with treatment team members or athletes. This sensitivity generally arises from coaches' 'feeling of culpability' for athletes' disordered eating behaviours. They therefore need to be held accountable for their athletes in a way that is not threatening. The best approach is to make disordered eating a 'health and safety issue' and not a coaching issue.

Prevention of eating disorders in sports

As an athlete, people automatically assumed that I was healthy. They thought that if I could compete without complaining, then I was fine. I would like to see a health care system that is more focused on early intervention in eating disorders, doctors who are sensitive to the fact that people with eating disorders come at all sizes and weight should not be the 'be all'. My sickest point had no relation to my lowest weight.

Kelly

Existing prevention programmes for athletes that have been evaluated are limited. Thus we will focus on issues that are expected to help prevent disordered eating and eating disorders in athletes (Drinkwater *et al.* 2005; Nattiv *et al.* 2007).

Information and guidelines

To adequately perform a supportive function, many coaches need factual information on nutrition, factors determining weight, risks and causes of disordered eating/eating disorders, menstrual (dys)function, and psychological factors that affect health and athletic performance. Coaches and athletes should be aware that female athletes with menstrual dysfunction are at increased risk for injuries. Sports-governing organizations and federations should give support to the coaches and provide education regarding disordered eating/eating disorders and have a strategy plan for eating disorders. The medical team should make the difficult decisions with respect to affected athletes as to whether they will remain in treatment or be allowed to train and compete.

De-emphasize weight

The best way to de-emphasize weight is to avoid weighing athletes for non-health-related reasons, avoid frequent measurements of the athlete's body composition, and avoid verbal and non-verbal comments regarding body composition and/or body weight. Dieting and measures of body composition or weight issues should never be a theme initiated by the coach, but should be considered according to the athlete's wishes. In such cases, the coach should take the athlete's initiative seriously and refer to professional help. The focus should be on performance enhancement via non-dieting strategies: improved nutrition, improved health, mental and psychological approaches.

Weight loss and dieting

Unnecessary dieting (dieting performed without having excess fat and unaccompanied by professional guidance) is considered a main risk factor for development of disordered eating and should be prevented. Coaches should avoid pressuring or telling an athlete to lose weight. This is especially important for athletes representing weight-class sports. Most weight-class athletes are fit and lean, but want to reduce weight to compete in a lower weight class, like Kelly. Most weight-class athletes consider this part 'of the game' and do not question methods or consequences. In such cases the coach and health-care team should motivate the athlete to improve strength and compete in a higher weight class. Health-care providers should teach the athletes and coaches that weight loss does not necessarily lead to improved athletic performance. Furthermore, since athletes are eager to perform, it is important to inform them also of the side effects of under-eating and abnormal eating behaviour. If the coach is concerned about an athlete's eating behaviour, body image and/or weight or body fat level, the athlete should be referred to a sports nutritionist for further evaluation and consultation. Athletes who do need to change weight or body composition should get professional guidance.

Conclusion

Emphasis on body weight and shape for performance puts athletes, especially those competing in leanness sports, at increased risk for eating disorders. Elite athletes also often have personality factors that predispose them to eating disorders. Early identification and management are extremely important, and the future challenge is mainly the prevention of eating disorders. Medical staff and coaches need to be updated on risks of disordered eating behaviour and eating disorders, and athletes must have adequate knowledge about sports nutrition.

References

American Psychiatric Association (APA) (1994) *DSM-IV: Diagnostic and Statistical Manual of Mental Disorders,* 4th edn, Washington DC: American Psychiatric Press.

Beumont, P. J., Arthur, B., Russell, J. D., and Touyz, S. W. (1994) 'Excessive physical activity in dieting disorder patients: Proposals for a supervised exercise program', *Int J Eat Disord* 15, 1: 21–36.

Bouchard, C., Blair, S. N., and Haskell, W. L. (2007) *Physical Activity and Health,* Champaign, IL: Human Kinetics.

Boyd, C., Abraham, S., and Luscombe, G. (2007) 'Exercise behaviours and feelings in eating disorder and non-eating disorder groups', *Eur Eat Disord Rev* 15, 2: 112–18.

Bratland-Sanda, S., Sundgot-Borgen, J., Ro, O., Rosenvinge, J. H., Hoffart, A., and Martinsen, E. W. (2010a) '"I'm not physically active – I only go for walks": Physical activity in patients with longstanding eating disorders', *Int J Eat Disord* 43, 1: 88–92.

Bratland-Sanda, S., Sundgot-Borgen, J., Ro, O., Rosenvinge, J. H., Hoffart, A., and Martinsen, E. W. (2010b) 'Physical activity and exercise dependence during inpatient treatment of longstanding eating disorders: An exploratory study of excessive and non-excessive exercisers', *Int J Eat Disord* 43, 3: 266–73.

Brewerton, T. D., Stellefson, E. J., Hibbs, N., Hodges, E. L., and Cochrane, C. E. (1995) 'Comparison of eating disorder patients with and without compulsive exercising', *Int J Eat Disord* 17, 4: 413–16.

Carraro, A., Cognolato, S., and Bernardis, A. L. F. (1998) 'Evaluation of a programme of adapted physical activity for ED patients', *Eat Weight Disord* 3: 110–14.

Chantler, I., Szabo, C. P., and Green, K. (2006) 'Muscular strength changes in hospitalized anorexic patients after an eight week resistance training program', *Int J Sports Med* 27, 8: 660–5.

Davis, C., Katzman, D. K., Kaptein, S., Kirsh, C., Brewer, H., Kalmbach, K., Olmsted, M. P., Woodside, D. B., and Kaplan, A. S. (1997) 'The prevalence of high-level exercise in the eating disorders: Etiological implications', *Compr Psychiatry* 38, 6: 321–6.

Drinkwater, B., Loucks, A. B., Sherman, R. T., Sundgot-Borgen, J., and Thompson, J. K. (2005) *Position Stand on the Female Athlete Triad,* International Olympic Committee

Medical Commission Working Group Women in Sport. Online. Available http://multimedia.olympic.org/pdf/en_report_917.pdf (accessed 22 August 2010).

Duesund, L. and Skårderud, F. (2003) 'Use the body and forget the body: Treating anorexia nervosa with adapted physical activity', *Clin Child Psychol Psychiatry* 8, 1: 53–72.

Haskell, W. L., Lee, I. M., Pate, R. R., Powell, K. E., Blair, S. N., Franklin, B. A., Macera, C. A., Heath, G. W., Thompson, P. D., and Bauman, A. (2007) 'Physical activity and public health: Updated recommendation for adults from the American College of Sports Medicine and the American Heart Association', *Med Sci Sports Exerc* 39, 8: 1423–34.

Kenttä, G., Hassmén, P., and Raglin, J. S. (2001) 'Training practices and overtraining syndrome in Swedish age-group athletes', *Int J Sports Med* 22: 460–5.

Martinsen, M., Bratland-Sanda, S., Eriksson, A. K., and Sundgot-Borgen, J. (2010) 'Dieting to win or to be thin? A study of dieting and disordered eating among adolescent elite athletes and non-athlete controls', *Br J Sports Med* 44, 1: 70–6.

Nattiv, A., Loucks, A. B., Manore, M. M., Sanborn, C. F., Sundgot-Borgen, J., and Warren, M. P. (2007) 'American College of Sports Medicine position stand. The female athlete triad', *Med Sci Sports Exerc* 39, 10: 1867–82.

O'Connor, H. and Caterson, I. (2006) 'Weight loss and the athlete', in L. Burke and V. Deakin (eds) *Clinical Sport Nutrition*, Sydney: McGraw-Hill.

Ravaldi, C., Vannacci, A., Zucchi, T., Mannucci, E., Cabras, P. L., Boldrini, M., Murciano, L., Rotella, C. M., and Ricca, V. (2003) 'Eating disorders and body image disturbances among ballet dancers, gymnasium users and body builders', *Psychopathology* 36, 5: 247–54.

Steinhausen, H. C., Grigoroiu-Serbanescu, M., Boyadjieva, S., Neumarker, K. J., and Winkler, M. C. (2008) 'Course and predictors of rehospitalization in adolescent anorexia nervosa in a multisite study', *Int J Eat Disord* 41, 1: 29–36.

Strober, M., Freeman, R., and Morrell, W. (1997) 'The long-term course of severe anorexia nervosa in adolescents: Survival analysis of recovery, relapse, and outcome predictors over 10–15 years in a prospective study', *Int J Eat Disord* 22, 4: 339–60.

Sundgot-Borgen, J. (1994) 'Risk and trigger factors for the development of eating disorders in female elite athletes', *Med Sci Sports Exerc* 26, 4: 414–19.

Sundgot-Borgen, J. and Torstveit, M. K. (2004) 'Prevalence of eating disorders in elite athletes is higher than in the general population', *Clin J Sport Med* 14: 25–32.

Sundgot-Borgen, J. and Torstveit, M. K. (2010) 'Aspects of disordered eating continuum in elite high-intensity sports', *Scand J Med Sci Sports* 20 (suppl. 2): 112–21.

Sundgot-Borgen, J., Rosenvinge, J. H., Bahr, R., and Schneider, L. S. (2002) 'The effect of exercise, cognitive therapy, and nutritional counseling in treating bulimia nervosa', *Med Sci Sports Exerc* 34, 2: 190–5.

Torstveit, M. K., Rosenvinge, J. H., and Sundgot-Borgen, J. (2008) 'Prevalence of eating disorders and the predictive power of risk models in female elite athletes: A controlled study', *Scand J Med Sci Sports* 18, 1: 108–18.

Vansteelandt, K., Rijmen, F., Pieters, G., Probst, M., and Vanderlinden, J. (2007) 'Drive for thinness, affect regulation and physical activity in eating disorders: A daily life study', *Behav Res Ther* 45, 8: 1717–34.

Chapter 24

Male eating disorders

John F. Morgan

Case study

I was born and raised in a small rural town by two devoted parents. The middle child of three, I was considered the wild one – having extreme potential but lacking direction. I loved sports, and my dream was to be my region's first lacrosse player to play Division One. I was a typical little boy growing up and my adolescent years were full of laughter and excitement. As a teenager, everything was effortless. I excelled socially, academically and athletically. Though physically small, my dream was to be a fierce athlete. I wanted to be bigger, faster, and stronger than anyone else. I pushed myself, worked out six days a week and took supplements to attain the ideal male athletic build.

Patrick

Men with eating disorders often describe an underlying drive to succeed that is never fully satisfied. Many men with eating disorders are high achievers but focus their ambitions on the toxic world of re-sculpting their bodies.

Often I was told that at 5 feet, 6 inches tall and 135 pounds, I was too small to play college lacrosse. I was driven to prove my critics wrong. My high school years were consumed with lacrosse, weightlifting and schoolwork. I set numerous records in lacrosse and weightlifting, played on the Senior All-State team and was nominated for the state Public School Player of the Year. When not training, I was the life of the party with a big ego and a chip on my shoulder. To stand out as a freshman, I partnered a very attractive junior to the prom. My boyish charm and confidence could win over any eye-catching female. I loved attention, popularity, and stardom. To those who thought they knew me best, I was a standout student athlete and a true ladies' man. But on the inside, nothing was good enough for me.

Patrick

To the outside world, some men with eating disorders can be seen as 'having it all', belying an intense existential dissatisfaction.

After breezing through my pubescent years, I graduated from high school and went to college, looking to continue my reign of greatness. My college years were all about partying, playing lacrosse, and my social image. I attended two universities, suffered sport injuries, saw my mother battle breast cancer, went through five coaches and drank excessively to numb the pain. I was 21 and in my senior year when my life spiralled out of control and an eating disorder began to develop. In an effort to escape my problems, I began working out more and eating less. I was trying to keep my starting spot on the lacrosse team, juggle two girlfriends, graduate and deal with a coach who, because of my size, didn't believe in my ability. Nobody noticed my growing chaos, possibly because I continued to excel in the classroom and producing on the lacrosse field. Even I didn't see that something was drastically wrong though the signs of anorexia nervosa were emerging – skipping meals, fatigue, mood swings and isolation.

Patrick

There are more similarities than differences between men and women with eating disorders. Fundamental is the psychological functionality: initially, a solution to emotional problems rather than a problem in its own right.

At my final college lacrosse game, I watched tearfully from the bench as our team lost the last playoff game. Despite my determined efforts, I would never be a great college lacrosse player. That day I put down my lacrosse stick for good, or so I thought.

My inner chaos accelerated: arrested twice for drinking, losing my lacrosse coach and mentor in a surfing accident, abusing alcohol, not eating, cheating on my girlfriend, dating two girls at once, and failing on the playing field. Yet nobody saw my life in a bad light. Guys thought I was cool, girls still thought I was a sweetheart, and my parents thought I was a wonderful son. Anorexia was settling in and I had no idea who I was.

For four years after college I bounced from job to job, drank too much, starved myself, and was in and out of a destructive relationship. I lived on energy drinks, and consumed less than one meal a day. I thought marriage would be my saving grace. I got engaged and thought my life would change. By now I was physically weak and pale, had no energy, wasn't sleeping and was periodically fainting.

Patrick

Eventually the fragile coping mechanism of disordered eating and excess alcohol becomes unsustainable, a sticking plaster concealing deeper scars. Stigma and isolation are the two biggest hurdles for men with eating disorders, as well as clinicians treating them. However, while many clinicians believe that men with eating disorders require male-specific therapeutic settings, most of the men with whom I have worked have been more concerned with having a sensitive well-informed therapist in a supportive milieu.

A month before my wedding day, I was lying on the ground crying for help. Two weeks later, I was diagnosed with anorexia nervosa and sent to an eating disorder treatment centre. My therapist said that my diagnosis was difficult. I was a successful and strong athlete, with no family history of anxiety, depression or disordered eating. I also remained in denial because of the shame and stigma of my problems. I thought I was the only guy dealing with body image issues, depression, substance abuse, and an eating disorder.

My therapist got the diagnosis right, but my primary care physician thought I solely had a drinking problem – I did, but it was a direct symptom of my anorexia. I spent thirty days in treatment in a partial residential programme, staying in my own apartment, doing my own grocery shopping and food preparation. During the day, I attended nutritional classes and cognitive-based individual and group therapy sessions. I was the only guy in treatment, and this is what I needed. Guys are known to be shutdown and unemotional. For years, I'd hid my feelings, and pretended nothing was wrong, yet inside I was dying. Being around sensitive females allowed me to open up and grow emotionally. My macho ego gave way to experiencing the simplicities of life. I participated in various therapies, particularly benefiting from the art, yoga and group sessions.

Patrick

Patrick had a strong bedrock from which to sustain his recovery, with the support of family and friends and, eventually, a talent for putting his feelings into words rather than behaviours.

> My treatment provided the foundation for a strong eating disorder recovery. I took an athletic approach with my healing, focusing on being part of a team – surrounding myself with family, friends and others. Being open about my struggles accelerated the mending and growth process. I have been in full remission from my anorexia for more than two years, and am back running and playing the sports I love.
>
> A fear of what others would say had kept me from seeking help for almost two years. After reaching out, this fear disappeared because I discovered most people were receptive to my illness. Anorexia nearly took my life because I was ashamed to get help, and those around me were afraid to address the issue.
>
> Patrick

Men with eating disorders consistently appear in early clinical descriptions of the condition (Morton 1694). Lord Byron's excessive pursuit of athleticism and weight loss covered similar emotional scars to those revealed by Patrick. Yet subsequently the plight of men with anorexia nervosa (AN) has been neglected by popular stereotypes.

Consistent evidence has suggested that 10 to 20 per cent of cases of AN and bulimia nervosa occur in men (Muise *et al.* 2003), though more recent community-based studies imply this may be an underestimation (Hudson 2007). Furthermore, the traditional classification of eating disorders emphasises concerns and methods of weight control common to women, such as thinness and dieting, rather than men, such as muscularity, low body fat, exercise and strength.

Just as core diagnostic criteria for eating disorders may differ between men and women, so too must those differences be reflected in treatment approaches. For example, gender differences are found in dimensions of body image, with men focused on re-sculpting body shape, in contrast to women's dissatisfaction with weight and drive to thinness (Garner 1997; Morgan and Arcelus 2009). Gender differences may partly reflect differences in societal beauty ideals. Men have enjoyed a degree of protection from body image disparagement, as masculine beauty ideals have more often overlapped with biological health than their feminine equivalents. However, gay men in particular have experienced discord between health and beauty for some time; this is also reflected in higher rates of eating disorders.

Unfortunately the same dissonance between health and beauty is beginning to be experienced by younger men in general, straight and gay, with a complex and sometimes contradictory drive towards both leanness and muscularity, leaving many men to feel small and weak (Stanford and McCabe 2002). We are only in the early stages of developing body image treatment interventions to target these issues (Morgan 2008).

Issues of weight control also differ between men and women. Andersen (1999) has noted common rationales for abnormal weight-control behaviours in men to include improvement of sports performance and avoidance of obesity-related teasing. Thus sportsmen can be seen as particularly vulnerable, and especially in those sports that emphasise weight control, including running, boxing, wrestling, gymnastics, bodybuilding and swimming.

Issues of sexual orientation can be highly relevant in some men with eating disorders, but equally can become overplayed among commentators, and should not be assumed. Feldman and Meyer found that more than 15 per cent of gay or bisexual men suffered AN or bulimia nervosa or 'eating order not otherwise specified' (EDNOS) (Feldman and Meyer 2007). Gay men may suffer a heightened focus on physical appearance, and stronger pressures to conform, giving rise to extreme body image dissatisfaction (Yager 2000), though it is possible that comparable trends are emerging among younger men in general, both gay and straight (Morgan and Arcelus 2009). Indeed the latter study found widespread body image dissatisfaction among younger men regardless of sexual orientation, and more similarities than differences between gay and straight men.

Social learning directs body image ideals for young boys as much as girls, and social pressures on boys to achieve leanness and muscularity are evident in studies of boys' action figures, with even more unrealistic body ideals set for boys than girls (Leit et al. 2001; Pope et al. 1999).

Issues of male eating disorders should also be considered in the context of changing social masculine roles, with men increasingly resorting to body image manipulation as the solitary source of masculinity (Pope et al. 2000). While this may lead to AN and bulimia, it also appears to have given rise to the excessive pursuit of muscularity found in the condition 'muscle dysmorphia' (Morgan 2000), with comparable rates of low self-esteem, perfectionism, low interoceptive awareness and lack of self-efficacy to those found in AN and bulimia nervosa (Blouin and Goldfield 1995).

Regardless of the above, the treatment of eating disorders in men shares more similarities than differences with the treatment of women. Weight loss should be addressed through evidence-based nutritional rehabilitation. Men require weight restoration to the point of normalisation of testosterone levels (Andersen et al. 1982), as for oestrogen deficiency in women. Men are likely to respond to a similar range of psychological treatments to women, but only small numbers of men appear in existing published outcome studies (Le Grange et al. 2007; Lock et al. 2005; Schmidt et al. 2007). Some men may respond better to a separate treatment programme, permitting more open discussion of issues including sexual identity. However, as exemplified by Patrick, it is more common for men to want accessible local treatment from therapists with a compassionate approach, regardless of the gender mix of therapist or patients. Nonetheless, therapists require sensitivity to anticipated gender differences in social functioning (Andersen and Holman 1997).

Conclusion

The causes and treatments of eating disorders in men and women have more similarities than differences, and the greatest challenge for men with eating disorders is to access local, evidence-based treatment despite personal and societal stigma. Men with eating disorders are particularly driven to a body image ideal combining leanness with muscularity, with compulsive over-exercise a common route into male eating disorders. Societal pressures on younger men in general appear to be growing, and young boys are under ever-increasing pressure to conform to an impossible body image ideal.

Eventually the same processes that would have aided a woman in the same predicament helped Patrick: evidence-based psychological therapy combined with nutritional rehabilitation, and a gradual return to healthy exercise. However, barriers to recovery for men are multiple. While at least one in ten cases of eating disorders are male, a far smaller proportion access treatment. All eating disorder services must consider why they are failing to reflect the gender diversity of the populations which they serve, and public health must embrace the fact that fat is more than a feminist issue.

References

Andersen, A. (1999) 'Gender related aspects of eating disorders: A guide to practice', *JGSM* 2, 1: 47–54.

Andersen, A. and Holman, J. (1997) 'Males with eating disorders: Challenges for treatment and research', *Psychopharmacol Bull* 33, 3: 391–7.

Andersen, A., Wirth, J.B., and Strahlman, E.R. (1982) 'Reversible weight related increase in plasma testosterone during treatment of male and female patients with anorexia nervosa', *Int J Eat Disord* 1, 2: 74–83.

Blouin, A.G. and Goldfield, G.S. (1995) 'Body image and steroid use in male bodybuilders', *Int J Eat Disord* 18, 2: 159–65.

Feldman, M.B. and Meyer, I.H. (2007) 'Eating disorders in diverse lesbian, gay, and bisexual populations', *Int J Eat Disord* 40, 3: 218–26.

Garner, D.M. (1997) 'The 1997 body-image survey results', *Psychol Today* 30, 1: 30–84.

Hudson, J.I., Hiripi, E., Pope, H.G., and Kessler, R.C. (2007) 'The prevalence and correlates of eating disorders in the national comorbidity survey replication', *Biol Psychiatry* 61, 3: 348–58.

Le Grange, D., Crosby, R., Rathouz, P., and Leventhal, B. (2007) 'A randomized controlled comparison of family-based treatment and supportive psychotherapy for adolescent bulimia nervosa', *Arch Gen Psychiatry* 64, 9: 1049–56.

Leit, R., Pope, H.G., and Gray, J. (2001) 'Cultural expectations of muscularity in men: The evolution of the Playgirl centerfolds', *Int J Eat Disord* 29, 1: 90–3.

Lock, J., Agras, W.S., Bryson, S., and Kraemer, H. (2005) 'A comparison of short- and long-term family therapy for adolescent anorexia nervosa', *J Am Acad Child Adolesc Psychiatry* 44, 7: 632–9.

Morgan, J.F. (2000) 'From Charles Atlas to the Adonis Complex – fat is more than a feminist issue', *The Lancet* 356, 9239: 1372–3.

Morgan, J.F. (2008) *The Invisible Man: A Self-Help Guide for Men with Eating Disorders, Compulsive Exercise and Bigorexia*, London: Routledge.

Morgan, J.F. and Arcelus, J. (2009) 'Body image in gay and straight men: A qualitative study', *Eur Eat Disord Rev* 17, 6: 435–43.

Morton, R. (1694) *Phthisiologica: Or, a Treatise of Consumptions*, London: Smith and Walford.

Muise, A., Stein, D., and Arbess, G. (2003) 'Eating disorders in adolescent boys: A review of the adolescent and adult literature', *J Adolesc Health* 33, 6: 427–35.

Pope, H.G., Olivardia, R., Gruber, A., and Borowiecki, J. (1999) 'Evolving ideals of male body image as seen through action toys', *Int J Eat Disord* 26, 1: 65–72.

Pope, H.G., Phillips, K.A., and Olivardia, R. (2000) *The Adonis Complex: How to Identify, Treat and Prevent Body Obsession in Men and Boys*, New York: Touchstone (Simon and Schuster).

Schmidt, U., Lee, S., Beecham, J., Perkins, S., Treasure, J., Yi, I., Winn, S., Robinson, P., Murphy, R., Keville, S., Johnson-Sabine, E., Jenkins, M., Frost, S., Dodge, L., Berelowitz, M., and Eisler, I. (2007) 'A randomized controlled trial of family therapy and cognitive behavior therapy guided self-care for adolescents with bulimia nervosa and related conditions', *Am J Psychiatry* 164, 4: 591–8.

Stanford, J.N. and McCabe, M.P. (2002) 'Body image ideal among males and females: Sociocultural influences and focus on different body parts', *J Health Psychol* 7, 6: 675–84.

Yager, J. (2000) 'Weighty perspectives: Contemporary challenges in obesity and eating disorders', *Am J Psychiatry* 157, 6: 851–3.

Part 4

Changing the culture

Introduction

Claire Vickery

Eating disorders must be considered on a par with other major illnesses. Medical access equal to that provided for people with cancer or even the common cold would be a good start.

We need increased research and better training. We need a whole government approach to prevention, early intervention, greater access to effective treatment, support of carers, health promotion, training and research. Eating disorders are too expensive to treat in the private health sector – they require multi-disciplinary teams, and intensive, no-time-frame healing environments. Treatment needs to be flexible and tailored to the individual. A cookie-cutter approach does not work.

As founder of the Butterfly Foundation, Australia's only national organisation for eating disorders, I am driven by this need to shift our toxic culture around thinness and appearances. Apart from my personal experience and the inspiration of my two beautiful daughters, now mothers themselves, I wanted to know why the mainstream eating disorder field was slow to accept family and/or carers as an integral part of a multi-disciplinary treatment team.

I was particularly driven by a comment from a stranger about starting our foundation: 'Well, that's interesting but you'll never get that up as it's not the kind of thing people would care about.'

Money should not stand between surviving eating disorders or dying.

I knew we had to change the whole system.

The biggest hurdle was getting to shift the culture gently without being aggressive or insulting. Health service professionals, I discovered, were victims of a fractured dysfunctional health system that didn't support them either. I had to bring them with me, not push or alienate them.

I have learnt that individuals can make a difference. Culture can change. I have discovered skills hidden beneath my own eating disorder and negative self-worth – and have grown into my wings.

Sufferers and their carers are experts too. Only they can provide the comfort to others in the words 'I know'.

We must work collaboratively to shift and shape our culture by establishing research funds, and ensuring eating disorders are part of the larger healthcare system.

Chapter 25

Narrowing the psychotherapy research–practice gap

Kristin M. von Ranson and Ann M. Laverty

Case study

Carolin describes seeking treatment for Billie, her youngest of three children, who developed anorexia nervosa (AN) at age 10.

Initially I was pleased when Billie lost some weight as she had been a little tubby and was teased at school. But when Billie began receiving praise on her slimness, she lost more and more weight. We approached our local general practice physician and shortly after a paediatrician confirmed AN. By now Billie was medically compromised, and was admitted to hospital.

The paediatrician and GP provided little information on treatment options. Initially Billie received treatment at our local rural hospital which had no eating disorder specialist staff.

After six weeks, she was discharged and remained out of hospital for the next eight months. Our local GP and dietician monitored weight and adjusted food requirements weekly. GP visits were conducted privately, parents confined to the waiting room. Clinicians said recovery was Billie's responsibility; her illness raged. We were unaware of AN behaviours, such as disposing of food and exercising behind closed doors.

After eight months Billie was not gaining weight and her GP suggested the best treatment option was at a tertiary hospital 200 km away. There was no facility for parents to accompany Billie nor was it recommended that we be involved in the treatment. Instead we chose a private outpatient eating disorder facility, 2,000 km from home. This was expensive but seemed our best hope. We could be involved but received no strategies or education on caring for Billie outside the one-hour therapy sessions. Again Billie was expected to eat and consume the necessary calories to increase weight with little or no involvement from family members. We were told not to make food the issue. Her weight plummeted so much in one month she required an emergency hospital admission in an intensive care unit followed by two weeks on a psychiatric ward and four months in a family therapy unit. Feeling stumped, clinicians suggested Billie be discharged with a nasal-gastric tube to be fed at home until she chose to eat.

Eighteen months of feeding with a nasogastric tube and weekly psycho-logical therapy, GP and dietician appointments, yielded no progress. Billie's identity and dependence on the tube was evident. Three years had lapsed since her original diagnosis of AN.

In desperation we agreed to participate in a new trial, called the Maudsley approach, being implemented at a hospital 800 km from home. Billie was admitted to this hospital's adolescent eating disorder unit but made little progress. I suggested care by parent as an option, similar to that operating for oncology patients/families, and the psychiatrist and hospital staff agreed. Supervision was around the clock. Slowly, over three months, Billie's weight increased and eventually the NG tube was withdrawn. Set target weight and bi-weekly therapy sessions kept us on track. Externalizing the illness from Billie helped avoid guilt over the AN's outrageous behaviours and emotions and we learnt to view these as symptoms of the illness.

Billie's suffering may have been considerably less if current information on evidence-based treatments had been supplied at the outset. If we, as parents, had been considered part of the treatment team we would have benefited from support and education on dealing with AN behaviours, and from feedback on how our reactions could maintain the illness.

During my three-year search to find a treatment to save Billie, I saw the need for clinicians to be proactive in implementing evidence-based treatments instead of waiting for change to occur when the child feels ready. Clinicians have a duty of care to provide treatment based on research evidence.

Discussion of complexities

Carolin's story highlights some complexities inherent in providing eating disorder treatment. Important points raised in the case study include the need for practitioners to provide comprehensive information about treatment options, including the evidence base underlying each option; for parents to take initiative in educating themselves about significant health problems facing their child; for both practitioners and parents to be proactive in initiating intervention; and for practitioners to plan for how to proceed if symptoms are resistant to initial treatment. Progress in eating disorders treatment often proceeds in fits and starts, and requires vigilance and persistence over a long period, as symptoms can be tenacious. Although a non-specialist with access to expert consultation may appropriately treat some individuals with mild eating disorders, a patient whose symptoms are severe, or whose symptoms do not resolve rapidly, must be referred to a specialist, multi-disciplinary team without delay to minimize the entrenchment of symptoms that Billie experienced. Members of a multi-disciplinary team should minimally include a psychotherapist, dietician, and physician, all with eating disorder expertise. Specialized knowledge is essential due to the complex nature of these problems, including the cognitive, emotional, and physical consequences of starvation, what Carolin aptly terms the 'outrageous behaviours' of an eating disorder, and the profound ambivalence felt by most individuals about overcoming their eating disorder.

Carolin's story illustrates that care for those with eating disorders is not always well coordinated or guided by best practice, i.e. shaped by research evidence about how best to treat an eating disorder (Shafran et al. 2009). In this chapter we aim to identify and discuss constructive ways to introduce evidence-based practice in eating disorders treatment. Our goals are: (1) to describe the research–practice gap in psychotherapy for eating disorders, (2) to consider why this gap exists, and (3) to explore ways we can move toward narrowing this gap.

Context of the research–practice gap

Historically, therapists were free to select treatment approaches they deemed most useful, and were subject to minimal oversight. With the advent of evidence-based practice, however, the status quo has been changing dramatically (Chambless and Ollendick 2001; Satterfield et al. 2009).

Research-related considerations further contribute to the research–practice gap. Clinical observation, qualitative and quantitative research all have value, including uncontrolled studies as well as randomized controlled trials (Banker and Klump, 2010). In recent years, researchers have worked to identify the psychotherapies most efficacious in improving eating disorder symptoms, particularly symptoms of bulimia nervosa (BN) and binge eating disorder (BED) (Wilson et al. 2007). However, surveys of psychotherapists have consistently shown that few practitioners actually administer these empirically-supported psychotherapies (ESTs) to their patients with eating disorders, citing a desire to tailor treatment to an individual's needs, among other reasons (e.g. Simmons et al. 2008; von Ranson and Robinson 2006). Although practitioners and researchers both hold the interests of individuals with eating disorders at the forefront, often they hold different views of how to optimize decisions about treatment. Understandably, practitioners may resent intrusion into what was traditionally their domain: decision-making about therapy. However, we argue that there are good reasons for practitioners to apply knowledge derived from systematic research to their everyday practice.

Defining what constitutes valid evidence can be contentious, and research has rarely identified absolutes regarding optimal treatment of eating disorders, the exception being the primary need to re-feed someone with AN to a minimally normal body weight. However, as in other areas of health care, the standard in mental health for identifying an EST is a randomized controlled trial (RCT, or 'efficacy' study), which involves, for example, randomized assignment of patients to treatment conditions, and use of a manual in which treatment sessions and techniques are specified for the therapist (Chambless and Ollendick 2001). The principle underlying an RCT is to control as many variables as possible (e.g. choice of therapy, patients' severity of symptoms, how treatment is delivered) to provide a test of a treatment's efficacy that is uncontaminated by biases, of which researchers may or may not be aware. Ideally, the only difference between groups in an RCT is the treatment that participants receive. Once an EST has been identified via efficacy studies, 'effectiveness' studies next aim to test the generalizability of RCT findings from efficacy trials to less structured clinical practice (Chambless and Ollendick 2001). There is a hierarchy of evidence that starts with simple observation of a case and culminates with RCTs, which are considered the gold standard by which to evaluate the efficacy of treatments (Satterfield *et al.* 2009).

ESTs may change over time and can be subject to dispute. Best practices depend on an evolving evidence base and interpretation. Over time, theories are introduced, refined, and discarded, as experts work to translate research findings into practice and as practice influences research questions. At present, cognitive-behavioural therapy (CBT) is the best-supported psychotherapy for BN and BED, although interpersonal psychotherapy, dialectical behaviour therapy and behavioural weight loss treatments enjoy some empirical support (Keel and Haedt 2008; Wilson *et al.* 2007). Few RCTs have examined psychotherapies for AN; the greatest empirical support to date is for family-based treatment, also known as the Maudsley approach, mentioned in our case study, particularly for younger adolescents (Keel and Haedt 2008).

However, other researchers conclude that the evidence base remains too limited to indicate that the Maudsley approach is superior to individual therapy for AN (Wilson *et al.* 2007). This inconsistency illustrates the debate that can exist over interpreting research evidence. A recent meta-analysis echoes this conflict: although two small studies suggest family therapy may be more efficacious than treatment as usual in the short term, these gains were not sustained at follow-up (Fisher *et al.* 2010).

Practitioners tend to endorse the use of many different psychotherapeutic approaches for their patients with eating disorders. Most therapists use an eclectic approach, indicating they do not adhere to a single theoretical model and may use an assortment of therapeutic techniques (von Ranson and Robinson 2006). The most common reason cited for choosing an eclectic therapeutic approach is that personal experience as a therapist indicates it is effective (von Ranson and Robinson 2006). The most common reason given for *not* choosing an EST is that manual-based treatments are viewed as 'too rigid or constraining and not a good fit for most patients' (Simmons *et al.* 2008: 347). However, manuals simply describe in detail how treatment should progress, and allow room for flexible application to suit individuals' needs.

Thus, while researchers have converged on a short list of ESTs for eating disorders, psychotherapists continue to draw on a variety of therapeutic approaches that only rarely include ESTs. We explore why the research–practice gap exists, in an effort to identify common ground and move the field forward in the best interests of patients.

Why is there a research–practice gap?

Contributions to the research–practice gap are manifold (Shafran *et al.* 2009). We focus on three broad domains: issues related to training, other considerations pertaining to selecting treatments, and practical concerns.

Training issues

The mental health professions are formulated around different, often overlapping, philosophies and values, which inevitably shape their respective academic training programmes. For example, counselling and clinical psychologists tend to work in different settings (e.g. counselling centres versus hospitals), help different populations (e.g. less versus more impairing problems), and embrace diverse philosophies toward assessment, diagnosis and treatment. Practitioners' training orientation and the theoretical model(s) in which they were trained influence their approach to practice and views about the applicability and utility of ESTs. Tradition also affects the type of research that tends to be conducted in disciplines, such as an emphasis on qualitative versus quantitative research, as well as philosophies on the utility of considering research literature when formulating a treatment plan.

Practitioners need to obtain skills in applying ESTs. Formal training under supervision by an expert is optimal but, as may have been the case for Billie's therapists, significant obstacles exist for many in receiving this sort of training. Therapists in rural or remote locations may have particularly limited access to such experts. Self-education through readings and conference attendance is essential, but it is also necessary to have someone with whom to problem-solve and consult on specific cases because the application of any treatment, even if standardized, is rarely straightforward. Regular consultation with experts who have experience applying an EST may be appropriate even for seasoned practitioners. As well, it takes time to become and remain current on best practices, and this time is often not reimbursed.

Once one is trained in administering an EST, ethical practice dictates that practitioners remain up-to-date about treatments. Therapists cannot assume that any single EST will suit, or work for, every patient with a particular problem, so they need to be prepared to apply different ESTs for the same problem(s) to maximize their therapeutic flexibility. Practitioners need to engage in such contingency planning to best serve their patients.

In the case study, Carolin's statement that Billie should have been offered evidence-based treatment at the outset is understandable. However, it suggests that evidence-based treatment was actively withheld, when the reality may have been less straightforward. Determining best practice at any given point and applying it is not always a simple matter. An often complex process of assessment, interpretation and decision-making, as well as familiarity with providing an EST, factor into treatment planning and implementation. Nevertheless, we agree with Carolin that, if practitioners lack eating disorders expertise, they should immediately refer a patient to specialized treatment.

Other influences in selecting treatment

Patient variables also influence selection of a psychotherapeutic approach in individual cases. For adults, patient needs and preferences impact the choice of treatment approach. If the patient is under the age of 18 – as in Billie's case – parents or guardians generally help determine the treatment approach. One important example of how patient needs may influence treatment choice is the level of care required because of the eating disorder's current severity – e.g. outpatient, inpatient, or day treatment. Another example of how patient needs influence treatment is the presence of any prominent, coexisting health and mental health concerns experienced by the patient, e.g. cardiac problems or ongoing substance abuse. An additional factor is the patient's readiness for change, which affects their willingness to participate in treatment (Geller *et al.* 2005). However, as Carolin notes in the case study, when health is at risk, re-feeding must proceed regardless of a patient's readiness for change. In sum, various competing demands may contribute to the under-utilization of ESTs and the research–practice gap.

Practical concerns

Third-party payers or agency policies often set limits on the number of psychotherapy sessions permitted, which can pose a problem for implementing ESTs that assume that a full twenty sessions (for example) will be available. Familiarity with research literature can provide compelling justification in requesting additional sessions from a third-party payer or manager.

Geographic location affects patients' ability to obtain ESTs near home, and patients' ability to pay privately for treatment may affect treatment choice. Both of these issues factored into Billie's eating disorder treatment.

Bridging the research–practice gap

As described, differences in perspectives, priorities, and training across individuals and disciplines, plus practical issues, contribute to the research–practice gap. Due to time demands, it is easy to neglect practices that might enrich research or clinical practice. However, all professionals have as a paramount concern the best interests of the patient or research participant and steps can be taken to narrow the research–practice gap in our field. Our suggestions are as follows:

1   *Pursue inter-professional collaboration.* We exhort researchers and practitioners to pursue inter-professional collaboration, both during and after graduate training. Collaboration among professionals can have reciprocal benefits in helping practitioners apply research findings to their practice, and helping researchers identify important questions, identify clinical implications, and better translate study findings into practice. Collaboration of the patient and family with treatment providers is also important, as Carolin identifies in the case study, as is frequent communication among multi-disciplinary treatment team members.

2   *Integrate the empirical evidence in treatment approaches.* Complete agreement is unlikely on what constitutes optimal evidence in identifying efficacious treatments. Nevertheless, there is a growing consensus that specific EST approaches provide symptom relief above and beyond therapies that rely primarily on building a therapeutic alliance (Wilson *et al.* 2007). Judgement is involved in interpreting empirical research findings. Findings from studies using robust designs, such as RCTs, and which are replicated by different investigative teams, tend to describe systematically obtained knowledge in which we may have the most confidence. In general, unreplicated findings from small studies should inspire commensurately less confidence. Experts' opinions may vary legitimately in interpreting findings; critical thinking is essential in developing an informed opinion about best practices.

3   *Remain up-to-date about best practices.* Practitioners can learn about research developments through regular literature searches, table-of-contents alerts for key journals, and conference attendance. Britain's National Institute for Health and Clinical Excellence (www.nice.org.uk) (National Institute for Clinical Excellence 2004) has posted a comprehensive review of treatment for eating disorders, which provides a good starting point. Up-to-date information on ESTs is available via searching the empirical literature through free web-based databases such as PubMed (www.ncbi.nlm.nih.gov/pubmed) or Google Scholar (http://scholar.google.ca). Search more than one database, as no database is comprehensive. Published academic articles usually list a corresponding author and contact information; most authors are happy to email copies of their research to interested parties. Participation in research conferences supports knowledge transfer and provides access to information about the latest research developments.

4   *Use technology.* Technology, such as teleconferencing or internet conferencing, may assist in linking researchers and practitioners, and facilitate practitioners' consultation with experts about management of their eating disorder cases. Dialogue may help problem-solve to fit research recommendations to current practice realities, such as disjoints between research recommendations and managed care limits. Dialogue may also enhance advocacy to ensure that practitioners and agencies are able to deliver treatment as recommended by research, rather than as shaped by fiscal demands.

5   *Perform brief assessments to track progress.* Practitioners should identify and implement simple, standardized measures at each therapy session as a means to conduct patient-directed, outcome-informed clinical work, which can enable early detection of poor responders to treatment (Newnham and Page 2009). Banker and Klump (2010) list readily available, brief measures that may be suitable for individuals with eating disorders.

Conclusion

A sea change in perspective on the value of research evidence for practice has occurred with the advent of evidence-based medicine, which emphasizes the use of systematic research studies, including RCTs, to ascertain relative efficacy of treatments. A premise of evidence-based medicine is that all forms of evidence are not equal. Rather, preferred treatment approaches, or ESTs, are defined as observations that are based on large numbers of patients, that are systematically collected, and in which extraneous influences are held to a minimum and, where possible, randomized across treatment conditions. This viewpoint has substantial implications for mental health practitioners in everyday decision-making about treatments.

In essence, this chapter explains how to employ the best possible evidence in providing services to a patient with an eating disorder. Our suggestions are likely to involve additional work for practitioners as well as researchers. Practitioners should focus on being up-to-date in best practices for eating disorders, and learning how to carry out ESTs effectively. Researchers should focus on collaborating with practitioners, and routinely, carefully considering practical implications for their research findings as part of the dissemination process. We must consider the broad view: we are all primarily interested in ensuring the well-being and rapid return to health of patients with eating disorders. Both researchers and practitioners can contribute to narrowing the research–practice gap.

Carolin and Billie's story illustrates the personal impact of the research–practice gap in eating disorders on a family. Carolin believes Billie would have suffered less if she had received prompter, suitable intervention. We cannot know if earlier access to Maudsley family-based treatment would have changed Billie's eating disorder course, as efficacy research findings apply to group averages rather than any individual's specific symptoms. However, evidence suggests best outcomes occur when we work together in assisting practitioners to incorporate ESTs into their practices. We are optimistic that increased use of ESTs is feasible and is in the best interest of patients with eating disorders.

References

Banker, J. D. and Klump, K. L. (2010) 'The research-practice gap: Challenges and opportunities for the eating disorder treatment professional', in M. Maine, D. Bunnell and B. McGilley (eds) *Treatment of Eating Disorders: Bridging the Gap Between Research and Practice* (459–477), London: Elsevier.

Chambless, D. L. and Ollendick, T. H. (2001) 'Empirically supported psychological interventions: Controversies and evidence', *Annu Rev Psychol* 52: 685–716.

Fisher, C. A., Hetrick, S. E., and Rushford, N. (2010) 'Family therapy for anorexia nervosa', *Cochrane Database Syst Rev* 4: CD004780.

Geller, J., Zaitsoff, S. L., and Srikameswaran, S. (2005) 'Tracking readiness and motivation for change in individuals with eating disorders over the course of treatment', *Cognit Ther Res* 29: 611–25.

Keel, P. K. and Haedt, A. (2008) 'Evidence-based psychosocial treatments for eating problems and eating disorders', *J Clin Child Adolesc Psychol* 37: 39–61.

National Institute for Clinical Excellence (NICE) (2004) *Core Interventions in the Treatment and Management of Anorexia Nervosa, Bulimia Nervosa and Related Eating Disorders. Clinical Guideline 9*, London: National Collaborating Centre for Mental Health. Online. Available: http://www.nice.org.uk/page.aspx?o=102235 (accessed 25 August 2010).

Newnham, E. A. and Page, A. C. (2009) 'Bridging the gap between best evidence and best practice in mental health', *Clin Psychol Rev* 30: 127–42.

Satterfield, J. M., Spring, B., Brownson, R. C., Mullen, E. J., Newhouse, R. P., Walker, B. B., and Whitlock, E. P. (2009) 'Toward a transdisciplinary model of evidence-based practice', *Milbank Quarterly* 87: 368–90.

Shafran, R., Clark, D., Fairburn, C., Arntz, A., Barlow, D., Ehlers, A., Freeston, M., Garety, P., Hollon, S., Ost, L., Salkovskis, P., and Wilson, G. (2009) 'Mind the gap: Improving the dissemination of CBT', *Behav Res Ther* 47: 902–9.

Simmons, A. M., Milnes, S. M., and Anderson, D. A. (2008) 'Factors influencing the utilization of empirically supported treatments for eating disorders', *Eat Disord* 16: 342–54.

von Ranson, K. M. and Robinson, K. E. (2006) 'Who is providing what type of psychotherapy to eating disorder patients? A survey', *Int J Eat Disord* 39: 27–34.

Wilson, G. T., Grilo, C. M., and Vitousek, K. M. (2007) 'Psychological treatment of eating disorders', *Am Psychol* 62: 199–216.

Chapter 26

Why carers need to know about research

Susan Ringwood

Carers want and need to know if recovery from an eating disorder is possible; they want to know what causes an eating disorder, how long it will take for their child or partner's treatment to work, and where did they go wrong. Learning about the science, and the growing evidence base that informs the understanding, diagnosis and treatment of eating disorders, can help carers and families beat an eating disorder.

Beat is the UK's leading charitable organisation supporting people affected by eating disorders and campaigning on their behalf. We aim to change the way people think and talk about eating disorders; improve treatment and services; and help sufferers believe they can beat their eating disorder.

We work closely with researchers and clinicians, sharing the experience of family and sufferers. We are in daily contact with families and loved ones as well. People typically contact us at one of three points in their fight to beat an eating disorder. The first is when they have their initial worries about themselves, a friend or family member, or have received a diagnosis and want to find out the implications.

People calling with their first worries often don't know that their thoughts, feelings and behaviours are due to a recognised, treatable condition.

> I didn't know I had an eating disorder – I thought I was just a bad person.
> 12-year-old girl

Secondly, they call when they seek treatment. The publicly funded National Health Service in the UK is free at the point of delivery and provides world-class treatment – but huge variables remain in the availability and funding of services to provide this treatment. The health-care system relies on general practitioners – family doctors – to act as gatekeepers to the specialist services often needed to treat an eating disorder. This gateway is often a barrier rather than a straightforward access point.

> The GP said: 'Don't worry, your son can't have an eating disorder – he's a boy.'
> Mother of 14-year-old son

The third typical contact, and comprising almost 50 per cent of helpline calls, is from families in crisis.

We are glad that families can turn to us – but the support we can give seems inadequate. These daily contacts with families and individuals (more than 240,000 instances in 2010) inform our campaigning work too. Besides providing families with vital information we are committed to sharing their insights and experiences with the professionals working to provide treatment or conduct vital research. Working together with trust and transparency is the way to beat eating disorders.

Each family situation differs, but concerns often share a commonality that science can best answer. Families can gain much from being informed of research work – and from being involved in the studies too. Part of the challenge is to communicate the learning from this work and to embed it in sound clinical practice.

> Carers are concerned and appreciate the efforts of eating disorder researchers. The problem is the gap between those with the information, and those who need it.
>
> Husband whose wife suffers from anorexia nervosa

Parents appreciate evidence-based answers. Typically mothers want to know why the eating disorder happened and fathers want to know what to do now and what happens next.

> A discussion with my clinician helped me realise how far we've come in recognising and helping people with eating disorders. We are lucky our daughter has benefited from this research.
>
> Father of 22-year-old daughter

Our challenge as campaigners is to help clinicians understand the importance of answering questions. A carer's initial awareness of a condition that thrives on secrecy, and is shrouded in stigma and shame, is limited. Any knowledge families have is often formed of myths, misunderstandings and misinformation.

The myths include: 'no one ever really recovers'; 'it is a modern fad, a phase'; 'it's self-indulgent attention seeking'; and 'ignore it and it will pass'. These contradictory views perpetuate, influencing families and their loved ones – attitudes to treatment, and expectation for recovery.

Once a family learns that an eating disorder is a serious, recognised psychiatric illness and not a silly fad, other misunderstandings occur. 'If not a silly fad, then my daughter has gone mad', is an example of the thinking with which families struggle. Then there is misinformation – perhaps the most insidious of all because it can be delivered with pseudo-authority to make it credible and hard to refute from a position of frightened ignorance.

Outdated views formed before the evidence base developed, and drawn from personal opinion of limited perspective, abound. The media can drive this misinformation – relying on stereotypes and sensationalism illustrated with shocking images.

> When our daughter had a relapse, a good friend said: 'What? A relapse? But I thought you were better. Can't you take a pill or something to fix it?'
>
> Mother of 14-year-old daughter

Sadly some myths, misunderstandings and misinformation have their source in health-care professionals that families meet in their quest for treatment, recovery and hope.

So what does research give – and what hopes do families have for it?

> I've blamed myself for my daughter's situation. More research and publicity would help to alleviate the guilt that many parents and I feel.
>
> Father of 31-year-old daughter

Research gives reassurance that the condition is being taken seriously. This reassurance can include hope for answers, that objectivity is possible. It helps families to understand and make informed decisions about treatment and treatment options.

> You need to be confident you are making the right decisions – that it will be best for your child in the long run.
>
> Father of 12-year-old daughter

> It helps to know it's not just my family or me.
>
> Sister of 28-year-old woman

Research builds the evidence base too, by steering families away from the pot-luck of treatment by pet theory – or worse, no theory at all. But there is a downside – evidence is limited and can lack clear clinical applications. Most people naturally equate research with finding a cure. To learn that much research is tentative, inconclusive or of academic interest is a profound disappointment.

What can researchers and clinicians do?

Research can help families make sense of their experience and put it in perspective. But too often, research is seen as remote and not part of the patient's life.

> I am not that fussed about research because my priorities are more immediate – getting care for my daughter and keeping myself sane.
>
> Mother of 18-year-old daughter

The challenge is to make the science of eating disorders relevant to the lives of ordinary people. Professionals can help achieve this by breaking myths, bringing facts to bear and dispelling the harmful stereotypes. They can correct misinformation by voicing the latest findings and showing how thinking has changed. Families are experts in how they are affected by an eating disorder and treatment teams must recognise and acknowledge this hard-won expertise.

Chapter 27

Promoting a full agenda of rights

Lynn S. Grefe

> We cannot live only for ourselves. A thousand fibers connect us with our fellow men; and among those fibers, as sympathetic threads, our actions run as causes, and they come back to us as effects.
>
> Herman Melville

This is our time to strive together as connected fibers to fight eating disorders.

This field of eating disorders faces many challenges. Besides searching for causes, prevention techniques, and improved treatments, we fight for access to care for those struggling. We are lost in the ongoing mass confusion of obesity issues. We are challenged to rise above the self-serving interests of the diet industry and public health campaigns which are often nothing more than knee-jerk reactions with no evidence base. Although more people suffer from eating disorders than from Alzheimer's disease, schizophrenia, or autism, inaction prevails, research is minimally funded, and it is as if our patients and their families do not exist. A cultural change must be realized that treats our patients with the love, care and respect they deserve.

Although our challenges are evident, our actions are sometimes lacking. Our efforts to educate advertisers and legislators are akin to tackling terrorism with a fly swatter. So much more needs to be done to present our case effectively. It takes knowledge, commitment, and certainty. We must talk about health, not weight. We must promote empathy, not shame. We must present evidence-based treatments and statistics, and use them to turn the vision of advanced research into reality to eliminate eating disorders.

Showing up is half the battle, but there are times when we have been unorganized upon arrival. Why? The reasons are complex. People question the validity of an illness that is rarely or barely covered by their insurance company. Flowers, cards and candy are unlikely to be delivered to the room of an eating disorder patient; instead, secrets and whispering await their return home. Parents are mistakenly blamed when the culprit is biology.

Friends are known to say, 'Gee I wish I had one of those for a few weeks', idealizing these deadly disorders.

Stepping out of this mythical muck, which has debilitated the eating disorder field, is difficult. Major attitudinal changes have been achieved on health and behavioral issues such as cigarette smoking, alcohol consumption, seat belt use; and social issues such as race and sexual rights. Cultural change can occur with eating disorders too, so, let's examine our prerequisites.

First, we need good data to guide us. In 2003, the National Eating Disorders Association (NEDA) commissioned American Viewpoint to launch focus groups to gauge public thinking. We discovered people knew much more about eating disorders than we expected. But when asked if they would tell anyone if they themselves suffered, the answer from both adults and teens was: 'No.' The reason? Shame and embarrassment 'that people will think I brought this on myself'.

This survey research told us that we had to break new ground and bring eating disorders into the mainstream. But talking is not enough. We must follow the four 'I's: *Identify* our target audience; *Inform* them; *Involve* them; and get them to *Invest* in this cause. It is important to coordinate and follow these principles collaboratively to provide the best information and strongest supporters and advocates possible. NEDA's 2010 United States national survey data tell us that public awareness has significantly increased and most people are more likely to seek help. The people surveyed suggested we be more proactive in educating the public on early signs and symptoms. Further, we learned that many more people now understand that these are illnesses, not lifestyle choices. That was our directive from NEDA's 2003 research, and using the four 'I's approach, our field has made progress.

Second, we must be committed, united and clear on our roles, with realistic goals. Consumer, professional, and advocacy organizations should coordinate their activities and work towards a common purpose, with targeted goals and benchmarks.

Because our field is accustomed to being ignored, some people mistakenly believe 'something is better than nothing', and paying for treatment remains a bureaucratic hurdle. It is disheartening when medical institutions impede our push for compulsory eating disorder education for health care professionals.

Changes did not occur in civil rights by saying that only some African American people can sit in the front of the bus, or that some gay people should not be discriminated against in the workplace. The leadership in those cases demanded their full agenda of rights. We must do the same for eating disorders. Success requires an agenda of rights for our patients, and a bonded community of professional partnerships to focus on their health.

Where do we go from here? Together in certainty and with well-deserved public outcry, it is time to put our shoulders back and build a solid foundation. Let's exude confidence and wear our commitment and certainty like a badge. Too often, shame has been our justification for lack of advancement. Let's ditch the shame card when espousing our cause. Let's agree we have entered a time of enlightenment.

Let us change our behavior first, literally faking confidence if necessary, so we can take the hard first steps. As Dr Margo Maine reminds us, the concept in therapy is 'stand tall and unashamed and our feelings will follow'. I urge that we use this philosophy for outreach, to act purposefully and fiercely, with no shame, blame, stigma, or apologies. The changes we need in public attitudes and understanding will follow. Patients will benefit, and this is our purpose.

Empowered by our mission, as part of this eating disorder fabric – the professional field, the families, and the recovered patients – an expanded base of committed activists and financial support will emerge and engage in dialogue that expresses the certainty of our cause. The future in the field of eating disorders is ours to weave.

Chapter 28

The patient-family-clinician-researcher quest for quality care

Mary Tantillo

Apprehension, uncertainty, waiting, expectation, fear of surprise, do a patient more harm than any exertion. Remember, he is face to face with his enemy all the time, internally wrestling with him, having long imaginary conversations with him. You are thinking of something else. 'Rid him of his adversary quickly, is the first rule with the sick.'

Florence Nightingale (1860: 38)

I think that the source of hope lies in believing that one has or can move toward a sense of connection.

Jean Baker Miller (2004)

Nightingale's quote is apt in relation to the experience of people with eating disorders and their families. Previous chapters in this book describe how genes, neurobiology, malnutrition, and the environment contribute to the severe anxiety and fear experienced by people with eating disorders. Family members also experience fear and anxiety as they witness their loved one struggle with the disorder. Health care providers are affected too, often feeling the intense helplessness and frustration the eating disorder evokes. And researchers, while more removed from direct influence of the illness, can sense the highly concentrated emotions experienced by patients, families and clinicians. This 'disease of disconnection' perplexes all stakeholders (Tantillo 2006).

The patient's disconnection from their own genuine thoughts, feelings and needs ripples out to all stakeholders. Conflict and tension isolate family members from each other and the treatment team. The eating disorder promotes all or nothing thinking, often disconnecting treatment team members from each other. The disconnection between clinicians and researchers in relation to implementing evidence-based treatments has been described in Chapter 25. One main adverse outcome is the inability to develop fuller, richer understandings of the etiology and treatment of eating disorders – understandings based on expert consensus, randomized clinical trials, and the voices and lived experience of patients and families. Joining and connecting these different perspectives is essential (Miller and Stiver 1997; Tantillo 2006).

Approaches are being created to address this issue and ensure accessible, high quality, coordinated, continuous, and evidence-based care of eating disorders. For example, stakeholders can connect with evidence-based practice through the work of the Academy for Eating Disorders (AED) Credentialing Task Force and the World Wide Charter for Action that specifies patient/family rights and expectations during treatment.

The World Wide Charter for Action

The World Wide Charter for Action on Eating Disorders, developed through a collaboration of the Academy for Eating Disorders and other national and international professional and patient/carer organizations (www.aedweb,.org/public/WorldCharter.cfm) may be considered a global paragon of patient, family, clinician and researcher partnership. In March 2005 an international task force was designated to develop and distribute a web-based survey to individuals with eating disorders, families, carers, and eating disorder health professionals. In March 2006 survey responses were collected from 1,730 people in forty-six countries. These responses indicated there were: (a) large variations in accessibility to comprehensive, high quality care, and (b) similar core issues related to the experience/burden of illness and health care needs uniting individuals with eating disorders and their families, across the globe.

The World Charter, written in eight languages and based on the above survey findings, identifies patient/carer rights and expectations in regard to treatment. The six basic rights of patients and carers are listed in Table 28.1. It emphasizes that a partnership among patients, families and care providers is essential to quality care and positive health outcomes. The World Charter empowers patients and families to ask for what they require and deserve in regard to treatment. It also calls on providers, government officials, third party payers and patient/family advocates to enact public and organizational policies and improve education and training to meet patient/carer expectations of quality care. So far almost 1,000 individuals and eighty organizations across the world have endorsed the Charter, and patient/family advocacy groups continue to seek its endorsement. An example is the USA-based National Eating Disorders Association (NEDA) STAR (States for Treatment Access and Research) Program, which works with volunteer leaders

Table 28.1 World Wide Charter: rights of individuals with eating disorders and carers

1. Right to communication and partnership with health professionals
2. Right to comprehensive assessment and treatment planning
3. Right to accessible, high quality, fully funded, specialized care
4. Right to respectful, fully informed, age appropriate safe levels of care
5. Right of carers to be informed, valued, and respected as a treatment team resource
6. Right of carers to accessible, appropriate support and education resources

in each state to obtain Charter endorsement. The program accomplishes this through training volunteer state leaders who launch the Charter in their state during National Eating Disorders Awareness Week in partnership with state legislators and other policy makers. Whenever possible, each launch includes a press conference including the NEDA state leader, a government official, an AED professional and a recovering patient or family member.

The World Wide Charter for Action on Eating Disorders was the first initiative of the World Summit on Eating Disorders, an event the AED sponsors annually at each international conference. The annual AED World Summit Inaugural Session includes professionals, patient/carers and other stakeholders who gather in a united effort to discuss common concerns about the current and future status of eating disorders treatment and services.

Future steps: synthesizing the voices of all stakeholders

If we start with the assumption that healing, recovery, and wellness always happen in connection with others (Miller and Stiver 1997; Resnick *et al.* 1993; Tantillo 2006), this assumption must inform all our efforts involved in developing and delivering high quality, evidence-based treatments for eating disorders.

The future of best practices and good treatment outcome depends on our ability to listen to all stakeholders and strengthen our partnerships with each other – patients, families, clinicians and researchers. Research from various fields supports the notion that knowledge is most effectively assimilated and integrated when buy-in, mutual exchange, and understanding are experienced among all key stakeholders (Banker and Klump 2008; Reardon *et al.* 2006; Rogers 1995). Most importantly, we must practice being open to different perspectives, feelings, and needs of respective stakeholder groups and learn to build on our differences. This commitment to *embracing difference within strong connection* is the hallmark of true mutual connection and partnership (Miller and Stiver 1997; Tantillo 2006), and is a central force in promoting partnership in treatment and in our collaborative work with one another. It can disable the eating disorder, which grasps at every opportunity to create disconnection within and between patients, families, clinicians, and researchers. With these assumptions in mind this chapter ends with steps to strengthen patient–family–clinician–researcher collaboration in our joint quest for quality care (see Table 28.2).

Table 28.2 Future steps to strengthen collaboration

- Use the AED Credentialing Task Force as a benchmark for how to embrace diverse stakeholder perspectives within a context of strong connections. Adapt this model of stakeholder collaboration for use in other countries.
- Continue to use the World Wide Charter for Action on Eating Disorders as a benchmark for collaboration within and among countries across the globe when needing to

unite individuals with eating disorders, carers, clinicians, and researchers on critical issues such as quality health care.

- Increase collaboration among stakeholders to obtain data regarding how well programs across the globe fulfill stated Charter expectations.
- Develop an evaluation tool (e.g. in collaboration with the AED Credentialing Task Force and other recovering individual, carer, clinician and researcher stakeholder representatives) that programs can use to examine whether they fulfill Charter expectations as part of their regular quality improvement process.
- Work with patient/carer organizations like NEDA and the UK-based Beat to advocate for inclusion of the above measure in program accreditation as defined by the task force and other accreditation/licensing agencies.
- Create various forums for ongoing dialogue among all stakeholders in national and international organizations regarding best practices and quality care, e.g. patient/carer and other task forces involving all stakeholders, and newsletter columns and annual conference plenaries/key notes that require each stakeholder group to provide their perspective on a clinical case, use of an empirically-supported treatment, or other topic of interest.
- Continue to use the world summit meeting at the AED annual conference as a forum for international collaboration and exchange of ideas in our quest for quality care.

References and further reading

American Psychiatric Association (APA) (2006) *Practice Guidelines for the Treatment of Patients with Eating Disorders,* 3rd edn, Washington, DC: APA.

Banker, J.D. and Klump, K.L. (2008) 'Research and Clinical Practice: A Dynamic Tension in the Eating Disorder Field', in I.F. Dancyger and V.M. Fornari (eds) *Evidence-Based Treatments for Eating Disorders*, New York: Nova Science Publishers.

Beale, B., McMaster, R., and Hillege, S. (2004/5) 'Eating Disorders: A Qualitative Analysis of the Parents' Journey', *Contemporary Nurse* 18, 1–2: 124–32.

Berkman, N.D., Bulik, C.M., Brownley, K.A., Lohr, K.N., Sedway, J.A., Rooks, A., and Gartlehner, G. (2006) *Management of Eating Disorders, Evidence Report/Technology Assessment No. 135*, Rockville, MD: AHRQ Publications.

Grover, M., Williams, C., Eisler, I., Fairbairn, P., McCloskey, C., Smith, G., Treasure, J., and Schmidt, U. (in press) 'An Off-Line Pilot Evaluation of a Web-Based Systemic Cognitive-Behavioral Intervention for Carers of People with Anorexia Nervosa', *Int J Eat Disord.*

Kazdin, A.E. (2008) 'Evidence-Based Treatment and Practice – New Opportunities to Bridge Clinical Research and Practice, Enhance the Knowledge Base, and Improve Patient Care', *Am Psychol* 63, 3: 146–59.

Lock, J., Le Grange, D., Agras, S., Bryson, S., and Booil, J. (in press) 'Randomized Clinical Trial Comparing Family-Based Treatment to Adolescent Focused Individual Therapy for Adolescents with Anorexia Nervosa', *Arch Gen Psychiatry.*

Miller, J.B. (2004) ''Encouraging an Era of Connection', paper presented at the Jean Baker Miller Training Institute, Wellesley, MA: June.

Miller, J.B. and Stiver, I.P. (1997) *The Healing Connection: How Women form Relationships in Therapy and in Life*, Boston, MA: Beacon Press.

National Institute for Clinical Excellence (NICE) (2004) *Eating Disorders: Core Interventions in the Treatment and Management of Anorexia Nervosa, Bulimia Nervosa and Related Eating Disorders*, Clinical Guideline 9, London: NICE.

National Institutes of Health (NIH) (2009) *Reengineering the Clinical Research Enterprise: Translational Research*, Bethesda, MD: NIH. Online. Available: http://nihroadmap.nih.gov/clinicalresearch/overview-translational.asp (accessed 12 April 2010).

Nightingale, F. (1860) *Notes on Nursing: What It Is, and What It Is Not*, New York: D. Appleton and Company.

Norcross, J. (ed.) (2002) *Psychotherapy Relationships that Work*, New York: Oxford University Press.

Polit, D.F. and Hungler, P. (1999) *Nursing Research and Methods*, 6th edn, Philadelphia: Lippincott Williams & Wilkins.

Reardon, R., Lavis, J., and Gibson, J. (2006) *From Research to Practice: A Knowledge Transfer Planning Guide*, Toronto: Institute for Work and Health.

Resnick, M.D., Harris, L.J., and Blum, R.W. (1993) 'The Impact of Caring and Connectedness on Adolescent Health and Well-Being', *J Paediatr Child Health* 29, S1: A1–S71.

Rogers, E.M. (1995) *Diffusion of Innovations*, 4th edn, New York: Free Press.

Tantillo, M. (2006) 'A Relational Approach to Eating Disorders Multifamily Therapy Group: Moving from Difference and Disconnection to Mutual Connection', *Families, Systems, and Health*, 24, 1: 82–102.

Tobin, D.L., Banker, J.D., Weisberg, L., and Bowers, W. (2007) 'I Know What You Did Last Summer (and It Was Not CBT): A Factor Analytic Model of International Psychotherapeutic Practice in the Eating Disorders', *Int J Eat Disord* 40: 754–7.

Whittal, M.L., Agras, W.S., and Gould, R.A. (1999) 'Bulimia Nervosa: A Meta-Analysis of Psychosocial and Psychopharmacological Treatments', *Behav Ther* 30: 117–35.

Websites

Academy for Eating Disorders: www.aedweb.org

Andrea's Voice: www.andreasvoice.org

APA Practice Guideline: www.psychiatryonline.com/pracGuide/pracGuideTopic_12.aspx

Beating Eating Disorders (Beat): www.b-eat.co.uk

Butterfly Foundation: www.thebutterflyfoundation.org.au

Eating Disorders Coalition for Research Policy and Action: www.eatingdisorderscoalition.org

Eating Disorders in Adolescents: Position paper of the Society for Adolescent Medicine: www.adolescenthealth.org/Content/NavigationMenu/Advocacy/PositionPapers/PositionPaper_Eating_Disorders_in_Adolescents.pdf

Families Empowered and Supporting Treatment of Eating Disorders (FEAST): www.feast-ed.org

International Association for Eating Disorder Professionals: www.iaedp.com

Maudsley Parents: www.maudsleyparents.org

National Eating Disorders Association: www.nationaleatingdisorders.org

New York State Comprehensive Care Centres for Eating Disorders: www.health.state.ny.us/diseases/chronic/eating_disorders/comprehensive_care_Centres.htm

NICE Guideline: www.nice.org.uk/CG009

Royal Australian and New Zealand College of Psychiatrists Anorexia Nervosa Guidelines: www.nzgg.org.nz/guidelines/0091/Anorexia_Full_Clinician_published_Sept_2004.pdf

STAR Program: Contact Lara Gregorio: lgregorio@nationaleatingdisorders.org

World Wide Charter: www.aedweb.org/public/WorldCharter.cfm

Videos and resources

Parents Do Not Cause Eating Disorders: www.aedweb.org/video/parents.cfm
End Fat Talk Week: www.endfattalk.org

The following are also found at: http://maudsleyparents.org/videos.html

- *Brain Imaging and Eating Disorders* (Walter Kaye MD): www.vimeo.com/1678383
- *Fighting Stigma with Science* (Cindy Bulik PhD): www.vimeo.com/1715091
- *AN in Teens: What Parents Need to Know* (Katharine Loeb PhD): www.vimeo.com/6351950
- *Eating Disorders in Teens* (Daniel Le Grange PhD): www.vimeo.com/2408156
- *Understanding Eating Disorders* (Thomas Insel MD, NIH): www.vimeo.com/6399719
- *Cognitive Styles in Eating Disorders* (James Lock MD, PhD): www.vimeo.com/6706759

Bulimia Nervosa Resource Guide for Family and Friends: www.bulimiaguide.org
Eating Disorders (NIMH booklet): www.nimh.nih.gov/health/publications/eating-disorders/complete-index.shtml

Index